New York City

David Ellis

New York City

1st edition

Published by
Lonely Planet Publications
Head Office: PO Box 617, Hawthorn, Vic 3122, Australia
Branches: 150 Linden St, Oakland, CA 94607, USA
             10a Spring Place, London NW5 3BH, UK
             1 rue du Dahomey, 75011 Paris, France

Printed by
Colorcraft Ltd, Hong Kong

Photographs by
David Ellis, Kim Grant, Jane Lloyd, Tom Smallman, Tony Wheeler

Front cover: Will & Deni McIntyre, Tony Stone Images
Title page: Kim Grant, Chrysler Building

Published
September 1997

Although the author and publisher have tried to make the information as accurate as possible, they accept no responsibility for any loss, injury or inconvenience sustained by any person using this book.

National Library of Australia Cataloguing in Publication Data

Ellis, David, 1962-
    New York.

    1st ed.
    Includes index.
    ISBN 0 86442 502 3.

    1. New York (N.Y.) – Guidebooks. I. Title.

917.471

text & maps © Lonely Planet 1997
photos © photographers as indicated 1997
climate charts compiled from information supplied by Patrick J Tyson, © Patrick J Tyson, 1997
New York City Transit Map © New York City Transit Authority 1997, used with permission

David Ellis

David was born in the heart of Greenwich Village and grew up on the New Jersey shore, where Bruce Springsteen was regarded as something of a demi god. He attended university in Boston and Dublin, Ireland, and, after earning a degree in journalism and international affairs, he spent a year in London writing for the *Economist* before returning to New York City. Over the past decade he's worked as a writer, editor and reviewer at *Time* and *People* magazines covering politics and culture, though he often takes time out to explore various parts of the globe. His work has appeared in many publications, including the *New Republic*, *New York*, the *Australian*, the *Times* of London and *Europe*. He has lived in three of New York's five boroughs (Brooklyn, Manhattan and the Bronx) and currently resides on New York's Roosevelt Island in the middle of the East River – a site described inside this guidebook.

JANE LLOYD

From the Author

I must thank Jane Lloyd for her uncommon patience, unstinting energy, infectious enthusiasm and constant support throughout this project. I couldn't have dreamed for a better partner to join me in my exploration of the city.

Lisa and David Furrule were always there when I needed them – people I could count on for support at all times.

Special thanks goes to a number of people for their assistance along the way, including Larry Mondi, Richard Lacayo, Susan Reed and David Anderson for their companionship and help while researching this project. Bud Kliment, Tom Meltzer, Paul Foglino, Lisa McLaughlin, David Seideman and Lynn Schnurnberger kindly shared their knowledge. Daniel Levy helped with his knowledge of architecture and city history.

Many people assisted me with information along the way, including Barry Popik, Theresa Osborne and Illana Harlow of the Queens Council on the Arts, Byron Saunders of the Queens Historical Society, Jennifer McGuire of the New York Convention & Visitors Bureau, Joy Farber and Jane Pope of the New Jersey Division of Travel and Tourism, the Staten Island Borough President's Office, and Rob Fariel of Amagansett, Long Island.

From the Publisher

This first edition was edited by Tom Downs. Many thanks to Carolyn Hubbard for proofing and advising and to Jeff Campbell for proofing.

Production and design were executed by Scott Summers. Spot illustrations were drawn by Hugh D'Andrade and portraits were contributed by Hayden Foell. Special thanks to photographer Kim Grant for her efforts.

Maps were drawn by Bo-sock Hayden Foell, with the omniscient guidance of Alex Guilbert.

Some of the sidebar material was contributed by Dan Levy (Architectural Walk), Tom Downs (Hip Hop) and Tom Smallman (Sultan of Swat).

Warning & Request

Things change – prices go up, schedules change, good places go bad and bad places go bankrupt – nothing stays the same. So, if you find things better or worse, recently opened or long since closed, please tell us and help make the next edition even more accurate and useful.

We value all of the feedback we receive from travelers. Julie Young coordinates a small team that reads and acknowledges every letter, postcard and email, and ensures that every morsel of information finds its way to the appropriate authors, editors and publishers. Everyone who writes to us will find their name in the next edition of the appropriate guide and will also receive a free subscription to our quarterly newsletter, *Planet Talk*. The very best contributions will be rewarded with a free Lonely Planet guide.

Excerpts from your correspondence may appear in updates (which we add to the end pages of reprints); new editions of this guide; in our newsletter, *Planet Talk*; or in the Postcards section of our Website – so please let us know if you don't want your letter published or your name acknowledged.

Contents

PLACES TO EAT 172

ENTERTAINMENT 194

SHOPPING 208

EXCURSIONS 218

ARCHITECTURAL GLOSSARY 244

INDEX 245

NEW YORK CITY MAP SECTION 256

Map Legend

BOUNDARIES

— · — · — · — · — International Boundary

— ·· — ·· — ·· — State/Provincial Boundary

AREA FEATURES

Park

NATIONAL PARK National Park

National/State Forest

Reservation

HYDROGRAPHIC FEATURES

Water

Coastline

River, Waterfall

Swamp, Spring

ROUTES

Freeway

Toll Freeway

Primary Road

Secondary Road

Tertiary Road

Unpaved Road

Trail

Ferry Route

Railway, Train Station

Mass Transit Line & Station

ROUTE SHIELDS

(10) Interstate Freeway

(1) US Highway

(100) New York State Highway

SYMBOLS

✪ **NATIONAL CAPITAL**
◉ **State Capital**
● **City**
● City, Small
● Town

■ Hotel, B&B
▲ Campground
⌂ Hostel
⊕ RV Park
▼ Restaurant
🍺 Bar (Place to Drink)
☕ Cafe

✚ Airfield
✈ Airport
∴ Archaeological Site, Ruins
🏦 Bank, ATM
⚾ Baseball Diamond
✕ Battlefield
🏖 Beach
◆ Border Crossing
⊥ Buddhist Temple
● Bus Depot, Bus Stop
⛪ Cathedral
⌒ Cave
✝ Church
🏛 Embassy
⤐ Foot Bridge
❖ Garden

⛽ Gas Station
⛳ Golf Course
♨ Hindu Temple
✛ Hospital, Clinic
ℹ Information
☡ Lighthouse
☀ Lookout
▲ Monument
☪ Mosque
▲ Mountain
🏛 Museum
♪ Music, Live
← One-Way Street
⌂ Observatory
▲ Park
Ⓟ Parking

)(Pass
⊼ Picnic Area
★ Police Station
▭ Pool
▽ Post Office
⛵ Shipwreck
❖ Shopping Mall
⛷ Skiing, Alpine
⛷ Skiing, Nordic
🏛 Stately Home
✡ Synagogue
☎ Telephone
■ Tomb, Mausoleum
🚶 Trailhead
🍷 Winery
🐘 Zoo

Note: Not all symbols displayed above appear in this book.

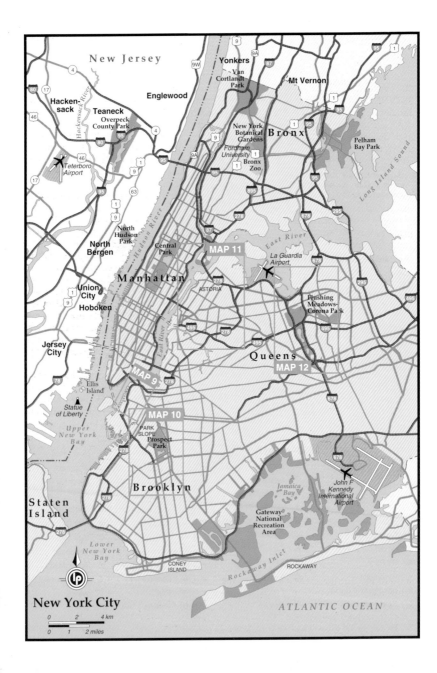

Introduction

More modest municipalities are content to be known as centers of manufacturing and agriculture, or even serve as their nation's capital. But New York City reserves for itself the only title that matters – 'Capital of the World' – and has the arrogance to hang banners saying so along its avenues.

That boast has plenty of validity: long after it ceased to be the absolute center of the US, New York continues to dominate the popular imagination. Throughout its 300-year history it has gained, then lost, primacy in many different important endeavors, including politics, agriculture, manufacturing, shipping, broadcasting and film production. New Yorkers are thus conditioned to expect that their city will continue to find fresh activities to exploit, and remain ever-confident that no rival will ever equal it as a center for cultural and intellectual pursuits.

Numbers tell much of the story: with seven million residents, New York City has more than twice as many people as Los Angeles, the second largest US city. All these people are packed into 309 sq miles of space, just about 75% of Los Angeles County's total land mass. From this density comes New York's intensity.

The city's energy is perhaps its most marketable commodity, attracting people from around the world as residents, drawing fans to its sports teams and patrons to its entertainment meccas, even tempting upright values hawkers to condemn its excesses.

Among those excesses is its enormity of scale, something not much noticed by the natives. Every day, New Yorkers blithely stroll past – or live in – buildings that would dominate the skyline of almost any other major city. Yet this immensity – and the crowding of so many colors and cultures within the city's borders – is what stuns visitors from more homogeneous locales.

Even the visitors are a sign of New York's excess, since there are so many of them: 30 million annually at last count. Most are conditioned by Hollywood (and lazy journalists) to assume that New York is a mayhem-ridden nightmare and often arrive gripped by a caution that borders on paranoia. Yet even the fearful – who you'd think would shun such a scary place – are still drawn to visit.

Yes, some of the clichés are true: a New Yorker talks faster – and closer to your face – than just about anyone else. The European *pension* tradition never took hold here, making it difficult, and at some times of the year nearly impossible, to find decent, low-cost accommodation. To survive in this crowded atmosphere, people close in on themselves. It could be argued that the city's reputation for rudeness is simply the survival instinct carried to the *nth* degree. It doesn't help that residents are a bit proud of the city's reputation as an edgy place – it gives them a cache simply for living there.

It's oddly sad to see the hundreds of people sunbathing in Central Park on a weekend day with their noses buried in their books because the urban social contract generally prohibits talking to strangers (unless you're both walking dogs). And it's oddly touching to see a subway rider – who hasn't spoken a word to any other passenger – neatly fold his tabloid newspaper and leave it on the seat at departure. It's not littering, just a courtesy to the next person who will board without a book and needs an excuse not to engage anyone in conversation.

Contrary to New York's down and dirty image, locals are regularly gracious and helpful to tourists. Sometimes they actually excuse themselves if they bump into you, and they love to give directions, if only because visitor queries cater to their self-perceived expertise on the city.

As for crime, thanks to well-targeted

community policing, along with the aging of the baby boom generation that helped contribute to a general decline in crime nationwide, New York continues to be one of the safest cities in the country. It is not even in the top 10 of the major US cities for violent crimes. Here's a fact for the fearful to slowly consider: New York ranks *144th* among cities with populations of 100,000 people or more, with a crime rate lower than Washington, DC, Atlanta, St Petersburg and Birmingham. It is ranked among the bottom in specific felonies among the nation's 25 largest cities, and the crime rate has dropped 39% since 1993. So the bottom line is that you should exercise sensible caution when visiting – just as you would in a city with a calmer reputation.

Yes, this is a very good time to visit – even live in – New York. But all the required energy makes it an exhausting holiday destination. This mega-city demands that you assault it with a game plan. Use this book to define your sightseeing priorities and get to them ahead of anyone else. Force yourself to walk around new neighborhoods, even get a little lost. Along the way, serendipitous occurrences will unfold, if only because some of the city's best entertainment can be found free on the streets.

That's why people feel a rush when they hit the streets from a hotel doorway or emerge from a subway station. They're about to be experience something of a dysfunctional miracle.

Facts about New York City

HISTORY
The Europeans Arrive

The area now known as New York City had been occupied by Native Americans for more than 11,000 years before Giovanni da Verrazano, a Florentine hired by the French to explore the northeastern coast, arrived in 1524. He is believed to be the first European to visit New York Bay. Though history records that a black Portuguese named Esteban Gomez sailed part of the river two years later, no serious attempt was made to document the topography of area or its peoples until September 1609, when English explorer Henry Hudson, on a mission to find the Northwest Passage, anchored *Halve Maen* in the harbor for 10 days before continuing up the river. Although one of his men was killed by Native Americans while walking the shoreline, Hudson was impressed by what he saw. 'It is as beautiful a land as one can hope to tread upon,' reported Hudson, who claimed the place for his employer, the Dutch East India Company.

It appears that the land mass that makes up New York City was home to several tribes. The local Munsee Indians had several names for the region, including *Manahatouh* ('place of gathering bow wood'), *Manahactanienk* ('place of general inebriation') and *Menatay* ('the island'). The name Manhattan – and Manhattoes, the name of another local tribe – can be traced to any one of these words.

The Struggle to Control New York

By 1625, the Dutch settlers had established a fur trade with the natives and were augmented by a group that established a post they eventually called New Amsterdam, the seat of a much larger colony called New Netherland. The government of Holland, eager to thwart England's interest in the new world, allowed a group of businessmen to create the new Dutch West India Company to control affairs in the colony. While advertisements in Europe attempted to lure settlers to New Amsterdam with promises of a temperate climate and bountiful land, the harsh winters claimed many lives.

Historians generally agree that Peter Minuit, the director of the Dutch West India Company, purchased the island from local tribes for goods worth 60 guilders at a meeting, somewhere near the southern tip of Manhattan. But the goods were worth a bit more than the $24 commonly recorded. A more up-to-date estimate of the exchange rate would value them at about $600, still a bargain.

The Big Apple

It has long been thought that New York City was dubbed 'The Big Apple' by jazz musicians who regarded a gig in Harlem as a sure sign that they had made it to the top. But Barry Popik, a judge with the city's Parking Violations Bureau and an amateur historian, did extensive research into the phrase and came up with a surprising new answer. He discovered that the term first appeared in the 1920s when it was used by a writer named John FitzGerald who covered the horse races for the *Morning Telegraph*. Apparently stable hands in a New Orleans racetrack called a trip to a New York racecourse 'the Big Apple' – or greatest reward – for any talented thoroughbred. The slang passed into popular usage long after the newspaper – and FitzGerald – had disappeared. Popik's persistence in publicizing his research finally paid off in 1997, when the city government agreed to set the record straight and amend tourist literature to tell the real story. ■

For 20 years, the frontier town was a rough place to live. There were numerous confrontations with hostile natives, and drunken fights often broke out among the colonists. In 1647, the Dutch dispatched a new governor named Peter Stuyvesant to impose order on an unruly colony. His ban on alcohol and curtailment of religious freedoms caused unrest among the settlers, and few regretted the bloodless takeover of New Amsterdam by the British in 1664. Though New Amsterdam briefly returned to Dutch rule the following decade and retained much of its Dutch character well into the mid-18th century, the military might of England eventually prevailed.

Under British rule, New Amsterdam was renamed New York, in honor of the Duke of York, brother of King Charles II. Though colonists began cultivating farms in New Jersey and on Long Island, the port town remained geographically tiny – the area that today runs from Wall St south to the tip of Manhattan. By the 1730s, opposition to the excesses of British colonial rule had developed and was given voice by John Peter Zenger's influential newspaper the *Weekly Journal*. Zenger was brought to trial for his commentaries against the British governor, but he was acquitted of libel charges in a case that conveyed the colonists' desire for freedom of expression and democratic representation.

Though many influential New Yorkers resisted the growing calls for a war for independence, New York's Commons – where City Hall stands today – was the center of many anti-British protests. The complaints intensified in 1765 with the infamous Stamp Act, through which Britain collected taxes on goods from colonists to pay for its standing army in America, the measure that more than anything else triggered the Revolutionary War. But King George III's troops controlled New York for most of the war and took their time going home, finally withdrawing in 1783, a full two years after the fighting stopped.

The Emerging Seaport

By the time George Washington was sworn in as president of the new republic on the balcony of Federal Hall on Wall St in 1789, New York was a bustling seaport of 33,000 people, but lagged behind Philadelphia as a cultural capital. The new Congress abandoned the city for the District of Columbia the following year. The move was driven in part by an intense dislike of the city by the founding fathers – Thomas Jefferson later said that he regarded New York to be a 'cloacina (sewer) of all the depravities of human nature.'

New York boomed in the early 19th century. Its population swelled from about 65,000 in 1800 to 250,000 two decades later. The growing pains forced a city government into being. In 1828 Christmas riots by the poor prompted the establishment of the city's first police force, and the mayor became an elected official soon afterward. In 1832, a cholera epidemic swept through the city, which then did not have an adequate supply of drinkable water, killing more than 3000 people. That tragedy led to the building of the $12 million Croton Aqueduct, which was completed in 1842. It brought 72 million gallons of fresh water to the city each day, which not only improved public health conditions but finally allowed residents the opportunity to bathe regularly.

Civil War & the Gilded Age

Before his election, Abraham Lincoln had traveled to New York to test his political prospects and build the new Republican party out of the ashes of the old Whig movement. He impressed many with his 'might makes right' speech at the Great Hall of the city's Cooper Union. When the Southern states seceded from the Union and the Civil War broke out, immediately following Lincoln's election in 1860, New York provided many volunteers for the Union cause. It was also home to many of the best-known polemicists for slave emancipation – including newspaper editor and writer Horace Greeley.

But as the war dragged on, many of the city's poorest citizens turned against the effort, especially after mandatory conscription was introduced. Several mass meetings were addressed by New York's Southern-born mayor, Fernando Wood, and in the summer of 1863, Irish immigrants launched the 'draft riots,' in large part because of a provision that allowed wealthy men to pay $300 in order to avoid fighting. Within days the rioters turned their anger on black citizens, who they considered the real reason for the war and their main competition for work. More than 11 men were lynched in the streets and a black orphans' home was burned to the ground.

The remainder of the century in New York was a boom time for the city's population, which grew thanks to European immigration, and for businessmen, who took advantage of lax oversight of industry and stock trading during the so-called 'Gilded Age.' Robber barons like railroad speculator Jay Gould were able to amass tax-free fortunes that approached $100 million. Plenty of public officials lined their own pockets as well, none as aggressively as William Magear 'Boss' Tweed, notorious head of the city's Tammany Hall Democratic organization. Tweed used public works projects to steal millions of dollars from the public treasury before being toppled from power. These men built grand mansions along 'millionaires row' on lower Fifth Ave and entertained at hotels that stunned European visitors with their fine furniture and huge ballrooms. Along Broadway from City Hall to Union Square, multi-story buildings – the first 'skyscrapers' – were built to house corporate headquarters and newspaper offices.

The Melting Pot

As New York City's population more than doubled from 515,547 in 1850 to 1,164,673 in 1880, a tenement culture developed. The poorest New Yorkers invariably worked in dangerous factories and lived in squalid apartment blocks. The work of crusading journalist Jacob Riis, who chronicled how this 'other half' lived, shocked the city's middle class and led to the establishment of an independent health board as well as a series of workplace reforms led by religious activists. At the same time, prostitution was on the rise, and by the 1870s, some 500 brothels were operating in SoHo, then New York's red light district.

One of those affected by Riis's reporting was Theodore Roosevelt, a reform-minded state legislator who was revolted by the corruption of the Democratic machine. After running unsuccessfully for mayor as a Republican, Roosevelt became Police Commissioner in 1895. He later moved to the nation's capital, where he served as vice president to William McKinley, becoming president after McKinley's assassination in 1901.

Meanwhile, millionaires like Andrew Carnegie, John Jacob Astor and John D Rockefeller (see the sidebar on the Rockefellers in this chapter) began pouring money into public works, leading to the creation of institutions such as the New York Public Library (1895), and Carnegie Hall, built for $2 million in 1891.

The burgeoning of New York's population beyond the city's official borders led to the consolidation movement, as the city and its neighboring districts struggled to service the growing numbers. Residents of the independent districts of Queens, Staten Island, the Bronx and financially strapped Brooklyn voted to become 'boroughs' of New York City in 1898.

This new metropolis absorbed a second huge wave of European immigrants who arrived at New York's Ellis Island, and its population exploded once again, from just over three million in 1900 to seven million in 1930. During this period, horse-drawn trolleys disappeared from the city's streets as a major network of underground subways and elevated trains ('els') made the city's outer reaches easily accessible.

Still, New York was slow to respond to the needs of a crowded city in trouble. Time and again, pestilent conditions and disease made life miserable for the city's poorest, and preventable disasters often struck the immigrant community. One such tragedy was the fire aboard the steamship *General Slocum* on June 4, 1904, which

The Rockefeller Legacy

No family has had more influence on 20th century US history than the Rockefellers, who have left their stamp not only on business but also domestic politics and international relations. Their works and deeds have had a particular impact upon New York City.

It all started when the wily Ohio-born patriarch John D Rockefeller (1839-1937) bought into an oil refinery in 1859 with three partners, including his brother William (1841-1922). In the years following the Civil War, John successfully built an empire of oil refineries in the Midwest while William, a genius with money, organized the finances in New York (which included shady stock dealing). By the 1880s, the Rockefellers' Standard Oil Company had a hammerlock on crude oil processing and sales in the US.

The Rockefellers put their business interests in a trust and for a time even forced the railroad companies that shipped their product to give them a 'rebate' on shipments of petroleum. But John D's ruthless behavior attracted the attention of state and federal officials who normally gave corporate chieftains free rein on matters of business. After the trust was declared illegal by the Ohio state supreme court, Rockefeller incorporated Standard Oil in New Jersey and continued to make millions as the internal combustion engine made automobile travel part of the American lifestyle.

By the time the Standard Oil monopoly was broken up into 34 different companies by the US Supreme Court in 1911, John D Rockefeller had amassed a fortune worth more than $1 billion. (Standard Oil's constituent parts are now huge businesses in their own right, including Exxon, Mobil, Texaco, Amoco, British Petroleum, Shell, Chevron and Atlantic Richfield.) Rockefeller spent the rest of his days looking after the various charitable and educational institutions he founded, including the University of Chicago and a New York City based medical research facility now known as Rockefeller University.

John D Rockefeller Jr (1874-1960) took over control of the family's fortune after his father retired, and also left his mark on society, particularly on New York City. In the height of the Depression, the younger Rockefeller proposed the building of a new Metropolitan Opera House on property owned by Columbia University that was occupied by hundreds

---

was carrying a group of German Americans from the Lower East Side on a church outing. More than 1000 people, many of them women and children, died in the conflagration.

As the immigrant population collected political strength, demands for change became overwhelming, and during the Depression, a crusader named Fiorello La Guardia (who previously worked as an interpreter at Ellis Island) was elected mayor. In three terms in office, the popular 'Little Flower' fought municipal corruption and expanded the social service network. He even read the Sunday comics to the city's children on the radio during a newspaper strike. Meanwhile civic planner Robert Moses used his politically appointed position as a parks commissioner to garner power without the obligation of answering to voters. He used that influence to remake the city's landscape through public works projects, highways and big events like the World's Fairs of 1939 and 1964. Unfortunately, Moses had the power of a modern-day Baron Haussmann but none of the master's aesthetic sense; his projects (which include the Triborough Bridge, Lincoln Center, several highways and massive housing projects) often destroyed entire neighborhoods and routed huge numbers of residents.

A Proud City Stumbles

New York emerged from WWII proud and ready for business. As one of the few world-class cities untouched by war, New York seemed the place to be. But prosperity wasn't limited to the city. In the 1950s, highways made access to the suburbs easy and hundreds of thousands of New Yorkers took advantage of them to move away permanently.

It wasn't just an understandable desire

of small brownstone apartment blocks. When that plan fell through, Rockefeller proceeded with a massive project that became known as Rockefeller Center; the limestone office and shop complex single-handedly changed the face of central Manhattan. He also built Riverside Church in upper Manhattan, and donated $8.5 million to purchase the East Side land for the headquarters of the United Nations.

John D Jr's six children all played prominent roles in public life. Among them were John D III (1906-78), one of the founders of New York's Lincoln Center, Winthrop (1912-73), who settled in Arkansas and became that state's Republican governor from 1967 to 1970, and David (1925–), the chairman of Chase Manhattan Bank and a recognized leader of the American business establishment.

But perhaps the most famous scion was Nelson Rockefeller (1908-79). He served Presidents Roosevelt, Truman and Eisenhower in a variety of positions and helped establish the current site of the Museum of Modern Art in New York. He was also elected Governor of New York State for four terms, and built the massive Albany State Mall complex. Rockefeller was a socially liberal Republican who was so self-conscious of his wealth he used the phrase 'thanks a thousand' to express gratitude. A leading contender for the Republican nomination in the 1960, 1964 and 1968 presidential elections, Nelson was appointed by Gerald Ford to serve as Vice President following Richard Nixon's resignation in 1974. Even today, upholders of the shrinking GOP left are known, derisively, as 'Rockefeller Republicans.'

Today the Rockefeller billions are spread among dozens of cousins, and the family name is not as prominent in the public eye. But John D IV, the great grandson of the patriarch, continued the tradition of public service by moving to West Virginia to work with poor people in Appalachia. Known as 'Jay' Rockefeller, he served as Democratic governor of that state and is now a US Senator, and is considered one of the most articulate liberal voices in the country. The $2.5 billion New York-based Rockefeller Foundation, created by John D Sr in 1913, continues to award over $100 million in grants every year to promote reforms in education, health and the environment worldwide. ■

for upward mobility that drew them away: many white residents left neighborhoods they felt had 'gone bad,' which was a barely polite way of saying that blacks and Puerto Ricans had taken their rightful place there too. Contributing to the problem was New York's narcoleptic political leadership in the post-La Guardia era. Tainted by municipal corruption, one mayor – William O'Dwyer – was appointed Ambassador to Mexico as a face-saving device. The most prominent Democrat of the time, Robert Wagner, served three terms without significantly dealing with the economic and demographic changes in the city.

While the politicos dithered and played to various entrenched constituencies, the city began to slide. TV production, manufacturing jobs and even the fabled Brooklyn Dodgers baseball team moved to the West Coast, along with the Dodgers' cross-town rivals the New York Giants. Like most of the US, New York looked to the West for cultural direction, and eventually corporations began abandoning the city as innovation in communications technology made it possible to do business anywhere.

Time and again, public works projects were either badly executed (the highways that destroyed entire neighborhoods) or started and then abandoned altogether (a subway line under Second Ave). Local officials fought to keep the subway fare cheap – first a nickel, then a dime and finally 15¢ well into the 1960s – which had the effect of keeping money out of the system for desperately needed improvements and expansion.

By the '70s, the unreliable, graffiti-ridden transit system became an internationally recognized symbol of New York's psychic and economic tailspin. Only a massive federal loan program saved the city from bankruptcy.

KIM GRANT

The World Trade Center's twin towers dwarf neighboring
buildings that would dominate most other skylines.

The Big Apple Comes Back

During the anything-goes Reagan years, the city regained much of its swagger as billions were made on Wall St. Ed Koch, the colorful and opinionated three-term mayor, seemed to embody the New Yorker's ability to charm and irritate at the same time. But in 1989, Koch was defeated in a Democratic primary election by David Dinkins, who became the city's first African American mayor. Dinkins, a career Democratic-machine politician, was rightly criticized for merely presiding over a city government in need of reform, though his moves to put more police on the streets helped curb crime. He was narrowly defeated for a second term in 1993 by moderate Republican Rudolph Giuliani. Thanks to the big drop in crime and the weakness of his Democratic-machine opponents, Giuliani was widely regarded as unbeatable in the 1997 mayoral election. For the first time in decades, the city is talking about starting huge (and necessary) projects to augment its infrastructure, such as a new rail tunnel under the Hudson River. (For more on Giuliani see Government & Politics, below.)

Strangely enough, New Yorkers head into the next millennium with the somewhat grudging feeling that, perhaps, the city has found a way to thrive as well as survive.

GEOGRAPHY

New York City is largely made up of some 50 islands besides its most famous one, Manhattan. Some islands are mere clumps of land set in the water, but others include the borough of Staten Island as well as Queens and Brooklyn, which together comprise the westernmost end of Long Island (a fact not made clear by maps of the city).

In fact, only the borough of the Bronx is physically connected to the US continental mainland, though its official borders include the offshore fishing port of City Island.

CLIMATE

Books will usually tell you that New York's weather is 'temperate,' but the yearly averages do not convey the extremes in climate here, which can make life unbearable sometimes. It's unbelievably hot and humid for days on end in summer, then glacially cold and windy in December, January and February, with the odd day of warmish weather.

Each year, about 45 inches of rain falls on New York, with long wet stretches common in November and April. Snow falls almost exclusively from December to February and the average total is about 30 inches, though major blizzards occur about once every four years.

In winter, high winds and Canadian weather fronts can combine to drive temperatures well below the freezing mark of 32°F (which happens to be the mean daily temperature in January). These winds are especially strong on the West Side of Manhattan off the Hudson River, and local weather reports invariably estimate the wind chill factor on these days.

In summer, the mean daily temperature is 77°F, and days can be comfortable until the humidity rises to about 60%. In general, temperatures tend to be a bit higher in Manhattan, because the heat is absorbed by concrete and asphalt. On particularly bad days, New Yorkers will complain how 'it's not the heat, its the humidity' that's driving them to sweat-drenched distraction.

ENVIRONMENT

New York has come a long way in recent years in improving the quality of its air and surrounding waterways, as its docks suffered decades of decline while heavy shipping moved away from Manhattan to a 'superport' in New Jersey. But visitors will note that the city's narrow streets are anything but pristine, and its infrastructure is in desperate need of improvement (potholes riddle the streets, and flooding from century-old water mains that crack are nearly a bi-weekly occurrence). The city also needs to find a new spot for its garbage now that Staten Island's dump – the world's largest – is scheduled to be closed within a few years.

The Hudson River, a fetid body of water where kids swam off piers as recently as the 1950s, used to be a dumping ground for 200 million gallons of sewage daily. But that changed with the opening of a sewage treatment plant on W 125th St in 1986. The worst pollution actually came from two now closed General Electric manufacturing facilities near Albany, which dumped PCBs (polychlorinated biphenyls) into the river and poisoned the fish supply. Today it's actually possible to catch striped bass, blueback herring, yellow perch and blue crab in the Hudson, and health officials say they're safe to eat if you're so inclined. Those who are still uneasy about eating anything out of the Hudson will be heartened by the state's 1996 Clean Water/Clean Air Bond Act, which provides $1.7 billion to continue the clean-up.

Whatever the conditions of the air and water, visitors will probably suffer most from the 24-hour noise pollution in New York – the car horns, sirens and trucks bedevil those used to quieter climes.

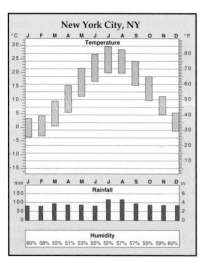

GOVERNMENT & POLITICS

New York has a long record of voting for the Democratic Party, though there are conservative pockets in the blue collar sections of Queens and Brooklyn, and suburban-flavored Staten Island is almost exclusively Republican. Despite the Democratic tradition, socially liberal Republican reformers can be elected mayor, as proven by the current mayor, Rudolph Giuliani.

A former federal prosecutor, Giuliani was elected to City Hall on his second attempt in 1993, defeating the beleaguered David Dinkins. Giuliani has shaken up the city bureaucracy and taken credit for the continuing drop in crime, but he also has a well deserved reputation as a control freak who cannot allow his administrators any independence, while being highly reluctant to take the blame for administration failures. In recent years he has run both the public schools chancellor and police chief out of town when they began garnering credit for good performances that threatened to diminish Giuliani's own ability to take credit for innovations in the education system and law enforcement.

In late 1997, Giuliani ran for reelection and was widely expected to win big, due to a combination of his genuinely decent record and the great weakness of his potential Democratic opponents.

The city's political structure also includes five borough presidents, who have their own local staffs and smaller budgets for community-level works and patronage. Historically, these positions are held by career political hacks and/or mayoral candidates in waiting. There is also a city wide comptroller (who serves as budget administrator and auditor) and a public advocate (who largely is concerned with consumer affairs).

New York also has a 51-member city council, perhaps the most disgraceful and useless governing body of any major city in the world. These elected officials, who are paid over $70,000 a year, are meant to represent individual neighborhoods and serve as a check on mayoral power. But in reality, city council members spend little time on their four-year jobs and many of them are lawyers who conduct full time legal practices.

In 1994, a law was passed limiting city council members, the mayor and major office holders to just two terms. The council unsuccessfully tried to fight the law in court, and in 1996 placed another issue on the ballot allowing current members a third term before dismissal. Although the politicos cleverly worded the ballot item so that a 'yes' vote on the measure actually meant approving the term extensions, it was convincingly rejected, and most current city council members must clear out in 2001.

KIM GRANT
Art Deco bas relief detail on Fifth Avenue

ECONOMY

New York could stand alone as its own city state. It is either the nation's leader or a major player in the worlds of finance, tourism, shipping and transportation, and is still a prestige address for major US corporations and nearly all prominent foreign concerns.

Though the city fell seriously behind in manufacturing in the post WWII era, it is still the country's leading producer of fashion and the world's communication center. And even in this time of electronic 24-hour global communications, New York is still the leading financial center. In fact, the market's success has a major impact on the local economy – though it is responsible for only 4% of city jobs, Wall St tax payments account for 17% of revenues, and there is a ripple effect on restaurants, bars and real estate when local fat cats are doing well.

Tourism cannot be underestimated in importance to New York's financial health. Some 30 million visitors come to the city each year (10 million in the Christmas holiday season alone), and they pour $18 billion into the local economy. In all some 25,000 different New York businesses directly benefit from the tourist trade.

POPULATION & PEOPLE

Approximately half of all New York state residents live in the New York City area, with the majority of those belonging to major ethnic groups. In fact, 28% of the city's 7,322,000 residents are foreign-born, buttressing its reputation as the nation's 'melting pot,' though that term seems somewhat quaint and misapplied in this era of increased ethnic identity and, sometimes, division.

The latest census count (1990) indicates that some 52% of the population is white, though immigration patterns in the middle of the decade virtually guarantee that non-Hispanic whites are now no longer in the majority. Blacks make up 29% of the population, and Asians some 7%. People of

The Immigrant Explosion

The city famously developed by immigrants is currently in the middle of one of its periodic émigré booms. Perhaps more than one million foreign-born persons will move into the city in the 1990s. About one-third of all residents are immigrants, adding to the countless ethnic subcultures in New York.

Official estimates indicate that in the early '90s, the largest group of immigrants came from the Dominican Republic (about 25,000) and most settled in Washington Heights, making that the neighborhood with the largest influx of foreign-born residents. At the same time, about 20,000 people from the former Soviet Union flooded into the Brighton Beach section of Brooklyn. A like number of immigrants from China, Taiwan and Hong Kong settled in Chinatown, pushing the borders of that neighborhood north toward the East Village.

Moreover, a federal lottery handed out a disproportionate number of resident visas to immigrants from Poland and Ireland. As a result, many Poles moved to the already established Eastern European neighborhoods of Williamsburg and Greenpoint in Brooklyn, while the Irish (who are basically everywhere) have added to their traditional stronghold in the Riverdale section of the Bronx.

Some of the new subcultures may be here just temporarily. It is estimated that more than 5000 young Japanese are currently living in the East Village. They have been attracted by the neighborhood's cutting edge reputation and the fact that a cheap dollar takes the sting out of ever-increasing rent rates. Walking around the East Village you'll see young Japanese boys puffing cigarettes in cafes and their female counterparts wearing hot pink plastic pants. ■

Hispanic origin (all races) comprise some 24%. There are about one million people in other racial categories.

New York City is a singular example of racial diversity. Visitors from abroad are often stunned at the variety of color in a single subway car. The city is home to the largest Chinese population in the US, along with the country's largest bloc of Asian Indians. On Labor Day, the Caribbean Day Parade in Brooklyn is attended by hundreds of thousands of Caribbean-born immigrants. New York City claims to have more Jews than anywhere outside of Israel, more native Greeks than anywhere outside of Athens, more native Russians than anywhere outside of Moscow, and perhaps more native Irish than anywhere outside of the British isles. Differences in culture and undocumented immigration may make some of these boasts statistically unprovable, but a walk through several of the city's neighborhoods leaves the impression that the statement is probably not far off the mark.

Blacks

There are about two million blacks living in New York City. African slaves first arrived in New York in 1644, when it was still part of the Dutch colony of New Netherland. By the time the American colonies went to war with Britain, New York's black population numbered about two thousand, and slaves fought on both sides of the conflict in the hope of winning their freedom. (After the war New York state freed those who fought in the local armed forces.) By the early 19th century, the abolitionist movement had been established in New York City, along with *Freedom's Journal*, the nation's first black newspaper. But voting rights were not bestowed on black males until well after the Civil War, in 1870. At the same time, black citizens found themselves losing economic ground to immigrants from Ireland and Eastern Europe.

By the early 20th century, migrating blacks from the south triggered the development of Harlem in Upper Manhattan, helping to create a well-defined community with churches, black-owned businesses and nightclubs that welcomed whites from other neighborhoods. For the first time, West Indians became a significant part of the area's population. But the 'Harlem Renaissance' – as captured in writing by Langston Hughes and in photographs by James VanDerZee – ended with the economic devastation of the Depression. After WWII, it became clear that blacks were again lagging behind more entrenched second and third generation white ethnic groups, but city officials did little to address the situation until riots broke out in Harlem in 1964. As in many US cities, lower-income black residents were stuck in ugly, decaying housing projects. By the 1970s, much of what was left of the black middle class had abandoned the city and followed the path paved by earlier white residents to the suburbs.

Hispanics

About half of New York City's 1.8 million Hispanic residents are of Puerto Rican descent. They began migrating from the island in significant numbers during the Depression and began displacing Italians in East Harlem. Throughout the 1960s, political activism by 'Nuyoricans' led to increased recognition of their contribution to city life, and the establishment of several important cultural institutions, including the Museo del Barrio near East Harlem.

Over the past 20 years there has been an influx of Latinos from many other countries. Immigrants from Ecuador and Colombia have created new communities in Queens, and the Washington Heights neighborhood in Manhattan is home to many former citizens of the Dominican Republic and El Salvador.

Jews

The first Jews, a group of 24 refugees fleeing persecution in Brazil, came to New York in 1654, when it was still a Dutch colony. They have been an important part of the city's population and politics ever since. Until the early 20th century, most of this population lived in Manhattan's Lower East Side, and the neighborhood still retains its traditional character, even though most New Yorkers of Jewish background now live elsewhere. In Brooklyn, the neighborhoods of Crown Heights and Williamsburg are still home to large numbers of Orthodox Jews, and an influx of immigrants from the Soviet Union during the

'80s added to their numbers. Today New York's Jews comprise about 12% of New York City's total population. They are the city's second largest ethnic voting bloc, behind blacks, but are the most effective ethnic group because they vote in higher numbers.

Racial Tensions

Former mayor David Dinkins often spoke of New York City as a 'gorgeous mosaic' of differing peoples. But several well-publicized incidents have painted an uglier picture, largely because of a growing level of distrust between African Americans and other ethnic groups. In 1986, a black man confronted by a gang of white teens was beaten to death in Howard Beach, Brooklyn, leading city officials to promise a vigorous crackdown on so-called 'bias crimes.' The following year, a black teenage girl from the upstate town of Wappingers Falls said officials ignored her claims of being raped by a group of white men. Accusations of a cover-up were silenced after her tale was revealed to be a hoax.

Tensions between Jews and African Americans have resulted in two separate incidents that have rocked the city. When a black child was accidentally run over by a member of a Hasidic Jewish sect in Brooklyn's Crown Heights neighborhood during the summer 1991, rumors quickly spread that the girl had been refused treatment by a Jewish ambulance crew. During several days of rioting that followed, an innocent Hasidic man was murdered by an angry mob.

More recently, African American anger has grown about the absence of black-owned businesses in the inner city. In late 1995, protesters hurled anti-Semitic insults in front of a Jewish-run clothing store in Harlem after the owner (oddly enough, a local black church) tried to evict the black-owned record shop from the building. Soon afterward, a disturbed African American man named Roland Smith stormed the place and burned it to the ground, killing himself and seven workers. City officials said they were determined to use Civil Rights laws against some demonstrators for inciting the tragedy, but didn't follow up on that potentially explosive promise.

It needs to be emphasized that despite these well-publicized tragedies, millions of New Yorkers live with each other and walk the streets together every day, usually without incident, and visitors who refuse to visit ethnic neighborhoods, are, in their own way, giving in to irrational fears.

ARTS
Literature

The publishing capital of the world has been featured in thousands of books. What follows is a highly selective sampling of my favorites.

KIM GRANT

Statue of Romeo and Juliet at the Delacort Theatre, Central Park

Three New York Film Directors: Scorsese, Allen and Lumet

Martin Scorsese This quirky, nervous and visionary director is celebrated for bringing the dark side of New York to life. Born in Queens in 1942, Scorsese grew up on Elizabeth St in Manhattan's Little Italy. After working as an editor on the documentary *Woodstock* (1970), he made *Mean Streets* (1973), a drama about Little Italy – actually shot in the Bronx – with Robert De Niro and Harvey Keitel. Both actors would become closely associated with Scorsese's films, starring together in *Taxi Driver* (1975), about psychopaths in the East Village. De Niro won an Oscar for his performance in *Raging Bull* (1980), a brutal biography of boxer Jake La Motta that was considered an instant classic.

In recent years, Scorsese has won praise for *Goodfellas* (1990), another true-life mob drama, and *The Age of Innocence* (1993), a detail-rich costume drama of 19th century New York based on the Edith Wharton novel. Scorsese cast his colorful parents in small roles in all his films until their deaths in the 1990s – he even featured them in an affectionate documentary called *Italianamerican* (1974). Lately, Scorsese has led the fight to preserve American film heritage through the restoration of classic films.

Woody Allen This filmmaker equals Scorsese in prominence, but certainly Woody Allen has no equal among US filmmakers in enjoying so much control over his final product (though the younger Spike Lee is challenging Allen's position as all-round *auteur*). Allen, who writes, directs and often stars in his own films, turns out motion pictures the way others produce short stories – about one per year. Born Allen Stewart Konigsberg in 1935 in Brooklyn, he began writing gags for TV comedians, and got a job on Sid Caesar's legendary *Your Show of Shows* in the mid-1950s. He then graduated to stand-up comedy, perfecting the now familiar persona of a sex-obsessed, intellectual 'nebbish' who nonetheless gets the girl in the end. He made his Hollywood debut as an actor and screenwriter in *What's New Pussycat?* (1965) and followed that up a year later with *What's Up Tiger Lilly?*, in which he redubbed comic dialogue onto a Japanese James Bond-style spy movie. While he was writing and directing the purely comic *Take the Money and Run* (1969), *Bananas* (1971) and *Sleeper* (1972), among others, he also began writing feisty comic essays for the *New Yorker*, and had a Broadway hit in *Play It Again, Sam*. The play, in which his loser character gets advice from the ghost of Humphrey Bogart, became a hit movie in 1972.

O Henry (1862-1910), author of *The Gift of the Magi*, and F Scott Fitzgerald (1896-1940) are 'New York' writers who specialized in writing short stories that brought two distinct New York social eras (late 19th century and the 'Roaring '20s') to life. Seek out Fitzgerald's *Tales of the Jazz Age* and *A Diamond as Big as the Ritz*.

Though largely an expatriate throughout his life, American writer Henry James (1843-1916) described New York upperclass life before the Civil War in *Washington Square*. The row houses that were then occupied by New York society still line the northern edge of Washington Square Park today. James's contemporary Edith Wharton (1862-1937) chronicled the Gilded Age New York City in the Pulitzer Prize winning *Age of Innocence* and the collection *Old New York*. Unfortunately most of her New York – the original Metropolitan Opera house, the Metropolitan Museum of Art and the mansions of Fifth Ave's 'Millionaire's Row' – has disappeared or been altered beyond recognition.

There are at least two more recent bestselling novels that provide a historical context for contemporary readers. Jack Finney's *Time and Again* is a perennially popular work about a man from the 20th century who somehow winds up in the New York City of the 1880s. Finney creates a descriptive, factually accurate portrayal of the period. *The Alienist*, by historian

It was with the classic *Annie Hall* (1975), one of the rare comedies to ever win an Oscar for Best Picture, that Allen's reputation as a comic artist was assured. He followed it up with the serious drama *Interiors* (1978) and *Manhattan* (1979), an unabashed (and beautifully shot in B&W) love letter to the city.

His private and professional partnership with actress Mia Farrow produced (among others) *Zelig* (1983), *Broadway Danny Rose* (1984) and *Hannah & Her Sisters* (1986), for which he won an Oscar for best screenplay. His nasty breakup with Farrow came after he began an affair with Soon-Yi Previn, Farrow's adopted daughter, in 1992. Allen still produces celebrated films, including the unlikely musical *Everyone Says I Love You* (1996), a quirky musical comedy featuring Goldie Hawn, Alan Alda and Allen himself crooning famous love songs in New York, Paris and Venice. He has since shot another work based on his court battles, while still playing clarinet in a traditional jazz band at Michael's Pub in Midtown every Monday night.

Sidney Lumet Born in 1924, Sidney Lumet represents an older, more idealistic New York liberal sensibility, one formulated in the '50s, when he got his start directing live TV drama. Even when most directors went out to Hollywood, Lumet preferred to shoot many of his films in the city. His first feature was *12 Angry Men* (1957) with Henry Fonda, a reprise of one of the best live TV dramas. He went on to direct *Serpico* (1974), a true-life story of a policeman who exposed widespread department corruption; *Dog Day Afternoon* (1975), another true-life drama – filmed entirely within 20 blocks of the actual event – about a bank robber (played by Al Pacino) who has a bizarre scheme to get his lover the money for a sex change operation; and *Network* (1976), a stinging satire of TV's excesses that foreshadowed the '90s era of junk talk shows. Lumet has also proven his versatility as a director with the Baroque costume melodrama *Murder on the Orient Express* (1974), set entirely in Europe. In all, his films – which in later years have included *The Verdict* (1982) , *Q&A* (1990, shot in Spanish Harlem) and *Night Falls on Manhattan* (1997) – have garnered more than 50 Academy Award nominations.

Today, Lumet still holds extensive pre-shoot rehearsals for his actors in the East Village, in a large room in the Ukrainian National Home on Second Ave between 8th and 9th Sts. He has written a wonderful treatise on his craft called *Making Movies*, essential reading for film buffs. ■

Caleb Carr, is set in roughly the same era but concentrates on a mass murderer on the loose in tenement society. This work features many real-life characters – including a crusading police commissioner named Theodore Roosevelt – and serves as a reminder that 'olde New York' was a dangerous place to be, particularly if you were young and poor.

Though it is not solely set in New York, Celine's *Journey to the End of the Night* is worth a mention because of its portrayal of a vagabond Frenchman on the loose in a triumphant city just after WWI. This New York is proud, booming and more than a little bit arrogant. The noted essayist Christopher Morley (1890-1957) brings the same times to life in his *Christopher Morley's New York* – a city of elevated streetcars, late night speakeasies and great literary arguments.

The Greenwich Village Beats left their mark on literature when Allen Ginsberg (1926-97) published *Howl and Other Poems* in 1956 amid great controversy, followed a year later by Jack Kerouac's (1922-69) *On the Road*, which was written, it was said, in one sitting in the Chelsea Hotel on a roll of teletype paper.

JD Salinger's (born 1919) *Catcher in the Rye* has spoken to three generations of manic teenagers with its portrayal of the misadventures of Holden Caulfield that culminate at the Museum of Natural History.

Of the many works by black artists set in New York, perhaps the most acclaimed is Ralph Ellison's (1914-94) *Invisible Man*, a classic rumination on race and the US.

EL Doctorow's (born 1931) works – including *Ragtime*, *The Book of Daniel* and *World's Fair* – reflect on New York in its various eras, from turn of the century boomtown to Cold War ideological battleground. Mario Puzo's *The Godfather* describes the West Side's Hell Kitchen neighborhood as it was in the years just after WWI.

Thomas Pynchon's debut novel *V* hopscotches from the New York of the late 1950s to various points around the globe, and illustrates the feverish attitudes of the young people who 'yo-yo'd' their way through the city at the time.

Pynchon was the forerunner of those who brought a newer, more energetic style of writing that dominated the '70s and '80s, with some authors adopting phantasmagoric or Gothic styles. Don DeLillo's *Great Jones Street* and Mark Helprin's *A Winter's Tale* are two prime examples of this disturbing new view of society. Paul Auster, who lives in the Park Slope section of Brooklyn, has won many followers abroad for his modern noir *New York Trilogy* and more recently he wrote the screenplay for the Brooklyn-based movie *Smoke*. Author-screenwriter Richard Price has also created a number of edgy works, including *The Wanderers*, *Ladies' Man* and *Clockers*.

Jay McInerney was first blessed, then cursed by his association with the yuppified early '80s, occasioned by his blockbuster first novel *Bright Lights, Big City*. Tom Wolfe's *Bonfire of the Vanities* followed that up with a comic canvass of a city out of control and noticeably split along racial lines. Tama Janowitz, author of *Slaves of New York* covers much of the same ground and has enjoyed a life of literary celebrity.

In recent years, many new writers and spoken word performers have emerged in the East Village of New York City debuting their work at various cafes, but for the most part the Generation X novelists have been based elsewhere.

For an overview of the city in literature, pick up Shaun O'Connell's *Remarkable, Unspeakable, New York*, a survey of how American writers have regarded the metropolis over two centuries.

Film

Just as it's nearly impossible to define the perfect New York book, there's almost no way to present a definitive list of films about the city. For years, 'New York movies' were shot on Hollywood sound stages, or perhaps cheated a bit by bringing in actors for a few days to shoot exteriors (a practice that continues to this day for TV shows such as *Seinfeld* and *NYPD Blue*).

That began to change substantially in the '70s, when directors began striving for realism and equipment became more mobile, making location shooting a less expensive alternative to the studio. Today, it's common to see film production trucks on the streets of New York (see the sidebar Filming on the Streets in Things to See & Do) – though some lower budget films try to pass off Canadian cities as New York (such as Jackie Chan's *Rumble in the Bronx*, which was shot in Vancouver). With a few noted exceptions, the following films were authentically set in New York and represent some sort of unique aspect of the city. They are all available on video.

On the Town (1949), about three sailors on shore leave in New York City, stars Gene Kelly and Frank Sinatra. Because Sinatra was at the height of his bobby-soxer popularity, director Stanley Donen would 'steal' a shot by setting up the cameras and sending the actors out at the last minute. It didn't always work – which is why you can spot hundreds of onlookers as Sinatra and Kelly sing 'New York, New York' in Rockefeller Center. The first major noir film to make use of the city streets was *Naked City*, in 1948, which was loosely based on the crime photos of the famous newspaper photographer named Weegee, who also inspired the Joe Pesci film, *The Public Eye* (1992).

Though it was filmed solely on a Hollywood soundstage, the setting of the melodrama *Dead End* (1937) captures the transformation, during the 1920s and '30s, of the East Side of Midtown Manhattan from a crowded tenement district to an enclave of fancy apartment blocks for high society.

The best B&W film ever shot in New York was the gritty *Sweet Smell of Success* (1957) starring Burt Lancaster as a ruthless gossip columnist (a barely disguised Walter Winchell) and Tony Curtis as the desperate press agent he manipulates. The cinematography, by the legendary James Wong Howe, captures the city's '50s nightlife perfectly, revolving around a Midtown nightclub scene that has pretty much disappeared thanks to the building of skyscrapers.

West Side Story (1961) depicted love and gang rivalry in Hell's Kitchen, and includes exterior shots of the tenements that were torn down to make way for the expansion of Lincoln Center.

A quintessential New York film is *The Taking of Pelham One, Two, Three* (1974) starring Walter Matthau as a beleaguered transit cop confronted with a subway hijacking. This cult classic, written by Peter Stone (the only writer to have won a Tony, an Oscar and an Emmy) includes a terrific twist in the last scene.

Three Days of the Condor (1975) is a great work of '70s anti-government paranoia starring Robert Redford as a rogue CIA officer on the run in New York who enlists the reluctant help of Faye Dunaway to bring his story to the authorities. Then there's *Saturday Night Fever* (1977), the Brooklyn take of the classic tale of a kid looking to make it in the big city of Manhattan.

In recent years, foreign directors have come to New York to provide domestic audiences with a look at the city from an outsider's sensibility.

Wayne Wang's *Smoke* (1995) and *Blue in the Face* (1996) both star Harvey Keitel as a cigar-store owner in Brooklyn. In Ang Lee's bittersweet comedy *The Wedding Banquet* (1993), New York represents the land of sexual freedom for a gay man from Taiwan, whose meddlesome parents arrive to supervise his 'marriage' to a woman. Manhattan's Chelsea and the Socrates Sculpture Park in Queen are featured settings.

In 1986, Spike Lee emerged as a major new New York filmmaker with *She's Gotta Have It*, and followed it up with the controversial *Do The Right Thing* (1989) about racial tensions in Brooklyn. Since then he's carved out a career combining fine works like *Malcolm X* (1992) and *Clockers* (1995), while gaining fame and wealth as a director of commercials for Nike.

Spike Lee

Music

Classical New York is home to some of the foremost classical music and operatic institutions in the world. Lincoln Center for the Performing Arts is the venue for such prestigious organizations as the New York Philharmonic Orchestra, the Metropolitan Opera Company and the New York City Opera. The century-old Carnegie Hall is the famous venue for solo and orchestral performances.

For years, New York attracted foreign-born composers and conductors, often because the city was home to some of the finest recording facilities in the world. Gustav Mahler (1860-1911) served as musical director of the New York Philharmonic in the last years of his life, and Arturo Toscanini (1867-1957) achieved great fame in the US as head of the Philharmonic and NBC Orchestras.

Though born and educated in Massachusetts, Leonard Bernstein (1918-90) became closely associated with New York and became the first major American-born classical conductor. He achieved fame in 1943 when, stepping in for the ailing Bruno Walter at the last minute, he conducted the New York Philharmonic Orchestra and wound up the subject of a front page article in the next day's *Times*. Later, Bernstein became musical director of the Philharmonic while making frequent forays into popular music, most notably with the stage works *On the Town*, *Candide* and *West Side Story*.

John Cage (1912-92) moved from his native Los Angeles to New York in the 1940s and became known as the leading avant-garde composer, using atonal structures and even silence in his famous works.

Jazz Ragtime, the progenitor of jazz, was widely popular in New York during the early 20th century thanks to Scott Joplin (1868-1917), whose 'Maple Leaf Rag' is a classic example of the form, and the young Irving Berlin (1888-1989), whose Tin Pan Alley brand of ragtime is represented by his 'Alexander's Ragtime Band.'

After cities like Kansas City and New Orleans gave way to New York as the US jazz capital in the 1940s, every performer of note (and thousands of wannabes) headed to Manhattan to be discovered. Jazz became mainstream, moving from clubs to orchestral spaces thanks to the works of George Gershwin (1898-1937) and Duke Ellington (1899-1974). (Ellington's famous recording 'Take the A Train' grew out of the first line of instructions he gave to composer Billy Strayhorn on how to get to his Harlem apartment.)

In the '40s, trumpeter Dizzy Gillespie (1917-93) and saxophonist Charlie Parker (1920-55) ushered in bebop, which quickly gave way to the freer expressions of trumpeter Miles Davis (1926-91) and Sonny Rollins (born 1929). Many old speakeasies of the '20s – particularly those on 52nd St – became jazz clubs in the post-WWII era.

In the early '60s, as jazz was caught in a struggle between structuralists and those seeking unfettered free expression, Rollins famously dropped out of sight to practice pieces. (His public solo sessions took place on the Williamsburg Bridge, contrary to the legend that places him on the more picturesque Brooklyn Bridge.) By the late '70s jazz was an expressive free for all, but a traditionalist movement has emerged in recent years, with trumpeter Wynton Marsalis and sax sensation Joshua Redman leading the way.

Today, Greenwich Village is still the site of many jazz clubs, including the 50-year-old Village Vanguard, arguably the most famous jazz venue in the world. Each summer there are at least three major jazz festivals held in the city, and in 1996, Wynton Marsalis began the annual 'Jazz at Lincoln Center' program, bringing dozens of major contemporary artists to the cultural mecca.

Rock, Folk & Punk Most of the preeminent figures in US popular music (Bob Dylan, The Doors, Jimi Hendrix) got their start elsewhere before heading to New York for validation and increased popularity. In fact, Alan Freed, the disc jockey credited with popularizing the term 'rock and roll'

Hip Hop

Unlike the many types of music that developed in other parts of the US before arriving in New York City, hip hop is a homegrown New York art form. In the mid-1970s, Bronx DJs Africa Bambaataa and Grandmaster Flash, not content to merely spin dance records, created original pieces by mixing songs and scratching, a sound effect caused by rotating records back and forth by hand. Rapping and breakdancing soon became an integral part of the live act, and by the late '70s the first hip hop groups began taking their grooves into recording studios.

The popularity of Grandmaster Flash and Harlem's Sugar Hill Gang (whose 'Rapper's Delight' was a Top-40 hit) helped spread the new form to other cities. By the mid-'80s more commercial albums by Run-DMC and by white exponents the Beastie Boys were selling largely to white audiences.

Rappers who upheld the hard-core, street-oriented New York style include LL Cool J, Public Enemy and Big Daddy Kane. Queen Latifa, from Newark, New Jersey, remains hip hop's leading feminist force.

Coinciding with the mainstreaming of hip hop, West Coast 'gangsta' rappers Snoop Doggy Dog and NWA ('Straight Outta Compton') emerged with controversial lawless attitudes that nevertheless met with tremendous commercial success. The criminal posturings of star gangsta performers were soon validated by convictions and jail sentences for several artists. Violence had already led major venues nationwide to ban hip hop shows, but record sales continued to climb. In late 1996, a war of words between leading West Coast and East Coast rappers Tupac Shakur and Biggie Smalls culminated in the shooting deaths of both artists in the space of a few months.

Hip hop enters its third decade in a metamorphic state. While computerized samplers have replaced turntables as the central element of the music, rapping is increasingly co-opted by other music forms – everyone from contemporary rocker Beck to acid jazz artists is rapping – and even popular hip hop groups like the Fugees seem to rely on rehashings of old Bob Marley songs, rather than deliver straight rap. ■

---

was a Cleveland broadcaster who moved to New York to seek a bigger audience.

The 'Tin Pan Alley' system of writers feeding songs to performers, which can be traced back to the early part of the 20th century, worked for the first wave of doo wop and rock groups. People like Jerry Leiber and Mike Stoller ('Hound Dog' and 'Don't be Cruel') and Carole King ('Be My Baby') eventually gave way to a new generation of singer-songwriters.

New York became the rock club capital of the world. By the '60s, performers like Hendrix were making waves in clubs like Cafe Wha? while Dylan headed a group of singers based out of Folk City. By the '70s, homegrown alternative rock groups such as The Ramones and The New York Dolls were appearing at the now-defunct club Max's Kansas City.

Certainly the most famous club of this era is CBGB on the Bowery in the East Village. Though its initials stand for 'Country, Bluegrass and Blues,' CBGB became known as ground zero for the punk and alternative movements. Talking Heads, The Police, Dead Kennedys and Black Flag are among the many groups that have appeared there in the past 20 years.

Perhaps the most influential New York-based contemporary musician is Lou Reed (born 1943), one of the founders of the Velvet Underground. Reed's work with that group and his subsequent solo works ('Sweet Jane,' 'A Perfect Day') created an edgy, druggy, urban sound that is echoed by dozens of bands worldwide. He now lives in the West Village with his companion, singer Laurie Anderson.

Dance

Since the time Isadora Duncan (1877-1927) brought modern dance to the attention of New York audiences, the city has been home to most of the country's prominent companies and choreographers, including Martha Graham (1894-1991). Graham choreographed over 140 dances and developed a new dance technique, still taught by her New York-based school emphasizing dramatic narrative.

The New York City Ballet was founded by Russian-born choreographer George Balanchine (1904-83) in 1948, who adapted traditional ballet to modern influences. Jerome Robbins (born 1918), who took over from Balanchine in 1983, had previously collaborated with Leonard Bernstein on several of Broadway's biggest musicals including *West Side Story* (1957). The NYC Ballet is currently directed by Peter Martins.

Paul Taylor (born 1930) and Twyla Tharp (born 1942), two students of Martha Graham, also borrow themes from popular culture. Taylor, who began with the Merce Cunningham company, heads his own group; Tharp is now associated with the American Ballet Theater.

Alvin Ailey (1931-89) set up his Alvin Ailey American Dance Theater in 1958, giving new prominence to African American dancers performing contemporary works. His most famous work is *Revelations* (1960), a dance suite set to gospel music. Mark Morris (born 1956) is a celebrated dancer and choreographer who formed his own dance group in 1988, which performs original works such as his reworking of *The Nutcracker* at the Brooklyn Academy of Music. The Dance Theater of Harlem, founded in Harlem by Arthur Mitchell in the late '60s, was the first major black classical company, and appears regularly at Lincoln Center. Today the Ailey, Graham and Taylor companies appear annually at City Center in Midtown, while Chelsea's Joyce Theater is the venue for the work of the Cunningham company and newer groups.

Theater

New York theater is, to a large extent, US theater. The first theater district was centered around the area now known as Herald Square. It was the site of the first Metropolitan Opera House and many musical theaters.

Vaudeville, the US version of British musical comedy, was largely performed in venues around Times Square, which is today's center of 'legitimate theater.' The first major theatrical impresario was Florenz Ziegfeld (1867-1932) who was best known for his 'Ziegfeld Follies,' featuring scantily-clad female dancers. Performers like Buster Keaton, James Cagney, George Burns, the Marx Brothers and Al Jolson got their start in vaudeville, honing the talents that would make them famous in other mediums.

Alternative, experimental drama arose in New York City in the 1930s. The most prominent playwright of the era is Eugene O'Neill (1888-1953) whose works include *The Iceman Cometh* and the autobiographical *Long Day's Journey into Night*.

Also American born is Arthur Miller (born 1915), whose *Death of a Salesman* won the Pulitzer Prize, is the most powerful living playwright. In 1953 he wrote *The Crucible*, which was about the Salem witch trials but had contemporary parallels with McCarthyism. Refelecting the decline of serious work on Broadway, Miller's most recent plays, *Broken Glass* and *The Ride Down Mount Morgan*, debuted in London before coming the US stage. In his 80s, he continues to be a presence in American theater and on film with his recent screen adaptation of *The Crucible*.

Alternative theater has produced some of the most prestigious American playwrights of recent decades, some of whose works have also shown on Broadway. Sam Shepard (born 1943) is known for his thought-provoking plays including *Buried Child*. August Wilson (born 1945), the country's best-known black playwright, has found success on Broadway with *The Piano Lesson, Fences* and *Seven Guitars*,

Hits and misses on 'The Great White Way'

KIM GRANT

along with other works examining the African American experience.

David Mamet (born 1947) has examined the seamier side of American life in plays like *Speed the Plow* and *American Buffalo*.

Neil Simon (born 1927), who got his start writing TV sketch comedy, is the modern playwright most closely associated with New York. His plays *The Odd Couple*, *Barefoot in the Park*, *Plaza Suite* and *Biloxi Blues* have all been made into films. Though a Broadway theater has been named after him, Simon's recent New York production, *London Suite*, actually opened in a smaller downtown theater.

Musicals have always been a mainstay of New York theater and the Tin Pan Alley composers George Gershwin *(Porgy & Bess)*, and Cole Porter (1893-1964; *Kiss Me Kate)*, produced many of the most enduring works. Stephen Sondheim (born

1930) has written varied and experimental popular Broadway fare including the lyrics for *West Side Story* and the music and words for *A Funny Thing Happened on the Way to the Forum* and *Sunday in the Park with George*.

Broadway and Times Square are currently experiencing a renaissance with big-dollar investment from companies like Disney, inspiring a uninspired retreads of projects that have appeared in other media, such as *Grease* and *Beauty and the Beast*. Mainstream theater relies mostly on big productions that run forever *(Miss Saigon, Cats)*, along with revivals and imports from London's West End.

Recently, off-Broadway attitudes (or perhaps poses) have been embraced as 'alternative' productions like *Chicago* and *Rent*, with more austere sets and offbeat themes, have become major Broadway hits.

Painting

When all is said and done, New York's place in art history looms largest as the home of many important collectors and gallery owners rather than as the inspirational center for artists.

In the mid-19th century, American artists became less influenced by the constraints of British portrait work and turned to more natural settings. The artists of the Hudson River School – among them Thomas Cole (1801-48) and Frederic Edwin Church (1826-1900) – gloried in the living world.

Impressionism in the US is best exemplified by the work of Childe Hassam (1859-1935), who explored revised forms of the style in his paintings of cityscapes and interiors – including his flag paintings, one of which is displayed in Bill Clinton's Oval Office in Washington, DC. Hassam, a member of the Coffee House Club, a leading literary and artistic organization, also helped start The Ten, a group of American impressionists who exhibited together up to WWI. Another impressionist painter was Mary Cassatt (1845-1926), noted for her etchings and oil paintings of domestic scenes. However Cassatt spent most of her working life in Europe.

In 1913, a young French painter named Marcel Duchamp (1887-1968) caused a sensation among the 300,000 people who attended the 1913 'Armory' show (officially called the International Exhibition of Modern Art) with his *Nude Descending a Staircase*. Critics noted that the cubist painting didn't seem to portray a recognizable nude *or* a staircase. Duchamp responded that that was exactly the point, and thus the New York school of 'dada,' named after the French slang for hobbyhorse, was begun. Duchamp, fellow countryman Francis Picabia (1879-1953) and American Man Ray (1890-1976) led a dadaist group known for its anti-war attitudes and deconstructive art that sought to shock and offend. By the '20s, most of the Dadaists had moved on – Ray to photography, Duchamp to full-time celebrity – but the movement remained influential for the rest of the century.

One of the best-known painters associated with New York is Edward Hopper (1882-1967), whose works portray a New York of long nights and solitary citizens, best represented in his *Night Hawks*, a portrait of late night patrons at a coffee shop that is displayed at the Art Institute in Chicago.

Painting also flourished in Harlem during the Harlem Renaissance of the 1920s and '30s. One of the most prominent artists was Aaron Douglas (1899-1979), who did illustrations for books and murals of black Americans and Africans.

American art flourished after WWII with the emergence of a new school of painting called abstract expressionism, which, because it centered on New York City, was also called the New York School. Simply defined, it combined spontaneity of expression with abstract forms composed haphazardly. Abstract expressionism dominated world art until the mid-1980s and two of its most famous exponents were Jackson Pollock (1912-56) and Willem de Kooning (1904-97). The Dutch painter Piet Mondrian (1872-1944) moved to New York in 1940 and used jazz music as his inspiration of his late series of famous abstract works.

From the 1950s modern art began to borrow images, items and themes from popular culture. New York was the home to Andy Warhol's Factory studio, where the artist and his hangers-on commented on culture through many media. Warhol (1928-87) created the pop art movement, which encompassed mass-produced art works, experimental films *(The Chelsea Girls)*, and the monthly downtown magazine *Interview*. The '60s also saw the emergence of modernists Jasper Johns and Roy Lichtenstein.

In the '80s, Warhol's legacy of the artist as celebrity spawned a host of well-known painters and illustrators whose work, to many critics, is somewhat questionable. But several of the artists/hustlers have broken out from the SoHo gallery scene to become internationally known, among them Julian Schnabel, Kenny Scharf and the late artist Keith Haring, who began his career as an underground graffiti artist.

Sculpture

The city's museums are filled with many examples of fine sculpture. On the street, most of the statuary celebrates the past. The first major example of public outdoor art was a statue of King George III constructed in 1770 in Bowling Green; it was torn down six years later after the first reading of the Declaration of Independence.

More recent public monuments have fared a bit more favorably. Among them are a statue to George Washington in Union Square (1856) and the Arch (1889) dedicated to the first president in Washington Square Park, along with the statue of Colonial patriot Nathan Hale (1890) at City Hall Park. The Mall in Central Park features bronze portrayals of famous artists and statesmen dedicated from 1876 to 1908, including Beethoven, Shakespeare and Robert Burns. Madison Square Park holds a number of statues of Union Army Civil War heroes. More contemporary monuments are found at the United Nations park on the East River and all throughout ornate Rockefeller Center, including Paul Manship's *Prometheus* (1934) overlooking the water fountain-skating rink and *News* (1940) by Isamu Noguchi, above the entrance of the Associated Press Building. Lincoln Center features Alexander Calder's *Le Guichet* (1963) at the New York Library for the Performing Arts, and Henry Moore's *Reclining Figure* (1965) in the reflecting pool in front of the Vivian Beaumont Theater. Louise Nevelson Plaza (where Maiden Lane, William and Liberty Sts all meet) appropriately enough has seven examples of the famous American sculptor's work.

There are many more contemporary examples of public art, but most can be dismissed with critic Robert Hughes' assessment of the sculpture in front of the Time Life Building, at 50th St and Sixth Ave, as 'Turd on a pedastal art.'

Photography

Photography developed as an art form at the end of the 19th century thanks to the work and influence of Alfred Stieglitz (1864-1946), who produced a number of images of New York City.

In the 1920s and '30s Man Ray (1890-1976), became a leading figure in the modernist movement away from traditional art forms, experimenting with new techniques in photography in which he used surreal images. But Ray moved from New York after his dada years to settle in Paris.

The city's role as a publishing center provided many opportunities for photographers, particularly with the addition of advertising agencies, fashion companies and news-gathering organizations. *Life* magazine was influential in the development of photojournalism, having spawned the famous Magnum photo agency. Among the most prominent photojournalists was the pioneering Margaret Bourke-White (1904-71), who was one of the first woman photographers attached to the US armed forces, and Alfred Eisenstaedt (1898-1995), a portraitist and news photographer who took the famous image of a sailor bussing a nurse in Times Square at the end of WWII.

Weegee (1899-1968), whose real name was Arthur H Fellig, was a tabloid photographer noted for his on-the-spot street photography. He also took portraits of celebrities and world leaders. William Klein and Richard Avedon are fashion photographers who worked for magazines like *Vogue* and *Harper's Bazaar* in the 1950s and '60s.

In more recent years, many photographers have become as famous for their commercial work as their more artistic endeavors. These include the American-born photographers Stephen Meisel, Herb Ritts and Annie Liebowitz. Others have forged careers with work that almost never reach the general public through advertising. Prominent in this latter group are Nan Goldin, who charted the lives (and deaths) of her transvestite and junkie friends from the '70s to the present day, and Cindy Sherman, who specializes in conceptual series of photographs (such as those inspired by movie stills and crime scene photos).

Architecture

New York is renowned worldwide for the great height and variety of its buildings. And while many past treasures have been lost (like the oft-lamented old Pennsylvania Station, which was demolished in the mid-1960s) visitors to New York will nevertheless be able to experience the city's history in its architecture.

Buildings all over New York are of interest to the student of architecture, but SoHo, Lower Manhattan and Midtown are areas where significant structures are concentrated. See the sections in Things to See & Do for more information on those neighborhoods, and also see the sidebar An Architectural Walk. There is a glossary of architectural terms in the back of this book.

If you're interested in making an in-depth exploration of New York's physical makeup, pick up a copy of the *AIA Guide to New York City* ($24). This superb companion from the American Institute of Architects is perfect for anyone interested in the city's aesthetic history, though its larger-than-a-brick size makes it difficult to carry around all day.

SOCIETY & CONDUCT

Being 'on' may be the New York style, but there isn't any particular look you can adopt to fit in here – practically anything goes, unless you're looking to dine in a fine restaurant on the Upper East Side, where jacket and tie are required. Yet even the most confident tourist can be marked as an outsider in dozens of tiny ways – by actually looking up at the buildings you pass, crossing the street at a corner instead of jaywalking, or attempting to read the *New York Times* on a packed subway train without first folding it lengthwise and then in half.

RELIGION

New York City, often derided by 'religious' outsiders as some sort of modern-day Sodom, has over 6000 places of worship – including Hindu and Buddhist temples and Jehovah's Witness kingdom halls.

Catholics are the biggest single religious group in New York City – about 44% of the population – and there are actually two dioceses here (one for Brooklyn and another for the rest of the city). Jews make up 12%

JANE LLOYD

Morning ritual

of the population, and there is an equal percentage of Baptists. Methodists, Lutherans, Presbyterians and Episcopalians total a combined 10%. About 8% of the population classifies itself as agnostic or non-believing.

Muslims have been part of the city's religious landscape since the late 1950s, and now number more than 500,000. Most adherents follow the Sunni Islam tradition. In 1991, a huge new mosque opened at 96th St and Third Ave, a monument to the city's fastest growing sect.

LANGUAGE

American English has borrowed words from the languages of successive waves of immigrants who made New York City their point of arrival. From German has came words like 'hoodlum,' from Yiddish-speaking Jews words like 'schmuck' (a 'fool'), from Irish words like 'galore.'

While you will immediately recognize the elongated vowels of New York City dwellers, the local accent (especially in Manhattan) sounds like a much milder version of the 'Noo Yawk Tawk' popularized in film and TV. Older residents often have a peculiar cadence in their voices, pronouncing 'Broadway' and 'receipt' with a heavy emphasis on the *first* syllable. The New York accent grows stronger in the outer boroughs, provided the person you're speaking to wasn't born in another country!

The city's huge Hispanic population has led to the emergence of Spanish as a semi-official second language. But so far, a Spanish-English hybrid has not developed for popular use, though everyone knows that *bodega* is slang for a corner convenience store.

It's easier to identify common phrases used, or at least recognized, by most New Yorkers, though even this is tricky because rap music is changing English in profound but as yet uncharted ways. But even the meaning of phrases changes from neighborhood to neighborhood: asking for a 'regular' coffee in Midtown means you'll get it with milk and a bit of sugar. The same request at a Wall St area shop will lead the server to immediately throw three heaping spoonfuls of the sweet stuff in the cup, because that's the way the hyper stock brokers and lawyers like it served. Some words and phrases that originated in New York include:

Big time – an all-out effort or massively good thing; eg, 'I'm going to get a big-time raise'

Enough already – a less than polite request to stop; eg, 'Enough already with your questions'

Potholes – the ubiquitous craters in city streets that can mangle car tires or send in-line skaters flying

Schlep – a long walk or the act of wandering around aimlessly; eg, 'we schlepped around all day looking for that hat'

Schmuck – an idiot

Step lively – a subway conductor's command to commuters as he closes the doors on a train

Straphanger – a standing subway rider, referring to the straps that used to be in the subway cars

The whole nine yards – an all-out effort, no costs spared; construction worker lingo derived from the maximum capacity of a cement truck, which is nine cubic yards

If all this is too confusing, then just remember the New Yorker's all-purpose phrase of general amazement and/or exasperation: 'You gotta be fuckin' kidding me.'

Facts for the Visitor

WHEN TO GO

New York is a year-round destination, so there isn't really an 'off-season' when local prices drop substantially. Winter bargains are sometimes available for airfares to the city, and many major hotels offer packages for the slower months from January to mid-March.

If you want to base your decision solely on the weather, generally the nicest and most temperate time to visit is in mid-September to October along with all of May and early June. Unfortunately, as these months are popular with tourists, hotel prices are scaled accordingly.

ORIENTATION

Islands make up most of New York City's 309-sq-mile land mass. Manhattan and Staten Island stand alone; Queens and Brooklyn comprise the western end of Long Island. Only the Bronx is connected to the continental mainland.

The water gap between Brooklyn and Staten Island – the 'narrows' through which the first Europeans entered the area – serves as the entrance to New York Harbor, which is also accessible to ships from the north via Long Island Sound. Manhattan is bordered on the west by the Hudson River and on the east by the East River, both technically estuaries subject to tidal fluctuations.

I-95, which runs from Maine to Florida, cuts through the city as the Cross Bronx Expressway. Via I-95, Boston is 194 miles to the north, Philadelphia 104 miles to the south and Washington, DC, is 235 miles south by car.

Manhattan

Most of Manhattan is extremely easy to navigate, thanks to a street plan imposed by a city planning commission in 1811 for the area north of Houston St. It created the current grid system of named or numbered avenues running the north-south length of

the island, cut across by numbered streets that run from east to west. (If you intend to do a lot of walking, keep in mind that along the avenues 20 blocks north or south is approximately one mile.)

Because the grid system was established long before the advent of the automobile, modern Manhattan suffers from tremendous traffic congestion, giving rise to the term 'gridlock.' This street plan had at least one other unintended consequence: the narrow streets precluded the creation of grand avenues in the European tradition, and discouraged the creation of buildings set back on large tracts of property. There was nowhere to go but up – and by the late 19th century Manhattan had a cluster of skyscrapers, as prominent multi-story office buildings came to be called.

Above Washington Square, Fifth Ave serves as the dividing line between the 'East Side' and the 'West Side.' Cross-street numbers begin there and grow higher toward each river, generally (but not exclusively) in 100-digit increments per block. Therefore, the Hard Rock Cafe, at 221 W 57th St, is slightly less than three blocks west of Fifth Ave.

Most New Yorkers give out addresses in shorthand by listing the cross street first and the avenue second, eg, 'we're at 33rd and Third.' If you are given an address on an avenue – such as '1271 Sixth Ave' – be sure to ask for the nearest cross street.

In the oldest part of New York City, from 14th St to the southern tip of Manhattan, travel becomes a bit trickier. Streets that perhaps began as cow paths or merchants' byways snake along in a haphazard manner, which is why it is possible today to stand at the corner of W 4th St and W 10th St in Greenwich Village (and even at the corner of Waverly Place and Waverly Place).

Broadway, the only avenue to cut diagonally across the island, was originally a woodland path used by Indians; it runs in some form from the southern tip of the island all the way to the state capital of Albany, 150 miles away. Today Wall St stands at the place where, in 1653, the Dutch residents of New Amsterdam constructed a wooden barrier at the town's northern border to ward off attacks from hostile Indians.

Outer Boroughs
The grid plan is repeated to a lesser extent in the other boroughs, with streets such as Northern Blvd in Queens laid over the old country pathways to the once-rural eastern areas of Long Island.

Address Information
If you're unsure of a local address dial 411 (information) on a NYNEX pay phone and ask for the *location* of the business. If you don't, the operator will immediately call up a computer message with the telephone number only, forcing you to spend 25¢ to obtain information they are supposed to provide gratis.

Neighborhoods
There's no method to the names that New Yorkers have given their neighborhoods. They can be purely geographical (the Lower East Side), ethnically descriptive (Chinatown) or just plain scary (Hell's Kitchen). Tribeca is the precious name given to the 'Triangle Below Canal St' that passed into popular use, as did SoHo, the square area south of Houston St.

Some have long outgrown their designations. Few residents of Chelsea know their area was named after an 18th century farm owned by a British army officer. Turtle Bay, a fashionable enclave surrounding the United Nations on the East Side of Manhattan, is named after a riverside cove that was drained way back in 1868.

The Upper East Side and Upper West Side include the areas above 59th St on either side of Central Park. Midtown generally refers to the largely commercial district from 59th St south to 34th St, an area which includes Rockefeller Center, Times Square, the Broadway theater district,

major hotels, Grand Central Station and the Port Authority Bus Terminal.

Significant neighborhoods in the outer boroughs include Arthur Ave and City Island in the Bronx; Brooklyn Heights, Park Slope, Williamsburg and Brighton Beach in Brooklyn; and Astoria, Jackson Heights and Flushing in Queens.

MAPS
Good street plans are usually given away free in the lobby of any decent hotel. The *Streetwise* series of laminated, pocket-sized maps covers many specific neighborhoods and these maps are available at bookstores and better newsstands. If you want to explore the city at large, buy a five-borough street atlas. *Geographia* and *Hagstrom* publish paperback-sized editions for under $10.

Most subway stations in Manhattan have 'Passenger Information Centers' next to the token booth with detailed maps of the surrounding neighborhood on which all points of interests are clearly marked. Taking a look before heading up the stairs may save you from getting lost.

You can get maps at the Hagstrom Map and Travel Center (☎ (212) 398-1222), 57 W 43rd St, and the Rand McNally Travel Store (☎ (212) 758-7488), 150 E 52nd St, which ships globes and atlases worldwide. Both stores sell colorful wall maps of Manhattan made by the Identity Map Company for about $25. Though not practical for walking the city, these wonderfully detailed maps make a great souvenir of your trip for the office wall back home.

TOURIST OFFICES
The New York Convention and Visitors Bureau (☎ (800) 692-8474, fax (212) 245-5943; subway: 59th St-Columbus Circle) is located at Two Columbus Circle and is open from 9 am to 6 pm Monday to Friday and 10 am to 3 pm weekends and holidays. The 24-hour toll-free line offers information on special events and reservations. Callers from outside the US and Canada can access the service by dialing ☎ (212) 397-8222.

The Manhattan Borough President's

office has established a Big Apple Greeters Program (☎ (212) 669-2896, fax (212) 669-4900), through which 500 volunteers welcome visitors to the city by offering free tours of lesser-known neighborhoods. Some greeters are multi-lingual and specialize in helping the disabled. Reservations must be made at least two days in advance.

The New York state tourist bureau (☎ (800) 225-5697) is located at 1515 Broadway at 45th St on the 52nd floor. The main office is at 1 Commerce Plaza, Albany, NY 12245 (☎ (800) 225-5697).

AAA (☎ (212) 757-2000), the 'auto club,' has offices at 1881 Broadway.

KIM GRANT

DOCUMENTS

Be sure to make photocopies of all documents and keep these separate from the originals.

Passports

If you are a foreign visitor you must bring your passport, which should remain valid for at least six months after your intended stay in the USA. If it's about to expire, renew it before you go. This may not be easy to do away from your home country.

Technically, Canadians may enter the US without a passport, but you must have proof of Canadian citizenship with photo ID. However it's always best to bring your passport, since immigration officials at the Canadian border have been giving people hassles about not having passports.

Applying for or renewing a passport can take from a few days to several months, so don't leave it till the last minute. Things will probably happen faster if you do everything in person, but check first on what you need to take with you. While traveling, carry your passport at all times and guard it carefully.

Once inside the US, you generally won't need to fill out government forms or deal with immigration bureaucracies unless you plan on traveling to Mexico or Canada, though it does help to have several passport-sized photos in your wallet should you need them; getting them done in a photo shop costs $10 or more and photo booths are not generally available in airports and train stations.

Visas

Travelers from most countries need to obtain a visa from a US consulate or embassy. Canadians do not need a visa. Visitors from a few other countries may also enter the US without a visa – see the sidebar on the Visa Waiver Pilot Program.

In most countries acquiring a visa can be done by mail. You'll need to submit a recent passport-sized (37 x 37 mm) photo with the application. Documents indicating financial stability and/or guarantees from a US resident are sometimes required, particularly for those from developing countries.

Visa applicants may be required to 'demonstrate binding obligations' that ensure their return home. Because of this requirement, if you're planning to travel through other countries before arriving in the USA you are generally better off applying for your US visa while still in your home country, rather than while on the road.

The validity period for US visitor visas depends on which country you're from. The length of time you'll be allowed to stay in the USA is ultimately determined by US immigration authorities at the port of entry.

Visa Extensions If you want, need or hope to stay in the USA beyond the date stamped on your passport, go to the local Immigration & Naturalization Service (INS) office (☎ (212) 206-6500), 26 Federal Plaza near Worth St (subway: Canal St or City Hall), *before* the stamped date to apply for an extension. Going *after* that date will usually lead to an unamusing conversation with an INS official who'll assume you want to work illegally. If you find yourself in that situation, it's a good idea to bring a US citizen with you to vouch for your character and to have some verification that you have enough currency to support yourself.

Other Documents

Travel Insurance This is highly recommended. Not only does it cover you for medical expenses (see Health, below) and luggage theft or loss, but also for cancellations or delays in your travel arrangements under certain circumstances (you might fall seriously ill two days before departure, for example) – and everyone should be covered for the worst possible case, such as an accident requiring hospital treatment and a flight home. Coverage depends on your insurance and type of ticket, so ask both your insurer and your ticket-issuing agency

> ## Visa Waiver Pilot Program
> The US has a reciprocal waiver program in which citizens of certain countries may enter for 90 days or less without first obtaining a US visa. Currently these countries are Andorra, Argentina, Australia, Austria, Belgium, Brunei, Denmark, Finland, France, Germany, Iceland, Ireland, Italy, Japan, Liechtenstein, Luxembourg, Monaco, the Netherlands, New Zealand, Norway, San Marino, Spain, Sweden, Switzerland, and the UK. Under this program you must have a round-trip ticket that's non-refundable in the USA and you cannot travel with the intention of extending your stay. ■

to explain where you stand. Ticket loss is also (usually) covered by travel insurance. Make sure you have a separate record of all your ticket details – or better still, a photocopy – in case the original is lost. Buy travel insurance as early as possible. If you buy it the week before you fly, you may find, for example, that you're not covered for delays to your flight caused by strikes or industrial action.

Driver's License You will need a driver's license and good driving record to rent a car. You may want to obtain an International Drivers Permit at your local auto club before arrival.

Although it's a strange policy, you should carry your license with you if you intend to drink or even enter a bar. By law you must be 21 years of age to drink anywhere in the US, but in New York it's rather easy to buy alcohol without ID if you look old enough. Some bouncers at bars want to see a driver's license with a photo before they'll admit you – especially in the East Village, where young drinkers congregate. Bouncers often don't consider a passport adequate documentation. But remember: you don't win arguments with dim bouncers.

EMBASSIES & CONSULATES
US Embassies & Consulates Abroad

US diplomatic offices abroad include the following:

Australia
Embassy:
21 Moonah Place,
Yarralumla, ACT 2600
(☎ (2) 6270 5900)

Consulate-General:
Level 59 MLC Center
19-29 Martin Place,
Sydney, NSW 2000
(☎ (2) 9373 9200)

There are also consulates
in Melbourne, Perth and
Brisbane.

Austria
Boltzmanngasse 16,
A-1091, Vienna
(☎ (1) 313-39)

Belgium
Blvd du Régent 27,
B-1000, Brussels
(☎ (2) 513 38 30)

Canada
Embassy:
100 Wellington St,
Ottawa, Ontario 1P 5T1
(☎ (613) 238-5335)

Consulate-General:
1095 West Pender St,
Vancouver, BC V6E 2M6
(☎ (604) 685-1930)

US Consulate-General:
1155 rue St Alexandre,
Montreal, Quebec
(☎ (514) 398-9695)

There are also consulates
in Toronto, Calgary and
Halifax.

Denmark
Dag Hammarskjolds Allé 24,
Copenhagen
(☎ 31 42 31 44)

Finland
Itainen Puistotie 14A, Helsinki
(☎ (0) 171-931)

France
2 rue St Florentin,
75001 Paris
(☎ 01.42.96.12.02)

There are consulates in
Bordeaux, Lyon, Marseilles,
Nice, Strasbourg and
Toulouse.

Germany
Deichmanns Aue 29,
53179 Bonn
(☎ (228) 33 91)

Greece
91 Vasilissis Sophias Blvd,
10160 Athens
(☎ (1) 721-2951)

India
Shanti Path, Chanakyapuri
110021, New Delhi
(☎ (11) 60-0651)

Indonesia
Medan Merdeka Selatan 5,
Jakarta
(☎ (21) 360-360)

Ireland
42 Elgin Rd,
Ballsbridge, Dublin 4
(☎ (1) 687 122)

Israel
71 Hayarkon St, Tel Aviv
(☎ (3) 517-4338)

Italy
Via Vittorio Veneto
119a-121, Rome
(☎ (6) 46 741)

Japan
1-10-5 Akasaka Chome,
Minato-ku, Tokyo
(☎ (3) 224-5000)

Korea
82 Sejong-Ro,
Chongro-ku, Seoul
(☎ (2) 397-4114)

Malaysia
376 Jalan Tun Razak,
50400 Kuala Lumpur
(☎ (3) 248-9011)

Mexico
Paseo de la Reforma 305,
Cuauhtémoc,
06500 Mexico City
(☎ (5) 211-00-42)

Netherlands
Embassy:
Lange Voorhout 102,
2514 EJ The Hague
(☎ (70) 310 92 09)

Netherlands cont.
Consulate:
Museumplein 19,
1071 DJ Amsterdam
(☎ (20) 310 9209)

New Zealand
29 Fitzherbert Terrace,
Thorndon, Wellington
(☎ (4) 722 068)

Norway
Drammensvein 18, Oslo
(☎ (22) 44 85 50)

Philippines
1201 Roxas Blvd,
Ermita, Manila 1000
(☎ (2) 521-7116)

Russia
Novinskiy Bul'var 19-23,
Moscow
(☎ (095) 252-2451)

Singapore
30 Hill St, Singapore 0617
(☎ 338-0251)

South Africa
877 Pretorius St, Box 9536,
Pretoria 0001
(☎ (12) 342-1048)

Spain
Calle Serrano 75,
28006 Madrid
(☎ (1) 577 4000)

Sweden
Strandvagen 101,
S-115 89 Stockholm
(☎ (8) 783 5300)

Switzerland
Jubilaumsstrasse 93,
3005 Berne
(☎ (31) 357 70 11)

Thailand
95 Wireless Rd, Bangkok
(☎ (2) 252-5040)

UK
Embassy:
5 Upper Grosvenor St,
London W1A 1AE
(☎ (171) 499 9000)

Consulate-General:
3 Regent Terrace,
Edinburgh EH7 5BW
(☎ (131) 556 8315)

Consulate-General:
Queens House,
Belfast BT1 6EQ
(☎ (1232) 328 239)

Foreign Consulates in New York City

The UN's presence in New York means that nearly every country in the world maintains diplomatic offices here. Most are listed in the white pages of the phone book under 'Consulate General of (country).' Some foreign consulates are:

Argentina
12 W 56th St
New York, NY 10019
(☎ (212) 603-0400)

Australia
636 Fifth Ave
New York, NY 10020
(☎ (212) 245-4000)

Austria
31 E 69th St
New York, NY 10021
(☎ 737-6400)

Belgium
1330 Sixth Ave
New York, NY 10019
(☎ (212) 586-5510)

Brazil
630 Fifth Ave
New York, NY 10011
(☎ (212) 757-3085)

Canada
1251 Sixth Ave
New York, NY 10020
(☎ (212) 596-1700)

Denmark
835 Second Ave
New York, NY 10017
(☎ (212) 223-4545)

France
934 Fifth Ave
New York, NY 10021
(☎ (212) 606-3600)

Germany
460 Park Ave
New York, NY 10022
(☎ (212) 308-8700)

Ireland
345 Park Ave
New York, NY 10154
(☎ (212) 319-2555)

Israel
800 Second Ave
New York, NY 10017
(☎ (212) 351-5200)

Italy
690 Park Ave
New York, NY 10021
(☎ (212) 737-9100)

Mexico
8 E 41st St
New York, NY 10017
(☎ (212) 689-0456)

The Netherlands
1 Rockefeller Center
New York, NY 10020
(☎ (212) 246-1429)

New Zealand
780 Third Ave Suite 1904
New York, NY 10017
(☎ (212) 832-4038)

Norway
825 Third Ave
New York, NY 10017
(☎ (212) 421-7333)

South Africa
333 E 38th St
New York, NY 10016
(☎ (212) 213-4880)

Spain
150 E 58th St
New York, NY 10155
(☎ (212) 355-4080)

UK
845 Third Ave
New York, NY 10017
(☎ (212) 745-0202)

CUSTOMS

US customs allows each person over the age of 21 to bring one liter of liquor and 200 cigarettes duty-free into the USA. US citizens are allowed to import, duty-free, $400 worth of gifts from abroad while non-US citizens are allowed to bring in $100 worth. See also Currency Regulations under Money.

MONEY
Currency

The US dollar is divided into 100 cents (¢). Coins come in denominations of 1¢ (penny), 5¢ (nickel), 10¢ (dime), 25¢ (quarter) and the seldom seen 50¢ (half dollar). Notes come in $1, $2, $5, $10, $20, $50 and $100 denominations (you'll only occasionally come across $2 bills – they're perfectly legal). There's also a $1 Susan B Anthony coin that the government tried unsuccessfully in the late '70s to bring into mass circulation; you may get them as change from ticket and stamp machines. Be aware that they look similar to quarters (which is why they failed to catch on with Americans).

The new $100 bill, on which Benjamin Franklin's portrait is not centered, might not always be accepted by merchants. Though you are likely to get this bill at foreign banks, it was designed largely to foil international counterfeiters and still looks weird to many Americans.

In New York, street vendors and movie theaters will resist accepting bills in denominations of $50 or more. This policy is not strictly legal, but rather than argue about the validity of your money, have $20 bills at hand for smaller purchases.

HIV & Entering the USA

Everyone entering the USA who isn't a US citizen is subject to the authority of the Immigration & Naturalization Service (INS), regardless of whether that person has legal immigration documents. The INS can keep someone from entering or staying in the USA by excluding or deporting them. This is especially relevant to travelers with the Human Immunodeficiency Virus (HIV). Though being HIV positive is not a ground for deportation, it is a 'ground of exclusion' and the INS can invoke it to refuse admission.

Although the INS doesn't test people for HIV at customs, it may try to exclude anyone who answers 'yes' to this question on the non-immigrant visa application form: 'Have you ever been afflicted with a communicable disease of public health significance?' INS officials may also stop people if they seem sick, are carrying AIDS/HIV medicine or, sadly, if the officer happens to think the person looks gay, though sexual orientation is not legally a ground of exclusion.

It's imperative that visitors know and assert their rights. Immigrants and visitors should avoid contact with the INS until they discuss their rights and options with a trained immigration advocate. For legal immigration information and referrals to immigration advocates, contact The National Immigration Project of the National Lawyers Guild (☎ (617) 227-9727), 14 Beacon St, Suite 506, Boston, MA 02108; or Immigrant HIV Assistance Project, Bar Association of San Francisco (☎ (415) 267-0795), 685 Market St, Suite 700, San Francisco, CA 94105. ■

Currency Regulations

If you're carrying more than $10,000 in US and foreign cash, traveler's checks, money orders and the like, you need to declare the excess amount. There is no legal restriction on the amount which may be imported, but undeclared sums in excess of $10,000 may be subject to confiscation.

Carrying Money

Most hotels and hostels provide safekeeping, so you can leave your money and jewelry there. Carry the money you'll need for each day somewhere inside your clothing (in a money belt, a bra or your socks) rather than in a handbag or an outside pocket. It helps to have money in several places, and don't venture around with an overstuffed wallet in your back pocket – it's the petty thief's dream.

Remember that using a simple safety pin to hold the zipper tags of a day pack together can help prevent theft of books and handbags.

Traveler's Checks

Traveler's checks offer protection from theft or loss. American Express and Thomas Cook are widely accepted and have efficient replacement policies.

Keeping a record of the check numbers and the checks you have used is vital when it comes to replacing lost checks. Keep this record in a separate place from the checks themselves.

You'll save yourself trouble and expense if you buy traveler's checks in US dollars. The savings you *might* make on exchange rates by carrying traveler's checks in a foreign currency don't make up for the hassle of exchanging them at banks and other facilities. Restaurants, hotels and most stores accept US-dollar traveler's checks as if they were cash, so if you're carrying traveler's checks in US dollars, the odds are you'll rarely have to use a bank or pay an exchange fee. Fast food restaurants and smaller businesses may refuse checks, so ask at the outset of a meal or a purchase if you can use them.

Take most of the checks in large denominations. It's only towards the end of a stay that you may want to change a small check to make sure you aren't left with too much local currency. Of course, traveler's checks are losing their popularity due to the explosion of ATMs (see below) and many visitors return home without using their entire supply.

Banks & ATMs

Banks are open from 9 am to 3:30 pm Monday to Friday. The Chase Manhattan branch in Chinatown at the corner of Mott and Canal Sts is open seven days, with Saturday and Sunday hours from 10 am to 2 pm. Several other banks along Canal St also offer weekend hours, so head there if you need major bank assistance on Sunday.

Given the prevalence of automated teller machines (ATMs) in New York City, you may save on commissions by drawing smaller amounts of cash directly from a home bank account, provided it is linked with the Cirrus or Plus networks. The banks offer better exchange rates for these electronic transactions and ATM fees are usually about $3. Most New York banks are linked by the NYCE (New York Cash Exchange) system, and you can use local bank cards interchangeably at ATMs. Contact your bank if you lose your ATM card. There are thousands of ATMs in Manhattan, especially in the midtown area.

Currency Exchange

A commission-free exchange service is offered at Chase Manhattan Bank's branch located at the corner of Liberty and William Sts from 8 am to 3 pm Monday to Friday. Other Chase Manhattan branches around the city offer foreign exchange near tourist spots (including the branch on Fifth Ave across from the Empire State Building and in Times Square). These banks advertise the service with a prominent sign in their windows.

Thomas Cook Foreign Exchange has eight locations in the city. The Times Square office (☎ (212) 265-6049), 1590 Broadway at 48th St, is open Monday to Saturday from 9 am to 6 pm and Sunday from 9 am to 5 pm. American Express has

KIM GRANT

She comes in all sizes.

an office in Bloomingdale's, at 59th St and Lexington Ave (☎ (212) 705-3171), as well as offices at 374 Park Ave (☎ (212) 421-8240), 65 Broadway (☎ (212) 493-6500) and 150 E 42nd St (☎ (212) 687-3700).

Chequepoint (☎ (212) 750-2400) offers less favorable rates at its office at 22 Central Park South and several other locations.

Companies offering foreign exchange services can be found in the Midtown area, and charge $3 to $5 commission fees.

Exchange Rates Exchange rates at press time were:

Australia	A1$	=	$0.86
Canada	C$1	=	$0.78
France	FF$10	=	$1.85
Germany	DM1	=	$0.62
Japan	¥100	=	$0.84
New Zealand	NZ$1	=	$0.75
UK	£1	=	$1.69

Credit & Debit Cards

Major credit and charge cards are widely accepted everywhere. Indeed, car rental agencies, travel agents and most hotels prefer them to cash. The most commonly accepted cards are Visa, MasterCard (which are both affiliated with European Access Cards) and the American Express card. Discover and Diners Club cards are also accepted by many businesses. It's probably a good idea to have an American Express card and another credit card since some places take one and not the other.

Banks that issue Visa and MasterCard also offer debit cards, which deduct payment directly from your savings or checking account. Smart Cards, which are used as cash substitutes (you put a certain amount on them and electronically spend it), are also being introduced on a pilot basis and are not yet widely accepted. The following are toll-free numbers for the main credit card companies:

American Express	(800) 528-4800
Diners Club	(800) 234-6377
Discover	(800) 347-2683
MasterCard	(800) 826-2181
Visa	(800) 336-8472

International Transfers

You can instruct your bank back home to send you a draft. Specify the city, bank and branch to which you want your money directed, or ask your home bank to tell you where a suitable one is, and make sure you get the details right. The procedure is easier if you've authorized someone back home to access your account.

Money sent by telegraphic transfer should reach you within a week; by mail allow at least two weeks. When it arrives it will most likely be converted into local currency – you can take it as it is or buy traveler's checks.

You can also transfer money by American Express, Thomas Cook or Western Union, though the latter has fewer international offices.

Tipping

Tipping is expected in restaurants, bars and better hotels, as well as by taxi drivers, hairdressers and baggage carriers. In restaurants, waitstaff are paid less than the minimum wage and rely upon tips to make a living. Tip at least 15% unless the service is terrible. Most New Yorkers tip about 20%, calculating the amount by doubling the 8.25 sales tax on a meal bill and rounding up a dollar or two. Never tip in fast-food, take-out or buffet-style restaurants where you serve yourself. And beware of restaurants that don't itemize the tax separately on a bill – it's a way to get you to tip on the tax amount as well.

Taxi drivers expect 10% and hairdressers get 15% if their service is satisfactory. Baggage carriers (skycaps in airports, bellhops in hotels) receive $1 for the first bag and 50¢ for each additional bag. In 1st-class and luxury hotels, tipping can reach ludicrous proportions – doormen, bellboys and parking attendants all expect to be tipped at least $1 for each service performed—including simply opening a taxi door for you. (Business travelers should tip the cleaning staff $5 a day.) However, simply saying 'thank you' to an attendant who does something you could just as easily have done it yourself is OK.

Taxes

Restaurants and retailers never include tax in their prices, so beware of ordering the $4.99 lunch special when you only have $5 in your pocket. New York state imposes a sales tax of 7% on goods, most services and prepared foods. New York City imposes an additional 1.25% tax, bringing the total surcharge to 8.25%. Several categories of so-called 'luxury items,' including rental cars and dry cleaning, carry an additional city surcharge of 5%, so you wind up seeing 13.25% added to those bills.

Hotel rooms in New York City are subject to a 13.25% tax plus a flat $2 per night occupancy tax. Believe it or not, that reflects a reduction in the previous hotel tax.

Tipping Bartenders

Many visitors, particularly those from countries where bartenders don't receive tips, don't understand that New York bartenders expect to be treated very generously and prefer a dollar thrown back at them for every drink they provide. You could argue that tipping a bottle-opening bartender at a higher level than a good restaurant waiter is ridiculous, but stiffing them is an unacceptable alternative. So here's a tip on tips: when New Yorkers are looking to make a night of it with friends, they usually place a $20 bill in front of them on the bar and have the bar person take the charge out of that, or they run up a 'tab,' saving the tip calculation for the total bill. It's also important to remember that a good bartender should 'buy back' a round – which means your fourth or fifth round should be free, especially if you're drinking only beer instead of expensive distilled spirits like whiskey. If the bar person neglects to give you a round (*and* you've been behaving yourself while quaffing all that booze), feel free to reduce the tip sharply. ∎

POST & COMMUNICATIONS

Mail

The main post office (☎ (212) 967-8585), 421 Eighth Ave at the corner of 33rd St (zip: 10001), is open 24 hours a day. The Rockefeller Center post office in the basement under 610 Fifth Ave is open Monday to Friday from 9:30 am to 5:30 pm.

The post office at Franklin D Roosevelt Station (☎ (212) 330-5549) at 909 Third Ave at 55th St (zip: 10022) is open for most postal and passport business from 9 am to 8 pm. Many post offices are open later (7:30 pm or thereabouts) on Thursday evenings and maintain some Saturday hours (10 am to 2 pm generally).

Poste restante services are not common in the US, but mail is accepted at the main post office provided it is marked 'General Delivery.' This method is not recommended or reliable. The American Express office at 150 E 42nd St (zip: 10022) also offers a mail hold for cardholders.

Postal Rates Rates for 1st-class mail within the USA are 32¢ for letters up to one ounce (23¢ for each additional ounce) and 20¢ for postcards. (Postal rates tend to go up – ask before you purchase stamps.)

International airmail rates (except Canada and Mexico) are 60¢ for a half-ounce letter, 95¢ for a one-ounce letter and 39¢ for each additional half ounce. International postcard rates are 40¢. Letters to Canada are 46¢ for a one-ounce letter, 23¢ for each additional ounce and 30¢ for a postcard. Letters to Mexico are 35¢ for a half-ounce letter, 45¢ for a one-ounce letter and 30¢ for a postcard. Aerogrammes are 45¢.

Parcels airmailed within the USA cost $3 for two pounds or less, increasing by $1 per pound up to $6 for five pounds. For heavier items, rates differ according to the distance mailed. Books, periodicals and computer disks can be sent by a cheaper 4th-class rate. Because of security concerns, the US Postal Service and other express carriers now require a signature for any package weighing over one pound – so you can no longer affix postage and drop packages in mailboxes.

Telephone

Phone numbers within the USA consist of a three-digit area code followed by a seven-digit local number. If you're calling locally, just dial the seven-digit number. If you're calling long distance, dial 1 + the three-digit area code + the seven-digit number.

If you're calling New York from abroad, the international country code for the USA is '1.'

Area Codes In New York City, Manhattan phone numbers are in the 212 area code, the four outer boroughs are in the 718 zone. Dial carefully, the explosion of phone lines in Manhattan means that neglecting to add 718 to an outer borough number will probably put you through to the wrong party in Manhattan. Note that Manhattan will soon have a second area code sometime within the life span of this book. But borders for the new area code have not yet been determined, and if you ring a Manhattan phone that has been switched over, you'll probably get a recording telling you so.

All toll-free numbers are given with an 800 or 888 area code. Some toll-free numbers for local businesses or government offices are accessible only regionally.

Rates Hotels (especially the more expensive ones) add a service charge of 50¢ to $1 for *every* call made from a room phone; they also have hefty surcharges for long-distance calls. Public pay phones, which can be found in most lobbies, are always cheaper. You can pump in quarters, or use a phone or credit card, or make collect calls from pay phones. An alternative is a phone debit card, which allows purchasers to pay in advance. Many convenience stores sell pre-paid phone cards, but the key is to use these cards on a reliable public phone.

When using phone cards in a public place, be aware of people watching you punch in your personal identification number (PIN). New York airports and especially the Port Authority are notorious for this scam: thieves memorize numbers and use them to make costly international calls. Some newer pay phones (like those in Penn Station) provide shields at the telephone pad to prevent a stranger from viewing your number.

Long-distance rates vary depending on the destination and which telephone company you use – call the operator (0) for rate information. Don't ask the operator to put your call through, however, because

operator-assisted calls are much more expensive than direct-dial calls. Generally, nights (11 pm to 8 am), all day Saturday and from 8 am to 5 pm Sunday are the cheapest times to call (60% discount). A 35% discount applies in the evenings from 5 to 11 pm Sunday to Friday. Daytime calls (8 am to 5 pm Monday to Friday) are full-price calls within the USA.

International Calls To make an international call direct, dial 011 then the country code, followed by the area code and the phone number. (To find the country code, check a local phone directory or dial 411 and ask for an international operator.) You may need to wait as long as 45 seconds for the ringing to start. International rates vary depending on the time of day and the destination. For example, the cheapest rates to London are available between 6 pm and 7 am, but to Sydney the cheapest time to call is from 3 am to 2 pm. Again, rates vary depending on the telephone company used and the destination. Call the operator (☎ 0) for rates.

KIM GRANT
Equitable Building in Lower Manhattan

Directory Assistance Local directory assistance can be reached by dialing ☎ 411. For directory assistance outside your area code, dial 1 + the three-digit area code of the place you want to call + 555-1212. (These requests are charged as one-minute long distance calls.) Regional and US area code maps are found in telephone directories.

Pay Phones There are thousands of pay telephones on the New York City streets, but those maintained by NYNEX, the local utility (soon to be called Bell Atlantic following a merger) are much more reliable

than the others. Be particularly careful about dialing long distance with a credit card on an unaffiliated phone; you may end up with a whopping bill from an unscrupulous long distance firm. It's much better to use the access lines of major carriers such as AT&T (☎ (800) 321-0288) or MCI (☎ (800) 888-8000).

Petty vandalism has led NYNEX to install dozens of telecard-operated phones on subway platforms and near heavily trafficked street corners. Unfortunately, $5 and $10 telecards for these distinctive yellow phones are sold only at a handful of newsstands and pharmacies – and the phones themselves have been disappearing because most of them don't work.

Directories are no longer provided at outdoor phone booths, so if you're unsure of a local address dial 411 (information) on a NYNEX pay phone and ask for the *location* of the business. If you don't, the operator will immediately call up a computer message with the telephone number only, forcing you to spend 25¢ to obtain information they are supposed to provide gratis.

Fax, Telegraph & Internet

Kinko's offers 24-hour fax in addition to its computer and photocopying services. They have 10 locations in Manhattan, including 16 E 52nd St (☎ (212) 308-2679), and 24 E 12th St (☎ (212) 924-0802). (They also take passport-sized headshots.) Check the yellow pages under 'copying' for the closest location of a Kinko's or equivalent service.

Telegrams can be sent from Western Union (☎ (800) 325-6000).

There are several 'cyber cafes' in the city where you can surf the net for an hourly fee, but they tend to go out of business rather quickly. As yet the yellow pages don't have a listing for 'internet' but might be by the time you read this – try 'computer rentals' or visit *Cyberfeld's* (☎ (212) 647-8830), 20 E 13th St off Fifth Ave, for computer rental, or *Cyber Cafe* (212) 334-5140), 273 Lafayette St. You can also find out the locations of cyber cafes in New York and around the world by connecting to www.cyberiacafe.net before your departure.

BOOKS

To find the following books, head to any large New York book shop – it will have a special section dedicated to tomes about the city.

New York on the Web

There are literally hundreds of sites dedicated to New York City in cyberspace, and of late a number of companies, including behemoth Microsoft, have been developing sites with visitor and resident listings and information. The following are some of the more useful sites for people gathering data for a visit.

Time Out New York – It isn't nearly as comprehensive as its Web pages for London, Amsterdam and Paris, but they promised an improvement by late 1997. (www.timeout.co.uk)

New York City Search – At the moment the best general guide for someone planning a visit. It's particularly good on upcoming events and updates on museum hours, etc. (citysearchnyc.com)

New York Times – Not really for tourists, but you can pick up the paper's daily reporting and collect recent restaurant and movie reviews from its archive. The Friday Weekend section is the most useful for travelers, since it often carries neighborhood profiles. (www.nytimes.com)

Sidewalk – Microsoft's new comprehensive service to several US cities. They promise to use local journalists, but the New York Sidewalk site was not fully up at press time. (www.sidewalk.com)

Total New York – A savvy and trendy site run by a former writer at *Time* magazine that's perhaps more useful to residents than visitors, but it's worth checking out. (www.totalny.com)

Lycos – A service that's best used as a link to more obscure sites – through it you can find web pages dedicated to the subway system and other minutia. (cityguide.lycos.com) ■

Guidebooks

Ethnic New York (Passport Books), by Mark Leeds, is a good neighborhood by neighborhood guide. *Wonderful Weekends* (Frommer), by Marilyn Wood, has information on trips within a 200-mile radius of New York City; it's a good trip planner, but has little on public transportation – you'll need a car to use it effectively. *Away for the Weekend* (Crown), by Eleanor Berman, covers much of the same ground.

For those interested in New York City's architecture, the American Institute of Architects' *Guide to New York City* (1988), edited by Norval White & Elliot Willinsky, is the classic text on the subject.

History

Though it is a work of fiction rather than straight history, Washington Irving's satirical *History of New York* (1809), published under the pseudonym of Dietrich Knickerbocker, includes glimpses of colonial-era New York. Those looking for a more historical (but well written) perspective should seek out *Colonial New York* by historian Michael Kammen.

Edward Robb Ellis's *The Epic of New York City* is an anecdotal history of New York covering most major events from colonial times to the mid-20th century. It is particularly good on the late 19th century corruption of 'Boss' Tweed and his Tammany Hall gang. The same author has kept an extensive *Diary of Edward Robb Ellis* for his entire adult life that was published in abridged form in 1995.

World of Our Fathers by Irving Howe is a comprehensive look at how the Eastern European Jewish immigrants who began coming to New York in the later 19th century were assimilated into the mainstream. It's a perfect book for anyone interested in the history of the East Village and Lower East Side.

Luc Sante has published two fine and colorful works dealing with the gamier aspects of early 20th century New York.

Low Life examines the world of the tenements occupied by immigrants, while *Evidence* is a picture book and essay focusing on the mayhem wrought in this world, with old police crime scene photos to illustrate the point.

Robert Caro's *The Power Broker*, one of the most monumental biographies of the 20th century, is the story of the ruthless civil servant Robert Moses, who used politically appointed positions to remake the face of New York from the late 1920s until the '60s.

Clifton Hood's *722 Miles - The Building of the Subways and How they Transformed New York* is a history of the city's confusing and frustrating transit system.

1939: The Lost World of the Fair by David Gelernter is a fictional memoir based on the collected recollections of the people who were affected by the optimistic atmosphere of the World's Fair that symbolized the country's emergence from the Great Depression.

True New York mavens will love the *Encyclopedia of New York City* (Yale University Press and New-York Historical Society), edited by historian Kenneth Jackson, but you'll need to buy a separate piece of luggage to haul this massive 1350-page volume home.

Memoirs

The city has inspired and attracted more than its share of affectionate memories. *Here is New York* by EB White is an essay written in 1949 that still stands today as an affectionate summing up of fast-paced city life. ('To bring New York up to date,' he writes, 'a man would have to be published with the speed of light.')

Kafka was all the Rage by Anatole Broyard, the late book reviewer for the *New York Times*, is a bittersweet look at living in Greenwich Village just after WWII, a time also recalled by journalist Dan Wakefield in *New York in the '50s*. Jack Kerouac's *Lonesome Traveler* focuses on his days in New York.

New York Days (1993) by Willie Morris, tells how, as a young man, he came from the South to New York City to seek his literary fortune and found it as editor of *Harper's Magazine* in that magazine's heyday. It's wonderfully descriptive of the 1960s literary era and new journalism, as well as the back-stabbing in the profession. *New York When I was Young* by Mary Cantwell is a female coming of age tale by an editorial writer for the *New York Times*.

Pete Hamill, one of New York's most famous newspaper columnists and current editor of the *Daily News*, recalls his Irish American Brooklyn childhood in *A Drinking Life*, an evocative look at the culture of drink and its effect on his career and relationships.

The Andy Warhol Diaries is a bitchy and colorful account of the '70s night culture by the man who may well be the most influential artist of the 20th century.

DAVID ELLIS

The *WPA Guide to New York City*, published in 1939 as a Depression-era employment project for the city's writers (including John Cheever), is back in print as a time-frozen look at a lost metropolis. This is a wonderful read for anyone who has lived in or explored the city in recent days.

NEWSPAPERS & MAGAZINES

Want a definition of 'information overload'? Walk into a well-stocked Manhattan newsstand. The world's major periodicals are all available in the city. Locally, it's hard to determine a single best source for listings – each periodical tends to emphasize a particular type of entertainment.

The *New York Times* (60¢, $2.50 Sunday) is still the nation's premier newspaper, with more foreign bureaus and reporters than any other publication in the world. Its Friday Weekend section is an invaluable guide to cultural events. The *Wall Street Journal* is must-reading for financial workers, but the paper's daily one-column digest of world events won't be enough to satisfy news junkies. It has an excellent Washington bureau and the nation's most rabidly conservative editorial page, which specializes in childish ad hominem attacks on Democrats.

The *Daily News*, a solid working class newspaper edited by Pete Hamill and owned by real estate developer Mort Zuckerman, and *New York Post*, Rupert Murdoch's pale imitation of a London tabloid, are locked in permanent combat for readers. The *Post*'s business section is a great source for industry gossip, and the *Post* and *News* regularly poke fun of their rival owner's financial interests.

The fabled *New Yorker* magazine continues its 70-year tradition of news, fiction and critical reviews, along with a new fixation on celebrity, introduced by editor Tina Brown, that has offended many older readers. The magazine's 'Goings on about Town' section lists major art, cinema and music events. *New York* magazine does the same thing for its younger and more restaurant-oriented readers. The *Village Voice* (distributed free in Manhattan each Wednesday), is well known for its night life listings for the mainstream clubs and music venues. It's also the best-known source for rental apartments and roommate situations. The *New York Observer*, a weekly newspaper for people obsessed with the local media and politics, strives for a quirkier listings of literary readings and parties in its 'Eight Day Week' column.

KIM GRANT

Information overload

The year 1995 saw the introduction of *Time Out New York*, which is published Wednesdays and costs $1.95. It has the same format as its London cousin and has a very good section on gay and lesbian events. The magazine's features are unimpressive, but the comprehensive listings are the main selling point.

Where New York is the best free monthly guide to mainstream city events. Available at most hotels, it's more useful than two pocket-sized rivals, *The New York Quick Guide*, a monthly, and *City Guide*, published weekly.

RADIO

There are over 100 radio stations in the city, but most 'narrowcast' only one type of programming. This is particularly true on FM, where 'radio apartheid' exists and it's nearly impossible to hear hip hop and rock on the same frequency.

On AM frequencies, WABC (770) is a talk radio station and home to conservative icon Rush Limbaugh. WOR (710), one of the nation's oldest stations, carries a calmer type of talk and WFAN (660) is a 24-hour sports station. WQEW (1560) broadcasts big band music and Sinatra standards. Spanish speakers listen to WKDM (1380) and WADO (1280); WWRL (1660) is a talk station aimed at the city's African American community.

WCBS (880) and WINS (1010) carry news and weather updates every 10 minutes and WNYC-AM (820) broadcasts National Public Radio.

On FM, classical music lovers turn to WNYC (93.9) and WQXR (96.3), which includes reviews and news reports from its owner, the *New York Times*. WBGO (88.3) carries NPR in the morning and commercial-free jazz the rest of the day.

The best top-40/rock mixture can be found on WHTZ (100.3). WBLS (107.5) is a premier spot for soft soul music, while WQHT (97.1) is known as 'Hot 97' for its hip hop and rap programming. At the moment, there are at least five stations broadcasting the tired format of 'classic rock.'

Those seeking the widest musical variety should listen to WKCR (89.9) and WFMU (90.1), fringe stations with eclectic programming.

TV

The comedian Fred Allen once said that TV was called a medium because 'nothing on it was either rare or well done.' A night watching the tube will prove the truth of his quip. The flagship stations of all four major networks – NBC, CBS, NBC and FOX – are located in New York City and carry familiar evening prime time fare.

Cable carries well-known networks like CNN, MTV and HBO. Channels dedicated to sports, culture, history and old movies are available. News broadcasts from Britain, Ireland, France, Mexico, Greece, Korea, Japan and Germany also appear on international cable channels each night between 7 and 11 pm. Manhattan cable also carries dozens of local amateur programs on the 'public access' channels. You can find everything from a strip show to a discussion of city real estate values on the air.

PHOTOGRAPHY & VIDEO
Film & Equipment

Print film is widely available at supermarkets and discount drugstores (which offer the best prices). See the Shopping chapter for more on camera and photographic supply stores.

Drugstores are a good place to get your film cheaply processed. If you drop it off by noon, you can usually pick it up the next day.

If you want your pictures right away, you can find one-hour processing services in the yellow pages under 'Photo Processing.' Be prepared to pay double the overnight cost.

Video Systems

The USA uses NTSC color TV standard, which is not compatible with other standards (PAL or SECAM) used in Africa, Asia, Australia and Europe unless it is converted.

TIME

New York City is in the Eastern Standard Time (EST) zone – five hours behind GMT/UTC, two hours ahead of Mountain Standard Time (including Denver, Colorado) and three hours ahead of Pacific Standard Time (San Francisco and Los Angeles, California). Almost all of the US observes daylight-saving time: clocks go forward one hour from the first Sunday in April to the last Saturday in October, when the clocks are turned back one hour. (It's easy to remember by the phrase 'spring ahead, fall backwards.')

In the US, dates are usually given with the month first, then the day, then the year.

ELECTRICITY

The USA uses 110V and 60 cycles and plugs have two or three pins (two flat pins often with a round 'grounding' pin). Plugs with three pins don't fit into a two-hole socket, but adapters are available at Radio Shack and other electronic stores as well as hardware stores.

LAUNDRY

Many New Yorkers live in apartments without laundry facilities, so most residential neighborhoods have an abundance of laundries. The Suds Cafe and Laundromat (☎ (212) 741-2366), at 141 W 10th St, has a reputation as a social scene. It is open from 7 am to 10 pm daily.

Washing machines generally cost $1.25 for a 25-minute cycle; dryers are $1.50 for 30 minutes. Almost all laundries have change-making machines so you won't have to visit a bank for quarters before doing laundry.

Many of these facilities also offer pick-up laundry services at a rate of about $1 per pound of clothing. Hotels charge very high prices for this service, so it's smart to look for an outside laundry.

WEIGHTS & MEASURES

Americans hate the metric system, and continue to resist it nearly 20 years after it was supposed to be fully introduced.

Distances are in feet (ft), yards (yds) and miles (mi). Near the Canadian border you may see some distances marked in kilometers as well as miles.

Dry weights are measured by the ounce (oz), the pound (lb; 16 ounces equal one pound) and ton (2000 pounds are one ton), but liquid measures differ from dry measures. One pint equals 16 fluid ounces. Two pints equal one quart, a common measure for liquids like milk, which is also sold in half gallons (two quarts) and gallons (four quarts). Gasoline is dispensed by the US gallon, which is about 20% less than the imperial gallon. US pints and quarts are also 20% less than imperial ones.

See the Metric Conversion Chart inside the back cover.

HEALTH

You don't need any special immunization to visit the US, and in New York your greatest health threat is heartburn from the more deleterious streetside food vendors.

Travel Insurance

It is important to have travel insurance, especially if you come from a country with a nationalized health program that doesn't extend beyond the country's borders. Most coverage will refund the entire amount of non-refundable deposits of a cancelled trip, lost bag replacement and emergency medical assistance. Coverage usually costs between $80 and $150 for a 21-day trip, with surcharges for additional days running $3 to $5 extra for each day.

When inquiring about insurance, make sure that the policy is for primary coverage and includes a 24-hour help line for emergencies. All insurance you consider *must* cover medivac transport out of areas with dodgy health facilities.

Travel Guard (☎ (800) 826-1300) is one of the better insurers available in the US, offering comprehensive service. Access America (☎ (800) 284-8300) offers similar options. The international student travel policies handled by STA Travel are usually reasonably priced.

KIM GRANT

Autumn in New York

Medical Services

If possible, avoid going to emergency rooms, which are incredibly expensive. Although all hospital emergency rooms are obligated to receive sick visitors without regard to an ability to pay, showing up without insurance or money will virtually guarantee a long wait unless you are in extremis.

The New York University Medical Center (☎ (212) 561-4347), 462 First Ave (32nd St), is easily reached by taxi and offers a kind of 'urgent-care clinic,' designed to deal with walk-in clients with less-than-catastrophic injuries or illnesses.

Pharmacies

There are several 24-hour Duane Reade Pharmacy locations, including one on the corner of W 57th St and Broadway (☎ (212) 541-9708) and one on Sixth Ave and Waverly Pl near the W 8th St subway entrance (☎ (212) 674-5357). Kaufman's Pharmacy (☎ (212) 755-2266), 557 Lexington Ave at 50th St, is also always open and delivers medicine all hours.

Planned Parenthood (☎ (212) 677-6474) has its main clinic at 380 Second Ave.

TOILETS

New York is not friendly to the weak of bladder. The explosion in the homeless population in the 1970s led to the closure of subway bathrooms and most facilities turn away non-patrons from bathrooms. It's possible to walk into a crowded bar or restaurant to use the bathroom if you are discreet and well dressed.

WOMEN TRAVELERS

Women need not be particularly concerned about traveling on their own in New York City. Though many shun the subways, this fear is unjustified since the transit system has a lower crime rate than the city streets. It's wise for solo women to make a habit of riding in the conductor's car (in the middle of the train). If someone stares or acts in an annoying manner, simply move to another part of the car or near the conductor's booth.

Women are far more likely to encounter obnoxious behavior on the street, being greeted with whistles, muttered 'compliments' and even the occasional kissing sound. Any engagement amounts to encouragement – your best bet is to ignore it and simply walk on.

DISABLED TRAVELERS

Federal laws guarantee that all government offices and facilities are available to the disabled. Most restaurant listings also note whether the location is wheelchair accessible. The mayor's office for People with Disabilities can be reached at ☎ (212) 788-2830. If you encounter problems, the state advocate for disabled people is available at ☎ (800) 772-1213.

SATH, the Society for the Advancement of Travel for the Handicapped (☎ (212) 447-7284), is located at 347 Fifth Ave, suite 610.

GAY & LESBIAN TRAVELERS

New York is one of the most gay friendly cities on earth, and several neighborhoods – particularly Greenwich Village and Chelsea in Manhattan and Jackson Heights in Queens – are populated by many gays and lesbians.

The Gay and Lesbian Switchboard (☎ (212) 777-1800) is the best all-around information source on what's happening in town. This 24-hour service has a very extensive automated information system that offers descriptions of the newest club scenes and specific support services. The line is also staffed by volunteers from noon to midnight.

The Lesbian and Gay Community Services Center (☎ (212) 620-7310), 208 W 13th St, serves some 5000 people each week through its legal aid workshops and social events. They also provide assistance to travelers and visitor information. A calendar of events at 'The Center' is available for those who stop in from 9 am to 11 pm.

Gay Men's Health Crisis (☎ (212) 807-6664) and the Community Health project (☎ (212) 675-3559) offer blood testing, health care for those with HIV and a wide range of counseling. The Anti-Violence Project hotline (☎ (212) 807-0197) is staffed 24 hours a day.

Gay-oriented tours and holidays are booked by many New York-based agencies, including One on One Travel (☎ (212) 213-3412) and RSVP travel (☎ (212) 800-328-7787). Check the gay publications for more information.

See the sidebar Gay & Lesbian New York in the Things to See & Do chapter for more information on gay life in the city. Also see related sidebars in the Places to Stay and Entertainment chapters.

KIM GRANT

Above the treetops – more buildings

Public Toilets: No Relief in Sight

Anyone who spends time walking around New York City will no doubt learn, to their discomfort, that there's a serious dearth of accessible public toilets. Most restaurants have signs specifically noting that bathrooms are for 'customers only,' and many of the big department stores (such as Macy's) keep their bathrooms in rather shabby conditions, presumably to discourage their use; other stores like the uptown Barney's refuse to list toilets in their directories forcing you to submit to scrutiny when you ask for one. (At Barney's uptown the men's rooms are on the 2nd and 4th floors, the women's room is on the 3rd floor.) You can often find a lobby level toilet in a hotel, but the tonier facilities frown on obvious outsiders cruising in for the call of nature, and those around Times Square don't usually offer public bathrooms. Museum toilets are invariably located *behind* their admission booth, and subway toilets are almost never open, with the erratic exception of the bathrooms in the 34th St/Sixth Ave station, which appear to be available but a few hours a day.

And then there's the city's single *new* public toilet, just behind City Hall.

Only *one* new toilet? That's right. One that's clean, safe, and plays space-age music while you attend to business in the 20 minutes allotted. It costs only 25¢ and has instructions in English, German, French and Chinese. Yet almost no one uses it – even at rush hour – and hundreds of New Yorkers pass it by without a second look, as if they don't believe it exists.

There's a reason for that attitude. For years, city officials talked about providing clean and well maintained public toilets throughout the city, identical to those found in London and Paris. In fact, in the late '80s then-mayor David Dinkins invited a French company to install a few sets of four toilets throughout the city. But suddenly the company was tied up in lawsuits by advocates for the disabled who believed that since only one out of every

SENIOR TRAVELERS

Travelers 50 years old or more (particularly those over 65) can often avail themselves of reduced transit fares, and cut rates on hotels, drug store prescriptions and museum admissions. New York restaurants don't generally offer age-specific discounts, but seniors are about the only class of person who can get a reduction in the $8.50 movie admission price.

Seniors over 65 with ID can obtain a free return trip transfer slip when purchasing a token on the subway.

The country's most powerful elder organization is the American Association of Retired Persons (AARP; ☎ (800) 424-3410), 601 E St NW, Washington, DC 20049. It's a good resource for travel bargains and information. One-year membership for US residents costs $8.

NEW YORK CITY FOR CHILDREN

With its abundance of world-famous sites, tours and attractions, New York is an ideal place to bring children. There are three museums dedicated to children (see the Children's Museum of Manhattan in the Upper West Side section of Things to See & Do) and many annual events that appeal to kids.

Kids will also love the Central Park Zoo and the more elaborate Bronx Zoo. The Big Apple Circus visits takes place in Lincoln Center each winter and the Ringling Bros and Barnum & Bailey Circus takes over Madison Square Garden every May and June.

Check the sections on Entertainment and Special Events for further information.

LIBRARIES

The main branch of the New York Public Library (☎ (212) 930-0800) on Fifth Ave at 42nd St is a significant architectural attraction and worth visiting if only to see the famous 3rd-floor reading room. Those looking for periodicals and book information will find fewer crowds at the Midtown

■■

four toilets would be wheelchair accessible, their installation was a violation of federal law guaranteeing equal access to public facilities for all.

Dinkins dithered and the French packed up their toilets in disgust at the bureaucratic snafu. A second project also ran aground, leaving the legacy of exactly one model toilet at City Hall, presumably for the comfort of the politicians therein.

In 1997, Dinkins' successor Rudolph Giuliani (voted in largely because he promised to break up the bureaucracy) announced that the city was finally going to restart the project for public facilities. But at time of writing, it remains to be seen whether this was just a pre-emptive election year ploy to deflect criticism for not doing something about the situation years earlier.

What's a traveler to do? The best rule is to plan bladder breaks around a trip to a cafe or bar. But failing that, here are a few places where you can find available (but not always clean) toilets:

Barnes & Noble – all superstores have well-marked toilets, though maintenance people are liable to keep the door open at all times. Check the listing in Shopping for locations.

McDonald's on Broadway just above E 4th St has a heavily trafficked toilet popular with local street people. (Other McDonald's and similar fast food facilities do not offer toilets.)

Bryant Park at 42nd St and Sixth Ave has a minimally acceptable public toilet, but a better bet is to visit the main branch of the Public Library just behind the park on Fifth Ave.

GE Building in Rockefeller Center has toilets in its lower level, but the line for the ladies' room can be astoundingly long during the holiday months, when thousands visit the area. ■

■■

Manhattan annex directly across the street, or at the Jefferson Market branch (☎ (212) 243-4334) at 425 Sixth Ave.

CAMPUSES

New York is home to many world-class private universities and fine public colleges, including Columbia, New York and Fordham Universities, The New School for Social Research, the Cooper Union, and the various colleges of the City University of New York (CUNY). These urban educational centers are not physically separated from the city – in fact NYU's campus and dorm facilities are distributed throughout Greenwich Village and the East Village.

Columbia's peaceful main campus is set back from Broadway in Upper Manhattan (subway: 116th St) and the City College campus of CUNY at St Nicholas Terrace is significant for its neo-gothic design and worth a visit (subway: 137th St-City College).

CULTURAL CENTERS

New York City's major cultural centers include:

Alliance Française
   22 E 60th St (☎ (212) 355-6100)

Asia Society
   725 Park Ave (☎ (212) 288-6400)

Czech Center
   1109 Madison Ave (☎ (212) 288-0830)

Goethe Institute
   1014 Fifth Ave (☎ (212) 439-8700)

Hispanic Society of America
   Broadway and 155th St (☎ (212) 690-0743)

Italian Cultural Institute
   686 Park Ave (☎ (212) 879-4242)

Japan House
   333 E 47th St (☎ (212) 832-1155)

Spanish Institute
   684 Park Ave (☎ (212) 628-0420)

Swiss Institute
   495 Broadway (☎ (212) 925-2035)

DANGERS & ANNOYANCES

Beggars

Criminal Willie Sutton, when asked why he robbed banks, replied that 'that's where the money is!' The same philosophy prompts panhandlers to set up shop at subway entrances, banks, landmarks and street corners heavily patronized by tourists. Requests for money come in dozens of forms, including appeals for a dubious support group ('I'm a member of the United Homeless Organization'), unsubtle appeals to tourist fear ('I don't want to hurt or rob anybody') or even guilt-trip opening lines ('I know you won't help me because I'm black/poor/homeless . . . '). It's impossible to differentiate between those truly in need and someone on the hustle, and many tourists assuage their guilt by giving. But New Yorkers know that money handed out even to genuinely destitute beggars will likely go to support a drug or alcohol habit rather than towards a meal or a room for the night – in which case it will certainly do nothing to change their condition.

It is the nature of life in New York that even some once-decent efforts to help panhandlers have been corrupted, such as the selling of *Street News*, a homeless publication. At least two subway beggars have taken to telling riders that the weather has prevented delivery of their copies or that they've nobly given their copies away to others. The upshot is that gullible listeners give these guys money anyway.

If you wish to give to a legitimate organization helping people in need, contact Citymeals-on-Wheels (☎ (212) 687-1234), which reaches out to feed hundreds of hungry people each day.

Scams

A prominent scam that targets out-of-towners takes the form of a shoulder-shrugging appeal for help. This differs from outright panhandling in that the person asking for money makes no pretense of being impoverished. Instead, they approach you with a sad story ('I just got locked out of my car and need money for a cab') and even promise to pay you back. Spare change isn't what they're after – they are very persuasive in trying to get $5 or even $20 from you, which they will never pay back. When approached by anyone asking for money, remember that the person is asking a tourist for help because the police and most locals are wise to scams.

In another frequent scam, hustlers set up three-card monte games – where 'players' try to pick the red card out of three shuffled on the top of a cardboard box. This variation on the shell game is widely known to be a no-win scam. Yet enough people play along (or get their wallets lifted while watching the proceedings) to make it a common sight on downtown streets during the weekends.

Drugs

There is heavy drug activity in the far East Village in Alphabet City (Aves A, B, C and

D), along Amsterdam Ave above 100th St and in Washington Heights near the George Washington Bridge bus stop. All three neighborhoods have the attendant dangers of such places. Expect to be approached by drug dealers if you wander into any of these places, and avoid walking through them with any amount of cash at night.

Prostitution

New York's strip joints are rather unspectacular (topless only), and either sleazy and cheap (in Midtown) or sleazy and expensive (near Wall St) and are not havens for prostitution. Elsewhere, there are sex clubs that cater to Japanese businessmen and pricey escort services that meet the demand for prostitution. Police have cracked down on street prostitutes, and instead of being on the stroll on Eleventh Avenue near the Lincoln Tunnel they ply their risky trade from vans.

Visiting businessmen are approached at public places, for example along Sixth Ave near Central Park South, the Bull and Bear pub at the Waldorf-Astoria and the lobby of the Grand Hyatt Hotel, one of the most open spots in the city for the hotel sex trade (perhaps because the hotel hosts many visiting professional athletic teams).

EMERGENCIES

For police, fire and ambulance calls, dial ☎ 911. The police department can be reached at ☎ (212) 374-5000 from 7:30 am to 6 pm Monday to Friday. All federal, state and city government offices appear in a special section in the white pages; the front of every phone book also contains a complete list of community organizations. Here are some useful numbers:

AIDS Hotline	☎ (212) 447-8200
Alcoholics Anonymous	☎ (212) 647-1680
Crime Victims Services	☎ (212) 577-7777
Gay &Lesbian Switchboard	☎ (212) 777-1800
Legal Aid Society	☎ (212) 577-3300
NYC Dept of Consumer Affairs	☎ (212) 487-4398

KIM GRANT

For New Yorkers, Union Square is an escape from the hustle and bustle.

LEGAL MATTERS

If you are arrested you are allowed to remain silent. There is no legal reason to speak to a police officer if you don't wish, but never walk away from an officer until given permission. All persons who are arrested are legally allowed (and given) the right to make one phone call. If you don't have a lawyer or family member to help you, call your consulate. The police will give you the number upon request.

In New York, police often ignore local laws against public drinking and even pot smoking in the park. But if you're arrested, there's no legal excuse in relating that we told you the cops don't enforce the law! And the police department is making an effort to crack down on 'quality of life' infractions, so beware.

BUSINESS HOURS

You can shop in New York for almost anything seven days a week, with some exceptions. Store hours from Monday to Saturday tend to be from 10 am to 6 pm, with big department stores open late on Thursday nights.

Bookstores and specialty shops often maintain regular night hours, and there are many 24-hour drug stores (Duane Reade, Rite Aid, Genovese) scattered throughout the city selling pharmaceuticals and a variety of items (toothpaste, candy, soft drinks and light groceries).

Sunday shopping hours tend to be noon to 6 pm. Bakeries and boutique clothing shops tend to be closed on Mondays.

In a barbaric holdover of the blue laws, liquor stores are closed on Sunday throughout New York state. But you can buy beer at grocery stores after noon Sunday.

SPECIAL EVENTS

Hardly a week goes by without a special event taking place in New York. In fact, there are some 50 officially recognized parades each year honoring certain causes or ethnic groups, along with more than 400 street fairs. Most of New York's street fairs offer a rather unremarkable selection of fast-food stands, house plants, athletic socks and cheap belts. You're bound to come across one as you stroll through town during the summer months.

Fifth Ave shuts down several times a year for the more elaborate major parades, including the granddaddy of all ethnic celebrations, the St Patrick's Day Parade on March 17th. Other parades take place on Salute to Israel Day (May), Puerto Rican

---

National Public Holidays

National public holidays are celebrated throughout the USA. Banks, schools and government offices (including post offices) are closed and transportation, museums and other services are on a Sunday schedule. Holidays falling on a weekend are usually observed the following Monday.

January 1	New Year's Day
3rd Monday in January	Martin Luther King Jr Day
3rd Monday in February	Presidents' Day
A Sunday in late March or early April	Easter
Last Monday in May	Memorial Day
July 4	Independence Day (Fourth of July)
1st Monday in September	Labor Day
2nd Monday in October	Columbus Day
November 11	Veterans' Day
4th Thursday in November	Thanksgiving Day
December 25	Christmas Day

Day (June), Labor Day (September), Columbus Day and Pulaski Day (both in October).

January

New Year's Eve – In addition to the annual New Year's Eve festivities in Times Square, there's a five-mile midnight run in Central Park (☎ (212) 364-3456) and fireworks at the South Street Seaport (☎ (212) 732-7678). *First Night* is a day-long festival of alcohol-free family events, including ballroom dancing in Grand Central Station's main concourse. It runs from 11 am on December 31 to 1 am New Year's Day. Tickets for adults/children are $20/5; call ☎ (212) 922-9393 for details.

Three Kings Parade – Every January 5, El Museo del Barrio (☎ (212) 831-7272) sponsors this parade in which thousands of schoolchildren, along with camels, donkeys and sheep, make their way up Fifth Ave to 116th St, in the heart of Spanish Harlem.

Winter Antiques Show – This show, held mid-month at the Armory at Park Ave and 67th St, features dealer stalls selling items like $30,000 couches and $15,000 tea services, and attracts many celebrities and everyday strollers who couldn't possibly afford the prices. Call ☎ (718) 292-7392 for information.

Chinese New Year – The date of the lunar new year varies from late January to early February each year, but the fireworks crackle in Chinatown for days before and after. Call the Chinatown History Museum (☎ (212) 619-4785) for information on community celebrations and cultural events.

February

Black History Month – The Martin Luther King Jr national holiday (in late January) serves as the unofficial kick-off to February's month-long celebration of African American history and culture. Call Harlem's Schomburg Center for Research in Black Culture (☎ (212) 491-2200) for details about related events.

March

St Patrick's Day Parade – For more than 200 years, the city's Irish population has honored their homeland's patron saint with this parade down Fifth Ave on March 17. In recent years a gay Irish group has protested their exclusion from the parade with a demonstration at Fifth Ave and 42nd St.

April

Avignon-New York Film Festival – This film festival is held at a prominent Midtown theater each year as a harbinger of cultural events to come later in the warmer weather.

May

Fleet Week – Thousands of sailors from many nations descend on New York for this annual convocation of naval ships and air rescue teams. Call the Intrepid Air & Space Museum (☎ (212) 245-2533) for scheduling information.

International Food Fair – In mid-May, just before the Memorial Day weekend that officially starts the summer, Ninth Ave between 42nd and 57th Sts literally teems with people eating ethnic fast food from stalls set up in the street.

Carnaval – On Memorial Day weekend Hispanic culture is celebrated.

June

Museum Mile Festival – On the second Tuesday in June, upper Fifth Ave is closed to traffic from 6 to 9 pm, and all nine museums in the area open their doors for free. Call ☎ (212) 603-9868 for information.

Change Your Mind Day – Tibetan Monks carry on a 2000-year-old tradition of philosophic debate by discussing transcendental matters in Central Park in early June. Call ☎ (212) 360-2756 for information.

JVC Jazz Festival – Nearly all the major concert halls in town are jumping with the top names in jazz. Call ☎ (212) 787-2020 for information.

What is Jazz? Festival – Meanwhile, smaller 'fringe' shows take place downtown at this event, sponsored by the Knitting Factory night club. Call ☎ (212) 219-3006 for information.

Toyota Comedy Festival – Comedians take to the stage of Carnegie Hall and a host of clubs. Call ☎ (212) 903-9600 for information.

Buskers Festival – A night of buskers highlights a series of free concerts and performances at the World Financial Center downtown. Call ☎ (212) 945-0505 for details.

Welcome Back to Brooklyn Celebration – This celebration of the self-assured borough lasts the entire summer. Events include concerts, Shakespeare plays and dance shows. Call ☎ (718) 855-7882 ext 52 for program updates.

NY Shakespeare Festival – The Public Theater (☎ (212) 861-7277) sponsors performances of the Bard's work from late June to September.

Major stars like Michelle Pfeiffer and Denzel Washington have appeared in the free performances in Central Park.

Lesbian and Gay Pride Week – On the last weekend of June a huge parade flows down Fifth Ave and dances are held on the Hudson River piers.

July

Independence Day – On July 4, Macy's sponsors its annual fireworks spectacular in the East River.

Lincoln Center Events – Lincoln Center has an astounding number of events throughout the summer, many of them free, including Lincoln Center Out-of-Doors (☎ (212) 875-5108), the Mostly Mozart concert series (☎ (212) 875-5103) , and the Lincoln Center Festival (☎ (212) 875-5400), an event (scheduled for 1998 and 2000) that brings many international actors, singers and acrobats to New York for the first time.

Central Park Summerstage – This is a series of musical performances and author readings held near the park's bandshell in July and August. Call ☎ (212) 360-2756 for information.

JANE LLOYD

Classic Movies in Bryant Park – On Mondays in July and August, the HBO cable network sponsors a series of open-air screenings.

Outdoor Concerts – Also in July and August the New York Philharmonic and the Metropolitan Opera perform under the stars in Central Park, with other performances in parks in all the boroughs. Call the Parks Department (☎ (212) 360-3456) for information on all outdoor events.

August

Harlem Week – The city's premier black neighborhood celebrates. For information call the Harlem Visitors Bureau (☎ (212) 427-3317).

Greenwich Village Jazz Festival – Jazz is back for an encore during a series of performances in intimate club settings. Call ☎ (212) 929-5149 for information.

September

US Open Tennis Tournament – This world-class event takes place in Flushing Meadows annually, with men's and women's finals played on Labor Day weekend. Call ☎ (718) 760-4700 for information.

Fall Festival – Also in Queens, the Fall Festival is sponsored by the Queens Council on the Arts (☎ (718) 647-3377) and lasts until November.

Caribbean Day – On Labor Day, over one million people take part in a parade in Brooklyn, making this the single largest event of the year. To get there, take the subway to Eastern Parkway or Grand Army Plaza. Call ☎ (718) 625-1515 for parade and event information.

New York is Book Country Festival – Publishers and rare book dealers set up all along Fifth Ave between 53rd and 57th Sts on a weekend in mid-September.

New York Film Festival – This major event takes place at Lincoln Center. For information call ☎ (212) 875-5600.

Jazz at Lincoln Center – Trumpeter Wynton Marsalis heads this up. For information call ☎ (212) 875-5599.

October

Halloween Parade – This colorful and sometimes wild parade winds its way down Sixth Ave in Greenwich Village, ending up in a street party on Christopher St.

New York Marathon – As the weather cools, the New York Road Runners Club (☎ (800) 697-7269) sponsors this annual 26-mile road race, in which some 25,000 runners travel through all five boroughs.

Paul Manship's *Prometheus* presides over the ice rink at Rockefeller Center.

November

Thanksgiving Day Parade – Macy's sponsors this big event with its huge balloons and floats down Broadway from W 72nd St to Herald Square.

December

Rockefeller Center Christmas Tree Lighting – At 7 pm on the Tuesday immediately following Thanksgiving, the big tree is plugged in. The event features celebrity performances and an appearance by the Radio City Music Hall Rockettes. Call ☎ (212) 632-3975 for information.

Radio City Christmas Spectacular – The Rockettes, of course, are on display all month at the famous theater (☎ (212) 247-4777).

Christmas Windows – Strollers along Fifth and Madison Aves can check out the elaborate holiday window displays at Barney's, Sak's Fifth Ave, Lord & Taylor and Macy's.

Singing Christmas Tree Celebration – At South Street Seaport, dozens of costumed carolers perform several times a day. Call ☎ (212) 732-7678) for information.

WORK

US law makes it difficult to work in the country without a prearranged permit from an employer. It is possible to overstay a J1 summer work visa, and thousands of foreign students do just that every year.

If you're a visitor from abroad, word of mouth is usually the way to find out about working illegally at restaurants and bars. It helps if you do not have a discernible accent. Illegal white collar work is pretty much out of the questions, since employers who hire illegal workers are subject to big fines.

Getting There & Away

Served by three major airports, two train terminals and a massive bus depot, New York City is the most important transportation hub in the northeastern USA.

AIR
Airports
John F Kennedy airport (JFK), 15 miles from Midtown Manhattan in southeastern Queens, is where most international flights land. La Guardia airport in northern Queens is eight miles away and services mostly domestic flights, including air shuttles to Boston and Washington, DC.

Newark airport is in New Jersey, directly 10 miles to the west. It's the hub for Continental Airlines and its brand new international arrivals terminal is used by many major carriers.

For information about getting to/from the airports see Getting Around.

JFK Airport JFK, which serves 30 million passengers a year, was recently voted the third-worst airport facility in the world by business travelers, and it deserves the dishonor. US airlines used to build separate showcase terminals at JFK – check out the TWA terminal, a landmark structure designed by Eero Saarinen in 1962. But the airport grew into a sprawling mess with no coherent plan to it as a whole. While some of the original airlines (Eastern, National, Pan Am) have disappeared, the terminals remain in use, linked by the JFK Expressway and a free shuttle bus. American Airlines, British Airways, Delta and TWA still have their own terminals; most other airlines use the crowded International Arrivals Building. The airport information line (☎ (718) 244-4444) will tell you if the airport is closed in bad weather. The airlines themselves, however, are usually reluctant to give honest information about flight delays over the phone.

Until the airport undergoes a much needed multi-million dollar renovation, it's a place best avoided. JFK's Duty Free shops, like those in most US cities, are absolutely useless – you can get alcohol, electronics and clothes cheaper in town, so don't expect to embark on a last minute purchasing spree for anything other than cigarettes.

La Guardia Airport If you're arriving or departing in the middle of the day, La Guardia (☎ (718) 533-3400) is a more convenient choice than JFK. US Airways and the Delta shuttle each have dedicated terminals; all other airlines use the Central Terminal Building in front of the parking garage.

Newark Airport Flights to/from Newark airport (☎ (201) 961-6000) are sometimes a bit cheaper because of the erroneous perception that the airport is less accessible than JFK or La Guardia. In fact, Newark has a large and spanking-new international arrivals terminal. Plus, the airport's four terminals are now linked by a monorail system that will also be connected to the New Jersey Transit train system by the year 2000, offering a traffic-free trip to the airport from Manhattan's Penn Station.

Airlines
Every major national carrier has a presence in New York – check the yellow pages under 'airlines.' The following airlines have offices downtown or at the airports:

Aer Lingus
    509 Madison Ave (☎ (800) 223-6537
Aeromexico
    37 W 57th St (☎ (800) 237-6639)
Air Canada
    15 W 50th St (☎ (800) 776-3000)
Air France
    120 W 56th St (☎ (800) 237-2747)
American Airlines
    18 W 49th St (☎ (800) 433-7300)

British Airways
530 Fifth Ave (☎ (800) 247-9297)
Continental Airlines
100 E 42nd St (☎ (800) 525-0280)
Delta Airlines
100 E 42nd St (☎ (800) 221-1212)
Finnair
228 E 45th St (☎ (800) 950-5000)
Japan Air Lines
JFK Airport (☎ (800) 525-3663)
KLM
437 Madison Ave (☎ (800) 374-7747
Korean Air
609 Fifth Ave (☎ (800) 438-5000)
Northwest Airlines
437 Madison Ave (☎ (800)447-4747)
Olympic Airways
647 Fifth Ave (☎ (800) 223-1226)
Philippine Airlines
JFK Airport (☎ (800) 435-9725)
Qantas
712 Fifth Ave (☎ (800) 227-4500)
Singapore Airlines
55 E 59th St (☎ (800) 742-3333)
Swissair
608 Fifth Ave (☎ (800) 221-4750)
Tower Air
JFK Airport (☎ (800) 221-2500)
TWA
1 E 59th St (☎ (800) 221-2000)
United Airlines
100 E 42nd St (☎ (800) 241-6522)
USAirways
101 Park Ave (☎ (800) 428-4322)
Virgin Atlantic
96 Morton St (☎ (800) 862-8621)

Buying Tickets

The plane ticket will probably be the single most expensive item in your budget and buying it can be intimidating. Rather than just walking into the nearest travel agent or airline office, it pays to do some research of the current market. Start looking early – some of the cheapest tickets and best deals must be bought months in advance, some popular flights sell out early and special offers may be advertised.

Look at the travel sections of magazines like *Time Out* and *TNT* in the UK, or the Sunday editions of newspapers like the *New York Times* and *Los Angeles Times* in the US, or the *Sydney Morning Herald* and *The Age* in Australia. Ads in these publications offer cheap fares, but don't be surprised if they're sold out when you contact the agents. They're usually low-season fares on obscure airlines with conditions attached. Talk to other recent travelers if possible – they may be able to stop you from making some of the same old mistakes.

Note that high season in the USA is mid-June to mid-September (summer) and one week before and after Christmas. The best rates for travel to and in the USA are found November through March.

Call travel agents for bargains (airlines can supply information on routes and timetables; however, except at times of fare wars, they don't supply the cheapest tickets). Airlines often have competitive low-season, student and senior citizens' fares. Find out the fare, route, duration of the journey and any restrictions on the ticket. Fare levels change constantly and some fares that include accommodations may be as cheap as roundtrip fares.

Outside the US cheap tickets are available in two distinct categories: official and unofficial. Official tickets have a variety of names, including budget, advance-purchase, Apex and super-Apex. Unofficial tickets are simply discounted tickets that the airlines release through selected travel agents (not through airline offices).

Wherever you buy your tickets, the cheapest are often nonrefundable and require an extra fee for changing your flight, if you're allowed to change your flight at all. Many insurance policies cover this loss if you have to change your flight for emergency reasons. Roundtrip (return) tickets are often much cheaper than two one-way fares.

The fares quoted in this book should be used as a guide only and don't necessarily constitute a recommendation for the carrier.

If you're traveling from the UK, you'll probably find that the cheapest flights are advertised by obscure bucket shops. Many are honest and solvent, but there are a few rogues who'll take your money and disappear, to reopen elsewhere a month or two later under a new name. If you feel suspicious, don't give them all the money at once – leave a deposit of 20% or so and pay the balance on receiving the ticket. If they insist on cash in advance, go elsewhere. Once you have the ticket, phone the airline to confirm that you are booked on the flight.

You may decide to pay more than the rock-bottom fare by opting for the safety of a better-known travel agent. Established firms like Council Travel or STA Travel, which have offices internationally, or Travel CUTS in Canada, offer competitive prices to most destinations.

Once you have your ticket, write down its number, together with the flight number and other details, and keep the information somewhere separate. If the ticket is lost or stolen, this will help you get a replacement.

Visit USA Passes Most US carriers offer special deals for non-US citizens who book abroad. These passes are usually in the form of coupons – you use one for each leg of your flight. Ask a travel agent about these offers.

A typical Visit USA scheme is the one offered by Continental Airlines, which can be used with an international airline ticket from anywhere outside the USA except Canada and Mexico. You must have your trip planned in advance and complete your travels within 60 days of the first domestic flight in the USA or 81 days after arrival in the USA, whichever comes first. If you decide to change destinations once you're in the USA, you'll be penalized at least $50. High-season prices are $379 for three coupons (minimum purchase; one coupon equals one flight) and $769 for eight (maximum purchase). The pass includes two free transits. American Airlines offers a similar deal.

Round-the-World Tickets Round-the-World (RTW) tickets that include travel within the US are popular and can be bargains. Prices start at about UK£900, A$1800 or US$1300.

Official RTW tickets are usually put together by a combination of two airlines, and permit you to fly anywhere you want on their route systems as long as you do not

backtrack. Other restrictions are that you must usually book the first sector in advance and be liable to normal cancellation penalties. There may be restrictions on the number of stops permitted and tickets are usually valid up to a year. You can also see if your travel agent can create a de facto RTW pass using a combination of discounted tickets.

Although most airlines restrict the number of sectors that can be flown within the USA and Canada to four, and some airlines black out a few popular routes (like Honolulu to Tokyo), stopovers are otherwise generally unlimited. In most cases a 14-day advance purchase is required. After the ticket is purchased, dates can be changed without penalty and tickets can be rewritten to add or delete stops for $50 each.

Many other airlines also offer RTW tickets, including Qantas, British Airways and TWA. TWA's lowest priced RTW, linking up with Korean Air, costs US$2087 and allows stops in Honolulu, Seoul, Tel Aviv, Amsterdam and Paris or London. (This one is not available in Australia.)

Travelers with Special Needs

If you have a special need – a broken leg, dietary restrictions, dependence on a wheelchair, responsibility for a baby, fear of flying – let the airline know as soon as possible so that it can make arrangements accordingly. Remind them when you reconfirm your booking (at least 72 hours before departure) and again when you check in at the airport. It may also be worth phoning several airlines before you make your booking to find out how they handle your particular needs.

Airports and airlines can be surprisingly accommodating to passengers in wheelchairs, but they do need advance warning. Most international airports provide escorts from the check-in desk to the airplane if necessary, and there should be ramps, lifts, accessible toilets and reachable phones. Aircraft toilets, on the other hand, are likely to present a problem; travelers should discuss this with the airline at an early stage and, if necessary, with their doctor.

TONY WHEELER

This service is not available.

Guide dogs for the blind often have to travel in a specially pressurized baggage compartment with other animals, away from their owners, though smaller guide dogs may be admitted to the cabin. Guide dogs are not subject to quarantine as long as they have proof of being vaccinated against rabies.

Deaf travelers can ask for airport and in-flight announcements to be written down for them.

Children under two travel for 10% of the standard fare (or free, on some airlines), as long as they don't occupy a seat. (They don't get a baggage allowance either.) 'Skycots' should be provided by the airline if requested in advance; these take a child weighing up to about 22 lbs. Children between two and 12 usually occupy a seat for half to two-thirds of the full fare, and do get a baggage allowance. Strollers can often be taken on as hand luggage.

Baggage
On most domestic and international flights you're limited to two checked bags, or three if you don't have carry-on luggage. There could be a charge if you bring more or if the size of the bags exceeds the airline's limits. It's best to check with the individual airline if you're worried about this. On some international flights the luggage allowance is based on weight, not numbers; again, check with the airline.

If your luggage is delayed upon arrival (which is rare), some airlines give a cash advance to purchase necessities. If sporting equipment is misplaced, the airline may pay for rentals. Should the luggage be lost, it's important to submit a claim. The airline doesn't have to pay the full amount of the claim, but can estimate the value of your lost items. It may take them anywhere from six weeks to three months to process the claim and pay you.

Illegal Items Items that are illegal to take on a plane, either checked in with your baggage or as hand luggage, include aerosols of polishes, waxes, etc; tear gas and pepper spray; camp stoves with fuel; and divers' tanks that are full. Matches shouldn't be checked in with your baggage.

Getting Bumped

Airlines chronically overbook and bet that a certain percentage of passengers won't show up. When this planning fails and flights are full, some passengers get 'bumped' off a flight. By volunteering to be a bumpee, you can take advantage of the system.

When you check in at the airline counter ask if they'll need volunteers to be bumped and what the compensation will be. Depending on the desirability of the flight, this can range from a $200 voucher toward your next flight to a pass allowing you a free roundtrip economy ticket within the US. (Hold out for the latter if you are asked to get off the flight.)

If you have to spend the night, the airline should foot the hotel bill, which will invariably be at an airport motel. Remember that if you are late for boarding, you could get bumped and receive none of the benefits.

Arriving in the USA

Aboard the airplane, on the international leg of the flight, passengers are given standard immigration and customs forms to fill out. The cabin crew will help you if you have any questions. After the plane lands, you first go through immigration. There are two lines: one for US citizens and residents, the other for nonresidents. Immigration formalities are usually straightforward if you have the necessary documents (passport and visa). Occasionally, you may be asked to show your ticket out of the US, but this doesn't happen often.

You then collect your baggage and pass through customs. If you have nothing to declare, you'll probably clear customs quickly and without a luggage search, but you can't rely on it. (See also Customs in

---

Edible Airline Food

Many travelers complain about the 'snacks' and meals served on US domestic airlines. But you can increase your chances of getting something resembling real food if you request a 'low fat' meal when booking your flight. Instead of being handed a prepackaged meal, you'll probably receive a sandwich prepared specifically before departure with real meat (usually turkey), decent bread and a salad that doesn't resemble something flash frozen on Mars. Of course, you'll most likely forfeit any chance of getting dessert! ■

---

the Facts for the Visitor chapter.) Once through customs, you're officially in the country.

Leaving the USA

You should check in for international flights two hours early. During check-in procedures, you'll be asked questions about whether you packed your own bags, whether anyone else has had access to them since you packed them and whether you've received any parcels to carry. These questions are security measures, which tightened after the crash of TWA flight 800 off the Long Island coast in 1996.

Within the USA

The *New York Times*, *Los Angeles Times*, *Chicago Tribune*, *San Francisco Examiner* and other major newspapers all produce weekly travel sections with numerous travel agents' ads. Council Travel (☎ (800) 226-8624) and STA Travel (☎ (800) 777-0112) have offices in major cities nationwide.

The magazine *Travel Unlimited*, PO Box 1058, Allston, MA 02134, publishes details of the cheapest air fares and courier possibilities.

Domestic airfares vary tremendously depending on the season you travel, the day of the week you fly, the length of your stay, how far in advance you pay and the flexibility of the ticket (in allowing for flight changes and refunds). There's also much competition and at any given time any one of the airlines could have the cheapest fare.

Canada

Travel CUTS has offices in all major cities. The *Toronto Globe & Mail* and *Vancouver Sun* carry travel agents' ads; the magazine *Great Expeditions*, PO Box 8000-411, Abbotsford, BC V2S 6H1, is also useful. Roundtrip fares to/from Toronto with US Airways and Delta Airlines start from around C$320 (US$237), to/from Montreal for around C$300 (US$215), though there are good deals from Montreal for under US$200 on offer periodically.

UK & Ireland

Check the ads in magazines like *Time Out* and *City Limits*, plus the Sunday papers and *Exchange & Mart*. Also check the free magazines widely available in London – start by looking outside the main railway stations.

Most British travel agents are registered with the Association of British Travel Agents (ABTA). If you've paid for your flight at an ABTA-registered agent who then goes out of business, ABTA will guarantee a refund or an alternative. Unregistered bucket shops are riskier but sometimes cheaper.

London is arguably the world's headquarters for bucket shops, which frequently place ads and can usually beat published airline fares. Two good, reliable agents for cheap tickets in the UK are Trailfinders (☎ (0171) 937-5400), 194 Kensington High St, London W8 7RG, and STA Travel (☎ (0171) 937-9971), 86 Old Brompton Rd, London SW7 3LQ. Trailfinders produces a lavishly illustrated brochure including airfare details.

Virgin Atlantic has a standard, roundtrip, weekday, high-season fare from London to New York City for £500 (US$600), but cheaper advance-purchase tickets are available. Aer Lingus has direct flights from Shannon and Dublin to New York City, but because competition on flights from London is fiercer, it's generally cheaper to fly to London first. Virgin Atlantic via

London is often the cheapest option, especially in the high season.

The Globetrotters Club, BCM Roving, London WC1N 3XX, publishes a newsletter called *Globe* that covers obscure destinations and can help you find traveling companions.

Continental Europe

Though London is the travel-discount capital of Europe, several other cities offer a range of good deals, especially Amsterdam and Athens. Many travel agents in Europe have ties with STA Travel, where cheap tickets can be bought and STA Travel tickets can be altered free of charge (first change only).

In the Netherlands, NBBS Reizen is a popular nationwide travel agency; it has offices in Amsterdam at Roken 38 (☎ 624 0989) and Leidestraat 53 (☎ 638 1736). In Paris, Council Travel (☎ 01 44 55 55 65) has its main office at 22 rue des Pyramides (1er). In Athens try International Student & Youth Travel Service (☎ (01) 323-3767), Nikis 11.

On Virgin Atlantic flights from Paris to New York, a standard, roundtrip, weekday, high-season fare usually costs FF4400 (US$800), but cheaper advance-purchase fares are available.

Australia & New Zealand

In Australia and New Zealand, STA Travel and Flight Centres International are major dealers in cheap airfares; check the travel agents' ads in the yellow pages and call around. The STA toll free number is ☎ (800) 637-444. Qantas flies to Los Angeles from Sydney, Melbourne (via Sydney or Auckland) and Cairns (weekly) with onward connections to New York City on a domestic US carrier. United Airlines flies to San Francisco and Los Angeles from Sydney.

The cheapest tickets have a 21-day advance-purchase requirement, a minimum stay of seven days and a maximum stay of 30 days. Qantas flies from Melbourne or Sydney to New York for a top price of A$2582 (US$2013) in the high season, but the usual standard, advance purchase fare runs A$1800 (US$1400). Flying with Air New Zealand can sometimes run cheaper, and both Qantas and Air New Zealand offer tickets with longer stays or stopovers, but you pay more. Full-time students can save A$80 (US$62) to A$140 (US$109) on roundtrip fares to the USA with proper ID.

Roundtrip flights from Auckland to Los Angeles on Qantas cost NZ$1720 (US$1170) in the low season.

Asia

Hong Kong is the discount plane ticket capital of the region, but its bucket shops can be unreliable. Ask the advice of other travelers before buying a ticket. STA Travel has branches in Hong Kong, Tokyo, Singapore, Bangkok and Kuala Lumpur. Many flights to the USA go via Honolulu. Others, to the East Coast, make a stopover in Anchorage, Alaska.

Japan United Airlines has three flights a day to Honolulu from Tokyo with connections to West Coast cities like Los Angeles, San Francisco and Seattle. Northwest Airlines and Japan Air Lines also have daily flights to the West Coast from Tokyo; Japan Air Lines also flies to Honolulu from Osaka, Nagoya, Fukuoka and Sapporo, and offers the only non-stop flight from Tokyo to New York City.

Southeast Asia Numerous airlines fly to the USA from Southeast Asia; bucket shops in places like Bangkok and Singapore should be able to come up with the best deals. Tickets to the US West Coast often allow a free stopover in Honolulu.

Northwest Airlines flies to Honolulu from Hong Kong, Bangkok, Manila, Seoul and Singapore, with connections to the West Coast. Korean Air and Philippine Airlines also have flights from a number of Southeast Asian cities to Honolulu, with onward connections.

Mexico & South America

Most flights from Mexico and Central and South America go via Miami, Houston or

Los Angeles and some fly direct to New York City. Most countries' international flag carriers, like Aerolíneas Argentinas and LANChile Airlines, as well as US airlines like United and American, serve these destinations. Continental has flights from about 20 cities in Mexico, Central and South America, including Lima, San José, Guatemala City, Cancún and Mérida, most of which arrive at Dallas-Fort Worth airport, with connections to the rest of the US.

BUS

All suburban and long-haul buses leave and depart from the Port Authority Bus Terminal (☎ (212) 564-8484), at 41st St and Eighth Ave. Greyhound (☎ (212) 971-6300, (800) 231-2222) links New York with major cities across the country. Peter Pan Trailways (☎ (800) 343-9999) runs buses to the nearest major cities, including a daily express to Boston for $24.95 one way and $47.95 roundtrip.

Short Line (☎ (212) 736-4700) has numerous departures to towns in northern New Jersey and upstate New York. New Jersey Transit buses (☎ (201) 762-5100) serve the entire Garden State, with direct service to Atlantic City for $15 one way.

Port Authority has been modernized in recent years and is much improved. Though it's not as rough as its reputation, expect to be met by beggars asking for handouts or offering to carry bags for tips.

Short-haul buses run by companies catering to commuters (Short Line, New Jersey Transit) also leave for New Jersey from the terminal near the George Washington Bridge (☎ (212) 568-5323; subway: 175th St).

Bus Passes

Greyhound's Ameripass is potentially useful if you plan on doing a lot of bus traveling out of New York. It costs $179 for seven days of unlimited travel, $289 for 15 days and $399 for 30 days (these rates apply in any season). Children under 11 travel for half price. You can get on and off at any Greyhound terminal. There is an International Ameripass that costs a bit less that international travelers can purchase at overseas travel agencies or from the Greyhound International Office (☎ (212) 971-0492, fax (212) 967-2239) at the subway level of the Port Authority Bus Terminal. It's open Monday to Thursday from 8:30 am to 4:30 pm, Friday to 4 pm.

TRAIN

Pennsylvania Station, on 33rd St between Seventh and Eighth Aves, is the departure point for all Amtrak trains (☎ (212) 582-6875, (800) 872-7245), including the frequent daily *Metroliner* service to Princeton ($9 one way), Philadelphia ($39 one way) and Washington, DC ($66 one way).

The Long Island Rail Road (LIRR; ☎ (718) 217-5477) serves several hundred thousand commuters each day from a newly renovated platform area to points in Brooklyn, Queens and the suburbs of Long Island, including the resort areas. Fares vary by distance and run from $5 to $15 one way.

New Jersey Transit (☎ (201) 763-5100) also operates trains from Penn Station to the suburbs and the Jersey Shore, with the top ticket price being $12 one way. Of all the train services, only New Jersey Transit regularly offers substantial roundtrip discounts (sample fare: $9 one way, $14 roundtrip).

One commuter company departs from Grand Central Station, at Park Ave and 42nd St: the Metro North Railroad (☎ (212) 532-4900), which serves the northern New York City suburbs and Connecticut. Fares are generally $15 and under, depending on distance.

CAR & MOTORCYCLE

It's a nightmare to have a car in New York, but getting there is easy. I-95, which runs from Maine to Florida, cuts east-west through the city as the Cross Bronx Expressway. It continues south, after crossing into New Jersey as the George Washington Bridge, and north as the Connecticut Turnpike.

The Long Island Expressway can be reached by taking the Queens Midtown Tunnel out of Manhattan (a stretch of road often choked by traffic). Alternately, you can get out of town by taking the Grand Central Parkway (right off the Triborough Bridge) which cuts through Queens on its way to Long Island. Northern Blvd in Queens become Rt 25A, which runs the northern length of Long Island.

Taking the Lincoln or Holland tunnels out of town connects you with the New Jersey Turnpike, which runs roughly diagonally across the state to Philadelphia as I-95. The Turnpike also connects to the Garden State Parkway (which includes Jersey Shore points and Atlantic City). Leaving Manhattan by the Lincoln Tunnel also connects you (via Rt 3) to the westbound I-80, which cuts through the middle of Pennsylvania. I-78, which goes to Harrisburg, Pennsylvania, can be reached by taking the Holland Tunnel.

Via I-95, Boston is 194 miles to the north, Philadelphia 104 miles to the south and Washington, DC, 235 miles south.

Highway speed limits in Connecticut and upstate New York are 65 mph; in New Jersey they remain 55 mph.

HITCHING

Hitching has a bad reputation throughout the US and it is extremely rare to see anyone trying to thumb a ride, even at spots where it might be easy to do so (the entrance to the Lincoln Tunnel, for example). This is due, in part, to the fact that most non-urban dwellers have cars and see hitchers as part of a wandering criminal element.

Generally, most Americans regard hitchhikers as probable homicidal maniacs or potential victims of same. Given that attitude, women attempting to hitch rides alone are highly likely to attract people who regard them as either crazy or fair game. It is certainly not recommended.

BOAT

It's highly unusual for anyone to yacht their way into town, but there is an exclusive boat slip at the World Trade Center and a long term tie-up available at the W 79th St

Boat Basin. Manhattan, on the whole, does not welcome temporary tie-up of recreational boats.

Visiting boaters should contact City Island Yacht (☎ (718) 885-0101), which is a full-service marina on City Island off the mainland of the Bronx. City Island is also the site of Kretzer Boat Works Marina (☎ (718) 885-2600).

TRAVEL AGENCIES

Council Travel offers bookings at three locations: 148 W 4th St (☎ (212) 254-2525), 895 Amsterdam Ave (☎ (212) 666-4177), and 205 E 42nd St (☎ (212) 661-1450). STA Travel (☎ (212) 627-3111) is at 10 Downing St on Sixth Ave. The main American Express travel office (☎ (212) 421-8240), at 374 Park Ave, offers package deals.

Bucket Shops

Consolidators, or 'bucket shops,' are travel agencies that sell last-minute flights on scheduled carriers. They are located in Midtown office buildings and advertise weekly in the *Village Voice* and the Sunday travel section of the *New York Times*. Call around to get the best price, since some agencies have consolidator deals with only a handful of specific airlines. TFI Tours (☎ (212) 736-1140), 34 W 32nd St, is one agency that accepts credit cards.

Courier Flights

Given its importance as a cargo port, New York is the best place in the US to arrange courier flights around the globe.

Now Voyager (☎ (212) 431-1616) books courier flights and last-minute domestic specials. It's best to call their busy office after business hours to hear a comprehensive voice menu of locations and conditions.

Several other agencies maintain offices in midtown or at JFK airport. For courier flights to/from Asia, try Discount Travel International (☎ (212) 362-3636) and East-West Express (☎ (718) 656-6246); for courier flights to Central America, try Air Facility (☎ (718) 712-1769); for Europe try Virgin Express (☎ (718) 244-7244) or Air Tech (☎ (212) 219-7000).

ORGANIZED TOURS

Larry Lustig's East Coast Explorer (☎ (718) 694-9667, (800) 610-2680), is a low-cost tour and travel service based in Queens. Once a week, passenger vans carrying up to 14 people leave for Boston ($35 one way) or Washington, DC ($35 one way), stopping at places of interest en route to and from New York City. The vans pick up and drop off at hostels in town and are very popular with budget travelers.

The well-known West Coast firm Green Tortoise (☎ (415) 956-7500, (800) 867-8647), 494 Broadway, San Francisco, CA 94133, offers alternative bus transportation to New York with stops at picturesque places along the way. The 10-day trips cross the country on southern or northern routes, depending on the seasonal weather, and cost $329 for passage with $81 additional charge for food. (Call ahead for information on current routes.) It isn't exactly luxury travel, but it's fun and a cheap way to see the country.

Getting Around

It's hard to exaggerate the problem of grid-lock in Manhattan's streets. The entire center of the island's grid system is packed with cars during the day, and major avenues – primarily Lexington and Broad-way – get tied up by double-parked trucks making deliveries to stores. The subway is the fastest way to get between uptown and downtown points, and contrary to popular belief, taking it is statistically safer than walking the streets in broad daylight.

Like most New Yorkers, you should use the city buses exclusively to get to points located along the same avenue or cross-town, when it's easy to calculate the amount of travel time by looking at the traffic.

The best overall plan is to use the subway all day until 10 pm, then use taxis at night. It's very important to note that taxis are obligated to take you anywhere you want to go within the five boroughs, as well as to Newark airport. During rush hours, taxi drivers often brazenly refuse fares from airport-bound customers (particularly during bad weather) because they can pick up easier fares in town. *Do not* ask permission to get into the cab if you're going to the airports, and do not negotiate a higher price for the job above the metered fare. If the cabbie refuses your business, threaten to report his/her license number to the Taxi and Limousine Commission. Even if this is an empty threat, the cab driver should take it seriously enough to relent. See the entry on taxis later in this chapter.

TO/FROM THE AIRPORTS

When departing for the airports in the middle of the day, allow *at least* 90 minutes travel time. The Port Authority of New York and New Jersey's Air Ride line (☎ (800) 247-7433) offers comprehensive information on ground transportation to/ from all three airports.

No matter what airport you fly into, there are several advantages to ordering a taxi by phone. You will be met by a car that is newer and larger than the yellow cabs hailed from the street, and you do not have to tip the driver. You can also order a pickup a day in advance and pay by credit card. If you ask for a 'price check' while ordering the taxi, the dispatcher can tell you the exact cost of the journey, which should run between $35 and $50, depending on your departure point and the airport destination. Some of the better services include:

Big Apple	☎ (718) 232-1015
Carmel (Manhattan only)	☎ (212) 666-6666
Citywide	☎ (718) 405-9393
Twin	☎ (718) 898-8888

JFK Airport

Carey Transportation buses (☎ (718) 632-0500) run to/from JFK at least every 30 minutes from 5 am to 1 am daily. Buses leave from 125 Park Ave, just a block south of Grand Central Terminal, and from the Port Authority Airport Bus Center near the 42nd St and Eighth Ave entrance, from 7:15 am to 11:15 pm each day. One-way fare to JFK is $13, with half-price tickets available for students. The journey takes at least one hour.

You can also take the subway to the Howard Beach-JFK station on the subway's A train, which takes at least an hour, and then switch to a free yellow and blue bus at the long-term parking lot to the terminals, which takes another 15 minutes. (You have to haul your luggage up and over several flights of stairs at the Howard Beach terminal.)

Taxi fare from the airport is about $45. (In 1996, New York City introduced a policy mandating that taxis must offer a flat rate of $30 from JFK to any location in Manhattan. If the fare is still available when you arrive, there will be signs indi-cating the price at the JFK taxi stands.)

Long-term parking at JFK costs $6 a day; short-term parking closer to the termi-nals costs $4 for four hours.

La Guardia Airport

Carey Transportation buses leave from Port Authority Airport Bus Center from 7:15 am to 12:45 am daily and from 125 Park Ave a block south of Grand Central Terminal from 5 am to 1 am daily. Buses depart at least every 30 minutes and cost $10 one way; the trip takes 45 minutes to an hour. The Delta Water Shuttle (☎ (800) 221-1212) leaves frequently for La Guardia with pickups at Pier 11 (at South and Wall Sts) and E 34th St on the East River. Fare is $20 one way, $30 roundtrip.

La Guardia is also accessible via public transportation by taking the subway to the Roosevelt Ave-Jackson Heights and 74th St-Broadway stops in Queens (two linked stations served by five lines). You then take the Q33 bus to the La Guardia main terminals or the Q47 bus to the Delta Shuttle's Marine Air Terminal. Since this journey takes well over an hour and costs two tokens ($3), it is recommended only for those who absolutely can't afford the additional $7 for the direct Carey bus. If you're in upper Manhattan, you can go directly to La Guardia by catching the M60 bus anywhere along 125th St for the price of a token or $1.50 in change (or use a Metrocard).

Taxis to La Guardia from Midtown cost about $35.

Newark Airport

Olympia Trails (☎ (212) 964-6233) travels to Newark from stops near Grand Central Terminal at Park Ave and 41st St from 5 am to 11 pm daily. Another bus departs to Newark from Lower Manhattan at One World Trade Center on West St from 6 am to 8 pm Monday to Friday and 7 am to 8 pm Saturday and Sunday. Both buses cost $7.

The Subway System

The city's subway system began in 1904 as a nine-mile, privately operated line along Broadway between City Hall and W 145th St. Over the next 30 years, this Interborough Rapid Transit (IRT) line expanded service to the Bronx, Queens and Brooklyn, including several elevated lines called 'els.' Competition also came from the rival Brooklyn-Manhattan Transit company (BMT), and the city-owned Independent Line (IND) on Eighth Ave. The private companies basically collapsed during the Depression, and the city wound up owning all three lines – designed to *compete* with rather than augment each other – by 1940. To this day, many New Yorkers refer to the West Side 1, 2, 3, and 9 trains as the IRT line, and a few even use the designations BMT and IND for the rest of the system.

New York's subway system is older than those found in many European cities, but even when it was relatively new the system was considered 'drab and noisy' by the editors of the *WPA Guide to New York*, published in 1939. The book went on to describe a subway where 'intent and humorless hordes cover uptown and downtown platforms, choke narrow stairways, swamp change-booths, wrestle with closing train doors . . . [and] a few of the homeless use the subway as a flophouse.' But, then, as now, 'the romance of the subways of New York may be found in their trajectories, and in the intricacy of their construction and operation.'

The problems and the physical plan of the subways are basically the same as they were when those words were written. Entryways are unprotected from the weather and stairs tend to be icy, snowy or just plain wet, depending on the season. Stations are close to the surface of the street, and you can hear the noise and sense the smells of the avenue above. And platforms, supported by ugly steel beams, are too narrow, leading rush hour crowds to back up the stairs at over-capacity stations like Rockefeller Center.

One reason there have been few major improvements was the short-sighted policy of artificially holding down the subway fare. For decades, politicians promised to 'keep the nickel fare' and admission to the subway was a heavily subsidized 15¢ into the 1960s.

New Jersey Transit (☎ (201) 762-5100) runs a No 300 bus from Port Authority Airport Bus Center to Newark airport 24 hours a day; it costs $7 one way and $12 roundtrip.

A taxi to Newark will cost about $45, plus tolls for the driver there and back that will add $10 to the total.

SUBWAY

As American humorist Calvin Trillin has noted, 'New Yorkers hate the idea of out of towners being able to find their way around the city,' speculating that is why the New York City Subway map is 'similar in design to spaghetti primavera.' It's noisy and confusing, and during summer the stations can feel like an inner circle of hell. But with a little attention to detail, you can figure out the 656-mile New York City subway system, used by 3.6 million people daily.

(It was as low as 60¢ in 1980.) Meanwhile, the system was falling apart, and the building of a needed underground line to replace the razed Second Ave 'el' was abandoned for lack of funds even though excavation had begun for the project. By the '80s, a consensus grew that the subways needed a major overhaul, but this multi-billion dollar program went largely to stop the great decline in equipment and reliability rather than actually bring the system into the late 20th century.

The subway system benefited greatly from a huge infusion of federal, state and local funding during the '80s, and now trains are generally quieter, more reliable and free of graffiti. Almost every token booth offers bus and subway maps, and even pamphlets on such ludicrous subjects as 'Riding Escalators Safely.' But nothing as ambitious as actually building a new line seems likely to happen in the near term, though subway officials still maintain the hole in the ground under Second Ave in the hope that a new line will eventually be built.

In 1995, the system began introducing magnetic strip Metrocards in certain stations, widely seen as a prelude to imposing a staged fare system sometime after 2000. You can buy the reusable plastic Metrocard at all stations in increments of the $1.50 subway fare.

After a year of solid resistance to the cards – New Yorkers feel a great affinity to their subway tokens, akin to what Americans in general feel about their useless one cent coin – the transit authority introduced free Metrocard transfers between subways and city buses as a way of encouraging their use among people who must pay two fares to get to work. At press time, the agency is considering promotions like free rides on weekends to bribe passengers into using the cards, which are cheaper to maintain.

Unfortunately, the December 1995 25¢ boost in the subway fare – the biggest ever – was accompanied by huge reductions in the budgets for system maintenance and improvement. Some of the stations most in need of repair – Times Square, 59th St and 72nd St-Broadway – remain in atrocious states with confusing, narrow and badly marked passageways, and are likely to remain that way in the near term. ■

The subway is the fastest and most reliable way to get around town, especially for trips totaling more than 20 blocks in north-south directions during the day. Taking a bus or a taxi guarantees that you'll hit traffic choke points at places like Times Square and wind up arriving at your destination only after a long and frustrating ride.

Most major Manhattan attractions – especially those on the West Side and downtown – are easily accessible by several subway lines. Madison Square Garden, for example, is within four blocks walking distance of three subway stations on 34th St served by a total of 12 different lines.

Subway tokens, which allow you to ride the system for any distance, cost $1.50 and are available at booths near the turnstiles. The system also sells Metrocards, which are 'swiped' through the turnstile and are convenient for travelers. It's a very good idea to buy enough tokens for a day or week's travel in one shot – the tokens can be used on the blue-and-white city buses (which do not accept dollar bills or make change), and rush-hour lines at token booths can be wicked. Subway clerks sometimes appear irascible, since they barely slide the tokens through the booth slot and try to give you back as many singles as possible in change to avoid a big count-up of dollar bills at the end of their shift. But they are the single best source for information on how to get around.

The common mistake most visitors make (other than getting turned around and taking a train in the opposite direction) is to board an express train only to see it blow by the local stop they desired. Pay particular attention to the subway map – local stops are shown with solid lines, and express stops are circles.

As for safety, standing in the middle of the platform will bring you to the conductor's car. The conductor can direct you through the system when he/she is not closing the doors of the train. Of course, it's not a good idea to leave a fat wallet bulging in your back pocket on a crowded subway, and all day packs should be secured with a safety pin.

The subway runs 24 hours. For information call ☎ (718) 330-1234.

PATH

New Jersey PATH (Port Authority Trans-Hudson) trains (☎ (800) 234-7284) are part of a separate-fare system that runs down Sixth Ave with stops at 34th, 23rd, 14th, 9th and Christopher Sts to Jersey City and Newark. A second line runs from the World Trade Center to northern New Jersey. These reliable trains (called the 'Hudson Tubes' when they first opened) run every 15 minutes and fare is $1 (machines take dollar bills).

BUS

City buses operate 24 hours a day, generally along avenues in a south or north direction, and cross-town along the major thoroughfares (including 34th, 42nd and 57th Sts). Buses that begin and end in a certain borough are prefixed accordingly: ie, M5 for Manhattan, Q32 for Queens, B51 for Brooklyn, and Bx13 for Bronx.

You need exact change of $1.50 or a token to board the bus, and if you plan on switching to a connecting route, you must ask for a transfer slip upon boarding. (Metrocards are also accepted on buses.) Drivers will be happy to tell you if their bus stops near a specific site, but don't engage them in a conversation about directions unless you want to endure poisonous stares from the old-timers who prefer using the bus to the subway.

Bus maps for each borough are available at subway and train stations, and well-marked bus stops have 'Guide-a-Ride' maps showing the stops for each bus and nearby landmarks. Remember that some 'Limited Stop' buses along major routes pull over only every 10 blocks or so at major cross streets. 'Express' buses are generally for outer borough commuters and cost $4 and should not be used for short trips.

As a safety precaution, you can request to be let off at any location along a bus route – even if it is not a designated bus stop – from 10 pm to 5 am.

Of course, you will discover the same woes found in every other major city during bad weather: after a 25-minute wait for a bus, three will come along in a row.

Call ☎ (718) 927-7499 for all bus information.

TAXI

Is there a category of worker more maligned than the New York City cab driver? No, not all of them are thieves, incompetent or in desperate need of a shower. The most common tension between driver and passenger comes from arguments about the fastest route from one place to another. Most cabbies *will* attempt to ride down Broadway in bad traffic, or cross town on crowded 59th St rather than use a faster Central Park 'transverse' – they're making money on the metered trip.

Taxis cost $2 for the initial charge, with 30¢ for every additional quarter mile and 20¢ a minute while stuck in traffic. There's an additional 50¢ surcharge for rides after 8 pm. Tampered meters turn over every 20 seconds or so while the cab is stopped in traffic or at a light, and if you notice it happening, don't hesitate to ask if it is 'running too fast.' If the driver apologizes a bit too energetically you've probably busted him and can negotiate a lower fare than the meter. Tips are expected to run 10% to 15% with a minimum of 50¢. If you feel ripped off, ask for a receipt and note the driver's license number. The city's Taxi and Limousine Commission (☎ (212) 302-8294) is particularly aggressive and the threat of a complaint puts the fear of god into obnoxious cabbies.

For hauls that will last 50 blocks or more, it's a good idea to instruct the driver to take a road well away from Midtown traffic. Suggest the West Side Hwy or Eleventh Ave if you hail a taxi west of Broadway; on the East Side, the best choice may be Second Ave (heading downtown) or First Ave (uptown), since you can hit a string of green lights in either direction.

One cab cliché does hold: only about one in five cab drivers actually thanks you for the tip, no matter how generous.

CAR

In New York, the cost, the traffic, and the high incidence of petty thievery more than offset any convenience having a car may offer. The city adds to the problem with Byzantine street cleaning rules that require you to move your car several times a week if you park on the street. Meanwhile parking garages in Midtown are usually operated by the Kinney Corporation, which has a hammer lock on the industry and garaging a car will cost at least $30 during daylight hours. Cheaper lots can be found in Manhattan along West St in Chelsea, but even those $10 to $15 daily deals aren't a bargain after the city's phenomenal 18.25% parking tax is added. Using a hotel lot is no bargain either – Midtown hotels can charge $40 a day, even for their customers.

Rentals

Hopefully, there is a special section of hell reserved for the people who set car rental rates in New York. Though rental agencies advertise bargain rates for weekend or week-long rentals, these deals are almost *always* blacked out in New York or can only be obtained in conjunction with an airline ticket.

If you want to rent for a few days, book through your travel agent before leaving home. A spot rental will cost at least $70 for a mid-sized car, though you'll probably have to spend $95 or more a day. And that's before extra charges like the 13.25% tax.

The rental agencies will also try to sell you options on personal insurance coverage (about $15 a day), which you don't need if you have medical coverage, as well as a 'Collision Damage Waiver,' (also called Liability Damage Waiver) which for another $15 covers the full value of the vehicle in case of an accident, except those caused by acts of nature or fire. (Some credit cards, such as MasterCard Gold and American Express, cover collision insurance if you rent for 15 days or less and charge the full cost of rental to your card.)

Agencies also add a $5 daily fee for each additional driver in the car. In all, you're talking about $100 a day – plus the option to prepay for a tank of gas to avoid filling up before a return, which costs $20 but is worth it due to the high price of gasoline in the city (about $1.60 a gallon).

With costs running well over $300 for a three day weekend rental, you may be better off renting a car on a weekly basis to save money in the long run. It used to be possible to play agencies against each other, or to rent cars at a cheaper rate at the airport, but the companies have gotten wise to just about any money-saving move and have blocked them by bureaucratic rules, or the statement on coupons and airline tickets that 'agreements can be revised or discontinued without prior notice.' That about covers any possibility that you'll beat them at this game.

If you don't find the above discouraging … then you must be on an expense account.

To rent a car you must have a valid driver's license and present a major credit card. In March of 1997, the New York state supreme court ruled that the nationwide policy of restricting rentals to those at least 25 years of age was discriminatory. Though the major companies now must offer cars to teens, they are allowed to charge a higher rate and will no doubt make it prohibitively expensive for college age consumers to take advantage of their new rights.

Call the agencies' toll free numbers to inquire about the most convenient office for you in town:

Avis	☎ (800) 331-1212
Budget	☎ (800) 527-0700
Dollar	☎ (800) 800-4000
Hertz	☎ (800) 654-3131
Thrifty (in Brooklyn)	☎ (800) 367-2277

BOAT

In the late 19th century, hundreds of ferries operated on New York's rivers, but disappeared with the opening of several East Side bridges. Now New Yorkers are rediscovering the convenience of ferries. New York Waterway (☎ (800) 533-3779) operates several routes including boats up the Hudson River Valley and from Midtown to Yankee Stadium in the Bronx. Its main ferry route is between Hoboken's Erie Lackawanna Train Terminal and the World Financial Center in Lower Manhattan. Ferries leave every 20 minutes at peak times. The trip takes eight minutes and costs $2 each way.

In the summer of 1997, the New York Water Taxi company (☎ (212) 681-8111) began running ferries from various points along the Hudson and East Rivers, offering a combination deal with Gray Line Bus Tours with a $22 two-day unlimited-stop pass for tourists. Call for up-to-date information.

BICYCLE

There are some US towns where you can leave your bike unattended and even unlocked – but New York is not one of them. The hassles of bike ownership may have contributed to the move toward in-line skaters, since thieves can pick bike locks with the greatest of ease – an expensive new bike can vaporize within minutes of being left on the street. The only solution is to use a banged-up bike that no one would really want, and lock it up anyway.

See Activities in Things to See & Do for information on recreational bicycling in New York.

ORGANIZED TOURS
Bus Tours

In general, bus tours of the city cannot be recommended because, at $15 to $50, they are too expensive and the buses are certainly not immune to getting caught in traffic jams – in fact they cause quite a few on their own. Residents in Greenwich Village hate the tour buses, which choke the narrow streets, and people in Harlem don't much like them either, since they are filled with white European tourists who gawk from the second deck of the bus at a neighborhood they're too terrified to explore on their own.

The premier tourist bus service is Gray Line (☎ (212) 397-2620), which offers more than 29 different tours of the city from the Port Authority Bus Terminal at Eighth Ave and 42nd St, including a hop-on, hop-off loop of Manhattan. The cheapest tours begin at $15/7.50 for adults/children and go as high as $50/37.50. There are big downsides to these tours: often you get a non-native guide who knows far less about the city than some of the passengers. (They're usually hired because of their ability to speak more than one language.)

New York Apple Tours (☎ (800) 876-9868) offers tours on rumbling old London double decker buses that sometimes break down in mid-tour. Buses make a loop of Manhattan from the Plaza Hotel and W 50th St and Seventh Ave; it costs $25/16 for two days unlimited use of the buses.

Boat Tours

More than one million people a year take the three-hour, 35-mile Circle Line cruise around Manhattan (☎ (212) 563-3200), which leaves from Pier 83, at 42nd St on the Hudson River, from March to December. This is the tour to take, provided the weather is good and you can enjoy the breezes on the outside deck. The quality of the narration depends on the enthusiasm of the guide; be sure to sit well away from the narrator to avoid the inevitable 'where are you from?' banter. Tickets for adults/seniors/children cost $18/16/9.

Circle Line also runs a 2½-hour Tuesday night Jazz Cruise from Pier 83 and a Thursday night Country Music Cruise during the summer. Tickets are $20; call ☎ (212) 563-3200 for reservations.

World Yacht (☎ (212) 563-3347) has well-regarded culinary cruises around Manhattan year round that leave from Pier 81 at W 41st St. Reservations and proper dress are required, and tickets for adults/children range from $29/16 for a two-hour lunch to $75 for a three-hour dinner.

Helicopter Tours

Gray Lines has three different helicopter tours of Manhattan that depart on the half

KIM GRANT

The World Trade Center has a way of appearing in photos of other monuments, like the Washington Square Arch.

hour from the heliport (☎ (212) 397-2600) at E 34th St and First Ave. Tours last up to four hours and cost $61/52.50 to $91/82.50 for adults/children depending on the duration. Island Helicopter Sightseeing (☎ (212) 683-4575) has departures from the same site from 9 am to 9 pm daily; tickets range from $44 to $129, and they slap on a $5 additional charge for tickets purchased on the day of departure.

Things to See & Do

Manhattan

For most visitors, Manhattan (population 1,487,536) *is* New York City. Even the residents of the outer boroughs refer to it as 'the city,' a tacit acknowledgment of the island's primacy. But it's important to remember that the Bronx, Brooklyn, Queens and Staten Island each have their own attractions. If you're here for more than a week, plan at least one excursion out of Manhattan – that's the best way to take advantage of what the entire city has to offer.

The best way to get around are your own two feet. Pick a subway destination near a set of major attractions (W 4th St, 34th St, Rockefeller Center, Canal St) and head out from there. Manhattan's Midtown grid pattern and prominent north-south avenues make it difficult to get badly lost. And don't be shy about asking for directions if you find yourself confused.

The following sections divide Manhattan into neighborhoods from the island's south-ern tip to the north. Remember that the most popular sites, like the Statue of Liberty, attract large crowds year round. To see more than two famous sites in one day will require an early departure from your hotel in order to be at the first stop by 9 am.

LOWER MANHATTAN

Lower Manhattan is served by 15 subway lines and nearly 20 stations. With the exception of South Street Seaport, most sites in this part of town are within a block or two of a subway. If you are following the Lower Manhattan Walking Tour, take the 4, 5 or 6 subway train to Brooklyn Bridge-City Hall, where the tour begins. The Architectural Walk is best served by the 2, 3, 4 or 5 train to Fulton St. To get to the Statue of Liberty and Ellis Island ferries, take the 1/9 subway to South Ferry or the 4 or 5 to Bowling Green.

Lower Manhattan Walking Tour

It is essential to explore this area on a weekday, concentrated as it is on the Monday to Friday activities of business, politics and the law. Expect this walk to

---

Tourists' Top Targets

Metropolitan Museum of Art	5.2 million
Empire State Building	3.1 million
American Museum of Natural History	3.0 million
Statue of Liberty	2.8 million
Bronx Zoo	2.3 million
World Trade Center	1.8 million
Ellis Island	1.6 million
Museum of Modern Art	1.5 million
Circle Line	1.2 million
Guggenheim Museum/Guggenheim SoHo	1.0 million

In addition, multi-attraction areas, such as the Theater District, Rockfeller Center, Times Square and South Street Seaport, all attract more than 10 million annual visitors. ■

take anywhere from three hours to a whole day, depending on how often you stop for attractions. It's a good idea to get an early start, between 9 and 10 am, to avoid fellow travelers and midday crowds.

The best start-off point is **City Hall**, near the pedestrian approach to the Brooklyn Bridge. Directly behind City Hall stands the **Tweed Courthouse**, an inadvertent monument to late 19th century municipal corruption. Built in 1872, an estimated $10 million of the $14 million budget for this new city courthouse wound up being embezzled by William Magear 'Boss' Tweed, the ruthless leader of the Democratic Party's Tammany Hall organization. Tweed's gang at one point was stealing about $1 million a month from the city treasury. The subsequent scandal over the building's cost toppled Tweed from power – but left an architecturally significant site with an impressive central hall.

Nearby at the intersection of Chambers and Centre Sts sits the former **Surrogate's Court**, a structure completed in 1914 with an interior that deliberately imitates the Beaux Arts style of Charles Garnier's Paris Opera House. The building is now home to New York City's official archival collection.

Strolling north on Centre St brings you to **Foley Square**, a complex of city, state and federal courthouses. The Federal Courthouse at 40 Centre St, the familiar setting for organized crime trials, stands one block south of the New York County Courthouse, home to the state supreme court. Check out the lawyers holding noisy impromptu negotiations in its huge, bustling rotunda.

Heading west on Duane St (directly in front of the US Courthouse) brings you to the **African Burial Ground**, a cemetery for the city's early black residents that was unearthed in the late '80s and declared a national historic site. Many of the bodies discovered were of slaves wearing British uniforms – soldiers who were promised their freedom for fighting for the loyalists during the Revolutionary War.

Turning left down Broadway brings you past the Sun Building at the northeast corner of Chambers St. The newspaper –

one of many located in this area during the early 20th century – no longer exists, but its clock remains, promising that the publication 'shines for all.'

After passing City Hall again, you'll see the **Woolworth Building** at 233 Broadway on your right. It was the world's tallest building (792 feet, 60 stories) when completed in 1913. Frank Woolworth, head of the famous discount store chain, reputedly paid the $15 million costs of the building with nickels and dimes. The lobby of this so-called 'Cathedral of Commerce' includes a gargoyle of Woolworth counting his change.

Carrying on down Broadway will bring you to **St Paul's Chapel**, where noon music recitals take place every Monday and Thursday. Three blocks down, a right turn on Liberty St leads to the **World Trade Center**. On clear days the South Tower's 107th floor observatory affords unbeatable views of the city and beyond.

Head back to Broadway and continue down the corridor to **Trinity Church**, one of the city's oldest surviving religious landmarks (see individual listing).

Wall St, which begins directly across from Trinity Church, stands at the site where early Dutch settlers constructed a northern barrier to protect New Amsterdam from attacks by Indians and the British. Today it is the metaphorical home of US commerce. Check out the Bank of New York Building at 1 Wall St, which has an Art Deco lobby of blazing red and gold mosaic tiles, and the sleek and modern 1988 Morgan Bank headquarters at 60 Wall St. Both buildings symbolize their eras architecturally and stand as distinctive monuments to money. Wall St is also the site of **Federal Hall**, which is the starting point for four self-guided Heritage Trail walking tours (☎ (888) 487-2457) that go into the area's history in greater detail. A Heritage Trails map, which details the 42 cast-iron site markers explaining downtown history, is given away free in the lobby. Across the street from Federal Hall stands the **New York Stock Exchange**, officially at 8 Broad St.

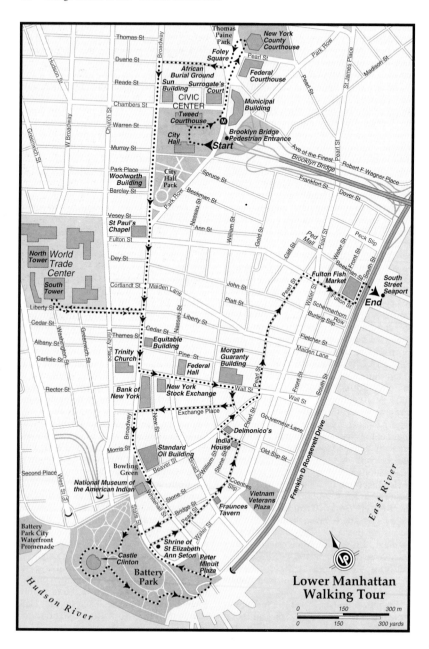

**Lower Manhattan
Walking Tour**

In front of Morgan Guaranty, turn down Hanover St and make the next right on Exchange Place, which leads back to Broadway. As Broadway veers east, just before becoming Whitehall St, note the **Standard Oil Building** at 26 Broadway. One of many early monuments to capitalism that line the Broadway corridor from St Paul's down to Battery Park, this curved edifice was built in 1922 by John D Rockefeller. Its 2nd floor houses the **Museum of American Financial History** (☎ (212) 908-4519), open Monday to Friday from 11:30 am to 2:30 pm.

Continue down Whitehall St, past Bowling Green, and you'll come upon the National Museum of the American Indian in the US **Customs House**. Just north of the museum is a bronze statue of a raging bull, the symbol of a healthy stock market. Turn right down Bridge St, which leads directly to Battery Park and Castle Clinton, a fortification built in 1811 to protect Manhattan from the British.

By walking east you'll exit Battery Park at **Peter Minuit Plaza**, reputedly the sight of the purchase of Manhattan for the equivalent of $24. Continuing up State St to Pearl St, you'll reach the **Shrine to St Elizabeth Ann Seton**, dedicated to America's first Roman Catholic saint. Tucked just behind this building is **New York Unearthed**, an interesting little exhibit of historical items discovered by archeologists and construction workers over the years. It's open Monday to Friday from noon to 6 pm.

Heading east up Pearl St will lead you to the historical block at Coenties Slip, a Dutch docking station that became a street as landfill extended the city further south. The archeological site of the old Dutch City hall is visible here, just across the street from the **Fraunces Tavern**. The current tavern is a 1907 renovation of the place where Washington gave his farewell address to Continental Army officers in 1783.

Continuing up Pearl St you will pass the **India House**, at 1 Hanover Square, a former bank building that's now an exclu-

KIM GRANT
Shrine to St Elizabeth Ann Seton

sive and somewhat secretive businessmen's club. Around the corner in a northerly direction on Beaver St (a name indicative of the trading activities of colonial New York) stands **Delmonico's**, part of the chain of famous restaurants that created the American notion of 'dining out' in the 19th century. This 1891 structure includes a marble portico supposedly bought in Pompeii; the storied restaurant was closed at press time, but is scheduled to reopen as a microbrewery and steak house.

Continue up Beaver St, and then up Pearl St. From here you can walk six blocks north to the intersection of Fulton St, and make a right turn towards the Hudson River and the **Fulton Fish Market**, the city's wholesale seafood distribution point, and the **South Street Seaport**. Try to arrive as night falls to watch the lights come on the Brooklyn and Manhattan bridges. The sight is worth the extra money you'll pay for a drink at a bar or cafe with a good view.

Lower Manhattan's Architectural Landmarks

Students of architecture will no doubt be drawn to New York City's far-flung landmarks: the brownstones of Brooklyn Heights, the marvelous medieval quiet of the Cloisters, or the sleek modernism of Ludwig Mies van der Rohe's Seagram Building (built in 1958) in Midtown. But if you want a short but comprehensive tour of the city's man-made landscape, it's best to spend a day downtown near Wall St. Though famous as the world's financial capital, this area of urban canyons is an unrivaled museum of architecture. Along these cramped and circuitous side streets and the grand avenue of Broadway you will find Federal homes, Greek revival temples, Gothic churches, Renaissance palazzos and one of the finest collections of early 20th century skyscrapers.

After the Dutch bought Manhattan from local Indians in the early 17th century, they protected their newfound home with a fort and erected a wood-and-mud wall to keep out hostile Indians as well as the British. While no Dutch buildings from this period have survived, the paths and lanes mapped out by the engineer Cryn Fredericksz in 1625 have since restrained and influenced every architect who ventured to build here.

Likewise, little lasts from the more than 100 years of British rule. Indeed, seven years of British military occupation during the Revolutionary War and major fires in 1776 and 1778 ruthlessly altered the face of the city. By the end of the war, a quarter of the settled area – more than 1000 shops and homes – lay in burnt decay. According to the diarist William Duer, 'The skeletons of the remaining walls cast their grim shadows upon the pavement, imparting an unearthly aspect to the street.'

Thankfully, during one of the blazes, citizens climbed to the roof of **St Paul's Chapel** on Broadway between Vesey and Fulton Sts and extinguished the flames threatening the schist and brownstone church. Designed in 1764 by Thomas McBean, the chapel is now the last remaining colonial building in the area, and one of the greatest Georgian structures ever built in the country. It was here, within the airy interior with its fluted Corinthian columns and Waterford chandeliers, that President George Washington attended services when New York served as the nation's capital. His personal pew is still on display. (See Fraunces Tavern in the Lower Manhattan section for more on existing traces of colonial architecture.)

On State St (between Pearl and Whitehall Sts) at the southern tip of the island stands the **Shrine to St Elizabeth Ann Seton**, lone survivor of a series of graceful row houses that once hugged the shoreline (due to landfill it's now set well back from the river). Today the shrine, dedicated to the first American Catholic saint, occupies the eastern portion of 7 State St. This delicate Georgian home with small marble plaques set in red brick dates from 1793. A Federal-style western wing was added in 1806, reputedly by John McComb, the first major New York-born architect. This section of the structure is enlivened with a curved porch and a double colonnade of attenuated Doric and Ionic columns supposedly made from recycled ship masts. Such an unusual building material apparently suited the so-called 'Peep-o'-Day Boys' – merchants who began each morning by walking out onto their porches and anxiously gazing through their telescopes to see if their far-flung cargo ships were approaching the port.

Just to the west in Battery Park looms the shell of **Castle Clinton**. Built in 1811 and indisputably designed by McComb, the imposing fortress with its eight-foot thick walls and rusticated gate once brimmed with 28 guns set in the embrasures. Back then the fort stood on an island hundreds of feet off the shore; landfill has since joined it with Manhattan. Its guns were never fired in anger, and in the 1820s the government decommissioned the fort and turned it into Castle Garden, a concert hall-cum-resort that is said to have hosted up to 6000 people beneath a domed roof. Castle Clinton has had a colorful history: in 1855 the government made it into a processing center for immigrants, and in 1896 the renowned firm of McKim, Mead and White remodeled the building as an aquarium that lasted until 1941. Today it is the site of the ticket office for the Statue of Liberty ferry.

As Americans sought a way to define their new nation, they looked to the ancient democracy of Greece and the republic of Rome for examples to emulate. Classic architecture, it was felt, gave expression to the aspirations of the young republic. The finest surviving example in Lower Manhattan is **Federal Hall** by the influential architects Ithiel Town and Alexander Jackson Davis. Standing on Wall and Nassau Sts on the site of the old British City Hall where Washington took his oath of office, the 1842 design with its hefty Doric porticoes, two-story rotunda, circular colonnade and paneled dome is truly a temple to purity.

By the mid-19th century, everything new, from courthouses and banks to privies, was designed to look like Greek temples, and people quickly tired of the austerity of the ancients. When British-born Richard Upjohn built **Trinity Church** on Broadway and Wall St in 1846, the brownstone church with its buttresses, finials and octagonal spire was the tallest and most richly decorated building in the city. Its appearance proved a revelation to a citizenry craving more transcendental and less rationalist forms. Upjohn's church helped launch the picturesque neo-Gothic movement in America.

By the early 1900s, as New York remained the center of US commercial trade, the federal government decided it needed a new **Customs House** to collect its revenues. Located near the foot of Broadway, the Customs House was completed in 1907. It was designed by Cass Gilbert, who went on to construct such landmarks as the Woolworth Building. Gilbert's vast seven-story limestone Customs House melds art and architecture in a tribute to the grandeur of trade. Walls, doors, ceilings and floors are festooned with marine ornamentation, shells, sails, sea creatures and sea signs. Dormers are the prows of galleons, and the glorious elliptical rotunda is a 135-foot-long room encircled by Reginald Marsh's murals (added in 1937) portraying everything from the great explorers of America to an uncredited cameo of Greta Garbo at an impromptu dockside press conference. It is simply one of the most sumptuous Beaux Arts buildings ever built.

The Customs House inspired a rash of new buildings near Bowling Green, most of them monuments to particular companies, and these skyscrapers started to dwarf neighboring landmarks. The 41-story **Equitable Building** on Broadway between Pine and Cedar Sts is a rather undistinguished but nevertheless influential example of the form. When it opened in just before WWI, its sheer unapologetic bulk changed the shape of Manhattan – and world architecture – forever. At 1.2 million sq feet it was the largest office building on the planet. Its size created such an uproar that four years after its opening New York enacted the nation's first zoning laws requiring building setbacks, thus stimulating countless architects to reinterpret the nature of the skyscraper. Their dizzyingly tall towers have sprung up all over Manhattan – and have subsequently filled other cities throughout the world.

– **Daniel S Levy**, architectural historian and reporter for *Time*. He is also the author of *Two-Gun Cohen* (St Martin's Press), a biography of the western adventurer who became a general in the Chinese army. ∎

Castle Clinton

Castle Clinton

The ticket office for the Statue of Liberty boats is in Castle Clinton, the fort built in 1811 to defend Manhattan from the British. Originally located 300 yards offshore before landfill engulfed it, Castle Clinton was converted to a theater in 1823, and has also served as an immigration station and aquarium. Today the Castle is literally just a shell of its former self – there's no roof on the building anymore.

Statue of Liberty

The most enduring symbol of New York City – and indeed, the USA – can trace its unlikely origins to a Parisian dinner party in 1865. There, a group of intellectuals opposed to the government of Napoleon III gathered in the house of political activist Edouard René Lefebvre de Laboulaye to discuss ways to promote French Republicanism. That notion of building a monument honoring the American conception

of political freedom intrigued sculptor Frédéric-Auguste Bartholdi, a fellow dinner guest, who dedicated most of the next 20 years to turning the dream into a reality.

Laboulaye and Bartholdi decided that the structure should wind up in the US, and the latter traveled to New York in 1871 to choose a site for the work he had modeled on the Colossus of Rhodes. Soon afterward, the pair created a lottery to cover the $250,000 cost of construction of the statue, which included a metal skeleton by railway engineer Alexandre Gustave Eiffel, who later became world-famous for his eponymous Parisian tower.

The statue's forearm and balcony-enclosed torch were displayed at the Centennial Exhibition in Philadelphia in July of 1876, and remained in New York for several years afterward to engender support for the project. But Americans seemed suspicious of the quixotic endeavor, and fundraising for a foundation for the 151-foot statue stalled. The completed work remained in Paris from 1884-85, attracting thousands of visitors.

Liberty's ticket to the States was punched by newspaper publisher Joseph Pulitzer, who turned the building of a base into a circulation-boosting public crusade. After the readers of Pulitzer's *New York World* donated $100,000, a 24,000-ton foundation was laid on Bedloe's Island. On October 28, 1886, the 151-foot *Liberty Enlightening the World* was finally unveiled in New York harbor before President Grover Cleveland and a harbor full of celebrating ships.

By the 1980s a restoration of the statue was in order, and more than $100 million was spent to shore up Liberty for her centennial. Substantial work was done on the rotting copper skin and a new gold-plated torch – the third in the statue's history – was installed. The older, stained-glass torch is now on display just inside the entrance to the staircase, near a museum describing the statue's history and its restoration. The exhibition also shows how the statue has always been exploited for commercial purposes.

The Statue of Liberty and Ellis Island are a 15-minute ferry ride from Battery Park, and attract some two million visitors each a year. Millions more take the boat ride just for the spectacular view of Manhattan but pass on taking the 354 steps to the Statue's crown, the equivalent of climbing a 22-story building. (No one is allowed onto the statue's torch balcony.)

A trip taking in both the Statue of Liberty and Ellis Island is an all-day affair. In the summer you may wait up to an hour to embark on an 800-person ferry, only to be confronted by a three-hour trek to the crown, followed by a bottleneck getting off both islands. If the statue is on your must-see list, get there at the very beginning of the day and make a beeline for the crown. Keep in mind, before waiting an hour or more to get to the top, that the view of Manhattan from the crown windows isn't any more or less spectacular than the one from ground level.

Though there is no charge to get off at Liberty Island, the ferries out of Manhattan cost $7/5/3 for adults/seniors/children. They leave every 30 minutes from 9 am to 5 pm with extended hours during the summer. (Ferries also leave from Liberty State Park on the New Jersey side of the harbor.) Call ☎ (212) 363-3200 for opening hours and ☎ (212) 269-5755 for ferry schedules.

KIM GRANT

Statue of Liberty

Ellis Island

Ferries make a second stop at Ellis Island, New York's main immigration station from 1892 to 1954. More than 15 million people passed through here before the island was abandoned. Barely visible further up the slip from the boat docks are the rotting remains of *Ellis Island*, a passenger ferry that sank in 1968 after years of neglect.

A $160 million restoration has turned the impressive red-brick main building into an **Immigration Museum** with a series of galleries on the history of the island. The exhibitions begin at the

KIM GRANT

Inside the Great Hall on Ellis Island

Baggage Room, and continue on to 2nd-story rooms where medical inspections took place and foreign currency was exchanged.

At all points, the exhibits emphasize that, contrary to popular myth, most of the ship-borne immigrants were processed within eight hours and that conditions were generally clean and safe. The 338-foot-long Registry Room includes a beautiful vaulted tile ceiling made by immigrants from Spain. But walking though the registry today – described as 'light and airy' in museum literature – surely can't compare to days when the same room housed a queue of 5000 confused and tired people waiting to be interviewed by overworked immigration officers and inspected by doctors.

There is a 50-minute audio tour of the facility available for an additional charge ($3.50/3/2.50) narrated by newsman Tom Brokaw that is a bit repetitive and padded with actor recreations of anonymous immigrant writings. Much more effecting are the recorded memories of real Ellis Island immigrants taped in the 1980s and available through phone banks in each display area.

A half-hour film on the immigrant experience is worth checking out, as is the exhibition of how the influx of immigrants just before WWI changed America. There's an interesting wall display of Tin Pan Alley sheet music that was aimed at this new foreign-born audience, including the songs *Yonkel the Cowboy Jew* and *Go On Good-a-Bye*, a 'characteristic Italian song' with words by one Joseph Murphy.

Trinity Church

This old Anglican parish (☎ (212) 602-0872), at the corner of Broadway and Wall St, was founded by King William III in 1697 and once had several constituent chapels, including the still-existent St Paul's Chapel at the corner of Fulton St and Broadway. Its huge land holdings in lower Manhattan made it the wealthiest and most influential church throughout the 18th century.

The current Trinity Church is the third structure on the site and was built in 1846 by English architect Richard Upjohn. Its 280-foot bell tower made it the tallest building in New York City before the advent of skyscrapers. A pamphlet describing the parish's history is available for a 25¢ donation.

The long, dark interior of the church includes a beautiful stained-glass window over the altar. Trinity, like other Anglican churches in the US, became part of the Episcopal faith following US independence, but instinctive connections with Mother England are made painfully obvious by a pavement plaque near the entrance. It informs visitors that 'on this spot stood her Majesty Queen Elizabeth II on the occasion of her gracious visit 9 July 1976.' The notice goes on to generously note that 'His Royal Highness the Prince Philip stood nearby.'

Trinity Church offers services Monday through Saturday at 8 am and noon, and free tours of the facility daily at 2 pm. Sunday services are held at 9 and 11:15 am. There are classical concerts held at 1 pm on Monday and Thursday during the winter. A small museum dedicated to church history is located at the back of the church and includes the original charter.

It is open to visitors Monday through Friday from 9 am to 3:45 pm, Saturday 10 am to 3:45 pm, and Sunday 1 to 3:45 pm, excluding the hour of lunchtime services.

Federal Hall

Distinguished by a huge statue of George Washington, Federal Hall (☎ (212) 767-0637), 26 Wall St, stands on the site where the first US Congress convened and where Washington later took the oath of office as the first US president. These events took place in the former city hall built by the British that was later replaced by the current Greek Revival structure in 1842. Today there is a small museum dedicated to post-colonial New York open from 9 am to 5 pm weekdays. Guided tours of the building leave every hour on the half hour from 12:30 to 3:30 pm.

New York Stock Exchange

Though 'Wall St' is the widely recognized metaphor for US capitalism, the world's best-known stock exchange (☎ (212) 656-5167) is actually around the corner at 8 Broad St, behind a portentous facade reminiscent of a Roman temple. A visitor's gallery overlooks the frenetic trading floor and includes an exhibit describing the exchange's history. The modern business of the exchange isn't explained very well, however, and not much is made of the famous 1929 stock market crash or even the 1987 debacle that led to restrictions on the computer-programmed stock dumping that triggered it off.

Free tickets to view the NYSE are distributed at a booth at 20 Broad St, Monday through Friday from 9:15 am to 4 pm. The tickets, which allow entrance to the visitor's center in 45-minute time periods throughout the day, are usually snapped up by noon. While waiting in line, you'll see dozens of brokers wearing color-coordinated trading jackets popping out of the NYSE for a quick cigarette or hot dog.

If you're lucky, you will receive a ticket for the time period that includes the 4 pm end of trading, when a retiring broker or other financial worthy is given the honor of ringing a bell that brings the business day to a close. Cheers arise if the market closes on a high note; groans and oaths abound on a down day.

National Museum of the American Indian

The National Museum of the American Indian (☎ (212) 668-6624), an affiliate of Washington's Smithsonian Institution, abandoned its uptown spot at 155th St in 1994 and moved to the former US Customs House on Bowling Green. The Beaux Arts monument to commerce was built to collect federal duties imposed on foreign goods in the days before income tax; it is a grand but somewhat incongruous space for the country's leading museum on Native American art, established by oil heir George Gustav Heye in 1916.

The galleries are on the 2nd floor, behind a vast rotunda featuring statues of famous navigators and murals celebrating shipping history. This museum does little to explain the history of Native Americans, but instead concentrates its collection on Indian identity as reflected in its million-item collection of crafts and everyday objects. Computer touch screens offer views on Native life and beliefs, and working artists are often on hand to explain their techniques. A gift shop sells Native American jewelry.

The museum is open daily from 10 am to 5 pm, and admission is free.

South Street Seaport

This 11-block enclave of shops and historic sights (☎ (212) 732-7678) is visited each year by over 10 million people, and combines the best and worst in historic preservation. Pier 17, beyond the elevated FDR Drive, is a waterfront development project that's home to a number of shops and over-priced restaurants. But the area also contains a number of genuinely significant buildings from the 18th and 19th centuries that once surrounded this old East River ferry port, which fell into disuse upon the building of the Brooklyn Bridge and the establishment of deep-water piers on the Hudson River.

A block of old warehouses bordered by Fulton, Front and South Sts, **Schermerhorn Row** contains novelty shops, seafood restaurants and a pub. The **Fulton Market Building**, built across the street in 1983 to reflect the red-brick style of its older neighbors, is nothing more than a glorified fast food hall and shopping arcade.

The **South Street Seaport Museum** (☎ (212) 748-8600) oversees several interesting sights in the area, including three galleries, an antique printing shop, a children's center, a maritime crafts center and the historic ships. These are all open daily from 10 am to 5 pm and admission to the collection is $6 for adults, $5 for seniors, $4 for students and $3 for children. You can also buy a combination ticket that includes a harbor cruise for an additional $10.

KIM GRANT

Trinity Church

KIM GRANT

St Paul's Chapel

KIM GRANT

Statue of George Washington, in front of Federal Hall

KIM GRANT

The former US Customs House, home of the National Museum of the American Indian

KIM GRANT

'After hours' at the Fulton Fish Market, which operates all night

Just south of Pier 17 stand several tall-masted sailing vessels, including the *Peking*, the *Wavertree*, the *Pioneer* and the lightship *Ambrose*. All can be inspected with the price of admission to the museum. A booth on Pier 16 also sells tickets for an hour-long riverboat excursion from the Seaport Liberty Cruise Line (☎ (212) 630-8888) that highlights Manhattan maritime history. Tours run at least three times each day from late March to the end of November and cost $12 for adults, $10 for seniors and $6 for children.

Pier 17 is also the site of the **Fulton Fish Market**, where most of the city's restaurants get their fresh seafood. The market (☎ (212) 669-9416) is a perfect example of how this area maintains its old character while still catering to tourists. Management of the facility has long been thought to be controlled by the Genovese organized crime family and a recent crackdown on corruption led to months of labor unrest and a suspicious 1995 fire that destroyed a part of the market. Nevertheless, the nightly working of the market can be seen by visitors from midnight to 8 am, and guided tours (☎ (212) 664-9416) are available from April to October.

If you make the trek down to the Seaport, be sure to venture away from the crowd by taking South St north a few blocks to Peck Slip, where you will see a few abandoned fish warehouses with their original signs intact.

Walk up Front St and turn left at Dover St, right under the Brooklyn Bridge, and take a look at the **Bridge Cafe**, a restaurant at the corner of Water St which was recently deemed by the *New York Times* to be the oldest tavern in the city – a distinction previously claimed by McSorley's Old Ale House in the East Village.

Federal Reserve Bank

The only reason to visit the Federal Reserve Bank (☎ (212) 720-6130), 31 Liberty St, is to see the facility's high-security vault, located 80 feet below ground and containing more than 10,000 tons of gold reserves. You'll only see a small part of that fortune, but it comes along with an informative tour about the US Federal Reserve System and an exhibit of coins and counterfeit currency. The catch is that you are expected to call a week before your intended visit to obtain a slot on the tour – but in reality you might be able to catch a tour by just showing up.

Fraunces Tavern

The Georgian-style Fraunces Tavern Restaurant & Museum (☎ (212) 425-1778), 54 Pearl St, is on a block of historic structures that, along with nearby Stone St and the South Street Seaport, are the final examples of colonial-era New York that remain largely intact – the buildings here can be traced to the early 18th century.

On this site stood the Queen's Head Tavern, owned by Samuel Fraunces, who changed the name to Fraunces Tavern after American victory in the War for Independence. It was in the 2nd-floor dining room on December 4, 1783, that George Washington bade farewell to the officers of the Continental Army after the British relinquished control of New York City. In the 19th century, the tavern closed and the building fell into disuse. It was also damaged in several massive fires that swept through downtown and destroyed most 18th century colonial buildings and nearly all structures built by the Dutch. In 1904, the building was bought by the Sons of the Revolution historical society and returned to an approximation of its colonial-era look – an act believed to be the first major attempt at historic preservation in the US.

The museum and restaurant are separate facilities, and eating a meal does not include entry to the museum, which is open Monday to Friday from 10 am to 4:45 pm and Saturday from noon to 4 pm. Admission for adults/children is $2.50/1.

Just across the street from the tavern are the excavated remains of the old Dutch **Stadt Huys**, which served as New Amsterdam's administrative center, courthouse and jail from 1641 until the peaceful British takeover in 1664. The building was destroyed in 1699.

World Trade Center

The massive twin towers of the World Trade Center (WTC; ☎ (212) 323-2340), which rise 1350 feet above the ground, are part of a complex that houses more than 350 different businesses employing 50,000 people. Built at a cost of $700 million from 1966-73, the sleek WTC has never stirred people's hearts in the same manner as the Empire State Building, though the project did change the city in a profound way: the one million cubic yards of rock and dirt unearthed for the WTC's foundation became the landfill on which the 24-acre Battery Park City development was built.

The center's twin towers have attracted two well-publicized daredevils: George Willig, who used mountain climbing equipment to scale the side of one building, and circus performer Philippe Petit, who claimed he was able to use a cross-bow to run a tightrope across both buildings and put on a show a quarter-mile above the ground without anyone in authority knowing about it. The center's array of federal and state government offices made it a tempting target for the terrorists who set off a truck bomb in the underground parking garage on February 26, 1993, killing six people. There is now a monument to those who died in the WTC central plaza.

The ticket booth for the WTC observation decks is open seven days a week from 9:30 am to 11:30 pm from June to September and 9:30 am to 9:30 pm the remainder of the year. Admission for adults/children is $7/3.50.

The **Commodities Exchange Center** (☎ (212) 938-2025) is on the 9th floor of 4 World Trade Center. You can view the trading floor – home to a group of traders far more emotional than their Wall St brethren – from 9:30 am to 3 pm weekdays. Admission is free. The shopping plaza on the subway level underneath the buildings was the first indoor mall to open in New York City, although the Manhattan Mall at Herald Square falsely claims that dubious distinction.

World Financial Center

The World Financial Center is just across West St from the WTC. This group of four office towers surrounds the **Winter Garden**, a glass atrium, an ostentatious centerpiece that is the site of free concerts during the summer and exclusive black-tie events year round. During good weather it's pleasant to walk, run or bike down the mile-long esplanade running from Hudson River Park past the World Financial Center and the residential **Battery Park City** apartments on to the southern tip of Manhattan; when it's rainy you can pass an hour in the shopping area or Liberty St Gallery, 225 Liberty Place, which has a number of worthwhile exhibitions and there's a museum-quality autograph store in the enclosed shopping plaza.

City Hall

City Hall (☎ (212) 788-6865) has been home to New York's government since 1812. In an example of the half-baked civic planning that has often plagued big New York projects, officials neglected to finish the building's northern side in marble, betting that the city would not expand uptown! That shortsightedness was finally rectified in 1954, completing a structure that architectural critic Ada Louise Huxtable has called a 'symbol of taste, excellence and quality not always matched by the policies inside.' On either side of the building stands 'The Key to City Hall,' an interactive video center with information on local landmarks and visitor services.

Walk to the 2nd floor to the spot at the top of the stairs where, in 1865, Abraham Lincoln's coffin was placed on its way from Washington, DC, to Springfield, Illinois. The Governor's Room, a reception area used by the mayor for important guests, contains 12 portraits of the founding fathers by John Trumbull, several examples of Federal furniture including George Washington's writing table, and the remnants of a flag flown at the first president's 1789 inaugural ceremony. Peeking into the City Council chambers may reveal the law-

Hidden Subway History

The ornate City Hall subway station was built in 1904 and served as the crown jewel of the first subway line. The station went out of active service in the 1940s, and was replaced by the adjacent Brooklyn Bridge-City Hall station, now servicing the 4, 5 and 6 Lexington Ave lines. Yet it's possible to catch a glimpse of the older station even today: it's used as a turn-around for the local 6 line, which terminates at Brooklyn Bridge-City Hall.

Get on (or stay on) the last car of a No 6 train on the downtown platform. (That way, the conductor who occupies the middle car won't see you and reveal the train has reached the end of the line.) Within a few minutes the train will begin its turnaround – and press your face to the windows on the right hand side of the car. You'll get a ghostly glimpse of the old City Hall station's terra cotta walls and cathedral-like roof structure. The Metropolitan Transit Authority plans to eventually open up the station to those who purchase tickets to the Transit Museum, which is located just over the bridge in Brooklyn Heights. ■

makers deliberating the renaming of a city street in someone's honor, an activity which accounts for 40% of all the bills passed by the 51-member body.

City Hall's steps are a popular site for demonstrations and press conferences by grandstanding politicians and the lobby now holds the World Championship trophy won by the New York Yankees in 1996. Don't be discouraged by the grumpy security presence – the building is open to the public Monday to Friday from 10 am to 4 pm.

Brooklyn Bridge

Regarded by many as the most beautiful bridge in the world and a magnificent example of fine urban design, the Brooklyn Bridge is the first steel suspension bridge ever built, and its 1596-foot span between the two support towers was the world's longest when it opened in 1883.

Plans for an East River suspension bridge were drawn up by the Prussian-born engineer John Roebling, who was knocked off a pier by a ferry at Fulton's landing in June of 1869 and died of tetanus poisoning before construction of the bridge began. His son Washington supervised construction of the bridge, which took 14 years and was plagued by budget overruns and the deaths of 20 workers. The younger Roebling himself was stricken by the bends while helping to excavate the riverbed for the bridge's western tower and remained bedridden for much of the project. There was one final tragedy, which came in June of 1883, when the bridge opened to pedestrian traffic. Someone in the crowd shouted, perhaps as a joke, that the bridge was collapsing into the river, setting off a mad rush in which 12 people were trampled to death.

There's no fear of collapse today, as the bridge enters its second century following an extensive renovation in the early '80s.

JANE LLOYD

The pedestrian walkway that begins just east of City Hall affords a wonderful view of Lower Manhattan, and you can stop at observation points under both stone support towers and view brass panorama histories of the waterfront at various points in New York's history. Once you reach the Brooklyn side (about a 20-minute walk) you can bear right to walk down to Cadman Plaza West to a park that will bring you to Middagh St, which runs east to west in the heart of Brooklyn Heights. Bearing left brings you to Brooklyn's downtown area, which includes the ornate Borough Hall and Fulton St pedestrian mall.

CHINATOWN & LITTLE ITALY

subway: 4, 5, 6, N, R to Canal St

Chinatown and Little Italy are renowned ethnic enclaves just north of the Civic Center and the financial district; Chinatown sprawls largely south of Canal St, while Little Italy is a narrow sliver extending north of the same thoroughfare.

The denizens of Chinatown now number about 100,000, many of whom are able to move and work in a mini-society each day without using a word of English. This community, with its own rhythms and traditions, is catered to in many different ways: some banks along Canal St keep Sunday hours, and no fewer than seven Chinese newspapers are available at newsstands. Throughout the '90s, Chinatown has also been home to a growing community of Vietnamese immigrants, who have set up their own shops and incredibly cheap restaurants here.

In recent times, Chinatown has moved east and north, and you can find Chinese bakeries and shops in the area above Canal St. In effect, the area known as the 'Lower East Side' is breaking up into two distinct neighborhoods: south of Delancey St it's Chinese, north of Delancey is becoming absorbed as a hopping adjunct of the East Village. Mott St above Canal also has a distinctly Chinese flavor for four blocks. And lately, Grand St, which runs parallel to

Canal St, is also dominated by Chinese-owned businesses, with busy fruit stands and fish stores open until 8 pm each night.

In contrast, Little Italy is confined largely to Mulberry St north of Canal St. This was once a very strong Italian neighborhood (film director Martin Scorsese grew up on Elizabeth St), and while many of the apartment buildings in this 10 block radius are still owned by former residents, there was an exodus from Little Italy in the mid-20th century to the Cobble Hill section of Brooklyn as well as the suburbs surrounding New York City.

For that reason, there are few cultural sites and most people come to Little Italy specifically to eat, even though there are many good restaurants serving better Italian cuisine at all price levels elsewhere in the city.

KIM GRANT

Doyers St in Chinatown

Off Mulberry St, on Elizabeth and Lafayette Sts, Little Italy begins to take on a more cosmopolitan character, as the overflow of SoHo-style shops, cafes and restaurants make their way into the area, taking over storefronts that once served as social clubs and stores for the old community. This neighborhood is being sold by realtors as having 'Montparnasse charm,' which means it's a hot area with overpriced, dumpy apartments. Take a special stroll along Elizabeth and Lafayette Sts – it's changing from month to month.

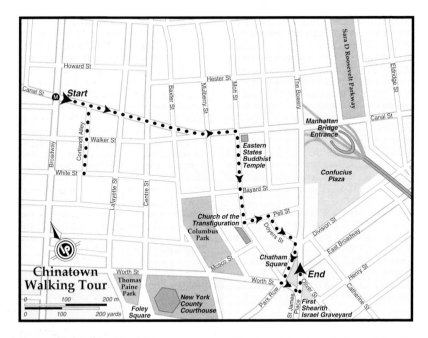

Chinatown Walking Tour

For a tour of Chinatown, start on Canal St near Broadway (subway: N, R to Canal St). Walking down the south side of the street for one block you will reach **Cortlandt Alley**, a perfectly preserved four-block enclave of gloomy old factories and warehouses that are often featured in movies – it's worth a quick look.

For several blocks Canal St maintains a decidedly seedy character, with hardware and electrical supply stores co-existing with street vendors selling phony designer clothing and bootleg videos of films still playing in theaters. If you buy anything off a street seller, make sure it's something you can wear or check out on the spot – a hat, a book, or a leather jacket. *(Never* buy electronics on the street.) The Chinese food shopping district begins past Baxter St, with several stands selling fresh fish and exotic produce, including guavas and durians, the infamous smelly fruit banned from the subways of Singapore.

Turning right (south) down Mott St brings you to most of the district's restaurants. The **Eastern States Buddhist Temple** (☎ (212) 966-4753), in a storefront at 64B Mott St, is a busy shrine with dozens of golden and porcelain Buddhas on display. You can buy a fortune for $1 and watch the devout make offerings.

The **Church of the Transfiguration**, 29 Mott St, began as an Episcopal church in 1801 and was purchased by the Roman Catholic Church 50 years later to meet the needs of what was then an Irish and Italian neighborhood. In the 1890s the ascendant and spiteful Irish church leaders forced Italian patrons to worship in the basement. The church got its first Chinese pastor in the 1970s and today holds services in Chinese.

Turning left on Pell St, an ancient road named for a butcher who plied his trade here in the colonial period, brings you to Doyers St. Chinatown began in this small enclave in the 1870s when Chinese railway workers, fed up with racial discrimination in the American West, moved to New York City in large numbers. During Chinese New Year celebrations in late January and early February, papier-mâché dragons snake their way around this corner to the sound of firecrackers shooing away evil spirits.

Exiting Doyers St brings you toward two examples of the neighborhood's previous ethnic history. **Chatham Square** is where public auctions took place to sell the goods of Irish debtors in the early 19th century. Walking 150 yards south on St James Place brings you to **First Shearith Israel Graveyard**. This cemetery, which dates back to the 1680s, is the final resting place of early Portuguese and Spanish immigrants, and is the oldest Jewish cemetery in the US.

At the end of the tour, you might want to seek out the restaurants on East Broadway or Catherine St, which are hardly ever patronized by tourists.

Chinatown History Museum

The nonprofit Museum of Chinese in the Americas (☎ (212) 619-4785), 70 Mulberry St, is in a century-old former public school building that reopened in early 1996 after a year-long renovation. The museum sponsors walking tours and crafts workshops on paper lantern making and other creative endeavors. Recent exhibits include 80 works made in captivity by the survivors of the *Golden Venture*, a ship full of illegal immigrants from China that ran aground near New York Bay in 1993. The Chinese who crossed over on the ship had been detained by the US immigration service for more than four years.

Admission to the museum is $3 for adults and $1 for children (under 12 are free). It's open Tuesday to Sunday from 10:30 am to 5 pm.

Little Italy Sights

The old **Police Headquarters** at 240 Centre St is an example of how public

---

The Stanford White Legacy

If you walk north out of Chinatown, take note of the old **Bowery Savings Bank** building at 130 Bowery. The bank's Romanesque archway and vaulted gold-leaf interior are a quiet respite from the noisy fruit stands and traffic on the corner of Bowery and Grand St. It was designed in 1894 by Stanford White, the most talented and colorful architect of the Gilded Age. His firm, McKim, Mead and White, created many of New York City's Beaux Arts masterpieces, including the original Pennsylvania Station, built in 1911. Widely considered to be White's greatest creation, Penn Station was demolished in 1965 for a newer facility, over the protests of many prominent public figures, including modernist architect Philip Johnson.

Once the elegant old train palace had been replaced by the ugly, inadequate and badly designed Penn Station/Madison Square Garden complex that now stands in Midtown Manhattan, public outcry forced the creation of the City's Landmarks Preservation Commission. Thanks to the laws protecting landmarks and increased public awareness of the city's architectural treasures, other works by White – including the Player's Club on Gramercy Park, the Washington Square Arch and the Brooklyn Museum – will remain untouched by the wrecker's ball.

White himself met an ignominious end. A roué and spendthrift art collector, he was nearly bankrupt by 1905. He engaged in a wild affair with the young married socialite Evelyn Nesbit, and they often met for trysts in his apartment located above an earlier version of Madison Square Garden. It was there on the roof garden restaurant that White was shot and killed by Nesbit's jealous husband Harry K Thaw. Subsequent revelations about the May-December romance during Thaw's trial permanently damaged White's reputation and led a jury to declare Thaw not guilty by reason of insanity. ■

officials in New York often approved the construction of European-style monuments without providing proper setback space or park land to allow passers-by to fully appreciate their grandeur. This building overwhelms its neighbors, just as it did upon its completion in 1909. It was converted into apartments in 1988.

The **Old St Patrick's Cathedral** at 263 Mulberry St appears bland and unimpressive because of a fire that destroyed much of its exterior. But the structure served as the city's first Roman Catholic Cathedral from 1809 to 1878, when its more famous successor was built uptown on Fifth Ave and 50th St. The old cathedral and its damaged Georgian interior can be viewed only during weekend services Saturday at 5 pm and Sunday at 9:30 am and 12:30 pm.

KIM GRANT

Puck Building

As you continue up Mulberry to Houston St, you will approach the back of the stunning red-brick **Puck Building**, the home of the turn-of-the-century American humor magazine. The building, with its two gold-leaf statues of the portly Puck, is a popular spot for wedding receptions and film shoots.

LOWER EAST SIDE
subway: F to Delancey St; B, D, Q to Grand St

Architecturally, this old tenement area still retains its hardscrabble character, with block after block of crumbling buildings. You can still see why early 20th century residents, about half a million Jews from Eastern Europe who worked in factories in the area, lamented that 'the sun was embarrassed to shine' on their benighted neighborhood.

Like Little Italy, the Lower East Side has lost most of its traditional ethnic flavor. There is no Jewish community left here, though many of the businesses remain. The people living behind the crumbling doorways of the contemporary Lower East Side are more likely to be young people living in their first city apartment or long-term residents holding onto the good deal on a rent controlled apartment. Also, a growing Latino community has spilled over the Lower East Side's northern border from Alphabet City, and the Chinese have been moving into the area south of Delancey St.

In recent years, more than a dozen no-name bars and late-night lounges have opened in the four-block area on and around Ludlow St, which runs south from Houston St. On Saturday nights, the streets are packed with grunge rockers, dance club addicts and underage drinkers. As the East Village, just above this area north of Houston St, continues its swift gentrification, the Lower East Side seems on track to become the city's quintessential outlaw neighborhood. And the opening of the Red Square building on E Houston St, with its $1300 per bedroom rents, statue of Lenin and huge clock, seemed a harbinger of the neighborhood's eventual transformation into a desirable place to live.

Orchard St

The 'Orchard St Bargain District' is the market area defined by Orchard, Ludlow and Essex Sts above Delancey St, which runs east to west. This is where Eastern European merchants used to set up pushcarts to sell their wares when the Lower East Side was still a largely Jewish neighborhood.

KIM GRANT

Today the 320 shops in this modern-day bazaar sell sporting goods, leather belts, hats and a wide array of off-name 'designer fashions.' While the businesses are not exclusively owned by Orthodox Jews, they still close early on Friday afternoon and remain shuttered Saturday in observance of the Sabbath. There's an unspoken rule that shop owners should offer a discount to their first customer of the day – usually 10% – for good luck, so it helps to arrive at 10 am if you're serious about buying something. Offering to pay in cash may also attract a discount. If you hate haggling, pick up a set of discount coupons and a store directory at the Orchard St Bargain District offices (☎ (212) 995-8258), 261 Broome St.

There's not much for sale in the Lower East Side that you couldn't pick up elsewhere in the city, with the exception of kosher food products, such as the wines at Schapiro's (☎ (212) 674-4404), 126 Rivington St, which offers a short tour of its facilities on Sunday. You can pick up unleavened bread at **Streit's Matzoh Company**, 150 Rivington St, potato knishes at **Yonah Shimmel Bakery**, 137 E Houston St, caviar at **Russ & Daughters**, 179 E Houston (check out the great neon sign) and sweet and sour pickles directly out of wooden barrels at **Essex Pickles**, 25 Essex St.

There are several young designers setting up eponymous stores in the Lower East Side, including Amy Downs (☎ (212) 598-4189), a maker of funky women's hats, at 103 Stanton St.

A free tour of the district leaves each Sunday at 11 am from Katz's Deli on the corner of Ludlow and Houston Sts. Call the Orchard St Bargain District offices (see above) to confirm the tour time.

Lower East Side Tenement Museum

The neighborhood's heartbreaking heritage is preserved at this museum. The gallery (☎ (212) 431-0233), 90 Orchard St, is open Tuesday through Sunday from 11 am to 5 pm, and offers a video on the difficult life endured by the people who once lived in the surrounding buildings, which often did not have running water or electricity.

Across the street, the museum has recreated a turn-of-the-century tenement owned by Lucas Glockner, a German-born tailor. This building, in which an estimated 10,000 people lived over 72 years, is accessible only by guided tour. The tours leave Tuesday through Friday at 1, 2 and 3 pm and every 45 minutes on the weekend from 11 am to 4:45 pm. Tickets to the museum, which include the tenement tour, are $7/6 for adults/children. From April to October the museum also sponsors a walking tour of the neighborhood. Call ahead for more information.

Synagogues

Nearby the tenement museum, near the corner of Rivington and Orchard Sts, is the **First Roumanian-American Congregation** (☎ (212) 673-2835), 89 Rivington St, one of the few remaining Orthodox synagogues in the Lower East Side (of the 400 that used to thrive in the neighborhood in the early 20th century). The building, currently under renovation, features a wonderfully ornate wooden sanctuary that can hold 1800 of the faithful, but now membership in the *shul* has dwindled to under 50 people.

The landmark **Eldridge St Synagogue** (☎ (212) 219-0888), at 12 Eldridge St between Canal and Division Sts east of the Bowery, is another struggling place of worship in an area that is now completely part of Chinatown. The Moorish synagogue stands across the street from what is one of the oldest surviving blocks of tenements in New York City. These old and dirty buildings are now occupied by recent Chinese immigrants, who patronize the employment agencies in the ground floor offices of those tenements. The synagogue has a museum and offers tours on the hour from 11 am to 4 pm Sunday, Tuesday, Wednesday and Thursday. Admission is $4/2.50.

SOHO

subway: B, D, F, Q to Broadway-Lafayette

This neighborhood is not named after its London counterpart but is a geographic conceit for the rectangular area south of Houston St extending as far down as Canal St. No one really knows for sure why Houston St is pronounced HOW-ston; though it is assumed that a man named William Houstoun who lived in the area pronounced his surname in that manner. (Somewhere along the line the second 'u' in the spelling of the street was dropped.)

SoHo is a paradigm of inadvertent modern urban renewal. The district is filled with block after block of cast-iron industrial buildings that date to the period just after the Civil War, when the area was the city's leading commercial district. These multi-story buildings housed linen, ribbon and clothing factories, and there were often showcase galleries located on the street level. But the area fell into disfavor as retail businesses relocated uptown and manufacturing concerns moved out of the city. By the 1950s the huge lofts and cheap rents attracted artists and other members of the avant-garde. Their political lobbying not only saved the neighborhood from destruction, but assured that a 26-block area was declared a legally protected historic district in 1973. Today, SoHo is the city's leading area for art galleries, clothing stores and boutiques selling oh-so-precious curios. Unadorned lofts sell for more than $300,000 and rental rates are simply impossible.

It's preferable to visit SoHo on a weekday morning, when the neighborhood is populated largely by the people who work in the galleries and assorted offices. True to the 'downtown' clichés, these office workers are dressed invariably in sleek black outfits and wear some of the most adventurous eye wear you'll see in the city. On Saturday and Sunday, West Broadway (a separate street from Broadway) becomes jam-packed with tourists and street artists selling homemade jewelry and paintings in defiance of the laws requiring a city license to sell such wares. A few vendors have been arrested for this, and a democracy wall protesting the police crackdown *was* located on Prince St near the corner of Mercer St. It's now an outlet of the catalogue retailer J Crew – that tells you everything you need to know about the current direction of SoHo.

SoHo Walking Tour

You can begin your exploration of SoHo by taking the subway to the Broadway-Lafayette St station and walking south down Broadway.

On the very first block you will encounter four fine art museums described in detail further on: the Alternative Museum, the African Museum, the New Museum of Contemporary Art and the Guggenheim/SoHo. Just past Prince St on the right, you will pass the **Singer Building**, at 561-563

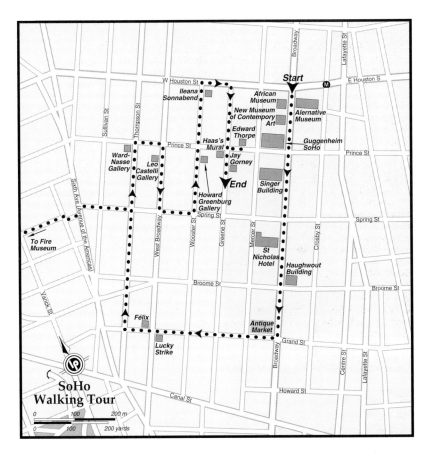

SoHo Walking Tour

Broadway, a very attractive iron and brick structure that was the main warehouse for the famous sewing machine company. At 521-523 Broadway, above the fabric store and gourmet food shop, you can view what's left of the marble-faced **St Nicholas Hotel**, the 1000-room luxury hotel that was *the* place to stay when it opened in 1854. The hotel, which closed by 1880, was the headquarters of Abraham Lincoln's War Department during the Civil War.

As you walk through SoHo, stop to look up at the buildings you're passing – many still have elaborate decorated flourishes that have been obscured or destroyed on the street level. A perfect example is the **Haughwout Building**, which houses the Staples office supply store at 488 Broadway. This was once the headquarters of the EV Haughwout crockery company. Built in 1857, it was the first building to use the exotic steam 'elevator' developed by Elisha Otis.

One block further south, at Grand St, you will encounter a parking lot that is the site of an **antique market** on Sunday. Turning right and walking west four blocks will bring you to West Broadway; near this

KIM GRANT
Haughwout Building

KIM GRANT
Richard Haas' apartment front mural

corner you will find a half dozen late night restaurants, including *Lucky Strike* and *Félix*, that have reputations for attitude rather than quality – though their bars are worth stepping into for a drink.

Continue west another block or two to SoHo's western edge and walk up Thompson St or Sullivan St and you'll reach the nicest spot in SoHo, particularly as you approach Houston St, where there are a few less pretentious boutiques and laid back restaurants. It's the best place for a quiet stroll before heading into the heart of SoHo's gallery district. Along the way you can detour over to the **Fire Museum**, at 278 Spring St, just west of Varick St.

At the corner of Thompson and Prince Sts, the **Ward-Nasse Gallery** (☎ (212) 925-6951), 178 Prince, specializes in yet-to-be-discovered artists. Turn right on Prince and turn right again on West Broadway. A few doors down on the right side of the street, at No 420, is a gallery owned by art titan **Leo Castelli** (☎ (212) 431-5160), who represents many contemporary greats. (Castelli owns galleries at two other SoHo locations as well.) Continuing down West Broadway, turn left on Spring St and after one block head up Wooster St. A number of influential galleries are on Wooster St, including the **Howard Greenberg Gallery** (☎ (212) 334-0010), No 120, which specializes in photography, and **Ileana Sonnabend** (☎ (212) 674-0766), No 149-155.

Take Wooster all the way up to Houston and turn right. Make another right on Greene St and head back down to Prince St. On the southeast corner of this intersection you will see a local landmark: artist Richard Haas' now fading mural of an apartment front painted on the bare brick wall of 112 Prince St. Important galleries near here include **Edward Thorpe** (☎ (212) 431-6880), 103 Prince St (half a block to the left), and **Jay Gorney** (☎ (212) 966-4480), 100 Greene St (half a block down).

KIM GRANT
(right) Try to ignore *this* public display.

Alternative Museum

The Alternative Museum (☎ (212) 966-4444), 594 Broadway, is more of a pay-to-view gallery of new art rather than a full-fledged museum. It's located on the 4th floor of a building that houses several other art galleries. There's a suggested admission charge of $3. The museum is open Tuesday through Saturday from 11 am to 6 pm.

Museum for African Art

This facility (☎ (212) 966-1313), 593 Broadway, is the city's only space dedicated solely to the works of African artists, and there's a heavy concentration on tribal crafts, musical instruments and depictions of spirituality. The interior was designed by Maya Lin, the young architect who first found fame for her stark and stunning Vietnam Veterans Memorial in Washington, DC.

The African Museum charges a $4/2 admission for adults/students and is open Tuesday to Friday from 10:30 am to 5:30 pm, and Saturday and Sunday from noon until 6 pm.

New Museum of Contemporary Art

This museum (☎ (212) 219-1222), 583 Broadway, is at the vanguard of the contemporary SoHo scene and offers exposure to art works that are less than 10 years old. That's probably why one of the museum's recent exhibits was called 'Temporarily Possessed: Works from the Semi-Permanent Collection.' Signage artist Jenny Holzer and sculptor Jeff Koons have had their work exhibited in this museum.

The museum is closed Monday and Tuesday. It is open Sunday and Wednesday through Friday from noon to 6 pm and Saturday from noon to 8 pm. Admission is $4 for adults, $3 for artists, students and seniors, and entry is free on Saturday evenings from 6 to 8 pm.

Guggenheim/SoHo

The Solomon R Guggenheim Museum's decision in 1992 to open a downtown branch (☎ (212) 423-3500), 575 Broadway,

was part of its extensive renovation and expansion that tripled its showcase space. The SoHo branch also lent legitimacy to the neighborhood's claim to being the center of the US arts scene. In addition to featuring works by living artists in mid-career such as sculptor Dan Flavin, the museum's two floors house overflow from the Guggenheim's permanent collection. The hustler-designer Kenny Scharf has set up the **Scharf Shack** to sell autographed T-shirts and other bric-a-brac from a kiosk in the shadow of the Guggenheim/SoHo.

The Guggenheim/SoHo is open Wednesday to Friday and Sunday from 11 am to 6 pm and Saturday from 11 am to 8 pm. Admission for adults/students is $5/3 (under 12 get in free). If you plan on visiting both branches of the Guggenheim, it's a wise idea to buy a ticket good for admission to both during a seven-day period, which costs $10/6 for students and seniors.

Fire Museum

The New York City Fire Museum (☎ (212) 691-1303), 278 Spring St, occupies a grand old firehouse dating back to 1904. It has a well-maintained collection of gleaming gold horse-drawn fire fighting carriages along with modern-day fire engines. The development of the New York City fire fighting system, which began with the 'bucket brigades,' is also explained along the way. All the colorful heavy equipment and the museum's particularly friendly staff make this a great place to bring children, even though they are not allowed to hop on any of the engines.

The museum is open Tuesday to Saturday from 10 am to 4 pm; suggested admission is $6 for adults, $4 for seniors and students, and $1 for children.

TRIBECA

subway: 1, 9 to Franklin St

This neighborhood of old warehouses, loft apartments and funky restaurants derives its name from its geographical location: the 'TRIangle BElow CAnal' St, an area roughly bordered by Broadway to the east and Chambers St to the south. Though not

Filming on the Streets

Don't be surprised if you chance upon a film crew shooting in New York during your visit. The city seems to be the setting for just about one out of three Hollywood films. The local government accommodates and encourages filmmaking by closing off streets, entire neighborhoods and even bridges. According to the latest figures from the Mayor's Office of Film, Theater and Broadcasting (1996), there were 21,286 production days on city streets, of which 4147 days were used for the making of 201 major feature films. In all, the city makes some $200 million in taxes from TV and film shoots.

At the time of writing, the following films were being shot in New York: *Men in Black* with Will Smith and Tommy Lee Jones (on King St in SoHo), *Conspiracy Theory* with Mel Gibson and Julia Roberts (on Roosevelt Island), a modern-day update of *Great Expectations* with Uma Thurman and Ethan Hawke (at Astor Place and Tribeca), and *Addicted to Love* with Matthew Broderick and Meg Ryan (on Cortlandt Alley near Chinatown).

TV series shot entirely in New York include *Law & Order*, *Spin City* with Michael J Fox and the studio-bound *Cosby* show.

If you see a film crew, here's a tip on how to find out what's being shot. Film crew members in charge of crowd control are the lowest on the production totem pole and often lie or walk away when you ask about who stars in the picture. (They don't want bystanders hanging around for the shot.) Instead, walk over to any vehicle connected to the production and look on the dashboard for a parking permit from the Office of Film, Theater and Broadcasting. The permit lists the name of the production, the director and studio, the action of the scene being shot and sometimes even the major stars. But don't be too disappointed if it's simply a TV commercial! ■

as touristy or architecturally significant as SoHo, its well-known northern neighbor, Tribeca nonetheless has its attractions, including a fair share of the 'scene' restaurants and bars, along with actor Robert De Niro's Tribeca Films production company.

The warehouses – most of which still retain long truck loading platforms covered by metal awnings – make great apartment spaces. As such the neighborhood is not yet overrun with boutiques and chain stores, which have driven some art galleries and plenty of well-heeled residents out of SoHo. Tribeca is home to more than a handful of famous people, including actor Harvey Keitel and magazine publisher-professional hunk John F Kennedy Jr.

In winter, it's not unusual to spot a star hanging out at a local restaurant or bar, though on summer weekends the place reverts back to its old character as a windswept industrial district as this same crowd flees the city for resort areas on Long Island and Cape Cod. Late afternoon summer light can be stunning in this neighborhood, and the desolation chic makes the area a favorite for fashion photographers. Make a special effort to walk the five blocks of Greenwich St just below Canal St. Here, there are many dry-goods warehouses that until a few years ago were mostly derelict. Almost right before your eyes, these huge spaces are being converted into luxury apartments. Within five years, this spot will be unrecognizable.

Harrison St

The eight townhouses on the block of Harrison St immediately west of Greenwich St were all built between 1804 and 1828 and constitute the largest collection of Federal-style buildings left in the city. But they were not always neighbors: six of them once stood two blocks away on a stretch of Washington St that no longer exists. In the early 1970s, that area was the site of Washington Market, a wholesale center that was the fruit and vegetable equivalent of the Fulton Fish Market. A new home had to be

KIM GRANT

Fire station in Greenwich Village

found for the row houses when the market was relocated uptown to allow the development of the waterfront, which now includes Manhattan Community College and the unattractive concrete apartment complex that now looms over the townhouses. Only the buildings at 31 and 33 Harrison St remain where they were originally constructed.

Clocktower Gallery

This free art space and studios (☎ (212) 233-1096), little-known to most visitors, is nestled inside the ornate old headquarters of the New York Life Insurance Company, and can be accessed by the entrance around the corner at 108 Leonard St. (The building is now the headquarters of the New York City Probation Department and the Public Health and Hospitals Corporation.) To get to the gallery, take the elevator to the 12th floor (which is as far as it goes) and walk up the clearly marked staircase to the tower.

The Clocktower's anonymity is probably attributable to the fact that it's only open on Monday and Friday from 10 am to 6 pm and Wednesday from 1 to about 6 pm. Artists sponsored by the Institute for Contemporary Art, which funds the gallery, are awarded space on the premises, and their works in progress are often on view.

If you're planning to be in the neighborhood when the gallery is closed and the weather is clear, take the elevator up to the tower anyway. You can look down Broadway, and walking to the right of the entrance to the gallery brings you to the northern face of the building, where there's an nice uptown panorama through dirty windows.

GREENWICH VILLAGE
subway: 1, 9 to Christopher St;
A, B, C, E, F, Q to W 4th St

This neighborhood is one of the city's most popular, and a symbol throughout the world for all things outlandish and bohemian. Generally defined by a northern border of 14th St and a southern demarcation of Houston St, Greenwich Village runs from Lafayette St all the way west to the Hudson River. The area just south of Washington Square Park (including Bleecker St running west all the way to Seventh Ave), is a lively and somewhat overcrowded collection of cafes, shops and restaurants. Beyond Seventh Ave is the West Village, a pleasant neighborhood of crooked streets and townhouses that is loaded with buildings of architectural or historic importance – look for bronze landmark plaques explaining their significance.

Greenwich Village began as a trading port for Indians, who liked the easy access to the shores of what is now Hoboken, New Jersey, just across the Hudson River. Dutch settlers established a number of tobacco plantations, and the peaceful wooded area was named Greenwich Village by their English successors. As the city began to develop a large servant class, Greenwich Village became New York's most prominent black neighborhood until many of those residents moved to Harlem just before the 1920s in search of better housing.

Its reputation as a creative enclave can be traced back to at least the early 1900s, when artists and writers moved in, and by the '40s the neighborhood was known as a gathering place for gays. The West Village today is a very mixed neighborhood – some of the bars and bookshops cater to gays and lesbians (the desired clientele can be gleaned by the names of the businesses, such as 'Rubyfruit' and 'Henrietta Hudson's'), but there are plenty of straight-friendly cafes and restaurants. The northern part of the West Village is occupied by the meat packing district, still active and fetid on weekday mornings – and, at night and on weekends, the site of several of the city's roughest gay bars.

The central Village is dominated by New York University, which owns most of the property around Washington Square Park, and the brownstone buildings abandoned by blacks all those years ago are now some of the most fashionable and valuable properties in the city.

KIM GRANT

Village denizens

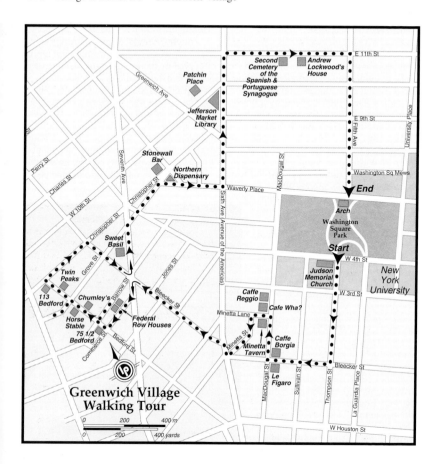

Greenwich Village
Walking Tour

| 0 | 200 | 400 m |
| 0 | 200 | 400 yards |

Greenwich Village Walking Tour

The best place to start a tour of the Village is the arch at **Washington Square Park**. Head south through the park to the **Judson Memorial Church**, which graces the park's south border. This yellow-brick Baptist church honors Adoniram Judson, an American missionary who served in Burma in the early 19th century. Designed by Stanford White, this national historic site features stained-glass windows by muralist John La Farge, who was born near the park, and a marble frontage by Augustus Saint-Gaudens.

Walk down Thompson St, past a series of chess shops where Village denizens meet to play the game for $1.50 an hour. At the intersection of Thompson and Bleecker Sts (Bleecker being the main east-west thoroughfare in Greenwich Village), look up at the southwest corner and you will see the old sign for the legendary jazz club the **Village Gate**, which recently relocated to Midtown. (The old Gate spot is now the site of a nightclub called Life.) Turn right on Bleecker St and head west for two blocks, which will bring you to two old coffeehouses associated with New York's '50s beatnik culture: **Le Figaro**, which still has a weekend jazz brunch, and **Caffe Borgia**. You're better off just taking a look around Bleecker St and then taking a right on MacDougal St where you'll find a great cup of cappuccino at **Caffe Reggio**, at No 119, which still retains some old-world character, thanks to its dark walls and massive trademark espresso machine. Double back half a block to **Minetta Tavern**, an old Village hangout that's a good Italian restaurant. It's a great place to stop for a beer or glass of wine while admiring old photos of '50s era celebrities that used to hang out there. On the opposite corner is **Cafe Wha?**, a legendary old club where Jimi Hendrix once played. (Its 'in' days are long past.) Going down Minetta Lane and making a left onto Minetta St takes you past a block of old 18th century slums that have been preserved and improved into desirable row houses. The old Minetta Brook still runs under some of the houses.

DAVID ELLIS

Crossing Sixth Ave and walking up Bleecker St brings you past a three-block stretch of record stores, leather shops, restaurants and great Italian pastry shops. Cross Seventh Ave and walk half a block down it before heading down quiet Commerce St and then turning right on Bedford St. You are already standing just a few yards from 75½ Bedford St, a quirky 9½-foot wide house that poet Edna St Vincent Millay lived in from 1923-24 that has recently been restored. (Cary Grant, John Barrymore and Margaret Mead also lived here at different times.) Right next door, at No 77, stands what is possibly the oldest house in the Village, a red-brick residence that was built in 1799.

Continuing up Bedford just beyond the corner of Barrow St brings you to a spare wooden door at No 86 – this is **Chumley's Bar**, a former speakeasy run by Lee Chumley, a socialist who welcomed many writers to his place in the late '20s. The bar's address is said to have inspired the slang phrase '86 it' – a shorthand imperative to get rid of something, which may have been whispered to warn Chumley's patrons to

drain their beverages as prohibition-era police raids were about to begin.

You might want to detour for a moment up Barrow St to check out the ivy-covered **Federal row houses** at Nos 49 and 51, and then have a look at the block of six perfectly preserved handsome red-brick

---

Greenwich Village's Rock Landmarks

In addition to checking out Cafe Wha? on the corner of MacDougal St and Minetta Lane, rock and roll fans will want to take note of 161 W 4th St, where Bob Dylan once lived and was inspired to write 'Positively 4th St.' He often performed (and reputedly smoked his first joint) at Gerdes Folk City, which originally stood at 11 W 4th St. Folk City moved to 130 W 3rd St in 1969, and closed in 1986. The site is now occupied by a bar called Kettle of Fish, but the old Folk City neon sign remains half-lit above the building.

Jimi Hendrix lived and recorded at the **Electric Lady Studios** just a few steps east of Sixth Ave at 55 W 8th St (check for the Hendrix photo in a 2nd-floor window), which was later used by the Rolling Stones during the session for the album *Tattoo You*. That's why Mick Jagger begins the song 'Dance Pt II' talking about standing on the corner of 8th St and Sixth Ave . . . . ■

KIM GRANT

Jefferson Market Courthouse

residences on the west side of the street before continuing up Bedford.

There's a wonderful old horse stable from 1894 at 95 Bedford St. Before continuing up Bedford, take a look at **Grove St** – a curved stretch of row houses that has been featured in several movies, including *Annie Hall*. Back on Bedford, note the early 19th century home called **Twin Peaks** at No 102, which got its name from the dual mock-Tudor tops that were added to it in the 1920s, and the 1843 Greek Revival residence at No 113 Bedford, which was built and occupied by a local saloon keeper. (Other buildings in this neighborhood have detailed plaques on them noting who built them.) Bedford ends at raucous Christopher St, the spiritual center of gay life in the Village – turn right and then head back down Bleecker St to Seventh Ave.

Going uptown on Seventh Ave, note the famous jazz club **Sweet Basil** on the left, and head north two blocks to Grove St, where a right turn will lead to **Stonewall Place**, site of the 1969 gay rebellion (see the sidebar Gay & Lesbian New York in this chapter). The **Stonewall Bar** (not the actual site of the incident) is on the north side of Christopher Park on Christopher St.

Heading east (right) on Waverly Place brings you to the oddly shaped **Northern Dispensary** at 165 Waverly Place. It was built in 1831 to combat a cholera epidemic that was then sweeping through this neighborhood and was New York's oldest public health facility until 1989, when it was shut down by city human rights officials after the dental clinic there refused to treat patients with the HIV virus. The three-sided Dispensary marks New York's strangest intersection: the corner of Waverly Place and Waverly Place!

Continue to Sixth Ave and turn left. Up two blocks is the red-brick **Jefferson Market Library**, and the **Jefferson Market Gardens**, which are sometimes open to the public on weekends. Just behind the building on W 10th St is **Patchin Place**, an enclosed courtyard block of flats that was home to both journalist John Reed and poet e.e. cummings.

Double back to Sixth Ave and head up a block to W 11th St and head east. On the right you'll find the tiny **Second Cemetery of the Spanish and Portuguese Synagogue**, which was used from 1805 to 1829. Continue along W 11th St and you'll pass by a series of traditional row houses, including builder **Andrew Lockwood's House** at No 60, which was built in 1842 on a lot that was originally part of the larger Wouter Van Twiller Farm dating to the Dutch colonial era.

Turn right when you reach Fifth Ave and you'll be heading directly back toward the arch in Washington Square Park. These last few apartment blocks on and around Fifth Ave are filled with the offices of psychologists and the area is thought to have the greatest concentration of shrinks in the entire world. Before you reach the end of Fifth Ave, wander up **Washington Square Mews**, a quiet, cobblestone street of stables that now house NYU offices.

Washington Square Park

Washington Square Park is purported to be, per inch, the most crowded recreational space in the world. A visitor from China or India might raise an eyebrow over that boast, but a stroll through the busy park on the weekend lends some credence to the claim.

The park, like many public spaces in the city, began as a 'potter's field' – a burial ground for the penniless. Its status as a cemetery protected it from development. It was also the site of public executions, including the hanging of several petty criminals to honor French statesman Marquis de Lafayette's visit to New York in 1824. The magnificent old tree near the northwestern corner of the park has a plaque stating it was the 'Hangman's Elm,' though no one is quite sure if it was actually used for executions.

Pay particular attention to the **arch**, originally designed in wood by Stanford White to celebrate the centennial of George Washington's inauguration in 1889. The arch proved so popular that it was replaced in stone six years later, and adorned with statues of the general in war and peace (the latter work is by A Stirling Calder, the father of mobile artist Alexander Calder). In 1916, artist Marcel Duchamp and a few of his friends climbed to the top of the arch by its internal stairway and declared the park the 'Free and Independent Republic of Washington Square.' These days the anarchy takes place on the ground level, as comedians and buskers use the park's almost permanently dry fountain as a performance space. The fountain was once used as terminus and turnaround for the Fifth Ave buses that ran under the arch. You'll probably notice that the park is also the site of the most

KIM GRANT

brazenly open drug dealing in the city, as hustlers conduct a brisk marijuana trade with the whispered come-on 'smoke, smoke?'

One block east of the park, at 245 Greene St, is the building where the Triangle Shirtwaist Fire took place on March 25, 1911. (A plaque declares it the 'site' of the fire, but it is the actual building.) This sweatshop had locked its doors to prevent the young seamstresses who toiled there from taking unauthorized breaks. The inferno killed 146 young women; many died jumping from the upper floors because the fire department's ladders did not extend to the top floors of the 10-story building. Every year, the New York Fire Department holds a solemn ceremony on the date in memory of the city's most deadly factory fire.

The row of townhouses at Washington Square North was the inspiration for *Washington Square*, Henry James's novel of late 19th century social morés, though James did not live here as is popularly assumed.

Forbes Galleries

The Forbes Galleries (☎ (212) 206-5549), at 60-62 Fifth Ave, house curios from the personal collection of the late publishing magnate Malcolm Forbes. This is an eclectic mix of Fabergé eggs, ship models, autographs, tin soldiers and Art Deco wood panels. Walking through here, you get the sense that the wily Forbes may have opened these galleries to the public as a way of giving his impulse purchases a tax-deductible status.

The Forbes Galleries are open free to the public Tuesday to Saturday from 10 am to 4 pm.

EAST VILLAGE

subway: 6 to Astor Place; F to Second Ave

This area of funky shops, bars and cafes, bordered by E 14th St to the north and E Houston St to the south, and stretching from Lafayette St to the East River, doesn't have much in common historically with Greenwich Village. The area was a series of rich and large farmland estates that were only overtaken by urban development in the late 19th century as New York became more industrial and moved northward from Lower Manhattan. By the early 20th century, this region was considered the northern section of the Lower East Side, a poorer cousin to Greenwich Village. But it has come into its own during the '90s, as the old tenements have been taken over by artists and restaurateurs in search of cheap rents.

The Ukrainian and Polish community that was established here more than 100 years ago is still very much in evidence, and senior citizens from this population hang out in **Tompkins Square Park** alongside punks, junkies, anarchists, drug dealers and dog-walking yuppies. (Jazzman Charlie Parker's house is located on the park's east border.) In recent years the East Village has

seen tensions sparked by the gentrification that has pushed poorer residents further east toward the river into Alphabet City, which is marked by Aves A, B, C and D. The police have clashed with protesters in the park and squatters in abandoned tenements.

The best way to explore the East Village is by simply walking up or down First Ave or Second Ave between 14th and Houston Sts. On this 15-minute walk you can see the neighborhood in rapid transition – the four- to six-story buildings that line both sides of First Ave house a succession of laundries, bars, coffee shops, Eastern European meat stores, pharmacies and restaurants offering a virtual world tour of cuisines – there are places serving Italian, Polish, Indian, Lebanese, Japanese and Thai fare. The same array of gastronomic choices can be found along Second Ave, though the bars and cafes are a bit more upscale.

A look at E 7th St gives you a sense of the ethnic and sociological crossroads that is the East Village. There's an herb shop, a used bookstore and Roman Catholic church on this single block. And directly across the street from St Stanislus Church is an S&M shop called Body Worship. At last glance, its window featured a leather-clad dummy with an impressive erection pointed in the direction of the bust of Pope John Paul II.

Boutiques selling antiques, furniture and clothing both new and used are springing up all over the East Village, but a good number of them can be found clustered on E 9th St just after Second Ave. There are also a number of herbal medicine stores nearby, in keeping with the naturalistic character of the neighborhood. You'll probably see a lot of young Japanese at the bars and clubs along here – coming to the East Village, getting their hair colored and dressing 'punk' has become something of a rite of passage for Japanese expats, who number at least 6000 here. Also, check out the police station on 5th St west of First Ave, which serves as the exterior for the police headquarters in the TV series *NYPD Blue*. The show regularly makes the neighborhood out to be far more chaotic and dangerous than it is in reality.

Tompkins Square Park is somewhat of an unofficial border between the gentrified part of the East Village (to the west) and the more dangerous **Alphabet City** (to the east). City officials have tried to polish up Alphabet City's reputation by dubbing the district 'Loisaida,' a derivative of the Spanish phrase for 'Lower East Side,' and a Carnaval takes place here every Memorial Day weekend. Hispanic culture is certainly in strong evidence throughout the neighborhood, and wall murals and paintings on store gates along Ave B have a distinctly Latino character, as do the 'botanicas' selling spirit votive candles and other items of faith. But the hard fact remains that Alphabet City is one of the city's most open drug dealing areas, mainly because some of the most cutting-edge (and sometimes illegal) dance clubs are located there. Ninth St between Ave A and First Ave is the site of heavy drug dealing, which can also be found the further east you travel.

Astor Place

This square is named after the Astor family, who built an early New York fortune on beaver trading and real estate and lived on **Colonnade Row** just south of the square at 429-434 Lafayette St. Four of the original nine marble-faced Greek Revival residences still exist, but they are entombed beneath a layer of black soot. Across the street, in the public library built by John Jacob Astor, stands the **Joseph Papp Public Theater**, one of the city's most important cultural centers and home to the New York Shakespeare Festival.

Astor Place itself is dominated by the large brownstone **Cooper Union**, the public college founded by glue millionaire Peter Cooper in 1859. Just after its completion, Abraham Lincoln gave his 'Right Makes Might' speech condemning slavery in the Union's Great Hall. The fringed lectern he used still exists, but the auditorium is only open to the public for special events.

Walking two blocks north and turning west on E 10th St brings you to **Grace Church** designed by James Renwick. This Gothic Revival Episcopal church was made of marble quarried by prisoners at Sing Sing, the state penitentiary in the upstate town of Ossining. After years of neglect, Grace Church has recently been restored, and its floodlit white marble make for a strangely elegant nighttime sight in this neighborhood of dance clubs, record stores and pizza parlors. The same architect is thought to have created **Renwick Triangle**, a movie-set-perfect group of brownstone Italianate houses one block to the east at 112-128 E 10th St.

Another significant church to note is **St Mark's-in-the-Bowery** at Second Ave and E 10th St, also an Episcopal place of worship that stands on the site of the farm, or *bouwerie*, owned by Dutch Governor Peter Stuyvesant, whose crypt is under the grounds. The church, damaged by fire in 1978, has been restored with abstract stained-glass windows and is open from 10 am to 6 pm Monday to Friday.

In this neighborhood, E 8th St is called **St Mark's Place**, once a nexus for the artistic fringe. Now the block beyond Astor Place contains a community center where local punks and junkies hang out alongside stalls selling books, illegal concert tapes, and T-shirts. East of Second Ave on St Mark's there are a half-dozen late-night cafes and bars.

Old Merchant's House

Not much remains of the neighborhood that existed here before the tenement boom, but this museum (☎ (212) 777-1089) in the 1831 house of drug importer Seabury Tredwell at 29 E 4th St is a remarkably well preserved example of how the business class lived. Occupied by Tredwell's youngest daughter Gertrude until her death in 1933, its original furnishings were still intact when it began life as a museum three years later.

The forlorn and abandoned building just past the empty lot was also owned by the Tredwell family, but not much has been done with it.

The Old Merchant's House is open Sunday to Thursday from 1 to 4 pm. Admission for adults/children is $4/2.

Gay & Lesbian New York

San Francisco's reputation notwithstanding, New York City has long been the true center of gay culture in the USA. At least two neighborhoods – Chelsea and Greenwich Village – are identified in popular consciousness with gay life. Gay and lesbian visitors will feel extremely comfortable there and practically anywhere else in the city.

At the beginning of the 20th century, gays and lesbians were widely known to meet in hidden clubs around the Bowery. Later, gay men gathered in the theater district, while lesbians attended drag clubs in Harlem. After WWII, Greenwich Village, once the city's largest black neighborhood, became the city's prime gay enclave, though quiet clubs and bars could be found uptown.

Throughout the '50s, the police regularly arrested gays and lesbians on morals charges, leading to the establishment of the Mattachine Society, the country's largest gay political organization. At one time, it was illegal for women to dress in men's clothing, and lesbians in drag were often arrested and transported to the Women's House of Detention on Sixth Ave and 8th St, now the site of the Jefferson Market public library. Gay men would gather in so-called 'tea houses' in Times Square, and cruise each other on the Midtown avenues, into the late '60s.

The signal moment of the modern gay rights movement occurred in New York on June 27, 1969. That night, the police launched a raid on the Stonewall Inn, a Christopher St men's bar. Its patrons were mourning the death of self-destructive singer Judy Garland, an icon for the gay community, and many angrily resisted the bust. Three nights of riots followed. The Stonewall Rebellion and other protests led to the introduction in 1971 of the first bill designed to ban discrimination on the basis of sexual orientation. The controversial measure was finally passed by the city council in 1986, and seven years later gay couples won important legal protections when New York allowed the registration of 'domestic partnerships.' Mayor David Dinkins also declared the area where the original bar once stood as 'Stonewall Place' and unveiled statues of two gay couples in Sheridan Square by artist George Segal.

Today the gay character of Greenwich Village has even become something of a visitor attraction. Even local gay residents complain that the area around Hudson and Christopher Sts is being ruined by day-tripping partygoers and tourists intent on getting a glimpse of gay life. That helps explain why Chelsea is now the hottest gay neighborhood in the city, with clubs, cafes, gyms and restaurants that cater to the community clustered around Eighth Ave between 14th and 23rd Sts. The leading zone for lesbian clubs and restaurants are the 10 blocks of Hudson St north of Houston St. There's also a thriving gay club scene in the East Village, along with a host of gay bars scattered uptown. See the sidebars Gay Accommodations in Places to Stay and Gay Entertainment in the Entertainment chapter. ■

10th St Baths

The waning of Eastern European traditions on the Lower East Side led to the closure of many old bath houses in Manhattan, and the AIDS crisis prevented their continuation as gay gathering places. But these historic old steam baths (☎ (212) 674-9250), 268 E 10th St, still remain. Here you can get a Russian-style oak-leaf massage followed by a plunge in an ice-cold bath, provided your heart can stand the strain. There's also a small cafe on the premises.

The baths' two owners had a serious falling out some time ago, and the reception desk hands out business cards indicating the week each man is in control of the facility so that loyalists for each can patronize at the appropriate time.

The 10th St Baths are open seven days a week from 9 am to 10 pm. Both sexes are admitted on Monday, Tuesday, Friday and Saturday. Thursday and Sunday are for men only, and women have exclusive entry on Wednesday. General admission is $19, with massage rates starting at $42.

CHELSEA

subway: 1, 9, A, C, E to 23rd St

In addition to being home to much of New York's gay and straight nightlife from Seventh Ave to the West Side piers, Chelsea is also the site of many 'districts' – areas where generally one type of business activity predominates. Roughly bordered by 14th St to the south running all the way up to 23rd St, west of Broadway, this neighborhood was the dry goods and retail area for the Gilded Age, and many of the emporia built to attract well-heeled shoppers are now office buildings. Closer to the Hudson River on Eighth and Ninth Aves, Chelsea is dominated by housing projects and warehouses. It's here that you'll find some of the city's most popular nightclubs, such as the Tunnel.

The prime site on noisy 23rd St is the **Chelsea Hotel**, the red-brick residential hotel with ornate iron balconies that is dominated at street level by no fewer than seven plaques declaring it a literary landmark. Even before Sid Vicious murdered his girlfriend there, the hotel was notorious for being a literary hangout for the likes of Mark Twain, Thomas Wolfe, Dylan Thomas and Arthur Miller. Jack Kerouac is famous for typing *On the Road* on a single roll of teletype paper during one marathon session at the Chelsea.

The Chelsea Piers Complex, on the Hudson River at the end of 23rd St, is a recent addition to the neighborhood. It is a large urban sports complex that caters to sporting types of all stripes – you can set out to hit a bucket of golf balls at the four-level driving range, then ice skate in the complex's indoor skating rink. You can even rent in-line skates to cruise along the Hudson River waterfront down to the Battery. Though the Piers Complex is somewhat cut off from the heart of Chelsea by busy West St, its wide array of attractions brings in the crowds. The Chelsea Studios are also here, where the TV series *Law & Order* and *Spin City* are shot. See Activities later in this chapter for more details.

Union Square

This garden square on the convergence of 14th St and Broadway was one of New York City's first uptown business districts, and throughout the mid-19th century it was the site of many worker rallies and political protests (the source of its name). By the 1960s, this was something of a depressed part of town, and the park in Union Square was one of the city's 'needle parks,' a hangout for junkies. It's been revived in recent years, and is home to the city's best-known open-air produce market, the Greenmarket, which operates Wednesday, Friday and Saturday mornings year round.

The area north of Union Square running to Madison Square, at 23rd St, was once known as **Ladies' Mile**. In the late 19th century commercial establishments such as B Altman's and Lord & Taylor catered to women shoppers. Variances in modern-day zoning laws have led to a return of large-scale retailing to Sixth Ave between 14th and 23rd Sts.

The late 19th century building that once housed the **Hugh O'Neill** dry goods store at 655 Sixth Ave is one of the few cast-iron palaces that have yet to be taken over by a big store. But it has been cleaned up and its flood-lit Corinthian columns look quite dramatic at night. This is the building that

KIM GRANT

Sheridan Square

The Gallery Scene

In early 1996, art dealer Mary Boone shocked the New York City cultural elite by announcing that she was moving her gallery from SoHo to a new space at 745 Fifth Ave. Boone, a pioneer in mixing art and commerce in the '80s who launched the careers of Julian Schnabel, David Salle and Jean-Michel Basquiat, claimed that the 'energy and focus of art has shifted uptown.' But skeptics believed that Boone's move was prompted by a class-driven distaste for the coffee houses and shops that have opened in SoHo, which attract crowds interested in looking at – but certainly not buying – overpriced contemporary art.

Chelsea is also becoming an art mecca, with galleries such as Paula Cooper (☎ (212) 255-1105) at 534 W 21st St. It's also the location of the cutting edge Dia Center for the Arts (☎ (212) 989-5512), at 548 W 22nd St, and Metro Pictures (☎ (212) 206-7100), 519 W 24th St. The most upscale galleries can be found on Madison Ave above 59th St.

But SoHo is still the best place to go if you're looking for galleries. Art titan Leo Castelli represents many contemporary greats at three SoHo locations, including 420 West Broadway (☎ (212) 431-5160). A number of influential galleries are on Wooster St, including the Howard Greenberg Gallery (☎ (212) 334-0010), No 120, which specializes in photography, and Ileana Sonnabend (☎ (212) 674-0766), No 149-155. Other important galleries near here include Edward Thorpe (☎ (212) 431-6880), 103 Prince St, and Jay Gorney (☎ (212) 966-4480), 100 Greene St. The Ward-Nasse Gallery (☎ (212) 925-6951), 178 Prince, specializes in yet-to-be-discovered artists.

You can find out what's on display by picking up the free monthly *NY/SOHO* listings map, available in downtown galleries, which also covers galleries in Tribeca and Chelsea. Or scan the Goings on about Town section in the *New Yorker* and the entertainment section of the Sunday *New York Times*. ■

was 'blown up' in the opening moments of the Bruce Willis thriller *Die Hard With a Vengeance*.

Theodore Roosevelt's Birthplace

This national historic site (☎ (212) 260-1616), at 28 E 20th St, is a bit of a cheat, since the house where the 26th President was born was demolished in his lifetime. His relatives recreated the house and joined it with another family residence next door. If you are interested in Roosevelt's extraordinary life, which has been somewhat overshadowed by time and the enduring legacy of his younger cousin Franklin, plan to visit here, especially if you don't have the time to see his summer home in Long Island's Oyster Bay.

The museum is open Wednesday through Sunday 9 am to 5 pm, with house tours on the hour to 4 pm; admission is $2/1.

Flatiron District

This neighborhood is named after the Flatiron Building that sits at the intersection of Broadway, Fifth Ave and 23rd St. Built in 1902, the Flatiron Building is famously featured in a haunting 1905 color-tinted photograph by Edward Steichen, and dominated this plaza when the neighborhood was the city's prime stretch of retail and entertainment establishments. The Flatiron was also renowned for being the world's tallest building until 1909, when it was overtaken by the nearby **Metropolitan Life Tower** at 24th St and Madison Ave, which has an impressive clock tower and golden top. For 10 blocks north along Broadway, the Flatiron District, loaded with loft buildings and boutiques, does a good imitation of SoHo without the European pretensions and crowds.

Just above the Flatiron Building is **Madison Square Park**, which defined the northern reaches of Manhattan until the city's population exploded just after the Civil War. It contains several statues of war heroes along with one dedicated to the man who may be the most obscure US president: former New York Governor Chester Allen Arthur, who became chief executive upon the assassination of James Garfield in 1881. On the site of the New York Life Building, at 51 Madison Ave, once stood the original Madison Square Garden, scene of various important public events and entertainment – sporting events, concerts and political conventions – from 1879 to the late 1920s.

Antiques

The Annex Flea Market (☎ (212) 243-5343) takes place every Saturday and Sunday from 10 am to 5 pm on Sixth Ave and 26th St, offering a generally high-quality selection of pocket watches, used cameras and one-of-a-kind items like gumball machines at its outdoor stalls. This market charges a $1 admission, but you can hover on the fence to see if there's anything you like before paying to get in. The popularity of the market has spurred the creation of other markets in empty parking lots nearby that charge no admission. The **Chelsea Antiques Building** (☎ (212) 929-0909), 110 W 25th St, has indoor stalls of first edition books, furniture and other items.

This same neighborhood is home to the **flower district**, a collection of florists who also offer large green houseplants to apartment dwellers from street stalls on weekends.

GRAMERCY PARK
subway: 6 to 23rd St

Gramercy Park is one of New York's loveliest spaces, the kind of garden area commonly found dotted throughout Paris and other French cities. Unfortunately, when the neighborhood was designed on the site of a marsh in 1830, admission to the park was restricted to residents. The tradition still holds, and mere mortals must peer through iron gates at the foliage.

Two other exclusive institutions are located here, worth noting for their architecture. The **National Arts Club** (☎ (212) 475-3424), 15 Gramercy Park South, was designed by Calvert Vaux, one of the men behind the creation of Central Park, and holds exhibitions sometimes open to the public. The club has a beautiful vaulted stained-glass ceiling above its wooden bar.

The **Players Club**, 16 Gramercy Park, is an actors' hangout built by the prominent Shakespearean actor Edwin Booth (brother of Lincoln assassin John Wilkes Booth) and designed by Stanford White that opened on the stroke of midnight on New Year's Eve in 1888. The club features many paintings of famous actors, and a few actually done by famous thespians, including John Barrymore's watercolors of a production of Hamlet.

Fortunately, you can get inside **Pete's Tavern** (☎ (212) 473-7676), 124 E 18th St, the place patronized by the short story writer O Henry, who is said to have written his Christmas story *The Gift of the Magi* in a front booth. The author probably didn't eat the free popcorn at Pete's, but it tastes as if it was made in his day. You can get a decent burger and beer here or find the same fare by walking a block away to the equally popular **Old Town Bar and Grill** (☎ (212) 529-6732), 45 E 18th St, a wood paneled 1892 pub.

MIDTOWN

You'll wind up spending a great deal of time in New York's teeming Midtown area, since it's where many of the city's most popular attractions are located. Very few people live in the center of Manhattan, and most apartment houses are found east of Third Ave and west of Eighth Ave. Midtown isn't the most dangerous part of town, but as in any similar district in cities around the world, you should be particularly savvy about moving about there, since you'll meet up with some of the city's most aggressive panhandlers and skilled pickpockets.

Midtown is the transportation hub of New York City. Five subway stations along the width of 42nd St are served by nearly 20 lines that connect Midtown directly to every part of the city.

Herald Square

This crowded convergence of Broadway and Sixth Ave at 34th St is the location for **Macy's**, which for years has inaccurately claimed to be the world's largest department store. The busy square doesn't offer much in the way of cultural landmarks, with two indoor malls south of Macy's on Sixth Ave that offer a boring array of shops, and a new HMV record store across the street.

Far more interesting is **Little Korea**, the small enclave of Korean-owned shops on 31st to 36th Sts between Broadway and Fifth Ave. Over the past few years this little neighborhood (particularly 32nd St) has seen an explosion of restaurants serving Korean fare. The best of the lot, *Soot Bull House* at 32 W 32nd St, is open 24 hours year round except Sundays and serves up delicious and filling barbecue dishes you cook yourself over white-hot charcoal.

The **Garment District**, where most of New York's fashion firms have their design offices, is to the west of Herald Square on Seventh Ave from 34th St to Times Square. During workdays the side streets are packed with delivery trucks picking up racks of name clothing. Broad-

KIM GRANT

View from the 102nd floor

way between 23rd St and Herald Square is called the **Accessories District** because of the many ribbon and button shops located there that serve the fashion industry. There are a number of stores on 36th and 37th Sts immediately west of Seventh Ave that sell so-called designer clothing at wholesale prices.

Empire State Building

New York's original skyline symbol (☎ (212) 736-3100), Fifth Ave and 34th St, is a limestone classic built in just 410 days during the depths of the Depression at a cost of $41 million. Located on the site of the original Waldorf-Astoria Hotel, the 102-story, 1454-foot Empire State Building opened in 1931 and was immediately the most exclusive business address in the city. The famous antenna was originally to be a mooring mast for zeppelins, but the Hindenberg disaster put a stop to that plan. One airship accidentally met up with the building: a B25 crashed into the 79th floor on a foggy day in July 1945, killing 14 people.

Since 1976, the building's top 30 floors have been floodlit in seasonal and holiday colors (eg, green for St Patrick's Day, red and green for Christmas, pink for Gay Pride weekend in June). This tradition has been copied by many other skyscrapers, including those with ornate golden tops around Union Square, lending elegance to the night sky.

Looking down on the city from the 102nd floor means standing in line for an elevator on the concourse level and sometimes being confronted with another line at the top. Getting there very early or very late helps you avoid this. Don't bother with the other exhibits on the concourse, which thrive purely on proximity to the ticket office.

The Empire State Building's observatories on the 86th and 102nd floors are open from 9:30 am to midnight daily, with the last tickets sold at 11:25 pm. Admission for adults/children is $4.50/2.25.

Pierpont Morgan Library

The Pierpont Morgan Library (☎ (212) 685-0008), 29 E 36th St off Madison Ave, is part of the 45-room mansion owned by steel magnate JP Morgan. This formerly private collection features cold temperatures (the better for the Morgan's manuscripts, tapestries and books), a study filled with Italian renaissance art works, a marble rotunda and a three-tiered East Room main library. Morgan spared little expense in his pursuit of ancient works of knowledge or art: there are no fewer than three Gutenberg Bibles here.

KIM GRANT

The Morgan Library has long had a stuffy reputation and its curator is trying to liven things up with a year-round program of lectures and concerts in the Garden Court. This lovely glass-enclosed space also contains an expensive cafe and bookstore. The Morgan is open Tuesday to Friday from 10:30 am to 5 pm, Saturday from 1:30 to 6 pm and Sunday from noon to 5 pm. Admission is $5/3.

Grand Central Station

When the New York Central Rail Road built this prestige terminal, at Park Ave and E 42nd St, in 1913, the 'cut and cover' installation of tracks for its new electric trains leading to the north created the unusually wide expanse of Park Ave. Grand

Central is no longer a romantic place to begin a cross-country journey – today it serves as a terminus for the Metro North commuter trains to the northern suburbs and Connecticut. It is also home to a large community of street people who live in the track areas under Park Ave.

The station is well worth seeking out because of its huge Romanesque south facade, marred a bit by an ugly car ramp, as well as the huge main concourse and its vaulted ceiling constellation. The starlight zodiac has been restored, as have the lower levels of the terminal, which include the Oyster Bar, a famous seafood restaurant that's quite noisy thanks to the vaulted tile ceiling. A nice bar on a balcony on the western side overlooks the concourse and its central clock and passenger information center.

The Municipal Art Society conducts free walks through Grand Central Station every Wednesday at 12:30 pm. During the hour-long tour, you will cross a glass catwalk high above the concourse and learn that the ceiling constellation was mistakenly laid out in a 'god's eye view,' with the stars appearing as they would from above rather than below. Remember that Grand Central gets very busy during the evening rush from 4:30 to 7:30 pm.

Chrysler Building

Just across from Grand Central Station at Lexington Ave and 42nd St is the 1048-foot Chrysler Building, an Art Deco masterpiece designed by William Van Allen in 1930 that briefly reigned as the tallest structure in the world until superseded by the Empire State Building. The Chrysler, a celebration of the car culture, features gargoyles that resemble hood ornaments (barely visible from the ground) and a 200-foot steel spire that was constructed as one piece and placed at the top of the building as a distinctive crowning touch. Nestled at the top is the Cloud Club, a businessmen's spot that closed years ago, and a private apartment built for Walter Chrysler, head of the company.

You can walk through the lobby and admire the African marble anytime, but the building doesn't offer much in the way of interest for visitors – no top-floor restaurant or observation deck. Until one exists, the Chrysler will be known primarily as the landmark most often mistaken by tourists for the Empire State Building.

New York Public Library

The New York Public Library's Main Branch (☎ (212) 930-0800), at 42nd St and Fifth Ave, which recently celebrated its centennial, contains more than 11 million books in its permanent collection, and display galleries of precious manuscripts by just about every author of note in the English language. The library's massive 3rd-floor reading room can hold 500 people and still has its original Tiffany lamps, and the notable stone lions on Fifth Ave are adorned by Christmas wreaths each holiday season.

It's open Tuesday and Wednesday from 11 am to 7:30 pm, Monday, Thursday, Friday and Saturday from 10 am to 6 pm. **Bryant Park**, located just behind the library, was once overrun by drug dealers but has been impressively restored and is a pleasant place to sit if you can claim one of the park's marble benches or folding chairs. It's a popular midday sunbathing site and a free outdoor movie festival is held there on Monday nights during the summer months.

United Nations

The United Nations (☎ (212) 963-7713), which has its visitors' entrance at First Ave and 46th St, is technically located on international territory overlooking the East River. Tours of the facility show you its **General Assembly**, where the annual autumn convocation of member nations takes place, the **Security Council**, where crisis hearings are held year round, and the **Economic and Social Council** chamber. A park south of the complex includes Henry Moore's *Reclining Figure* and several other sculptures with a peace theme.

The UN was created in 1945 by an international conference in San Francisco, and met for two years in Flushing Meadows-Corona Park in Queens before the Rockefeller family donated $8.5 million for the purchase of the land. The complex itself, appropriately enough, was designed by a large international committee of architects.

For years there have been complaints about the UN's spendthrift ways, but they are not much in evidence in the headquarters. The buildings have a dated, late '50s feel to them, with a lot of Norwegian wood, and the carpeting is woefully worn.

For a heady few years following the end of the Cold War, the UN was believed to have entered a new era of effectiveness. But the organization's failure to stem tribal brutality in Rwanda and Somalia – along with its Peacekeeping Force's three-year humiliation in Bosnia – has bumped it back down to talking shop status. With the 1997 election of the popular Kofi Annan as Secretary General, it is thought that the member states might finally pay some of the $2 billion in back payments to the world organization, about half of which is owed by the US.

It's open seven days a week during March to December from 9:15 am to 4:45 pm and maintains the same hours Monday to Friday in January and February. English tours of the complex leave every 45 minutes, and are available on a limited basis in several other languages. Admission is $6.50 for adults, $4.50 for seniors and students. Children ages five to 17 are $3.50 and children under five are not admitted.

Sutton Place to Third Ave

Sutton Place encompasses several blocks of European-style luxury apartments that run parallel to First Ave from 54th to 59th Sts. The dead-end streets have pleasant benches that look out on the East River and served as the setting for Diane Keaton and Woody Allen's first date in *Manhattan*. Under the 59th St Bridge, you will see Sir Terence Conran's Bridgemarket, a collection of food stalls and restaurants in the arches of the 1909 span. Depending on when you visit New York, the Bridgemarket will either be under construction or just recently opened.

At one time, Third Ave was the site of an elevated train line that cast shadows on the old speakeasies and middle-class businesses. Thanks to the destruction of the 'el' and a subsequent building boom, Third Ave is now almost exclusively large office and apartment blocks. (One remnant from the early days is PJ Clarke's, an old bar from the 1890s at the corner of Third and 55th St.) Second Ave, however, has lagged behind in this development and still retains much of its old character – there are dozens of look-alike modern Irish bars and moderate restaurants.

Rockefeller Center

The 19 buildings of the 22-acre Rockefeller Center comprise the most coherent and best-known public complex in the US, though some might find the '30s-era 'progress of man' theme of the architecture a little overbearing.

More than 200 small-scale dwellings were cleared away beginning in 1931 for Rockefeller Center, which took nine years to complete (one original holdout still survives: the building that houses Hurley's Bar at 49th St and Sixth Ave). The 70,000 construction workers on the project were watched constantly by 'sidewalk supervisors' – passers-by who peered through holes cut into the fence around the site. When the laborers set up a small Christmas tree on the site, a tradition began that continues to this day: the annual lighting of the Rockefeller Center Christmas tree the week after Thanksgiving invariably attracts thousands of visitors to the area.

The completion of the center was tainted by a controversy over artwork. A mural painted by Mexican artist Diego Rivera in the lobby of the 70-story RCA (now GE) Building was rejected by the Rockefeller family because it featured the face of Lenin. The fresco was covered during the opening ceremony and was later destroyed. Its replacement by José Maria Sert, called *American Progress*, features the more acceptable figure of Abraham Lincoln.

In 1989, controlling interest in Rockefeller Center was purchased by a Japanese

KIM GRANT

Radio City Music Hall This 6000-seat Art Deco movie palace (☎ (212) 247-4777) had its interior declared a protected landmark. Even the smoking rooms and toilets are elegant. Concerts here sell out quickly and tickets to the annual Christmas pageant featuring the hokey-but-enjoyable Rockettes dancers now run up to $65. But you can see the interior by taking a tour of the Music Hall. Tours leave every half-hour from 10 am to 5 pm weekdays and 11 am to 5 pm Sunday. Admission for adults/children is $12.50/9.

NBC Studios The NBC television network has its headquarters in the 70-story GE building that looms over Rockefeller Center, and the *Today* show broadcasts from 7 to 9 am seven days a week from a glass-enclosed street-level studio near the fountain area (an ice skating rink during the winter months). Tours of the NBC studios leave from the lobby of the GE Building, Monday to Saturday from 9:30 am to 4:30. Admission is $8.25, and children under six are not permitted.

St Patrick's Cathedral
St Patrick's Cathedral (☎ (212) 753-2261), just across from Rockefeller Center on 50th St and Fifth Ave, is the main place of worship for the 2.2 million Roman Catholics in the New York diocese headed by the conservative John Cardinal O'Connor, a major player in New York City political life and favorite of Pope John Paul II. Though past retirement age, O'Connor has not been replaced by the Vatican. (The diocese of Brooklyn, a separate district, serves 1.7 million Catholics.)

The cathedral, built at a cost of nearly $2 million during the Civil War, originally didn't include the two front spires (added in 1888). The well-lit St Patrick's isn't as gloomy as its Old World counterparts, and the new TV monitors in restricted view seats are testimony to the church's determination to have its place in the modern world.

consortium, triggering off bitter lamentations in the press about the selling of American icons to foreigners, as if the buildings were in danger of being relocated to Tokyo. The Japanese holding company went broke when real estate values plummeted. But the center's money travails have not seemed to result in a lack of exterior maintenance. Take special note of the tile work above the Sixth Ave entrance to the GE building, the three flood-lit cameos along the side of Radio City Music Hall, and the back-lit gilt and stained-glass entrance to the East River Savings Bank building at 41 Rockefeller Plaza, immediately to the north of the skating rink/outdoor garden cafe in the heart of the complex.

Passing by the eight small shrines along the side of the cathedral brings you past the main altar to the quiet **Lady Chapel**, dedicated to the Virgin Mary. Looking toward the front, you can see the handsome stained-glass **Rose Window** above the 7000-pipe church organ. A basement crypt behind the altar contains all of O'Connor's predecessors.

Unfortunately, St Patrick's is not a place for restful contemplation during the day because of the constant buzz from visitors. It's also a regular site of protest by gays who feel excluded by the church hierarchy. The exclusion of Irish gays from the St Patrick's Day Parade since 1993 (an event not sponsored by the Catholic Church per se, but identified with Catholic traditionalists) has triggered protests near the cathedral every year in March.

It's open from 6 am to 9 pm daily. Masses are held frequently on the weekend, and the Cardinal presides over the service at 10:15 am Sunday.

Fifth Ave

Fifth Ave's reputation as a high-class area dates back to the early part of the 20th century, when its uptown portion was known as Millionaire's Row due to the series of mansions that extended all the way up to 130th St. Uptown addresses were then considered very desirable for their 'country' air and open spaces. Today Fifth Ave is a hodgepodge of retail stores and residences reflecting the city's various economic strains. At its start, Washington Square Park in Greenwich Village, there are a number of high rise apartment buildings that date back to the '30s, giving way to retail clothing stores and carpet wholesalers from 14th St to 42nd St.

KIM GRANT

St Patrick's Cathedral

KIM GRANT

Tiffany's on Fifth Ave

Manhattan Bus Tour

Details on guided bus tours are available in the Organized Tours section in Getting Around. But a good cheap alternative to these tours is to take a self-guided loop of Manhattan on city buses. It's absolutely vital to start this tour in the morning, because traffic can turn this two-hour journey into a frustrating three-hour crawl. If you take in any sights along the way, you have the option of returning downtown via the A or 1/9 subway lines along Broadway. Many of the sights mentioned here are given greater attention in the Chelsea, Midtown, Upper West Side and Washington Heights sections in this chapter.

Catch the M5 bus anywhere along Sixth Ave above Houston St going uptown. Be sure to board a 'Limited Stop' bus, which picks up at W 3rd St and Sixth Ave as well as major cross streets (14th St, 23rd St, etc), since you're taking the bus far uptown and don't want your journey to include a stop every three blocks or so. Buses do not take dollar bills, so use a token, a Metrocard or exact change of $1.50 and ask for a transfer just in case you want to visit the Cloisters by switching to the M4 bus.

The M5 starts its journey from Houston St and Sixth Ave and travels first through **Chelsea**, past Ladies' Mile, where fashionable women shopped for millinery and china in the late 19th century. Today the old ornate buildings between 14th and 23rd Sts are being taken over by modern superstores (Staples office products, Bed Bath & Beyond, Barnes & Noble books, etc). The bus continues past Herald Square and Macy's department store and, to the right, passes the western edge of Bryant Park located behind the main branch of the New York Public Library. You then travel by **Rockefeller Center** including the GE building at 50th St and Radio City Music Hall on your right.

Turning left at 59th St, the bus skirts the southern end of Central Park before turning uptown at **Columbus Circle**. This circle, with the statue of Christopher Columbus (built 1892) as its centerpiece, is the closest thing New York has to a grand traffic circle in the European tradition. Any chance of improving on the idea was destroyed by the construction in 1969 of the Gulf + Western Building, north of the circle between Central Park West and Broadway, a huge, badly designed black and white office tower that has been remade into a more muted brown glass luxury apartment building and hotel by developer Donald Trump.

On Broadway to your left emerges **Lincoln Center**, the white marble home of the Metropolitan Opera, New York Philharmonic and the Julliard School of Music, above 62nd St. Ten blocks later the bus turns left over to Riverside Drive, upper Manhattan's westernmost street, which is bordered on its east side by block after block of well-kept apartment buildings. As the bus turns north, you'll see a statue of Eleanor Roosevelt dedicated in 1996 by Hillary Rodham Clinton.

In Midtown, the street is the site of airline offices and a few high-end shops and hotels, including the garish **Plaza** at Grand Army Plaza overlooking the corner of Central Park South (59th St) and Fifth Ave. The huge institution really doesn't have much of a grand lobby, but it is worth a walk through just to say you've been there. The fountain in front of the hotel, which features a statue of the Roman goddess Diana, is a good spot for a rest and a bit of lunch – provided you're not downwind from the horse-drawn carriages that line Central Park South during the summer months.

Most of the heirs of the millionaires that owned estates on Fifth Ave either sold their mansions for demolition or converted them to the cultural institutions that make up Museum Mile (see Upper East Side). The **Villard Houses**, actually located on Madison Ave behind St Patrick's Cathedral, comprise one surviving example of these grand estates. The six four-story townhouses were built by financier Henry Villard in 1881; they were

Riverside Park looks downright elegant in beautiful weather, with its sloping hills and view of the cliffs of northern New Jersey. (In the '60s, Riverside Park was known as a wind-swept gathering place for drug users, but now the main problem with the park isn't crime but rather dog owners who let their pets run wild.) There are a number of monuments in the park, and from the bus at 89th St (on your left) note the grand campanile of the 1902 **Soldiers' and Sailors' Monument** honoring those who served in the Civil War. There's also a statue of Joan of Arc at 93rd St.

Just as the bus returns to Broadway at 120th St, you may be tempted to hop off the bus and explore. **Grant's Tomb** is just a few hundred yards above you at 122nd St and Riverside Drive. Just to the right of Grant's Tomb is the magnificent **Riverside Church** with its grand organ and bell tower observation deck.

After 125th St – the southern end of Harlem – the neighborhood abruptly shifts from middle class collegiate to working class Hispanic, with blocks of *bodegas*, variety stores and fruit stands, before you see **Audubon Terrace** on the west side of the street at 155th St. Two under-appreciated museums are located at the former home of naturalist John James Audubon: the **American Numismatic Society** and the **Hispanic Society of America**.

Provided you haven't hopped off the bus for any extended period of time, you can use your transfer on Broadway to take the M4 further uptown to **The Cloisters** (☎ (212) 923-3700). This spectacular museum contains parts of several medieval European monasteries and was opened in the 1930s to house the Metropolitan Museum of Art's collection of medieval art. Nearby, on Broadway at 204th St, is **Dyckman House**, built in 1783, the last Dutch farmhouse to survive in Manhattan and situated on what used to be a 28-acre farm.

If you took time out to see anything on the way up, you'll want to take the subway back, using the A or 1/9 subway, depending on your location. To continue sightseeing from the bus, take the M4 back, which returns south along Broadway, cutting across at Central Park North (110th St) and continuing down 5th Ave to Midtown. (This will mean a separate fare.) The bus will pass the **Museo del Barrio**, the **Museum of the City of New York**, the **Guggenheim Museum** and the **Metropolitan Museum of Art** (see the section on Museum Mile for further details).

The M4 then passes by both Rockefeller Center's eastern edge and St Patrick's Cathedral. By this time you are bound to be caught in traffic or just fed up with the bus, so hop off by the time it reaches the Empire State Building on 34th St and Fifth Ave. ■

eventually owned by the Catholic Church, and then sold to become part of the expensive 1000-room New York Palace hotel. The Urban Center Bookstore (☎ (212) 935-3592), the city's leading shop for architectural works, is located in the north wing of the Villard Houses.

Most of the more exclusive boutiques are uptown on Madison Ave, but Gianni Versace, Liz Claiborne and Tiffany's are all still on Fifth Ave above 50th St. On 57th St nearby, you can shop at Burberry's, Chanel, Hermès and Charivari, among several other designer spots. On Fifth Ave, stores worth exploring are Saks Fifth Ave, Henri Bendel, Bergdorf Goodman and Tiffany's. See the Shopping chapter for details on what to expect and shop for.

Museum of Modern Art

The Museum of Modern Art (☎ (212) 708-9480), 11 W 53rd St, known as 'Moma' (pronounced with a long o), distinguishes itself by its manageable, three-floor layout. Among the first-rate works in its sculpture and painting galleries are a number of works by Picasso, Van Gogh's *Starry Night* and Matisse's *Dance 1*. A quiet stand-alone gallery is dedicated solely to Monet's three-paneled *Water Lilies*, and the Abby Aldrich Rockefeller Sculpture Garden is the setting for a summer series of concerts during July and August. A few years back, saxophonist Sonny Rollins came to the garden to give his first solo concert in decades, playing against the noises of the traffic on Fifth Ave.

At least once a year, Moma puts on an important exhibit of a single major artist's work – recent retrospectives focused on the abstractionist Piet Mondrian, Picasso's portraiture and American painter Jasper Johns. In 1998, there will be a major retrospective on the work of Jackson Pollock. The museum recently bought the Dorset Hotel and two brownstones behind it on 54th St and is undergoing a major expansion to be completed within the next seven years.

The museum places a special emphasis on photography and film, two areas of visual expression that get short shrift at the larger Metropolitan Museum of Art. There are daily film screenings in Moma's two basement theaters, and an Oscar, awarded to the museum's film department in 1978, is on permanent display along with an impressive collection of film posters.

If you're pressed for time or simply undecided where to go, it's a good idea to rent the $4 audio tour of the museum narrated by chief curator Kirk Varnedoe, which comes in a cell phone that you can program to get more information about specific works of interest.

The museum is one of the few major cultural institutions in New York City that is open on Monday, and instead closes on Wednesday. Hours are Saturday to Tuesday from 11 am to 6 pm, Thursday and Friday from noon to 8:30 pm. Admission is $8 for adults, $5 for seniors and students;

children under 16 are free. The museum offers free admission to everyone on Thursday and Friday after 5:30 pm.

American Craft Museum

Directly across from Moma is the American Craft Museum (☎ (212) 956-3535), at 40 W 53rd St, a spectacularly well-designed and airy space for innovative and traditional examples of style. The museum is completing a 10-year survey of American craft making, and examples of works from the eight identifiable periods of artisanship are on display. There is also a collection of 77 items of traditional craft making from the White House on exhibit.

It's open Tuesday from 10 am to 8 pm and Wednesday to Sunday from 10 am to 5 pm. Admission is $5/2.50 for adults/seniors; children are free.

Museum of Television & Radio

This couch potato's paradise (☎ (212) 621-6800), at 25 W 52nd St, contains a collection of over 75,000 US TV and radio programs available with the click of a mouse from the museum's computer catalog. It's a great place to head when its raining or when you're simply fed up with walking. Nearly everybody checks out their favorite childhood TV programs on the museum's 90 consoles, but the radio listening room is an unexpected pleasure. It's nice to remember – or discover – just how funny those old radio comedies really were. There are also daily screenings, and the museum recently featured the television work of Elvis Presley.

It's open Tuesday to Sunday from noon to 6 pm, with additional hours to 8 pm on

Thursday. Admission is $6 for adults, $4 for students and seniors, $3 for children under 12.

Intrepid Air & Space Museum

The Intrepid Air & Space Museum (☎ (212) 245-2533), on the waterfront at W 46th St, is on an aircraft carrier that served in WWII and Vietnam. It's a triumph of shipbuilding as well as an advertisement for US military might. The museum's deck features fighter planes and the pier area contains the Growler guided-missile submarine, an Apollo space capsule and Vietnam-era tanks.

During the museum-sponsored Fleet Week in May, the piers nearby are occupied by visiting carriers that deposit thousands of sailors into town. The area takes on the character of the movie *On the Town* – perhaps with a touch of Federico Fellini – as these young sailors roam about the city's night spots in starched white uniforms.

The museum is open daily from 10 am to 5 pm from June to August and 10 am to 5 pm Wednesday to Sunday the rest of the year. Admission is $10 for adults, $7.50 for seniors, veterans, students and persons 12 to 17, and $5 for kids six to 11 years old.

TIMES SQUARE

subway: 1, 2, 3, 9, N, R to
42nd St-Times Square
Before TV, Times Square was the nation's largest space for glittery advertising directed at a mass audience. Dubbed the 'Great White Way' after its bright lights, it has long been celebrated as New York's crossroads. But Times Square fell into a deep decline in the 1960s, as once-proud movie palaces that previously showed first-run films turned into 'triple X' porn theaters, and the square became known as a hangout for every colorful, crazy or dangerous character in Midtown.

For years the city tried to change Times Square's gamy reputation, and it finally seems to be working, as companies have reinstalled colorful billboards above the street and built theme showcases, such as the Virgin Megastore and the neighboring Official All Star Cafe, smack in the middle of the square. The combination of color, zipping message boards and (at last count) four massive color TV screens makes for quite a sight these days, and each year some 24 million people visit the square. Several media companies – among them German publisher Bertlesmann, Reuters and the US magazine group Condé Nast – have built headquarters in and around Times Square.

Up to a million people gather here every New Year's Eve to see a brightly lit ball descend from the roof of One Times Square at midnight, an event that lasts just 90 seconds and leaves most of the revelers spending the first few hours of the new year wondering what to do with themselves.

Strolling around Times Square gives you a good look at the city's many architectural styles, from the former **McGraw Hill Building**, an Art Deco curiosity at 330 W 42nd St, the Greek Revival **Town Hall**, a concert venue and lecture space at 113 W 43rd St, and the more garish office blocks built in the last few years on Broadway itself, including the **Morgan Stanley** tower at No 1589, with its 24-hour stock market ticker, a more colorful variant on the 'zipper' news wire that runs along the bland white building at One Times Square.

Hell's Kitchen

For years, the far West Side of Midtown was a working-class district of tenements and food warehouses known as 'Hell's Kitchen,' a neighborhood for Italian and Irish immigrants often romanticized in Hollywood films. (In fact, *Hell's Kitchen* was the name of a 1939 movie starring Ronald Reagan and the Dead End Kids.)

By the 1960s, the neighborhood had a solid reputation as a no-go area populated by junkies and prostitutes on the stroll. Even now, used condoms on the side streets off Eleventh Ave are evidence of the streetwalkers who service the tunnel trade.

While the East Side on Lexington and Third Aves exploded with new office buildings, companies shied away from the West Side. The construction of the World Wide Plaza building at W 50th St and Eighth Ave in 1989 was supposed to make a big difference. (The complex took over the site of the 1930s-era Madison Square Garden, which had been a parking lot in the interregnum.) Throughout the '90s, Hell's Kitchen, and especially W 49th St, hardly changed. Eighth and Ninth Aves from 50th to 35th Sts are still dotted with wholesale food stores, and few buildings rise more than eight stories above the street.

Though World Wide Plaza attracted high profile companies like advertising agency Young & Rubicam and the Polygram record company, few others followed. W 49th St, directly south of the complex, was a study in contrasts. Facing the building's plaza was a block of tenements, and the men from the neighborhood's largely Puerto Rican population could often been seen playing dominoes on the stoop during summer evenings.

But World Wide Plaza eventually did change W 49th St. The tenements' facades were cleaned up, and new security systems were installed in many of the apartments, improvements financed largely by the young professionals who moved in at high rents.

A walk down W 49th St today will reveal that the old neighborhood bodega is still there, now joined by a pet shop called Spoiled Brats. At the Coffee Pot cafe on W 49th and Ninth, workers from the complex mingle with staffers from nearby St Clare's Hospital. A long-forgotten (and illegal) nightclub has been remade into a bustling restaurant. And there are signs for monthly meetings of the '49-50th St Neighborhood Coalition.'

Yes, W 49th St between Eight and Ninth Aves has certainly changed. It's the old story: money talks, though sometimes slowly, and in a whisper. ■

The block of 42nd St between Times Square and Eighth Ave was for a long time a haven for porn shops, but aggressive zoning changes and tax breaks for 'legitimate' businesses led to their closure. This block is changing rapidly, with the restoration by architect Hugh Hardy of the neighborhood's oldest venue, the 1899 **New Victory Theater**, into a center for children's productions. Disney is updating the **New Amsterdam**, built in 1904, as a permanent home for its theatrical versions of children's classics. Madame Tussaud's waxworks palace and actor Dan Aykroyd's House of Blues nightclub are also slated to move in within a year or two. (At the moment, the porn industry thrives on a small stretch of Eighth Ave from 42nd to 48th Sts – a desultory array of video shops, strip joints and book shops that seems doomed to be overrun within a few years as property values increase.)

A free two-hour **walking tour** of the changing neighborhood is offered by the Times Square Business Improvement District every Friday at noon. It leaves from the Times Square Visitor's Center (☎ (212) 869-5453) at the **Selwyn Theater** on the north side of W 42nd St between Broadway and Eighth Aves. The Selwyn shares its front with the **Grand Luncheonette**, a magnificent artifact of 1940s New York life, complete with lunch counter and hot dogs grilling in its window. It seems straight out of a time capsule. Make sure to see it soon – it may disappear with the street's rapid redevelopment.

CENTRAL PARK
subway: 1, 9, A, B, C, D, E to
59th St-Columbus Circle
This 843-acre rectangular park in the middle of Manhattan was designed to be an oasis from the urban bustle, but on weekends it's packed with joggers, skaters, musicians and tourists. Its quieter areas are found above 72nd St, where the crowds thin out and the well-planned landscaping becomes more apparent to the visitor. The park is currently in the midst of a restoration program that has led to the reseeding of many open spaces.

The park's reputation as a place to avoid at night dates at least as far back as the Depression, when unemployed men camped out in its confines. You won't want to go there for a midnight stroll, but the fact that the Park is actually one of the safest spots in the city is obscured by a crime against a jogger or tourist, which gets city-wide and often international attention. You can actually walk crosstown through the park at night when there's a concert, and there's a midnight five-kilometer run held every New Year's Eve. Even so, jogging alone through the Park's northern reaches in the middle of the afternoon is probably unwise because so few people are around at that time. The most prevalent (and usually unsolved) crime is rape of solo female joggers, so women should avoid solo jaunts.

In 1844, newspaper editor William Cullen Bryant, concerned that the city's north-bound expansion would eliminate all remaining woodland, called for the establishment of a public park. It took 14 years for officials to purchase the tract of marshland, and 16 more years for English-born architect Calvert Vaux and park project supervisor Frederick Law Olmsted to build it. (The two later collaborated on Brooklyn's Prospect Park.)

The park displaced several rural settlements for ethnic groups, including Seneca Village, a largely black enclave of 300 people, which was located west of the park above 80th St. The park you see today – which opened officially in 1873 – is a totally landscaped affair. Almost nothing is indigenous to the area, and more than four million trees and shrubs were brought to the area during construction.

Central Park Walking Tour
A good stroll through the park begins at the Columbus Circle entrance, through the **Merchants' Gate** and up to Sheep Meadow, a wide expanse of green favored by sunbathers and Frisbee players. Turning right, a pathway (called a transverse) runs along the south side of the meadow to the Carousel, and then the Dairy building, where the park's visitor center is located not far from the Wollman skating rink.

Just north of the Dairy, past the statue of Christopher Columbus, is **The Mall**, enclosed on both sides by a group of 150 American Elms. These trees, which have not suffered from the Dutch Elm disease that destroyed most of the country's elms, are believed to be the largest surviving stand in the country. At the end of The Mall is **Bethesda Fountain** a hippie hangout in the '60s that has been restored. Continue on the path to the left to the Bow Bridge. You can cross the bridge to the **Ramble**, a lush wooden expanse that was once a gay pickup area but is now a meeting place for dog owners of all sexual persuasions. It offers stunning scenery during the autumn months.

The Ramble gives way to **Belvedere Castle** and the **Delacorte Theater**, where the Public Theater holds two free Shakespeare productions each summer. Immediately beyond is the **Great Lawn**, a grouping of softball fields where the occasional free concert is held, along with annual open-air performances of the New York Philharmonic and Metropolitan Opera in June and July. The Great Lawn is undergoing a much needed, two-year reseeding, moving the concerts to **North Meadow** above 97th St.

Turning left and walking down the West Drive to 72nd St brings you to **Strawberry Fields**, the three-acre landscape dedicated to the memory of John Lennon that contains plants from more than 100 nations.

This spot was frequently visited by Lennon, who lived in the massive **Dakota** apartment building across the street, where he was shot on December 8, 1980.

Central Park Wildlife Center

This small zoo (☎ (212) 861-6030) was built in the 1930s and has been renovated for the comfort of the animals housed there, including three polar bears and several seals whose frequent feedings delight the children who visit. The zoo is open from April to October Monday to Friday from 10 am to 5 pm and Saturday and Sunday from 10:30 am to 5:30 pm. In the winter the zoo is open daily from 10 am to 4:30 pm. Admission is $2.50/1.25 seniors, children from ages three to 12 pay 50¢.

Park Activities

There are many activities in the park, and more information on what's happening is available at the visitor center in the Dairy (☎ (212) 794-6564) in mid-park along the 65th St transverse. It's open Tuesday to Sunday from 11 am to 4 pm.

KIM GRANT

Jackie O

The Central Park roadway that loops around the park for six miles is closed to traffic in the evenings and on weekends, and is a popular track for runners, in-line skaters and bikers, though the wicked S-shaped curve near E 106th St near the Lasker Pool should be avoided by beginner skaters. A soft, 1.6-mile cinder path encircles the **reservoir**, named in 1994 after Jacqueline Kennedy Onassis, who regularly used the track. The **New York Road Runners Club** (☎ (212) 860-4455) sponsors regular runs through the park and operates an information booth near the reservoir entrance at E 90th St.

Bikes are available for rent in good weather at the Loeb Boathouse on the East Drive near 74th St from 10 am to 5 pm daily; call ☎ (212) 861-4137) for information. A separate office (☎ (212) 517-2233) rents out rowboats. Ice skating is available in the winter at the Wollman Rink (☎ (212) 875-8410), mid-park at 62nd St. A far less crowded alternative is the Lasker Rink (☎ (212) 543-7639) uptown near E 106th St.

Kids can fish in the newly restored and stocked **Harlem Meer**, at 110th St and Fifth Ave, which includes the Dana Center (☎ (212) 860-1370), an environmental educational facility that's open Tuesday to Sunday from 11 am to 5 pm. The **Carousel** (☎ (212) 879-0244) has been popular with generations of children. It's in the east side of the park near 64th St and is open Monday to Friday from 10:30 am to 5 pm and Saturday and Sunday from 10:30 am to 6 pm. The **Alice in Wonderland** statue, on the east side of the park near the 76th St entrance, is the site of Saturday storytelling sessions. Call the visitor center for a schedule.

Without a doubt the most touristy thing to do in the park is to rent a **horse-drawn carriage** for a short spin along the smelly carriage paths. The carriages line up along Central Park South and cost $34 for 20 minutes and $15 for every additional 15-minute bloc. Drivers expect a tip on top of that charge.

UPPER WEST SIDE
subway: 1, 9 to 66th St, 116th St-Columbia; B, C to 81st St
The Upper West Side begins as Broadway emerges from Midtown at Columbus Circle. A number of middle to high end hotels can be found along Central Park South, and many celebrities live in the massive apartment buildings that line Central Park West all the way up to 96th St.

Lincoln Center
Lincoln Center (☎ (212) 875-5400) is a complex of seven large performance spaces built in the 1960s, replacing a group of tenements that were the real-life inspiration for the musical *West Side Story*. There's a clean, if architecturally uninspired look to Lincoln Center during the day, but at night the chandeliered interiors make a beautiful sight from across Columbus Ave. If you are at all interested in high culture, Lincoln Center is a must-see, since it contains the **Metropolitan Opera** adorned by two colorful lobby tapestries by Marc Chagall, the **New York State Theater**, home of the New York City Ballet, and the **New York City Opera**, the low-cost and more daring alternative to the Met. The New York Philharmonic holds its season in **Avery Fisher Hall**.

The Lincoln Center Theater group has its home at the 1000-seat **Vivian Beaumont Theater**, which also contains the smaller and more intimate Mitzi Newhouse Theater in the round. To the right of the theaters stands the **New York Public Library for the Performing Arts**, containing the city's largest collection of recorded sound, video and books on film and theater. The library always has an exhibition drawn from its permanent archive of dance, theater and recorded music materials. It's also a good place to while away some bad-weather hours listening to a hard-to-find old album while watching young theater people try to pick each other up.

The Julliard School of Music, attached to the complex by a walkway over W 65th St, contains **Alice Tully Hall**, home to the Chamber Music Society of Lincoln Center, and the **Walter Reade Theater**, the city's most comfortable film revival space and the major screening site of the New York Film Festival, held every September.

Each summer Lincoln Center holds Serious Fun and Out-of-Doors festivals, two separate series of free or low-cost dance, spoken-word and music performances at the Guggenheim Bandshell and other facilities. In the winter, the Big Apple Circus sets up a tent in Damrosch Park next to the Metropolitan Opera for two months of holiday performances, and trumpeter Wynton Marsalis organizes the Jazz at Lincoln Center Festival. In June of 1996, Lincoln Center inaugurated an ambitious biannual International Arts Festival.

Tours of the complex leave from the concourse level each day, and explore at least three of the theaters, though just which ones you see depends on production schedules. It's a good idea to call ahead for a space (☎ (212) 875-5350). Tours cost $8.23 for adults, $7 for students and seniors and $4.50 for children six to 17.

New-York Historical Society

As the antiquated, hyphenated name implies, the New-York Historical Society (☎ (212) 873-2400), 2 W 77th St, is the city's oldest museum, founded in 1804 to preserve artifacts of history and culture. It was also New York's only public art museum until the founding of the Metropolitan Museum of Art in the late 19th century, and in this capacity obtained John James Audubon's original watercolors for his *Birds of America* survey, which are on display in a 2nd-floor gallery.

The museum is somewhat overshadowed by its neighbor, the American Museum of Natural History, and has suffered severe financial problems in recent years. But it is well worth a visit, since viewing its quirky permanent collection is like traipsing through New York City's attic: there's even an army cot that George Washington actually slept in.

It's open Wednesday to Sunday from noon to 5 pm.

American Museum of Natural History

The American Museum of Natural History (☎ (212) 769-5100), with its entrance at Central Park West and 79th St, was founded in 1869 and now has over 30 million artifacts in its collection. It is no doubt most famous for its three large dinosaur halls, which reopened in June of 1995 after a significant renovation that includes the latest knowledge on how these behemoths behaved and theories on why they disappeared. Knowledgeable guides roam the dinosaur halls ready to answer questions, and there are 'please touch' displays that allow you to handle, among other items, the skullcap of a *pachycephulasaurus*, a plant-eating dinosaur that roamed the earth 65 million years ago.

Perhaps to remind people that there's more to the museum than the dinos, an audio tour is available ($5/3) that directs you to 50 'treasures of the permanent collection' among its four floors, including the scary-looking plaster blue whale that hangs from the ceiling above the Hall of Ocean Life. While some of the mammal halls still

have a gloomy, Victorian-era look to them, the museum is aggressively trying to update the entire facility.

In 1997 the museum closed the antiquated Hayden Planetarium (circa 1935) and will replace it with a bigger and better facility that will use the latest technology and include hands-on exhibits and an updated universe. It's scheduled to be open by 2000.

The museum's Naturemax center (☎ (212) 769-5650) will remain open and continue to show films about space exploration and animal life on its massive IMAX screen every hour on the half-hour for an additional charge.

The museum is open every day of the year except Thanksgiving and Christmas. Hours are Sunday to Thursday from 10 am to 5:45 pm and Friday and Saturday from 10 am to 8:45 pm. Admission is $7/5/4. A combination ticket for the museum and a Naturemax show is $10/7/6 for adults/seniors/children. For Naturemax alone the charge is $7/5/4.

If all the bones on display at the museum whet your desire to own some of your own, head to the nearby Maxilla & Mandible (☎ (212) 724-6173), 451-5 Columbus Ave, a strange emporium that sells various animal skeletons, preserved butterflies and even human skulls.

Children's Museum of Manhattan

The Children's Museum of Manhattan (☎ (212) 721-1223), 212 W 83rd St (subway: 1, 9 to 86th St), features discovery centers for toddlers and a postmodern Media Center for kids under 16. Technologically savvy kids can work in a TV studio and the museum also runs crafts workshops on weekends. There are two affiliated children's museums elsewhere in the city: the Brooklyn Children's Museum emphasizes art and design, while the Staten Island Children's Museum specializes in science and nature (see the Outer Boroughs section).

The Children's Museum of Manhattan is open Monday, Wednesday and Thursday from 1:30 to 5:30 pm and Friday, Saturday and Sunday from 10 am to 5 pm. Admission is $5 for adults, $2.50 for seniors, children under one are free.

Columbia University

Columbia University (☎ (212) 854-1754) and the affiliated Barnard College are on upper Broadway in a spot once far removed from the downtown bustle. Today, the city has definitely enveloped and moved beyond Columbia's gated campus. But the school's main courtyard, with its statue *Alma Mater* perched on the steps of the Low Library, is still a quiet place to enjoy the sun and read a book. **Hamilton Hall**, in the southeast corner of the main square, was the famous site of a student takeover in 1968, and since then is periodically a place for protests as well as pretty wild student parties. As you would expect, the surrounding neighborhood is filled with inexpensive restaurants and good bookstores like Papyrus Books at 2915 Broadway. **Tom's Diner**, at 2880 Broadway, is an ordinary lunch spot that got a lot of attention when Suzanne Vega sang a song about sipping coffee at its window – and the exterior appears nearly every week on TV as the hangout for the crowd on *Seinfeld*. There are many cafes, including the landmark **Hungarian Pastry Shop** (☎ (212) 866-4230), 1030 Amsterdam Ave, where you can eavesdrop on the crisis-driven student conversations while waiting for your espresso. The **West End Cafe** is no longer a breeding ground for intellectuals as it was in Allen Ginsberg's day, but you can still find inexpensive food and decent jazz there on weekend nights.

Cathedral of St John the Divine

The Cathedral of St John the Divine (☎ (212) 316-7540) dominates Amsterdam Ave just behind the Columbia University campus. It is the largest place of worship in the US, a massive and dark 601-foot long Episcopal cathedral that, upon completion, will be the third largest church in the world (after St Peter's Basilica in Rome and the newly built Our Lady at Yamoussoukro in the Ivory Coast).

But it's unlikely that St John's (subway: 1, 9 to Cathedral Parkway), which had its cornerstone laid in 1892, will be finished in your lifetime. Work has yet to begin on the stone tower on the northwest part of the church or the crossing tower above the pulpit. In 1978, the Episcopal Diocese of New York began training local young people in stone cutting, and their work can be seen in the courtyard to the south of the church behind the sundial during warm weather. Other features shown on the church's cutaway floor plan near the front entrance, such as a Greek amphitheater, are merely wistful visions of the distant future.

Still, the cathedral is a flourishing place of worship and community activity, the site of holiday concerts, lectures and memorial services for famous New Yorkers, and even has a 'High Wire Artist in Residence' in Philippe Petit, the man who walked between the World Trade Center towers in the early 1970s. The cathedral also has a Poet's Corner just to the left of the front entrance – though, unlike at Westminster Abbey, no one is actually buried there.

The cathedral is open from 7 am to 5 pm Monday to Saturday and on Sunday from 7 am to 8 pm . Sermons at its Sunday High Mass at 11 am have featured well-known intellectuals such as Prince Charles's late guru Sir Laurens van der Post. (There is also a 9:30 am mass in Spanish.)

General Grant National Memorial

Popularly known as Grant's Tomb (☎ (212) 666-1640), this landmark monument at Riverside Drive and W 122nd St (subway: 1, 9 to 116th St-Columbia) is where Civil War hero and president Ulysses S Grant and his wife Julia are buried. Completed in 1897 – 12 years after Grant's death – the granite structure cost $600,000 and is the largest mausoleum in the country. The building was a graffiti-marred mess for years until the general's relatives threatened to move his body somewhere else and shamed the National Parks Service into cleaning it up. Now this two-level monument (which also houses maps showing Grant's progress in battle during the war and contains busts of his fellow Union generals) features a clean and attractive plaza.

It's open Wednesday to Sunday from 9 am to 4:30 pm.

Riverside Church

Riverside Church (☎ (212) 222-5900), 490 Riverside Drive at 122nd St, is a gothic marvel overlooking the Hudson River built by the Rockefeller family in 1930. The observation deck, 355 feet above the ground, is open to the public during good weather, and its 74 carillon bells, the largest grouping in the world, are rung every Sunday at noon and 3 pm.

It's open daily from 9 am to 4 pm, with inter-denominational services on Sunday at 10:45 am.

HARLEM

subway: 2, 3, A, B, C, D to 125th St

New York's most identifiable African American neighborhood is going through a bit of an identity crisis. Tourist dollars are certainly flowing in thanks to the many Japanese and European travelers eager to learn about Harlem's significant history. But the many bus tours that move through its streets give off an unseemly vibe – much like an urban safari undertaken by people too fearful to move about on foot. Over the past decade, Harlem has also become home to a community of about 10,000 West Africans, who have brought their own distinct culture and cuisine into the neighborhood.

For the visitor, traveling to Harlem is not a cause for self congratulation, but an exercise in smart exploration. Certainly, the run-down buildings and racial tensions between some blacks and 'outsider' shop owners (mostly Asian and Jewish) are signs that all is not perfect, or even very well, in Harlem. But you needn't exercise any more caution there than in any other neighborhood. Perhaps even less: the troubles have led the city to post police cars on 125th St every other block or so. The city has also aggressively promoted

Harlem to developers, and the plan seems to be working: by late 1998, a new 'Harlem USA' entertainment and retail complex is scheduled to open just a few steps away from the Apollo Theater, complete with a 12-screen cinema, a rooftop skating rink and a Disney store.

The best time to visit Harlem is on a Sunday morning, when people head to services at the dozens of small churches in the neighborhood. Wednesday is also good, since you can end the day at the Apollo Theater watching its famous amateur night.

To Tour or Not to Tour

Harlem has become a very popular destination for foreign visitors who want to see the neighborhood but don't wish to walk its streets. As a consequence, bus companies have been doing big business on guided tours to the neighborhood. But it's worth checking the true cost of the service. One operator offers a $70 trip to Amateur Night at the Apollo, with dinner at an unspecified soul food restaurant. Taking the subway yourself ($3 roundtrip), picking up a ticket at the Apollo Box office (prices range from $7 to $20) and finding your own restaurant ($15 or less) represents a huge savings for those on a budget.

Harlem Spirituals (☎ (212) 757-0425) offers several three-hour trips to Harlem that leave from in front of the Ed Sullivan Theater at Broadway and 53rd St. Prices for adults/children start at $32/23 and run much higher for nighttime excursions. Both Harlem Spirituals and Musical Fest of Harlem (☎ (212) 222-6059) run Sunday morning tours of Gospel services in local churches, with prices starting at $55/45 including lunch. However, Big Onion Walking Tours (☎ (212) 439-1090) offers a very informative tour of historic Harlem for $9/7. Needless to say, Harlem residents give a better welcome to street-bound visitors than those who gawk at the neighborhood from the ersatz safety of a double-decker bus.

The bottom line: don't take a bus tour to Harlem, for reasons that have nothing to do with saving money. If you're too scared to go on your own, stay in Midtown. ■

As you explore Harlem, you should note that the major avenues have been renamed in honor of prominent African Americans, but that locals still call the streets by their original names, making getting around a little confusing. From west to east: Eighth Ave is Frederick Douglass Blvd, after the 19th century abolitionist writer. Seventh Ave is Adam Clayton Powell Jr Blvd, after the controversial preacher who served in Congress during the 1960s. Lenox Ave has been renamed for the Muslim activist Malcolm X. 125th St is also known as Martin Luther King Jr Blvd.

Getting There First-time visitors will probably be surprised to discover that Harlem is but one express stop away from the Columbus Circle-59th St station downtown. The trip on the A and D trains takes just five minutes, and they deposit you one block from the Apollo Theater and two blocks from Lenox Ave, where many soul food restaurants are located. The 2 and 3 trains from the West Side stop on Lenox Ave at 116th St, site of the Harlem open-air market, and at Lenox and 125th St.

Apollo Theater
The Apollo Theater (☎ (212) 749-5838) has been Harlem's leading space for political rallies and concerts since 1914. Virtually every major black artist of note in the '30s and '40s performed there, including Duke Ellington and Charlie Parker. After a brief desultory spell as a movie theater and several years of darkness, the Apollo was bought in 1983 by radio magnate Percy Sutton and revived as a live venue. It still holds its famous weekly amateur night – 'where stars are born and legends are made' – on Wednesdays at 7:30 pm. (Among those made legends were Billie Holliday and James Brown.) Watching the crowd call for the 'executioner' to yank hapless performers from the stage is

often the most entertaining part of amateur night. These days, German and Japanese tourists make up a big portion of the audience. On other nights the Apollo hosts performances by established R&B and hip hop artists. For other music venues in Harlem, see Harlem Jazz Clubs in the Entertainment chapter.

Studio Museum in Harlem
The Studio Museum in Harlem (☎ (212) 864-4500), at 144 W 125th St, has given exposure to the crafts and culture of African Americans for nearly 30 years, and provides working spaces to promising young artists. Its photography collection includes works by James VanDerZee, the master photographer who chronicled the Harlem Renaissance of the 1920s and '30s.

It's open Wednesday to Friday from

KIM GRANT

Where stars are born . . .

10 am to 5 pm and Saturday and Sunday from 1 to 5 pm. Admission is $5 for adults, $3 for seniors and students and $1 for children under 12.

Schomburg Center for Research in Black Culture

The nation's largest collection of documents, rare books and photographs is at the Schomburg Center for Research in Black Culture (☎ (212) 491-2200) at 515 Lenox Ave. Arthur Schomburg, a man born in Puerto Rico of a white father and black mother, started gathering works on black history during the early 20th century while becoming active in the movements for civil rights and Puerto Rican independence. His collection was bought by the Carnegie Foundation and eventually expanded and stored in this branch of the New York Public Library. The Schomburg Center has a theater where lectures and concerts are regularly held.

It's open Monday to Wednesday from noon to 8 pm and Friday and Saturday from 10 am to 6 pm. The center's gallery spaces are also open Sunday from 1 to 5 pm.

Striver's Row

While you're here, check out Striver's Row, also known as the St Nicholas Historic District. These row houses and apartments, many of which were designed by Stanford White's firm in the 1890s, were much prized (check out the alleyway signs advising visitors to 'walk their horses'). When whites moved out of the neighborhood, they were then occupied by Harlem's black elite, thus giving the area its colloquial name. This is one of the most visited blocks in Harlem – so try to be a bit discreet, since the locals (modern day Harlem elites) are a little sick of all the tourists. Streetside plaques explain more of the area's history.

Sunday Gospel Services

Some of the churches in Harlem have cut deals with bus operators, and their services are packed with visitors who attempt to take pictures during the services or even leave early. It's much better to go on your own to a place that welcomes visitors but not tour groups. Just show up respectfully well dressed – *sans* camera, and under no circumstances should you leave the service before it's over.

The **Abyssinian Baptist Church** (☎ (212) 862-7474), 132 W 138th St, was a downtown institution started by an Ethiopian businessman that moved north to Harlem in 1923, mirroring the migration of the city's black population. Its charismatic pastor, Calvin O Butts, is an important community activist whose support is sought by politicians of all parties. The church has a superb choir and holds services every Sunday at 9 am, 11 am and 3 pm.

The **Canaan Baptist Church** (☎ (212) 866-0301), 132 W 116th St, may be Harlem's friendliest church. It's a good idea to show up a bit early and introduce yourself to the parishioners before the Sunday 10:45 am service (10 am during the summer).

The **Bethelite Community Church** (☎ (212) 427-2839), at 36-28 W 123rd St, holds a service to heal the sick every Sunday at 6 pm.

Harlem Market

Vendors at the Harlem Market, at W 116th St and Lenox Ave, do a brisk business selling tribal masks, oils, traditional clothing and assorted African bric-a-brac. Most of the people at the market used to sell their wares from tables set up along 125th St, but were moved to the open-air site, amid great controversy, in 1995 after retailers complained about their presence. You can also get cheap clothing, leather goods, music cassettes and bootleg videos of films still in first-run theaters. The market is operated by the **Malcolm Shabazz Mosque**, the former pulpit of Muslim orator Malcolm X, which stands across the street.

The market is open daily from about 10 am to 5 pm and stays shut only in the coldest weather.

Spanish Harlem

Spanish Harlem is the name given to the area above E 96th St from Fifth Ave east to the River. Formerly an Italian neighborhood, it now contains one of the biggest Latino communities in the city. **La Marqueta**, a colorful, ad-hoc collection of produce, meat and fish stalls, is a signature attraction in 'El Barrio' on Park Ave above 110th St, underneath the elevated bridge for the trains to the northern suburbs. There you will find fruits, meat, oils and sacred candles for sale. (It's closed on Sunday.)

El Museo del Barrio This museum (☎ (212) 831-7272), 1230 Fifth Ave (subway: 6 to 103rd St), in an unprepossessing office block, began in 1969 as a celebration of Puerto Rican art and culture and has since expanded to include the folk art of Latin America and Spain. Its galleries now feature pre-Columbian artifacts and a collection of more than 300 *santos*, hand-carved wooden saints in the Spanish Catholic tradition. Temporary exhibits feature the work of local artists who live in East Harlem.

El Museo del Barrio is the best starting point for any exploration of Spanish Harlem. Every January 5, the museum holds a Three Kings Parade in which thousands of schoolchildren, along with camels, donkeys and sheep, make their way up Fifth Ave to 116th St, the heart of Spanish Harlem.

It's open Wednesday to Sunday from 11 am to 5 pm, with extended summer hours on Thursday to 7 pm. Admission is $4 for adults, $2 for seniors and students, free for children under 12.

Italian Landmarks Several landmark remnants of Italian East Harlem remain in business, though Italian resident moved out decades ago and return here only to eat. Check out *Morrone's Bakery* (☎ 212-722-2972), 324 E 116th St, for great peasant bread. *Rao's Restaurant* (☎ (212) 722-6709), 455 E 114th St, is an expensive restaurant with just 12 tables that's famous

for claiming to be booked months in advance (the rules are bent if you're Woody Allen or a local politician). If you want to go, show up early in the evening well dressed and polite. If you're in jeans, check out *Patsy's Pizzeria* (☎ (212) 534-9783) at 2287 First Ave (open from 10 am to 10 pm Monday through Saturday, from noon to 10 pm on Sunday).

WASHINGTON HEIGHTS

This neighborhood, located in northern Manhattan above Harlem, is named after the first US president, who set up a Continental Army fort here during the Revolutionary War. An isolated rural spot until the late 19th century, Washington Heights is today an unremarkable neighborhood of large apartment buildings. In the 1990s, the neighborhood has welcomed the arrival of thousands of new immigrants from the Dominican Republic.

There's a lot of drug activity in Washington Heights, and big business is done selling to downtowners and suburbanites who drive into the city on the George Washington Bridge. But there's no real need to fear a trip here – the area around the Cloisters, which includes **Fort Tryon Park**, is quite beautiful in warm weather and very safe. And those who fear the druggy reputation of Washington Heights will be happy to know that on Sunday the eight cultural institutions in the area offer an Uptown Treasures Tour, where free shuttle buses run between the museums from 11 am to 5 pm. Call any one of the following places to find out the schedule.

Audubon Terrace

Audubon Terrace, at Broadway between 153rd and 155th Sts (subway: 1, 9 to 157th St), is the former home of naturalist John James Audubon, and presently the site of three little-known museums. The **American Numismatic Society** (☎ (212) 234-3130) has a large permanent collection of coins, medals and paper money. It is open Tuesday to Saturday from 9 am to 4:30 pm and Sunday from 1 to 4 pm. Admission is free.

The **Hispanic Society of America** (☎ (212) 690-0743) has furniture and artifacts of Spanish and Portuguese culture, including significant artworks by El Greco. Few people make the journey up here – guards often outnumber visitors, and they'll have to go upstairs to turn on the lights so you can see the paintings. There are also some nice statues in the courtyard, including one of El Cid in full battle cry. It's open Tuesday to Saturday from 10 am to 4:30 pm and Sunday from 1 to 4 pm. Though admission is free, a donation to support this unfortunately ignored cultural institution is recommended.

The **American Academy and Institute of Arts and Letters** (☎ (212) 368-5900) opens its bronze doors to the public several times a year for temporary exhibitions; call ahead for the schedule. Admission is free.

Morris-Jumel Mansion

Built in 1765, the columned Morris-Jumel Mansion (☎ (212) 923-8008), 65 Jumel Terrace at 160th St east of St Nicholas Ave (subway: A, B, C to 163rd St-Amsterdam Ave), served as George Washington's Continental Army headquarters. After the war it returned to its former function as the summer residence of a wealthy local family. The mansion's interior is a designated landmark and contains many of the original furnishings, as well as a bed on the 2nd floor that reputedly belonged to Napoleon. The ghost of Eliza Jumel, the wealthy woman who lived here until her death in 1865, is said to still move about the place.

It's open Wednesday to Sunday from 10 am to 4 pm; admission is $3 for adults, $2 for seniors, students and children (under 10 are free).

The Cloisters

Built in the 1930s the Cloisters (☎ (212) 923-3700), in Fort Tryon Park (subway: A to 190th St), incorporates fragments of old French and Spanish monasteries and houses the Metropolitan Museum of Art's collection of medieval frescos, tapestries and paintings. In the summer, which is the best time to visit, concerts are held on the grounds, and more than 250 varieties of medieval flowers and herbs are on view. The museum and the surrounding gardens in Fort Tryon Park are very popular with visitors, so get here early during the warm months.

It's open Tuesday to Sunday from 9:30 am to 4:45 pm. Admission is $7/3.50 (under 12 free).

Dyckman House

The Dyckman House Museum (☎ (212) 304-9422), 4881 Broadway, was built in 1783 on the site of a 28-acre, 17th century farm and is the last remaining Dutch farmhouse to survive in Manhattan. Excavations of the property have turned up valuable clues about colonial life. To get to the Dyckman House take the subway to the 207th St station and walk one block south – many people mistakenly get off one stop too soon at Dyckman St.

It's open Tuesday to Sunday from 11 am to 4 pm, and admission is free.

DAVID ELLIS

The Cloisters

UPPER EAST SIDE

The Upper East Side is home to New York's greatest concentration of cultural centers, as Fifth Ave above 57th St is called Museum Mile. The neighborhood is filled with many of the city's most exclusive hotels and residential blocks. The side streets from Fifth Ave east to Third Ave between 57th to 86th Sts have some stunning townhouses and brownstones, and walking through this area at nightfall affords a voyeuristic opportunity to peer into the interiors and see the grand libraries and living rooms in these homes.

The East Side is served by just three subway lines running up and down Lexington Ave, and the stations listed for sites in this section are served by the 6 local line and the 4 and 5 express trains.

The **Abigail Adams Smith Museum** (☎ (212) 838-6878), at 421 E 61st St, is an 18th century carriage house that is angled to the street in an odd manner. It once was part of a riverside estate owned by the daughter of John Adams, the second US President. It's open Monday to Friday from noon to 4 pm and Sunday from 1 to 5 pm; admission is $3/2.

At 63rd St and York Ave, a jogger's path runs parallel to FDR Drive along the East River all the way up to the E 80s, where it becomes **Carl Shurtz Park**, a favorite spot for the elderly and women with baby strollers. **Gracie Mansion** (☎ (212) 570-4751), the 1799 country residence where New York's mayors now live, is at the end of the park at E 89th St. It's only open to the public on Wednesdays and you must call to reserve a tour slot. Eight blocks to the west is the heart of the Museum Mile district on Fifth Ave.

Museum Information

In recent years, attendance at New York's museums has exploded as tourists have discovered that they are low-cost family alternatives to Broadway shows (for which ticket prices begin at about $45) and the cinema (first-run films now cost $8.50). As a consequence, cultural centers have been brazenly boosting admission charges, and at the same time becoming unbelievably crowded. Though you wouldn't know it by the forbidding Checkpoint Charlie-like entrances, most admission charges are voluntary. If you're on a budget, keep a keen eye out for the words 'suggested donation' at the entrance. You can also call ahead to

KIM GRANT

The Roof Garden at the
Metropolitan Museum of Art

find out whether a museum has weekly 'pay as you wish/free admission' times, or pick up a copy of *Museums New York*, available free at most museum entrances, which offers discount admission coupons.

It would take several days to see all the institutions along Museum Mile, so it's best to pick just one or two sites and explore them thoroughly. Details on the museums and more can be obtained by dialing ☎ (212) 777-2787/ARTS, the Department of Cultural Affairs' 24-hour hotline listing events and concerts at cultural institutions, or by picking up *The Culture of NYC*, a guide and series of maps available at the Visitors Center and major museums.

Temple Emanu-El

Five blocks south of the Frick, at E 65th St and Fifth Ave, stands Temple Emanu-El (☎ (212) 744-1400), the world's largest reformed Jewish synagogue, which is significant for its Byzantine and Near-Eastern architecture. It's open to the general public daily from 10 am to 5 pm (it closes at 4 pm on Friday).

Frick Collection

The Frick Collection (☎ (212) 288-0700), 1 E 70th St (just off Fifth Ave), is located in a mansion built in 1914 by Pittsburgh steel magnate Henry Clay Frick, one of the many such residences that made up millionaire's row. Most of these mansions proved too expensive for succeeding generations and were eventually destroyed, but the wily and very wealthy Frick established a trust to open his private collection as a museum. It's a shame that the 2nd floor of the residence is not available for viewing, though the 12 rooms on the ground floor are grand enough. The Frick's Oval Room is graced by Jean-Antoine Houdon's stunning figure *Diana the Huntress*, and you'll find works by Titian, Vermeer and Bellini, and portraits by Gilbert Stuart, Sir Joshua Reynolds, Thomas Gainsborough and John Constable. It's well worth picking up the small guide to the galleries ($1) to fully appreciate the significance of the works on display.

The Frick is open Tuesday to Saturday from 10 am to 6 pm and Sunday from 1 to 6 pm. Admission is $5/3; children under 10 are not permitted.

Whitney Museum of American Art

The Whitney Museum of American Art (☎ (212) 570-2676), 945 Madison Ave at 75th St (subway: 6 to 77th St), is part of Museum Mile in spirit if not exact location. It is housed in an extraordinarily ugly brutalist structure by Marcel Breuer that

virtually defines the institution's mission to provoke.

The collection was established by Gertrude Vanderbilt Whitney in the 1930s, who began a Greenwich Village salon for prominent artists such as Edward Hopper. The Whitney specializes in 20th century and contemporary art, and is known for its biennial celebration that gathers more attention for the political statements made by the artists than for the quality of their works. Recent major exhibits included a retrospective on the photographer Robert Frank and an assessment of American Beatnik culture.

The Whitney is open Wednesday from 11 am to 6 pm, Thursday from 1 to 8 pm and Friday and Sunday from 11 am to 6 pm. Admission is $8 for adults, $6 for seniors and students, children under 12 free. On Thursday from 6 to 8 pm admission is free for all ages.

The Whitney has smaller exhibits at its branch in the Philip Morris Building, 120 Park Ave, across the street from Grand Central Station; admission is free.

Metropolitan Museum of Art

The Metropolitan Museum of Art (☎ (212) 879-5500), at Fifth Ave and 82nd St, is New York's most popular single-site tourist attraction, and functions something like a self-contained cultural city-state with three million individual objects in its collection. As only one of its five million annual visitors, you must plan an assault on its collections, and arrive early or calculate the effects of the weather on museum attendance carefully. The Met crowds are impossible on rainy Sunday afternoons in the summer, but during horrible winter weather, you might find the 17-acre museum nearly deserted on a Friday evening.

Once inside the **Great Hall**, pick up a floor plan and head to the ticket booths, where you will find a list of exhibits closed for the day along with a line-up of special museum talks. The Met presents more than 30 special exhibitions and installations each year, and clearly marked floor plans show you how to get to those on offer. To the right of the hall, there is an information desk that offers guidance in several languages (these change depending on the volunteers) and $4 audio tours of the special exhibits.

It's best to target exactly what you want to see and head there first, before culture and crowd fatigue sets in (usually after 90 minutes). Then you can put the floor plan away and get lost trying to get back to the main hall. It's a virtual certainty that you will stumble across something interesting along the way.

If you do not want to see anything in particular, then make a loop of the 1st floor before heading to the 2nd-floor painting galleries. Entering the Egyptian Art section in the north wing, you will pass the tomb of Pernebi (circa 2415 BC), several mummies and incredibly well-preserved wall paintings before seeing the **Temple of Dendur**. The temple, threatened with submersion during the building of the Aswan dam, found a home in New York under this glass enclosure – if you look closely at its walls you can see the graffiti etched by European visitors to the site in the 1820s. (The accompanying history makes plain that the temple was a gift to the US in exchange for building a permanent space for it.)

Exiting the gallery door behind the temple brings a culture shock as you see the Met's collection of **baseball cards**, including the rarest and most expensive card in existence: a 1909 Honus Wagner worth some $200,000. Carrying on to the left brings you to the American Wing of **furniture and architecture**, with a quiet enclosed garden space that serves as a respite from the Met hordes. Along the garden are several stained-glass works by Louis Comfort Tiffany, as well as an entire two-story facade of the Branch Bank of the US, preserved when the building was destroyed downtown in the early 20th century.

You then pass through the dark galleries dedicated to **medieval art**. Turning right, you reach a pyramid-like addition that houses the Lehman collection of **impres-**

KIM GRANT

Temple of Dendur, detail

sionist and modern art, which includes several works by Pierre August Renoir (including *Young Girl Bathing*), Georges Seurat and Pierre Bonnard. An unexpected bonus in this gallery is the rear terra-cotta facade of the original 1880 Met building, now completely encased by later additions and standing mutely on view as its own piece of architectural art.

Heading back toward Fifth Ave brings you through the Rockefeller collection of **Africa and Pacific island arts**. At the museum cafe, turn left and wander through the **Greek and Roman art** section before winding up back at the south side of the Great Hall.

On the 2nd floor, you will see the Met's famous collection of **European paintings** in some of the museum's oldest galleries with colonnaded entryways. Here are works by every artist of note, including self-portraits by Rembrandt and Van Gogh, *Portrait of Juan de Parej* by Velázquez, and

KIM GRANT

The spiral Guggenheim Museum, designed by Frank Lloyd Wright

a suite of rooms dedicated to impressionist and post-impressionist art.

The Met offers free guided walking tours of museum highlights and specific galleries every half hour from 10:15 am to 4 pm Tuesday to Friday. Check the calendar, given away free at the Great Hall information desk, for the specific schedule.

The Met is open Tuesday to Thursday and Sunday from 9:30 am to 5:15 pm and Friday and Saturday from 9:30 am to 8:45 pm. Suggested admission is $7 for adults, $3 for seniors and students, children under 12 free.

Solomon R Guggenheim Museum

The Solomon R Guggenheim Museum (☎ (212) 423-3500), 1071 Fifth Ave, is the distinctive spiral art space designed by Frank Lloyd Wright to hold one of the 20th century's greatest private bequests. A 1993 renovation added a 10-story building behind Wright's structure that many com-plained made the museum resemble a commode, but it did add space for the 5000-work Guggenheim collection, including the major donation in 1976 of impressionist and modern works by Justin Thannhauser.

The museum is open Sunday to Wednesday from 10 am to 6 pm and Friday and Saturday from 10 am to 8 pm. Admission is $8/5, with children under 12 free; pay-as-you-wish hours are Friday from 6 to 8 pm. A combination ticket that includes admission to the SoHo branch of the Guggenheim is $10/6.

National Academy of Design

The National Academy of Design (☎ (212) 369-4880), 1083 Fifth Ave, was founded by painter-inventor Samuel Morse and has a permanent collection of paintings and sculptures. The academy's works have been housed since 1940 in a grand mansion designed by Ogden Codman, who also designed the Breakers mansion in Newport, Rhode Island. The house is notable for its marble foyer and spiral staircase.

It's open from Tuesday to Sunday from 11:30 am to 5:30 pm with late hours on Friday until 8 pm. Admission for adults/students is $5/3.50; for seniors and children under 16 it's free.

Cooper-Hewitt
National Museum of Design

The Cooper-Hewitt National Museum of Design (☎ (212) 860-6868), 2 E 91st St, stands in the 64-room mansion that billionaire Andrew Carnegie built in 1901 in a spot then far away from the downtown bustle. Within 20 years, the country surroundings that Carnegie sought disappeared as other wealthy men followed his lead and built palaces around him.

The museum, a branch of the Smithsonian Institution in Washington, DC, is a must for anyone interested in architecture, engineering, jewelry or textiles. The museum has also examined advertising campaigns and household item design. If you only have a passing interest in any of this, the place is still worth a visit for its garden.

It's open Tuesday from 10 am to 9 pm, Wednesday to Saturday from 10 am to 5 pm and Sunday from noon to 5 pm. Admission is $3 for adults, $1.50 for seniors and students, and children are free. There is no admission charge Tuesday night from 5 to 9 pm.

Jewish Museum

The Jewish Museum (☎ (212) 423-3200), 1109 Fifth Ave, examines 4000 years of Jewish history, ceremony and art. A $25 million renovation of the building, a 1908 banker's mansion, greatly increased gallery space for its more than 30,000 items of Judaica and added a new gallery dedicated to teaching children about Jewish heritage. In 1996 the museum held the first comprehensive exhibition of 20th century Russian and Soviet Jewish artists.

It's open Sunday to Thursday from 11 am to 5:45 pm and Tuesday from 11 am to 8 pm. Admission is $7 for adults, $5 students and seniors, children under 12 are free; free admission is offered to everyone on Tuesday night from 5 to 8 pm.

International Center of Photography

The International Center of Photography (☎ (212) 860-1777), 1130 Fifth Ave (subway: 6 to 96th St), is the city's most important showplace for exhibitions on the careers of major figures in photography,

KIM GRANT

Cooper-Hewitt Museum

and has recently had retrospectives on fashion photographer and filmmaker William Klein and French photojournalist Henri Cartier-Bresson.

It's open from Wednesday to Sunday from 11 am to 6 pm and Tuesday from 11 am to 8 pm. Admission is $4 for adults, $2 for seniors and students, $1 for children under 12.

There is also an ICP gallery in Midtown (☎ (212) 768-4682), 1133 Sixth Ave (subway: B, D, Q, F to 42nd St), which has the same opening hours and admission price.

Museum of the City of New York

The Museum of the City of New York (☎ (212) 534-1672), at Fifth Ave and 103rd St (subway: 6 to 103rd St), doesn't seem to have a coherent plan to its displays and somewhat duplicates the function of the older New-York Historical Society across town (see Upper West Side). Consequently, both institutions – overshadowed by their many world-class neighbors – attract few visitors and have suffered financially since the 1980s. Nevertheless, the Museum of the City of New York is forging ahead with an expansion, tracing the city from its beaver trading port days to the modern era. It has a notable 2nd-floor gallery with entire rooms from demolished homes of New York *grandees*, an excellent collection of antique doll houses, teddy bears and toys, along with and an exhibition dedicated to Broadway musicals.

It's open Wednesday to Saturday from 10 am to 5 pm and Sunday from 1 to 5 pm. Admission is $5/3, or $8 for an entire family.

ROOSEVELT ISLAND

New York's most thoroughly planned neighborhood is on a tiny island no wider than a football field in the East River between Manhattan and Queens. Once known as Blackwell's Island after the farming family that lived there, the island was purchased by the city in 1828 and became the location of several public hospitals and an insane asylum. In the 1970s

New York State built apartments for 10,000 people along the island's only street. The planned area along the cobblestone roadway resembles an Olympic Village, or, as some less kindly put it, a college dorm complex.

Most visitors take the three-minute aerial tramway over, admire the stunning view of the East Side of Manhattan framed by the 59th St Bridge and head straight back. But it's worth spending an hour or so on the island during good weather, if only to enjoy the quiet and the flat roadway and paths that circle most of the island to make it a perfect spot for both running and picnicking. Roosevelt Island Tours (☎ (212) 223-0157) offers group excursions of the island and its six landmarks for $10 per person.

The Roosevelt Island tramway station (☎ (212) 832-4543) is located at 59th St and Second Ave. Trips leave every 15 minutes on the quarter hour from 6 am to 2:30 am daily. The cost is $1.50 each way, and the turnstiles accept tram and subway tokens. The tram is subject to closures for maintenance and bad weather but Roosevelt Island has its own subway station accessible from Manhattan via the Q line during the day and the B line on nights and weekends. Just make sure the train you get on (nearest stop: 63rd St-Lexington) lists '21st St-Queensbridge' as its final destination.

Outer Boroughs

THE BRONX

The Bronx – a geographic area that has a curious article before its name, like the Hague and the Yucatán – is named after the Bronck family, Dutch farmers who owned a huge tract of property in the area. They, in turn, gave their name to 'Bronck's River,' which led to the derivation used today. The Bronx has dubious world renown as a metaphor for urban decay, even though the southwestern part of the borough – the area unofficially referred to as the South Bronx – doesn't quite live up to its reputation, thanks to a 10-year, billion-dollar program to build low income housing.

The borough, once a forest-like respite from the rest of the city, is now home to 1.6 million people, and serves as a study in contrasts. The Morrisania section of the lower Bronx is still riddled with abandoned buildings, while Fieldston, in the northern reaches of the borough, is a privately owned community of Tudor homes occupied by some of the city's richest residents. The Bronx also boasts the quiet and isolated fishing community of City Island as well as the 2764-acre Pelham Bay Park, the city's largest.

The Bronx Tourism Council (☎ (718) 590-3518) offers a Visitor's Guide to the borough and keeps track of community events. The Bronx County Historical Society (☎ (718) 881-8900) sponsors weekend walking tours of various sites.

Yankee Stadium

Many people might be tempted to pass up a visit to Yankee Stadium, baseball's mecca, because of its location in the South Bronx. The area is really not at all hazardous, though its reputation for being crime-ridden has been exploited by New York Yankee owner George Steinbrenner, who seems intent on hustling the city into constructing a grander facility downtown or moving the team to the New Jersey suburbs.

Steinbrenner will probably make good on one of those threats just after the year 2000, when the Yankee Stadium lease expires. But for now you can still visit what

The Bronx Bombers & the Sultan of Swat

The New York Yankees are, without any doubt, the most successful team in the history of baseball. The 'Bronx Bombers' have been in the World Series 34 times and won it 23 times, including in 1996. Even foreign visitors have probably heard of the team's most famous player: left-handed slugger George Herman Ruth (1895-1948). Ruth – popularly known as 'The Babe,' and the 'Sultan of Swat' – was the sport's first superstar, an icon whose charisma on and off the field helped make baseball the national pastime.

In 1920, Ruth, then recognized as one of the best pitchers in the game, was sold to the Yanks by the Boston Red Sox, creating for that team the 'Curse of the Great Bambino,' which dictates that the Sox never again win the World Series (so far they haven't), and instigating a rivalry between the two teams that remains heated to this day. (One Boston Catholic priest has suggested performing an exorcism to rid the team of the curse.)

But the Yanks didn't want a pitcher – it was Ruth's bat they were interested in. In New York Ruth played the outfield exclusively; he took the field every day and began to hit home runs in numbers the game had never seen before. In 1927 he hit 60 homers, which remained a record for a single season until 1961. His career total of 714 home runs (659 for the Yankees) wasn't surpassed until Hank Aaron beat it in 1974.

Ruth helped the Yankees win their first American League pennant in 1921 and their first World Series in 1923. During the 1926 World Series, he became the first player to hit three home runs in one game (a feat he repeated in his very last game in 1935 when he was playing for the Boston Braves).

Yankee Stadium was built in 1923 and renovated in 1976. It is still commonly referred to as the 'House that Ruth Built,' because it was partly designed to suit his hitting style and was made large enough to fit the many fans who came just to see him.

A year after his retirement from baseball Ruth was one of the first players inducted to the Baseball Hall of Fame in Cooperstown, New York. After a brief coaching stint with the Brooklyn Dodgers he later starred as himself in the 1942 movie *Pride of the Yankees*, which was about his Yankee teammate Lou Gehrig. Ruth himself was the subject of two later films, *The Babe Ruth Story* in 1948 and *The Babe* in 1991. ∎

the team calls 'the most famous stadium since the Roman Coliseum' in all its active glory on summer game days. Gates open 90 minutes before game time, and fans can visit the left field **Memorial Park** where

JANE LLOYD
Dreaming at Yankee Stadium

plaques are dedicated to such baseball greats as Babe Ruth, Mickey Mantle and Joe DiMaggio. Across the street from the stadium stand several bustling memorabilia shops and restaurants. **Stan's Sports Bar** gets particularly raucous when the Yankees play the archrival Boston Red Sox.

Yankee Stadium is 15 minutes from Midtown via the 4 and D subway lines.

Bronx Museum of the Arts

If you're taking in a ballgame, you might want to make a slight detour to this museum (☎ (718) 681-6000), 1040 Grand Concourse at 165th St (the Grand Concourse, the Borough's largest avenue, is three blocks to the east of the Stadium). The museum often shows the work of young city artists, and is open Wednesday from 3 to 9 pm, Thursday and Friday from 10 am to 5 pm, and Saturday and Sunday from 1 to 6 pm. Admission is $3 for adults, $2 for students and $1 for seniors.

Hall of Fame for Great Americans

One of New York's most neglected sites is the Hall of Fame for Great Americans, in University Heights at Bronx Community College (☎ (718) 289-5100), 183rd St and Sedgwick Ave (subway: 4 to 183rd St). This outdoor colonnade, which overlooks the Hudson River and features the busts of more than 100 notables, was built by New York University, which had its main campus on this site until the early 1970s. When NYU abandoned the site, it was taken over by the local community college.

The Hall of Fame was in a very bad state until a $3 million restoration in the mid-'80s, and though it looks fine now, the updating was purely physical and not philosophical: the Hall contains the bust of but one woman, suffragette Susan B Anthony.

The neighborhood is still pretty dicey, so if you visit the Hall of Fame do so during the day, preferably when the college is in session. It's open daily from 10 am to 5 pm; admission is free.

New York Botanical Garden

The 250-acre New York Botanical Garden (☎ (718) 817-8705) has suffered financial woes in recent years, but it will be worth visiting once the **Enid A Haupt conservatory**, a grand Victorian iron and glass edifice, is restored (sometime in 1997). There's also an outdoor **Rose Garden** just next to the conservatory, and a **Rock Garden** with a multi-tiered waterfall. The shop in the museum building sells plants along with 'zoo doo' – manure manufactured by the residents of the nearby Bronx Zoo.

It's open Tuesday to Sunday from 10 am to 6 pm, with the same hours on Monday national holidays. Admission for adults/children is $3/1, with free entry all day Wednesday and on Saturday from 10 am to noon.

You can reach the Botanical Garden by taking the D subway train to Bedford Park Blvd and walking east down the hill seven blocks to the gate. Just before crossing Webster Ave, you'll pass **Mike's** (☎ (718) 365-5486), 380 Bedford Park Blvd, which serves the most delicious chicken hero sandwiches in the city that make for a perfect picnic lunch in the garden. Metro North trains (☎ (212) 532-4900) leave hourly from Grand Central Terminal to the Botanical Garden stop; the trip costs $3.50 each way.

Bronx Zoo

The Bronx Zoo (☎ (718) 367-1010), which recently changed its official name to the more politically correct Bronx Wildlife Conservation Society (subway: 4, 5 to Pelham Parkway), attracts more than two million visitors annually to its 265-acre site. Nearly 5000 animals are on exhibit, all in comfortable, naturalistic settings. It's best to visit the zoo in warm weather, since many of the outdoor rides are shuttered during the winter months and the animals retreat into shelter areas, and you're stuck touring the older buildings that are home to reptiles and birds.

The usual array of lions, tigers and bears is mostly observed along the Bengali Express Monorail (tickets: $2), which is open from May to October and offers a 25-minute narrated journey through the Wild Asia areas. The Jungle World indoor exhibit, open year round, is a 37,000-sq-foot recreation of the Asian tropics with 100 different species of animal and tropical plants. You'll either be delighted or terrified by the World of Darkness, where bats hover nearly unseen (but not unsmelled).

The zoo is open daily from 10 am to 4:30 pm during the winter, and closes an hour later during the summer months. Admission from November to March is $3/1.50; in the summer, when everything is open, it jumps to $6.75/3. Admission is free on Wednesdays year round.

You can reach the Bronx Zoo via the 2 or 5 subway trains, or with a car by taking the Bronx River Parkway (parking: $5). It's difficult – and also exhausting – to walk from the Botanical Garden to the Zoo, but if you must, they are best linked by going down Southern Blvd and taking a left at Bronx Park South to the Boston Rd entrance to the zoo. Liberty Lines Express (☎ (718) 652-8400) runs buses to the zoo

that pick up passengers along Madison Ave in Manhattan (at 26th, 47th, 54th, 63rd, 69th and 84th Sts) for $4.

Arthur Ave

Just south of Fordham University is the Belmont section of the Bronx, the most authentic Italian neighborhood in the city. This is a neighborhood for pure gastronomic exploration (see Places to Eat), and a place to soak up true Italian American culture.

Arthur Ave is the perfect place to stock up on Italian provisions, including live chickens at the **Arthur Ave Poultry Market**, at No 2356, and **Teitel Brothers Wholesalers** (☎ (718) 733-9400), on the corner of 186th St. The Arthur Ave Retail Market contains indoor food stalls, including **Mike & Sons**, a cheese shop with heartbreakingly good aged parmesan and prosciutto. The **Cosenza** fresh fish store, No 2354, sells clams on the half shell to pedestrians from a small table on the street, while clerks at the **Calabria Pork Store** (☎ (718) 367-5145), No 2338, offer free samples of hot and sweet homemade sausages that age on racks along the ceiling. The Belmont section continues along 187th St; where **Mt Carmel Liquors** (☎ (718) 367-7833), owned by Giancarlo and Rosa Paciullo, offers one of the largest selections of Chianti wines in the US.

The Belmont Italian American Playhouse (☎ (718) 364-4700), 2384 Arthur Ave, is the neighborhood's only performance spot. It's the site of a season of new theatrical works that runs from April to December, and a place where local authors and musicians perform year round. If you're lucky, you'll be in town for one of the rooftop doo wop concerts (a tradition reminiscent of the days when Dion and the Belmonts emerged from this neighborhood).

You can reach Arthur Ave by taking the Metro North train to Fordham Rd or the No 4 subway to the stop of the same name and walking east 11 blocks, then turning right at Arthur Ave and continuing south three blocks.

City Island

Surely the oddest and most unexpected neighborhood in the Bronx is City Island, a 1½-mile long fishing community 15 miles from Midtown. City Island has numerous boat slips, is home to three yacht clubs, and is the place to go if you're interested in diving, sailing or fishing in Long Island Sound (see the sidebar, City Island Water Sports). Perhaps the strangest thing about this self-contained little spot, cut off from the rest of the Bronx by Pelham Bay Park, is that there's hardly a trace of the New York accent found in conversation between the locals – in fact their inflections and accents betray a New England influence.

City Island Water Sports

If you're interested in fishing, sailing or ocean trips during your New York stay, head to City Island.

Land's End (☎ (718) 885-2424), 560 Minneford Ave, and NY Sailing School (☎ (718) 885-3103), 697 Bridge St, run sailing courses and rent boats during the summer. Boats offering early-morning trips include the *Riptide III* (☎ (718) 885-0236) and *Daybreak II* (☎ (718) 409-9765). (These boats also embark on nighttime bluefish trips during the summer.) Cost is around $40 per person. If you make the trip, have a seafood meal and check out the **Undersea Museum** (☎ (718) 885-0701), which contains a wealth of items obtained by local divers and a film about whaling. It's open in the summer Monday to Friday from 10 am to 5 pm and weekends from noon to 5 pm; admission is $4.50.

If you're going to concentrate on seafaring activities, you might want to consider staying at *Le Refuge Inn* (☎ (718) 885-2478), 620 City Island Ave, the island's only B&B, run by transplanted French chef Pierre Saint-Denis. It is open year round and has eight rooms (four with shared bath) with rates of $73/85. The owner also operates a fine restaurant at the Inn from Wednesday to Saturday, with a changing menu for $40 per person. ∎

All of its shops and 20-odd seafood restaurants are located along City Island Ave, which runs the length of the mile-long island. The short side streets are filled with attractive clapboard houses that overlook the surrounding water, and the main marinas are found on the western side.

You can reach City Island by taking the No 6 subway to its terminus at Pelham Bay Park and getting on the Bx 29 bus which runs directly to City Island Ave, or by taking an express bus from Madison Ave in Midtown directly to City Island ($4 each way). Call the City Island Chamber of Commerce at ☎ (718) 885-9100.

If you travel to City Island by car, be sure to check out the Bartow-Pell Mansion & Gardens (☎ (718) 885-1461), 895 Shore Road in nearby Pelham Bay Park. This elegant 19th century residence is open Wednesday, Saturday and Sunday from noon to 4 pm. Admission is $2.50 for adults, $1.25 for seniors and students, children under 12 free.

BROOKLYN

For years, a sign on the eastern side of the Brooklyn Bridge welcomed visitors to the 'fourth-largest city in the America.' The sign has been replaced by one with a less separatist sentiment, but Brooklyn's pride – and right to claim fourth-largest city status – still remains (it is home to 2.3 million people). The borough also makes the dubious claim that 'one out of every seven famous people' in the US was born in Brooklyn!

Officially called Kings County, Brooklyn derives its name from *breucklen*, the Dutch word for marshland. For most of its 350-year history, Brooklyn was a collection of farming villages, and its citizens joined greater New York City with great reluctance. Even after the 1898 consolidation, the borough remained independent in spirit: citizens enjoyed Prospect Park, Brooklyn's own version of Central Park, followed the fortunes of the Brooklyn Dodgers baseball team, and sun worshipped at the ritzy resort hotels on Coney Island. But much of Brooklyn's separate city pretensions were destroyed in the late '50s, when the Dodgers moved to the West Coast and many of the borough's residents began moving to the suburbs. Today Brooklyn's inner neighborhoods are home to newer immigrants from the Caribbean, Eastern Europe and the former Soviet Union. The old carriage houses and brownstones in neighborhoods along the eastern part of the borough have been snapped up by professionals looking for a nice space within commuting distance of Manhattan.

The Brooklyn Tourism and Festivals Project (☎ (718) 855-7882) issues a free calendar of events called *Meet Me in Brooklyn*. It's updated every three months and is available at all Brooklyn cultural institutions. *Brooklyn Bridge*, a $2.75 monthly magazine on sale in shops and newsstands throughout the borough, has a more extensive list of happenings.

Brooklyn Heights

This neighborhood of brownstones and mansions by the mouth of the East River developed as a ferry departure point for Lower Manhattan in the early 19th century. Walking along its promenade, you get a stunning view of Manhattan's skyscrapers framed at the bottom by the far less impressive metal storage warehouses along the waterfront.

Walking Tour You can begin a tour of 'The Heights' at the 1848 Beaux Arts **Brooklyn Borough Hall** (☎ (718) 875-4047), 209 Joralemon St (subway: A, C, F to Jay St-Borough Hall). If you are particularly energetic, you can get to Borough Hall from downtown Manhattan via a 20-minute walk across the Brooklyn Bridge and bearing right on the bridge's pedestrian walkway, which will bring you south along Adams St to the building. (You'll also see the imposing US Post Office building just north of Borough Hall.) The municipal offices are open from Monday to Friday from 9 am to 5 pm, and a free tour of the facility leaves from there every Tuesday at 1 pm. From behind Borough Hall, go down Montague St, the main

avenue for cafes and bars. One block north runs the parallel Pierrepont St, site of the Brooklyn Historical Society (see below).

Montague St ends at Pierrepont Place (pronounced PIER-pont) and the waterfront promenade, and here you can turn right and continue north on Columbia Heights toward **Fulton Landing**, the old ferry dock at the base of the Brooklyn Bridge. This was the main departure point for Manhattan-bound ferries before the bridge was completed in 1883. Now classical music concerts are held on a barge here and it's a perfect place to watch the sun set beyond Manhattan.

Heading back up the hill along Henry St, note the old wooden frame houses around Middagh St. Take a look at the brownstone at No 7 Middagh St. In the 1930s and '40s the building was something of an 'ivory tower boardinghouse,' as Truman Capote, who lived in the neighborhood, dubbed it. Owned by George Davis, a literary editor, 7 Middagh was at various times the home of writers Carson McCullers, Richard Wright and Paul and Jane Bowles as well as poet WH Auden.

Just before Atlantic Ave, check out **Sidney Place**, a quiet block of brownstones with an impressive carriage house at No 51 near the corner of State St. Many such carriage houses have been converted into exclusive residences. **Atlantic Ave** is a busy thoroughfare featuring several Middle Eastern spice shops and an array of restaurants catering to the growing population of Yemeni immigrants. Sahadi Importing Co (☎ (718) 624-4550), 187-189 Atlantic Ave, wholesales its dried fruits and nuts all over the country. Its also worth stopping in at the neighboring El-Asmar (☎ (718) 855-2455) at No 197 to say hello to the friendly folks there and pick up some snacks or simply to enjoy the exotic atmosphere of spices displayed in open barrels.

Cobble Hill & Carroll Gardens Walking south along Court St past Atlantic Ave brings you to the Italian enclave of Cobble Hill. Court St is mostly a commercial district, a good mix of pastry shops,

---

For Coffee Lovers Only

If you're a java aficionado, you *must* visit D'Amico Foods (☎ (718) 875-5403), 309 Court St. Visit the 'Coffee King of Brooklyn' in mid-morning. By that time, someone will be stoking the fire in the old gold-plated Royal roasting machine, filling the store with a wonderfully bitter aroma. D'Amico sells more than 70 types of coffee, many of which are roasted on the premises. D'Amico's is also a gourmet deli, so you can get a sandwich, cheese and brewed coffee for a Brooklyn Heights waterfront picnic. A pound of their wonderful coffee makes a great house gift for a host, or a nice souvenir to be consumed after returning home. ■

---

convenience stores and cafes, with brownstone residences on the surrounding streets.

Take in Court St for 11 blocks (see Places to Eat) making sure to stop in at the fine Bookcourt Book Shop (☎ (718) 875-3677) at No 163. Turn right at Carroll St and walk west one block to Clinton St, which brings you to the red-brick Greek Revival **Rankin residence** at No 440, on the southwest corner. Now a funeral home, this 1840 mansion was once the only house on a large farm with a view of New York Harbor. It sits today in the middle of the Carroll Gardens Historic District, a remarkably well-preserved neighborhood of brick and brownstone houses from the mid- to late 19th century, most with small fenced front yards. As you head north back on Clinton St to busy Atlantic Ave, it will be easy to see why Brooklyn is called the 'Borough of Churches' – you will have passed at least half a dozen on your walk around the neighborhood.

Brooklyn Historical Society

The Brooklyn Historical Society (☎ (718) 624-0890), 128 Pierrepont St (subway: N, R to Court St), has a research library and a museum dedicated to borough history in a fine terra cotta auditorium that's a national landmark. The Historical Society celebrated the 50th anniversary of Jackie Robinson's 1947 debut with the Brooklyn Dodgers, which broke professional baseball's undeclared ban on African American players. The Society has also digitized its collection of 31,000 photographs and prints, and you can explore these images on computers in the 2nd-floor library.

It's open Tuesday to Saturday from noon to 4:45 pm; admission is $2.50, free on Wednesday.

New York Transit Museum

The New York Transit Museum (☎ (718) 243-8601), located in a decommissioned subway station from the 1930s at the corner of Boerum Place and Schermerhorn St, a block north of Atlantic Ave (subway: A, C, F to Jay St-Borough Hall), has a distinctly low-tech look to it. Virtually unchanged since its opening in 1976, the museum does not have a video presentation, let alone a computer-driven exhibits. What it does have is an impressive collection of subway cars from the transit system's first 100 years on the platform of the old station; most have their original ads still intact. Keep an eye out for the silver car used in the 1995 film *Money Train*, as well as the R-1, the model that inspired Duke Ellington's *Take the A Train*. You will also see the 1947 R-11 model, which featured 'germicidal' lighting designed to sterilize tunnel air. The cars were discontinued amid fears that the lights would also sterilize subway conductors and trainmen.

The Transit Museum runs tours of the subway system in antique subway cars several times a year; call for a schedule. It's open Tuesday, Thursday and Friday from 10 am to 4 pm, Wednesday from 10 am to 6 pm and Saturday and Sunday from noon to 5 pm. Admission is $3/1.50.

Brooklyn Academy of Music

The Brooklyn Academy of Music, commonly called 'BAM' (☎ (718) 636-4100), 30 Lafayette Ave (subway: D, Q, 2, 3, 4, 5 to Atlantic Ave), is the oldest concert center in the US and consists of the Majestic Theater and the Brooklyn Opera House. BAM hosts visiting opera companies from around the world in subtitled productions and is home to the Mark Morris dance troupe. You can take public transportation to BAM or call to reserve a spot on the bus that leaves from the corner of 51st St and Lexington Ave in Manhattan an hour before the performance; it costs $10 roundtrip.

Prospect Park

Created in 1866, the 526-acre Prospect Park is considered the greatest achievement by Frederick Law Olmsted and Calvert Vaux, the same landscaping duo that designed Central Park. Though less crowded than its more famous Manhattan sister space, Prospect Park offers many of the same activities along its broad meadows, including ice skating at the **Kate Wollman rink** (☎ (718) 287-6431), which is open daily from October to early March. Admission costs $2.50/1, with skate rental for $3.50. There is also the **Lefferts Homestead Children's Museum** (☎ (718) 965-6505), open only on weekends, and a small **zoo** (☎ (718) 399-7339), open daily from 10 am to 4 pm with an admission charge of $2.50/50¢. Information on other activities, including park walks, carousel rides and art exhibitions, can be obtained by visiting the boathouse (subway: D, Q to Prospect Park) or calling ☎ (718) 965-8999.

Grand Army Plaza (subway: 2, 3 to Grand Army Plaza) stands at the northwest entrance to the park, marked by an 80-foot **Soldiers' and Sailors' Monument** constructed in 1898 to commemorate the Union Army's triumph during the Civil War. In the summer, you can visit a gallery in the arch that's dedicated to local artists, as well as climb an observation deck just below the four-horse bronze chariot. New York City's only structure honoring President John F Kennedy is located in a small fountain park just to the north of the Grand Army arch. The immense Art Deco **Brooklyn Public Library** faces the arch on its south side.

On Saturday and Sunday all year round, a free hourly trolley service makes a loop from the Brooklyn Museum (see Eastern Parkway for information) to Prospect Park, stopping at points of interest including the park zoo and ice rink, the botanical garden, and the Brooklyn Library. Ask at the museum information desk for the time it passes by the entrance.

Park Slope

This rectangular-shaped residential neighborhood is located immediately west of Prospect Park, and most of its shops and restaurants are located along 18 blocks of Seventh Ave bookended by two subway stations (subway: D, Q to Seventh Ave; F to Seventh Ave-Park Slope). There's a literary atmosphere to the area, which is home to author Ian Frazier and no fewer than two husband and wife novel-writing duos: Paul Auster *(The New York Trilogy)* and Siri Hustvedt, along with Colin Harrison *(Bodies Electric)* and Kathryn Harrison *(Exposure)*. Appropriately, there are four bookstores within easy walking distance, including Booklink (☎ (718) 965-9122), 320 Seventh Ave, which features the work of local writers. Park Slope is a pleasant place to have lunch or dinner or just linger over coffee after a trip to Prospect Park. **Ozzie's** (☎ (718) 398-6695), 57 Seventh Ave, is a coffee shop cum literary hangout patronized by Auster and actor John Turturro. There are several more cafes along the street.

JANE LLOYD

New York's finest

Eastern Parkway
Named after the six-lane boulevard that runs along the north end of Prospect Park, this area was once one of the most exclusive neighborhoods in Brooklyn. The area cuts through Prospect Heights and Crown Heights, home to the Lubavitch sect of Orthodox Jews and a large Caribbean community. There have been major tensions between the two groups in recent years, but it is quite safe to explore shops and restaurants along Washington Ave, which runs in front of the Brooklyn Museum of Art.

Brooklyn Museum of Art Were it located anywhere else, the Brooklyn Museum of Art (☎ (718) 638-5000), 200 Eastern Parkway (subway: 2, 3 to Eastern Parkway-Brooklyn Museum), would be considered a premier arts institution. Even though it is shadowed by the Metropolitan, this museum is very much worth a visit. It's never really crowded, even on Sunday, and you can take up an entire day exploring its collection and seeing the nearby Botanical Gardens and Brooklyn Children's Museum (☎ (718) 735-4400).

On the museum's first two floors, there are galleries dedicated to African, Islamic and Asian art. Particularly good are the modern 3rd-floor galleries containing colorful Egyptian cartonnages (mummy casings) and funerary figurines. The 4th floor, which overlooks a tiled court crowned by a skylight, has period rooms, including a reconstruction of the Jan Schenck House, a 17th century Dutch settlement in Brooklyn. The 5th floor has colonial portraiture, including a famous Gilbert Stuart painting of Washington in which the General looks particularly uncomfortable wearing his false teeth, along with a collection of 58 Auguste Rodin sculptures.

The Brooklyn Museum of Art is open Wednesday to Sunday from 10 am to 5 pm. Admission is $4 adults, $2 children, $1.50 seniors.

Botanic Garden The 52-acre Brooklyn Botanic Garden (☎ (718) 622-4433), 1000 Washington Ave (subway: 2, 3 to Eastern Parkway-Brooklyn Museum), has more than 12,000 different plants in its 15 gardens. There's a fanciful Celebrity Path with slate steps honoring famous Brooklynites, and a Fragrance Garden that makes for a wonderful walk. Unfortunately, someone recently made off with several of the Steinhardt Conservatory's Bonsai trees, a few of which were 250 years old or more.

The Botanic Garden is open Tuesday to Friday from 8 am to 6 pm and Saturday and Sunday from 8 am to 4:30 pm from April to September. Winter hours are Tuesday to Sunday from 10 am to 4:30 pm. Admission for adults/seniors/children is $3/1.50/50¢. Admission is free on Tuesday.

Coney Island
This former summer playground was where sweating city dwellers came to enjoy the fun house, minor games of chance and bumper-car rides in the Dreamland amusement park before WWI. It is a ghostly shadow of its former self, especially after Labor Day, when the Astroland Amusement Park closes for the season. But it's still worth the hour-long subway ride from Manhattan, especially since it is also the site of the New York Aquarium and just a quarter-mile boardwalk stroll from Brighton Beach, home to the nation's largest grouping of Russian émigrés.

As you emerge from the colorfully decrepit subway station (subway: B, D, F, N to Stillwell Ave-Coney Island), you'll see a 24-hour coffee shop right in the middle of the station. Hardbitten patrons sit at the countertop hunched over their meals and dozens of menu items are advertised on the bright yellow walls of the shop – meanwhile your nose is assaulted by the smell of sausages, hot dogs, home fries and other greasy delights. You then pass through the doors to Surf Ave, where Russian residents pick up odd tools and electronic equipment at **flea market stalls** along the street. There are a few obvious 'hot sheet hotels' along Surf Ave as well. Not far from here is the **Coney Island Sideshow** (☎ (718) 372-5159), 1208 Surf Ave, a small museum and freak show where you can see snake charmers, tattooed ladies and sword swallowers for a $3/2 admission charge. **Nathan's**, the city's prototypical fast-food stand, has been open at the same Surf Ave site for more than 75 years and still sells its famous hot dogs ($2) from 8 am to 4 am daily.

Along the Boardwalk you will see two disused relics of Coney Island's past glory: the bright red **parachute jump**, moved here from the 1939 World's Fair in Queens, and the ivy-covered **Thunderbolt** roller coaster, which operated from 1925 to 1983; it's older than Astroland's more famous Cyclone.

New York Aquarium The New York Aquarium (☎ (718) 265-3400), along the Coney Island boardwalk (subway: D, F to W 8th St-NY Aquarium), may look thoroughly unattractive from the outside and lack the computerized gadgetry of newer facilities elsewhere, but its manageable scale makes it a perfect place for young children. There's a touch pool where kids can handle starfish and other small forms of sea life, and a small amphitheater with Sea World-style dolphin shows several times daily. You can spend the better part of a day at the aquarium viewing its 10,000 specimens of sea life. Most kids love viewing whales and seals from the outside railing overlooking their tanks or from the observation windows that afford views of the animals' underwater habitats.

It's open every day from 10 am to 5 pm, and admission is $6.75/3.

Brighton Beach

There's more than a little bit of Russia to be found in Brighton Beach (subway: Q to Brighton Beach), just a five-minute walk north on the boardwalk from the New York Aquarium. Russian shops, bakeries and restaurants line Brighton Beach Ave, which runs parallel to the boardwalk just one block from the beach.

Brighton Beach has been identified as the main money laundering spot in the US for the Russian *mafiya*. But there's no reason to worry about crime on the street –

just about the only criminal behavior you'll observe are the *babushkas* selling illegal prescriptive medicine Moscow-style on the street corner. This community is so close-knit that a non-Russian speaker will stick out like a sore thumb. But the restaurants and shops are tolerant and friendly to outsiders, a category that includes Brooklynites from any other neighborhood.

Williamsburg

This neighborhood, located just over the namesake Williamsburg Bridge, is home to a large Orthodox Jewish community – a living embodiment of what Manhattan's Lower East Side once was in the early 20th century. But the windswept northern area of Williamsburg is much different and varied in character. The 'Northside' (subway: L to Bedford Ave) has long been home to a large population of Central European immigrants, mostly from Poland. In recent years, this aging community has been augmented by many aspiring artists and writers who are taking advantage of the cheap rents and large loft spaces. The two distinct communities coexist quite peacefully. On sunny Sunday afternoons, you can see Polish senior citizens hanging out on just about every other doorstep, exchanging greetings in their native language after church services, while paint-splattered younger folks gather in the local bars for brunch, beer and cigarettes.

Though the local press has noted Williamsburg's growing popularity with the cutting-edge art crowd, there has yet to be an invasion of art galleries or Manhattan-level rents. Inner Williamsburg (subway: L to Lorimer St) is a largely Italian neighborhood. Southern Williamsburg (subway: J, M, Z to Marcy Ave) is Jewish. A college campus atmosphere prevails along Bedford St, where locals looking for apartment shares post signs on mini 'democracy walls,' and musicians advertise for band mates.

For the moment, the local cafes and restaurants in Williamsburg serve as de facto galleries where artist hang out and display their work. To get into the rhythm of the place check out the *L Cafe* (☎ (718) 388-6792), 189 Bedford Ave, *Plan-eat Thailand* (☎ (718) 599-5758), just across the street at No 184, and *Teddy's Bar* (☎ (718) 384-9787), 96 Berry St (at N 8th St).

Though Williamsburg doesn't have much to offer culturally as yet, it's only a five-minute subway trip from Manhattan's Union Square and worth seeing in good weather: you can grab a good meal here and admire the sunset view of Manhattan from Kent Ave along the waterfront.

The Brooklyn Brewery For years, the award-winning Brooklyn Brewery made its award-winning Brooklyn Lager under contract at breweries outside of the borough. But the beer 'came home' to Brooklyn in 1996 with the opening of a microbrewery in Williamsburg (☎ (718) 486-7422), at 79 N 11th St (subway: L to Bedford St). Housed in a series of buildings that once made up the Hecla Ironworks factory (the firm that made the structural supports for the Waldorf-Astoria Hotel), the brewery offers free self-guided tours every Saturday from noon to 4 pm. Call ahead during high season to find out if the tours have been fully booked.

QUEENS
With a land area of 282 sq miles, Queens is the largest borough in New York City, and the residential neighborhoods near the East River have always attracted newer immigrants looking for affordable housing within easy commuting distance of Manhattan, and many have settled near the traditionally industrial neighborhoods of Long Island City, Astoria and Maspeth.

However, a strange phenomenon has happened over the years – most of the newer immigrant groups have augmented, rather than replaced, those already in Queens. It's now the most ethnically diverse place in the city, and perhaps even the world – more than 100 minority groups live there, speaking over 120 different languages or dialects – and the borough's population approaches two million.

As the British writer Michael Pye observes in *Maximum City*, his biographical history of New York: 'The city is an atlas that has been shuffled. If you grow up in Queens, you know Bombay is in the middle of Colombia, alongside Manila, down the road from Ireland and on the way to Argentina, Ecuador and Italy. It is only 10 miles to all those nations from the 59th St Bridge.'

One could add, more than six years after those words were written, that you can wind up your journey in both Korea and China, since Flushing, at the end of the No 7 subway line, happens to be one of the largest Asian neighborhoods in the city. (See the sidebar Ethnic Neighborhood Tour.)

As Queens segues into Long Island, the character of the neighborhoods becomes distinctly more suburban. Development did not entirely wipe away the space once given over to farming land and horse tracks; many of these neighborhoods are accessible only by car.

The Queens Council on the Arts has a 24-hour hotline (☎ (718) 291-2787) on community cultural events; in keeping with the multi-cultural demographics of the borough, it provides information in English, Spanish, Korean and Chinese.

Astoria
Home to the largest Greek community in the US, Astoria (subway: N to Broadway) also has a smattering of Eastern European immigrants. Astoria was a mid-19th century ferry depot named after millionaire fur merchant John Jacob Astor. It soon developed into a neighborhood of factories, including the Steinway piano company, which still operates there. The German and Italian artisans who lived in Astoria were replaced by Greek immigrants in the years following WWII.

Today, Astoria is a proud working class neighborhood of brick and concrete apartment blocks and two-story wooden homes. Posters advertising concerts by visiting Greek personalities dot the landscape along Steinway St, and down Broadway, the main area for shops.

Greek Astoria is also found north of the Triborough Bridge along 23rd Ave (subway: N to Ditmars Blvd). After dark Astoria keeps hopping with Greek shows and concerts. Visiting musical artists from Athens play at the **Grecian Cave** (☎ (718) 274-2227), 31-11 Broadway. There's Cypriot food and music on offer from 11 am to 4 am on weekends at *Taverna Vraka* (☎ (718) 721-3007), 23-15 31st St. A bland apartment building was refronted with a four-column temple entrance for the *Plato* nightclub (☎ (718) 274-6611), 31-84 33rd St off Broadway, frequented almost exclusively by locals 21 years of age and older. You can buy Greek sausages, dried fruit and nuts at *El Greco Superette* (☎ (718) 728-0029), 32-16 Broadway. (See Places to Eat for a list of restaurants.)

Artisans at Work You can view two very different examples of skilled craftsmanship in Astoria. The **Byzantion Woodworking Company** (☎ (718) 932-2960), 37-20 Astoria Blvd (subway: N to Astoria Blvd), doesn't offer tours, but you can drop by from Monday to Saturday to see artisans at work carving elaborate Greek Orthodox religious items for clients from around the US and Canada. The **Steinway Piano Company** (☎ (718) 721-2600, ext 164), at 19th Ave and 38th St (subway: N to Ditmars Blvd), offers free 2½-hour tours of its facility every Thursday; call ahead to reserve a place, since the tours are often booked by school groups months in advance.

American Museum of the Moving Image The American Museum of the Moving Image (☎ (718) 784-0077), at 35th Ave and 36th St (subway: R to Steinway St), stands in the middle of the Kaufman Astoria Studio complex, a 75-year-old film production center that has been the shooting site of various films from the Marx Brothers' *Coconuts* to *Glengarry Glen Ross*. Unfortunately, the studios are not open to public tours, but this museum makes a good effort at showing the mastery behind film making, with galleries showing the makeup and costumes from films like *The Exorcist* and movie sets from the 1987 version of *Glass Menagerie*, directed by Paul Newman. Film and TV serials are shown in a small theater built by conceptual artist Red Grooms, inspired by the '30s Egyptian-themed movie palaces.

Those familiar with London's far more ambitious Museum of the Moving Image will no doubt be disappointed by the smaller New York version. In early 1996, the museum spent several million dollars introducing interactive displays to its two floors of galleries. Now you can use computer screens to create your own video backdrop, listen to famous film soundtracks or re-dub dialogue from famous films. The museum also holds interesting retrospectives on famous filmmakers year round. If you decide to make the short (15-minutes from Midtown) subway trek out to Queens, go when there's an interesting film on offer – and end your day with a Greek meal on Broadway.

It's open from Tuesday to Friday from noon to 5 pm and Saturday and Sunday from noon to 6 pm. Admission is $7 adults, $4 seniors, $2.50 children and students.

Isamu Noguchi Garden Museum Tucked away among the East River warehouses in Long Island City, the cinderblock Isamu Noguchi Garden Museum (☎ (718) 721-1932), 32-37 Vernon Blvd, stands on the site of a studio designed by the Japanese American sculptor. (Noguchi died in 1988, just three years after the museum opened.) The 12 galleries and garden contain more than 300 examples of his work.

It's open from April to November only on Wednesday, Saturday and Sunday from 11 am to 6 pm, and a tour of all the galleries takes place at 2 pm. Admission is $4/2.

Just two blocks north, where Broadway meets Vernon Blvd, is the **Socrates Sculpture Park** (☎ (718) 545-5707), a year-round open-air public space with changing works by local artists on a former illegal waste dump overlooking the East

Ethnic Neighborhood Tour

The elevated 7 subway line, which cuts across the northern third of Queens and ends up in the Asian neighborhood of Flushing, passes through several colorful ethnic enclaves. Dr Illana Harlow, a folklorist employed by the borough, has put together a pamphlet on what she has dubbed the 'International Express.' If you want to make a more detailed exploration of these neighborhoods, you can obtain the publication by calling the Queens Council on the Arts (☎ (718) 647-3377), or by sending $1 to the organization at One Forest Park, Woodhaven, NY 11421-1166.

After leaving Manhattan on the 7 train (catch it at Grand Central Station or Times Square), you can reach the different neighborhoods by disembarking at the following stations and exploring the blocks nearby. You won't get lost if you keep Roosevelt Ave, which runs directly under the elevated train tracks for the final third of the line, as a reference point (Roosevelt Ave runs east-northeast through Queens). The second big thoroughfare is 37th Ave, located one block north of, and parallel to, Roosevelt Ave. The journey from Manhattan to the very end of the line at Main St-Flushing takes about 35 minutes.

Architecturally, most of these neighborhoods are uniformly bland, a landscape of brick buildings punctuated by wooden single-family houses. What changes from one stop to another is the ethnic character found around the subway.

In this section of Queens, the streets *and* avenues are numbered, making for some confusing addresses. But as a general guide, numbered streets run west to east; numbered avenues run north to south. Most of the following sites are located within a few blocks of the given subway stop. (Subway stops are in bold below.)

46th St-Bliss St/52nd St-Lincoln Ave/61st St-Woodside One of the city's oldest Irish neighborhoods, Woodside is served by these three stations. The area was reinvigorated in the '80s by an influx of young immigrants fleeing Ireland's depressed economy. There are so many bars that some are identified with certain regions of Ireland – Dubliners patronize one pub while folks from other counties hang out in another. *Sidetracks* (☎ (718) 786-3570), 45-08 Queens Blvd, is an upscale bar-restaurant that's a good place to begin a pub crawl. The *Starting Gate* (☎ (718) 429-9269), 59-10 Woodside Ave, is a singles joint and a good place to end up at on Friday and Saturday night.

74th St-Broadway At the heart of Jackson Heights is perhaps the most ethnically diverse neighborhood in Queens, with about 60% of its 100,000 residents foreign born. There are food shops catering to Korean, Filipino and Indian communities, who live in neat red-brick homes and apartment blocks.

Jackson Heights is also known to have the largest gay population outside of Manhattan, with a high percentage of lesbians. There are several clubs that attract Latin gays, and the neighborhood holds its very own lesbian and gay pride parade each June.

This is the neighborhood to find the legendary *Jackson Diner* (☎ (718) 672-1232), 37-03 74th St, which many consider the city's best southern Indian restaurant. This dingy converted coffee shop is famous for its Masala Dosa appetizer, a massive crepe with potato, onion and peas, and the Seekh Kabob, a long sausage made of tender lamb.

Around the corner from the Jackson Diner is *La Porteña* (☎ (718) 458-8111), 74-25 37th Ave, which serves Buenos Aires-style barbecue cooked on the storefront window. Meals come to the table along with *chimichurri*, a garlic-laden oil and vinegar sauce that's long-lasting and delicious.

82nd St-Jackson Heights There's also a large Colombian population served by such restaurant-nightclubs as *Chibcha* (☎ (718) 429-9033), 79-05 Roosevelt Ave, with salsa and jazz shows on Friday and Saturday nights beginning at 11 pm. *Taco Mexico* (☎ (718) 899-5800), 88-12 Roosevelt Ave, is a fast food restaurant that has homemade salsa and tortilla chips. There's also *Inti Raymi* (☎ (718) 424-1938), 86-14 37th Ave, serving Peruvian specialties like grilled cow's heart (open Thursday to Sunday).

Junction Blvd Several Latino subcultures exist side by side here at the dividing line between Jackson Heights and Corona. The *Broadway Sandwich Shop* (☎ (718) 898-4088), 96-01 Roosevelt Ave, serves garlicky toasted Cuban pork sandwiches for under $5 and steaming hot cups of strong *cafe con leche*. One block away is *Quisqueya Restaurant* (☎ (718) 478-0704), 97-03 Roosevelt Ave, which offers sweet *plantain* plates for $2 and Dominican specialties like young goat stew for $7.50.

103rd St-Corona Plaza Corona, traditionally an Italian neighborhood, was also a place where well-known black jazz musicians bought comfortable houses in the '20s and '30s. Louis Armstrong lived at 34-56 107th St from 1929 until his death in 1971, and the landmark is scheduled to be converted into a museum by 1998. Recently, Corona has seen an influx of Muslims from Pakistan and India, in addition to a large community of Mexicans. Tomas Gonzalez runs a mini-empire with his *La Espiga* (☎ (718) 779-7898), 42-13 102nd St, which is a combination bakery, taco bar restaurant and grocery store. People line up for the fresh tortillas (two pounds for $1) which are made several times a day. The shop also sells Mexican embroidery.

Just a block away is the **Masjid Alfala House of Worship** (☎ (718) 476-7968), a mosque serving the large local Muslim population.

Ben Faremo, The Lemon Ice King of Corona (☎ (718) 699-5133), 52-02 108th St, is open all year round (winter closing: 6 pm) and serves homemade ices – its signature ice has chunks of lemon and is the perfect refresher for a summer day. The Lemon Ice King is about a mile from the subway. Walk south on 104th St to Corona Ave, turn left and walk two blocks to 52nd Ave; or take the Q23 bus to Forest Hills and get off on 108th St and 52nd Ave on the opposite corner from the shop. ■

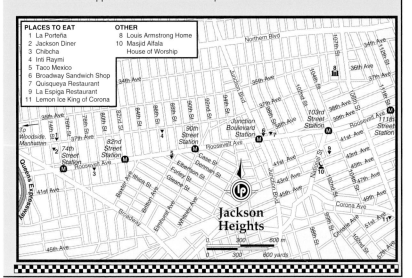

PLACES TO EAT
1 La Porteña
2 Jackson Diner
3 Chibcha
4 Inti Raymi
5 Taco Mexico
6 Broadway Sandwich Shop
7 Quisqueya Restaurant
9 La Espiga Restaurant
11 Lemon Ice King of Corona

OTHER
8 Louis Armstrong Home
10 Masjid Alfala
    House of Worship

Jackson Heights

JANE LLOYD

The Unisphere

River. The works on display, including the five wind chimes along the shoreline, have a stark industrial look to them, in keeping with its location right next to a steel company. It's open from 10 am to dusk; admission is free.

Flushing Meadows-Corona Park

Flushing Meadows Park (subway: 7 to Willets Point-Shea Stadium) is the site of **Shea Stadium**, the ballpark of the New York Mets, and the **National Tennis Center**, home of the US Open. It was also the site of the spectacular 1939 and 1964 World's Fairs.

The center of the park is dominated by the distinctive, 380-ton **Unisphere** globe, built for the '64 fair by US Steel. A few of the old buildings constructed for the fair are still in use, though Philip Johnson's **New York State Pavilion** is an embarrassing mess; rusty, overgrown with weeds and closed to the public.

Queens Museum of Art The former New York City building of the 1939 World's Fair has been completely renovated as a museum (☎ (718) 592-9700) and contains displays dedicated to both fairs held in the park. The building was also the site of the first sessions of the United Nations before the body moved into its permanent quarters on Manhattan's East Side (a gallery explains the history of those early peacemaking meetings).

The major attraction of the museum is the **Panorama of New York City**. This 9335-sq-foot model of the metropolis debuted at the 1964 World's Fair and was a big hit with visitors who marveled at its details reproduced at a scale of 1200:1. In 1994 the panorama was cut up into 273 four-by-10-foot sections and updated to include all of the significant new additions to the local skyline. Today it's a stunning sight with more than 835,000 tiny buildings. A glass-bottomed observation deck encircles the panorama, and every 15 minutes there's a mock sunset, prompting thousands of tiny lights to flicker on across the diorama.

The Queens museum is open Wednesday to Friday from 10 am to 5 pm and Saturday and Sunday from noon to 5 pm; admission is $3/1.50.

New York Hall of Science This former World's Fair pavilion (☎ (718) 699-0005), which resembles a Stalin-era concrete block, houses a children's museum dedicated to technology. It stands next to an outdoor park with a few early space-age rockets from the '60s, and specializes in hands-on exhibits. A small zoo and playground are nearby.

The New York Hall of Science (☎ (718) 699-0005), is open Wednesday through Sunday from 10 am to 5 pm. Admission for adults/children is $4.50/3; free on Wednesday and Thursday afternoons from 2 to 5 pm.

Flushing

It's hard to imagine that this bustling neighborhood (subway: 7 to Main St-Flushing) was once a secluded forest that in the mid-17th century served as a secret meeting place for Quakers determined to circumvent Dutch Governor Peter Stuyvesant's religious intolerance. Later a country village, this was the site of the first commercial nursery in the US, visited by George Washington soon after his inauguration as president. Flushing eventually became an urban eyesore, the site of a huge commercial ash heap (mentioned in F Scott Fitzgerald's novel *The Great Gatsby)* and a series of junkyards often noted by travelers to Long Island. The area was reclaimed as park land for the World's Fair of 1939, and saw a huge influx of Korean and Chinese immigrants in the 1980s.

Packed as it is with discount shops, 24-hour coffee shops and municipal offices, Flushing is anything but architecturally charming. But at some spots, with the prevalent signage in Korean, you could possibly believe you're in a residential neighborhood in Seoul. While some of the older residents resent the incursion of new Asian immigrants, Flushing has not suffered from any serious tensions between the various communities.

Flushing's center is at the corner of Roosevelt Ave, which runs east-west, and Main St, which runs north-south – right at the subway exit.

Queens Historical Society The Queens Historical Society (☎ (718) 939-0647), 143-35 37th St, is in the Kingsland Homestead, a wooden 1765 estate house, just beyond Margaret Carmen Green.

You can get there by walking two blocks east from the subway station on Roosevelt Ave, turning left, and walking two more blocks north. The Historical Society offers maps of 'Freedom Mile,' listing 19 places of religious significance, and brochures published in English, Korean, Spanish and Chinese. The tour is a bit of a cheat, since some of the sites are really the locations of important places that no longer exist. But

you can still see the 1661 **John Bowne House**, which stands today at 37-01 Bowne St, near the Kingsland Homestead. Quakers met in the house, which is the oldest residence in Queens.

A 10-minute walk south on Bowne St will bring you to what must be Flushing's most exotic sight: the **Hindu Temple Society of North America** (☎ (718) 460-8484), 45-57 Bowne St. The temple, complete with carved elephant-headed gods, was designed and built in India and reconstructed here in 1977. Take your shoes off and enter the 2nd floor of the temple to observe devotees offering coconut milk to the deity Maha Vallabha Ganapati. There are daily services at the temple, which is open from 8 am to 9 pm, and at the side of the building a cafe serves yogurt drinks and light fare.

In late August, the temple holds a festival to the god Ganesh that lasts nearly two weeks and includes visiting performers from India and a parade through Flushing.

Leaving the temple, you should turn right on Holly Ave, then right again on Kissena Blvd, which will eventually bring you back to Main St.

Town Hall There's a contemporary art museum and historical gallery at Flushing's Town Hall (☎ (718) 463-7700), 137-36 Northern Blvd. Built in 1864, this Romanesque revival building is also the site of a year-round series of jazz and classical concerts. The museum is open Monday to Friday from 10 am to 5 pm and Saturday and Sunday from noon to 5 pm; admission is $3/2.

STATEN ISLAND

Residents of the 'forgotten borough' of Staten Island have long entertained thoughts of secession from greater New York City. Its tiny population of 378,977 – largely white, middle class and politically Republican – has historically had little clout in predominately Democratic New York City. Most politicians have made little secret of their disdain for this suburban tract of land close to the New Jersey shoreline – in fact, former Mayor David Dinkins made his very first trip to Staten Island when campaigning for office in 1989. What's worse, the borough is home to the city's (and the world's) largest garbage dump – a fact snickered about in Manhattan and deeply resented on Staten Island (the dump is scheduled to be closed permanently by 2001). The borough's image is not helped by the gray, dirty and unimpressive waterfront near the ferry terminal.

Staten Island grew when railway magnate Cornelius Vanderbilt established a ferry service between it and the port of New York in the early years of the 19th century. The island retained its character of verdant farmlands and large estates for the rich, and there was little development there until the 1960s, after the construction of the Verrazano Narrows Bridge finally forged a land link with the rest of New York City. Even still, most New Yorkers know the borough as the place to turn around after a pleasantly breezy ferry ride when the weather turns hellish in the summer, or simply as the starting point of the New York City Marathon. Of course, there's more to Staten Island, and it's worth a day trip.

The Staten Island Chamber of Commerce (☎ (718) 727-1900) provides information on cultural events and attractions Monday to Friday from 9 am to 5 pm. The *Staten Island Advance* covers local news and events.

Eighteen bus routes converge on the St George Ferry Terminal in Staten Island; you can pick up buses from there to all the major sites. The buses leave within minutes of the ferry's arrival.

The Ferry

The Staten Island Ferry (☎ (212) 806-6940) is one of New York's enduring bargains, taking 70,000 passengers each day on the free 20-minute, six-mile journey from Lower Manhattan to Staten Island (the return trip is 50¢). It operates on the half hour 24 hours a day, and only the most brutal weather keeps ferries in their slips. (Ferries carrying cars operate from

early morning until 9:30 pm and charge $3 per vehicle.)

This is the low-cost, hassle-free alternative to the crowded boat trips to the Statue of Liberty and Ellis Island. You'll pass within a half-mile of both on the way out to Staten Island, and the view back at Manhattan and Brooklyn Heights is breathtaking. It's best to pack a lunch or snack before heading out to the ferry, since the food on the boat itself is dreadful and the South Ferry terminal, an outdated and ugly facility slated for replacement within a few years, doesn't have a decent restaurant.

Snug Harbor Cultural Center

The Snug Harbor Cultural Center (☎ (718) 448-2500), 1000 Richmond Terrace, is on the site of a retirement complex for about 1000 sailors built between 1831 and 1917. The five buildings just inside the north gate are the finest small-scale Greek Revival structures left in the US. The Great Hall and the Veterans Memorial Chapel nearby have impressive interiors.

In 1976, the city took control of the run-down 83-acre site, which overlooks the oil tankers and container ships docked in Bayonne, New Jersey, and restored it as a complex for the borough's cultural institutions. You can easily spend at least half a day exploring the **Botanical Garden** (☎ (718) 273-8200), the **Children's Museum** (☎ (718) 273-2060) and the **Newhouse Center for Contemporary Art** (no phone), open Wednesday to Sunday from noon to 5 pm. A free tour of the 28 landmark buildings on the site leaves from the visitors center every Saturday and Sunday at 2 pm.

You can get to the Snug Harbor Cultural Center by taking the S40 bus two miles west from the ferry terminal.

Jacques Marchais
Center of Tibetan Art

Home to one of the largest private collections of Tibetan art outside of China, the Jacques Marchais Center (☎ (718) 987-3478), 338 Lighthouse Ave, was built by art dealer Edna Koblentz, who collected the works under an alias that did not betray her gender. It was opened to the public in 1947, a year before her death, and includes a number of golden sculptures and religious objects made of human bone. Just about the only authentic thing missing from the home, built in the style of a Tibetan temple, is the smell of yak butter. The museum holds its annual weekend Tibetan cultural festival in the early part of October in the outdoor garden among the stone Buddhas.

There's a bonus in store for those who make the trek out to the museum: near the museum, you can get a glimpse of the only private home designed by **Frank Lloyd Wright** ever built in New York City. It's the low-slung, cliffside residence at 48 Manor Court, constructed in 1959.

The Marchais Center is open Wednesday to Sunday from 1 to 5 pm, with concerts and demonstrations each Sunday at 2 pm. Admission for adults/seniors/children is $3/2.50/1.

You can get to the Marchais Center by taking the S74 bus along Richmond Rd for 25 minutes and asking the driver to let you off at Lighthouse Ave. The museum is located at the top of a hill – it's a fairly strenuous climb.

Historic Richmond Town

The village of Richmond (☎ (718) 351-1611) was once the county seat of Staten Island, and 11 original buildings still stand in what is now a borough preservation project, including the 300-year-old redwood **Voorlezer's House**, which is believed to be the oldest surviving school building in the country. In the 1960s, 11 other historic structures from around the island were moved here in an ambitious attempt to protect local history.

Historic Richmond is best seen in warm weather, when you can enjoy the surrounding landscape along the old Richmond Creek. During the summer season, volunteers dressed in period garb roam around the grounds ready to explain the ways of 17th century rural colonial life.

You can begin an exploration of the 100-acre site at the village courthouse, which serves as a visitor center. Every hour, a guide embarks from there on key tours of the 15 buildings open to the public. There's also a historical museum in the former country clerk's office.

The town is open during the summer months Wednesday to Friday from 11 am to 5 pm and Saturday and Sunday from 1 to 5 pm. From September to June it's open Wednesday to Sunday from 1 to 5 pm; admission is $4/2.50. You can reach the center by taking the S74 bus from the ferry to Richmond Ave and St Patrick's Place, a journey of about 35 minutes.

Greenbelt Nature Walks

The 2500-acre Greenbelt environmental preserve (☎ (718) 667-2165) in the middle of Staten Island encompasses several parks with five different ecosystems, including swamp areas and freshwater wetlands. It's one of New York City's unexplored nature treasures, offering some spectacular walks not far from the bustle of downtown Manhattan. Casual walkers and aggressive hikers are served by its 28 miles of trails. Birders should also head to the Greenbelt to track its 60 different species of birds.

The **High Rock Park** section of the Greenbelt offers six trails through hardwood forest and three gardens. You can get there by taking the S74 bus from the ferry to Rockland Ave, walking up Rockland and bearing right at Nevada Ave to the park entrance.

The **William T Davis Wildlife Refuge** once housed the wells that gave Staten Islanders their drinking water; today it is a sanctuary for migrating birds and the site of the Greenbelt Native Plant Center. You can reach the refuge trails by taking the S62 or S92 buses from the ferry along Victory Blvd to Travis Ave.

ACTIVITIES

Unless you're ambitious enough to head out to Staten Island to hike (see above), the city offers little respite from the urban bustle. There is one spot that offers a wide array of activities: the Chelsea Piers Complex (☎ (212) 336-6000) on the

KIM GRANT

Sunday in the park

Hudson River and 23rd St. This huge complex has a four-level driving range overlooking the river and an indoor skating rink. A huge sports and fitness center there offers a running track, swimming pool, workout center, even sand volleyball and rock climbing. A day pass costs $26. The complex is open Monday to Friday from 6 am to 11 pm, Saturday from 7 am to 8 pm and Sunday from 8 am to 8 pm.

Organized Walking Tours

There are many companies and organizations that conduct urban treks, and their phone lines offer detailed information on the latest schedules. Big Onion Walking Tours (☎ (212) 439-1090), established in 1991 by two Columbia University history doctoral candidates, operates year round. They specialize in ethnic New York and run an annual Christmas Day tour of the Jewish Lower East Side. Their walks cost $9/7 adults/students. Howard Goldberg's Adventures on a Shoestring (☎ (212) 265-2663) has been charging the same $5 admission since 1963 for tours of historic houses and other places of interest.

Citywalks (☎ (212) 989-2456) has two-hour tours of specific neighborhoods from March to November at a cost of $12 per person. The Municipal Art Society (☎ (212) 439-1043) is famous for its free tours of Grand Central Station each Wednesday at 12:30 pm; other regularly scheduled tours cost $10 a person. Arthur Marks (☎ (212) 673-0477), a weekend fixture in Greenwich Village, leads more expensive $20 tours of the streets. He wears a floppy hat and is prone to rattle off a show tune or two to illustrate points of interest.

Perhaps the weirdest new tour available is one offered by Kenny Kramer, the real-life inspiration for TV's *Seinfeld* character of the same name. He offers weekend walks past major sites of the series for $27. Call ☎ (800) 572-6377 – that spells 'KRAMERS' – for information.

Gyms

Gyms all over the city offer day rates for about $15. Many advertise in the *Village Voice*. One well-located, no frills gym to keep in mind is the Prescriptive Fitness Gym (☎ (212) 307-7760) at 250 W 54th St. It offers $13 daily rates for its well-maintained machines, and there's no 'scene' at the club, which may explain why celebrities like Michael Douglas work out there. Crunch is a popular gym chain with several locations, including 162 W 83rd St (☎ (212) 875-1902).

Running

There are three traffic-free spots to run in Manhattan. Central Park's six-mile roadway loops around the park and is closed to cars each weekday from 10 am to 3 pm and all weekend. If you don't want to jockey for space with bladers and bikers, try the Jacqueline Kennedy Onassis Reservoir (subway: 86th St on either side of the park), which is encircled by a soft 1.6-mile path. West St has a runner's pathway along the Hudson River from 23rd St all the way down to Battery Park City, which passes a very pleasant stretch of public park and offers great views of the Jersey shoreline and the Statue of Liberty. Riverside Park on the Upper West Side runs from 72nd St to above 125th St and has nice paths. The Upper East Side boasts a path that runs along FDR Drive and the East River from 63rd St to about 115th St. If you're alone it's not advisable to run further north than 105th St, since the path isn't well lit beyond that point.

The New York Road Runners Club (☎ (212) 860-4455), 9 E 89th St, organizes weekend runs all over the city as well as the October New York Marathon. Information and assistance for runners can be found at the NYRRC booth at the Engineer's Gate entrance to the park at E 90th St.

Biking

If you hit the city's pockmarked streets, use a trail bike with wide wheels. Also wear a helmet and be alert so you don't get 'doored' by a passenger exiting a taxi. Transportation Alternatives (☎ (212) 475-4600), 92 St Marks Place, is a bike advocacy group that sponsors free or low-cost weekend trips to the outskirts of the city – their newsletter is available at major bike shops.

Many places rent bicycles for the day, including Metro Bicycle with seven stores (one at 6th St and Broadway; ☎ (212) 663-7531) and Sixth Ave Bicycles (☎ (212) 255-5100), 545 Sixth Ave. Frank's Bike Shop (☎ (212) 533-6332) is an out-of-the-way shop in the Lower East Side (subway: B, D, Q to Grand St) that attracts many customers thanks to its helpful staff and very low prices.

Of course, don't forget a very good lock – a new bike vaporizes on New York City's streets without one.

In-Line Skating

In-line skating is the hot sport of the moment, and daredevil skaters with great bodies can be seen darting in and out of traffic in warm weather. Central Park, on the mall that runs east of the Sheep Meadow, is the main place to show off your skills (or lack thereof). If you're just starting out, rent a pair from the nearby Blades West (☎ 787-3911), at 120 W 72nd St, and ask a volunteer at the W 72nd St Park entrance to show you how to stop. If you take the plunge and buy, do it at Paragon downtown (see Shopping).

Boating & Fishing

You can actually fish for striped bass on the piers overlooking the Hudson River, but the river's history of chemical contamination makes eating the fish inadvisable. For better fishing head to City Island in the Bronx (see the sidebar City Island Water Sports). There, you'll find Land's End (☎ (718) 885-2424), 560 Minneford Ave, and NY Sailing School (☎ (718) 885-3103), 697 Bridge St. Both run sailing courses and rent boats during the summer months.

Places to Stay

It's harsh but true: if you want to find a good, cheap place to stay in New York City, the best thing is to find a friend who lives there. Failing that, you must plan this part of your trip very carefully. Decent rooms under $100 a night have always been a rarity, and the low US dollar has brought in so many foreign visitors that hotels in all categories are experiencing astounding 90% occupancy rates. That makes the already limited bargain choices even harder to book. Unlike most places to stay in other US cities, few Manhattan hotels offer parking, though they will be happy to tell you in advance if there is an overpriced lot in their immediate neighborhood. Bear in mind that parking in a Midtown lot for a week could cost more than $150.

But don't despair: you just need to keep in mind that two phone calls made before your arrival could turn out to be the smartest money spent on the vacation – one to make a reservation as far in advance as possible, the other confirming the booking a week or so before you arrive.

If you do come to New York on the fly and with a limited budget, you might want to front load your costs by taking a night in a pricier hotel. After a shower and a good night's sleep, start making phone calls to cheaper places – or head to a select few in person, well before the checkout time.

HOSTELS

It's easy to figure out the high season for hostels – they're booked solid when college is out of session (the four summer months and the weeks around Christmas), and beds are generally available at other times.

Call ahead if you want to stay in a hostel. Some of the city facilities will only welcome customers holding a foreign passport. This policy is at the very least rude and possibly discriminatory and illegal – why should domestic college students be barred from a public accommodation available to kids from anywhere else?

The *New York International Hostel* (☎ (212) 932-2300), 891 Amsterdam Ave (subway: 103rd St), is the Hostelling International facility in the city, and it books up its 480 beds quickly during the summer. As it's open for check-in 24 hours a day, it's the place to head if you land in town at an odd time. A bed costs $20 for members, with a small $3 surcharge for non-members. The coffee bar on site is pretty expensive – try the neighborhood delis for coffee and snacks. The drug dealing on Amsterdam Ave led the hostel to install computer card keys for the rooms a few years ago.

The *Chelsea International Hostel* (☎ (212) 627-0010), 251 W 20th St, has a party atmosphere and beds for $18, with a limited number of private rooms at $40. A few blocks up and to the west is the quieter *Chelsea Center Hostel* (☎ (212) 643-0214), 313 W 29th St; its 22 beds are $20.

There are a few alternatives to the HI/AYH facility farther uptown: the *International Student Center* (☎ (212) 787-7706), 38 W 88th St, welcomes non-US residents under 30 for $12 a night. The *Big Apple Hostel* (☎ (212) 302-2603), 119 W 45th St, is a spare facility just off Times Square that's open all day and has a laundry along with $20 beds (foreign passport required). *Banana Bungalow* (☎ (212) 769-2441), 250 W 77th St, sleeps six in a room for $12 to $18 a night, but its dirty conditions have led to a number of second-night departures. This hostel, located in a hotel that also caters to those on public assistance, has gotten a very bad reputation among travelers for having a rude and unhelpful staff. The Gershwin Hotel (see Hotels) also has dorm facilities.

Columbia University's *International House* (☎ (212) 316-8436), 550 Riverside Drive at 122nd St, is a good bet with rooms from $30 with shared bath (May to August only).

If you want to say you stayed in Harlem, call the *New York Bed and Breakfast* (☎ (212) 666-0559), 134 W 119th St, a house run by Giséle Allard, a colorful, talkative expatriate from Montreal. All five rooms cost $20 per person and share a bath. Giséle also runs a 30-bed hostel nearby at 239 Lenox Ave, and she is very proud of the clean new mattresses on offer for an incredible $12 a night.

Sugar Hill (☎ (212) 926-7030), 722 St Nicholas Ave, and the *Blue Rabbit* (☎ (212) 491-3892), 730 St Nicholas Ave, are sister hostels with 30 beds in each facility. Dorm beds are $14 and private rooms that sleep two are $16 per person per night.

If you plan on staying in hostels across the USA, write for *The Hostel Handbook*, published by the Sugar Hill folks: 722 St Nicholas Ave, NY, NY 10031 (☎ (212) 926-7030). The handbook costs US$2, £1.50 or C$3.

HOTEL DISCOUNTERS

Hotel consolidators are copying the patterns of airline bucket shops by serving as last-minute clearinghouses for unsold rooms. The Hotel Reservations Network (☎ (800) 964-6835) books rooms in 20 US cities, and their service includes nearly 100 Manhattan hotels for as little as $70 a night. As with airline consolidators, you must pay in advance, though the room can be canceled on 24-hours notice. Accommodations Express (☎ (800) 444-7666; 7 am to 11 pm Eastern Time) offers smaller discounts – around 15% – but deals with a larger number of rooms in every price category.

Quickbook (☎ (800) 789-9887) discounts moderate Midtown hotels; the office is open from 9 am to 5 pm. You can ask them about room availability in many of the hotels listed below.

B&Bs

The city does not have a single clearinghouse for B&B reservations, so several rival companies vie for the business, many offering spots in 'outlaw' B&Bs not registered

---

The Hotel Price Game

Unless you're on an expense account, you'll probably be looking for decent, reasonably priced accommodation in New York. Three factors conspire to make that task more difficult than it already is in a crowded city that already doesn't offer much in the way of European-style pensions. The first is New York's enduring popularity as a year-round destination for foreign visitors, making it almost impossible to identify a true low season where prices drop accordingly, though some major top-end hotels offer package deals for about $200 a night from January to March. Check with the Convention and Visitors Bureau (☎ (800) 692-8474, fax (212) 245-5943; outside the US and Canada, ☎ (212) 397-8222).

Moreover, New York's hotels habitually advertise dubiously low room prices – an airline trick, which means deals are only available for a certain block of less-than-desirable rooms. (A great weekend deal in a 'name' hotel almost certainly means you'll be booked into a room overlooking the facility's ventilation system rather than one with a stunning vista of Central Park.) Don't be surprised if the prices listed here are actually $20 to $50 a night cheaper than the price you'll actually pay if the tourist boom continues.

Finally, there's the matter of New York City's hotel taxes: 8.25% plus a 5% additional surcharge *and* a $2 per room per night 'occupancy tax.' That levy means that a budget-straining $220 room is, in reality, a budget-busting $250.

For possible deals you can try the hotel discounters listed on this page. And don't forget to ask for a 'corporate discount' (just name your university or employer) if you're reserving in a mainstream hotel, which can shave 10% to 15% off the quoted price. Hotel clerks almost never ask for proof at check-in and are usually understanding if you 'forget' to bring along your employee ID. ■

with the city or any organization. Rooms tend to be the same price as at the cheapest hotels, about $75 to $120 a night, with two-night minimum stays in the summer. To avoid disappointments and misunderstandings, reservation services should be prepared to describe the level of contact you will have with a host and also provide a detailed description of the neighborhood and its nearest attractions. (Most services offer reduced rates for monthly rentals.)

Urban Adventures (☎ (212) 594-5650) has 600 rooms in its registry from $75 to $125 for double occupancy. New York Bed and Breakfast (☎ (800) 900-8134) has singles/doubles starting at $60/90, with a good selection of rooms in Greenwich Village. Manhattan Home-Run Bed and Breakfast (☎ (212) 879-4229) is a newer, smaller service with 250 rooms with private baths that range from $70 to $110 a night.

The Fund for the Borough of Brooklyn has information on Brooklyn B&Bs and mails out a list of locations; call ☎ (718) 855-7882, ext 51. The borough's premier B&B is the romantic (and expensive) *Bread and Breakfast on the Park* (☎ (718) 499-8961), in a beautiful brownstone on Prospect Park West between 6th and 7th Sts.

On City Island in the Bronx there's *Le Refuge Inn* (☎ (718) 885-2478), 620 City Island Ave, a B&B run by transplanted French chef Pierre Saint-Denis. It's open year round and has eight rooms (four with shared bath) with rates of $73/85.

SUITES & LONG STAYS

In addition to the B&B services, there's Manhattan East Side Suites Hotels (☎ (800) 637-8483), a group of nine East Side locations offering kitchen-equipped suites from $159 a night weekdays and $140 on weekends, with lower rates for extended stays. City Lights Bed and Breakfast (☎ (212) 737-7049) has a 'Live Like a Millionaire' service that offers entire private apartments in uptown locations for $170 to $245 a night.

HOTELS
Lower Manhattan
Most of the available hotels below Houston St cater to a business clientele, so most offer very good deals on weekends. The downside is that the area is quite dead once the office workers go home, and you'll even have to go uptown to eat, since most Wall St area restaurants open only for lunch.

One middle-range option, Best Western's *Seaport Inn* (☎ (212) 766-6600), 33 Peck Slip, sits in the shadow of the Brooklyn Bridge at the South Street Seaport. Rates for singles are $99 to $150.

The business-oriented *Millenium Hilton* (☎ (212) 693-2001), 55 Church St (subway: Cortlandt St), rises above the street like a black pillar but is still dwarfed by the World Trade Center across the street. It's good for free-spending travelers who want great views but care little about nightlife, which is reflected in the weekday prices – singles start at $290. On weekends, however, the rates drop to $139 and include buffet breakfast.

The *New York Marriott at the World Trade Center* (☎ (212) 938-9100), located right inside the complex, has doubles from $250 and weekend specials with breakfast starting at $189.

Chinatown
If you're on a strict budget and have ever stayed in a Chinese-run hotel in Southeast Asia, you might try the *World Hotel* (☎ (212) 226-5522), 101 Bowery. This transient place is relatively clean, with 130 tiny singles/doubles running $25/35 with shared bath, and a few closet-like spaces for $12. The World is only for those with little pocket money and a strong sense of adventure. Even the most adventurous travelers should avoid the nearby *Grand Hotel* and *Hotel Paradise*, which both have the look (and odor) of flophouses and are run by suspicious and unhelpful staffs.

If you can ignore the garish interior design, the *Off SoHo Suites Hotel* (☎ (800) 633-7646), 11 Rivington St (two blocks south of E Houston St), has efficiencies

KIM GRANT

starting at $85, though you may have to share a kitchen with another room. A party of four can book adjoining suites for a total of $140.

The *Pioneer Hotel* (☎ (212) 226-1482), 341 Broome St (subway: Grand St), is a no-frills traveler hotel on the outskirts of Chinatown with singles/doubles for $34/50 with shared bath; rooms with private bath are $60.

The *Holiday Inn Downtown* (☎ (212) 966-8898), 138 Lafayette St, offers its standard accommodations in a large 223-room facility near Canal St. Rates for singles/doubles start at $130 a night and generally don't go over $200.

SoHo

Zoning laws kept hotels out of this neighborhood for years, but a savvy real estate magnate built the *SoHo Grand* (☎ (212) 965-3000), 310 West Broadway, in a well-located spot near Canal St just outside the restricted area. Unfortunately the exterior of this 367-room facility looks like a college dorm building. Inside you'll find a cast-iron staircase, a staff dressed in black (naturally) and models and assorted Eurotrash lounging in overstuffed couches along the 2nd-floor bar area. Singles cost from $199 to $300, with doubles from $219 and up. Suites are available at $400 and up.

Greenwich Village

There are a number of hotels and inns downtown that cater to gay and lesbian travelers; see the sidebar Gay Accommodations for more information.

Budget Nearby in the East Village, the *St Marks Hotel* (☎ (212) 674-2192), 2 St Marks Place, has a great location in the East Village, but the block is noisy and you

won't want to inquire about the activities of your neighbors. Singles/doubles are $45/65.

The best feature of the *Riverview Hotel* (☎ (212) 929-0060), 113 Jane St (subway: 14th St-Eighth Ave), is its location in the West Village overlooking the Hudson River just west of some of the neighborhood's most beautiful blocks. The hotel's 220 rooms are very spare, with closet-like singles for $30 a night and $150 a week with baths at the end of the hall. Doubles are $49/250 for a night/week. It's not a particularly welcoming place for single women, but it is safe and cheap. A $5 key fee is refunded upon checkout.

A good and pretty much undiscovered place is the *Larchmont Hotel* (☎ (212) 989-9333), 27 W 11th St. Located on a quiet block just off Fifth Ave, the hotel's 52 rooms have sinks (baths and kitchens in the hallways) and cost $55/90.

Middle The 160-room *Washington Square Hotel* (☎ (212) 777-9515), 103 Waverly Place (subway: W 4th St), has earned a good reputation for its location and price, but its popularity makes last-minute booking difficult. Singles/doubles cost $90/110.

The *Incentra Village* (☎ (212) 206-0007), 32 Eighth Ave, is a charming 12-room inn that's gay and lesbian friendly and booked solid every weekend. This well-maintained, quiet place has a lovely parlor; rates are $100/129 for smaller rooms and $130/170 for suites.

Chelsea & Gramercy Park

Budget *Hotel 17* (☎ (212) 475-2845), 225 E 17th St, is a popular Gramercy Park choice that offers singles/doubles with shared bath at $65/75, with private bath for around $100 a night. (Check out their new Midtown sister facility, Hotel 31.)

The *Gershwin* (☎ (212) 545-8000), 3 E 27th St, is more a hostel than a hotel and has the aura of a performance space. Just four blocks north of the Flatiron Building, this increasingly popular spot features a funky lobby that's a shrine to Andy Warhol (it features a Campbell Soup can signed by Warhol). In many ways, it's more bohemian in character than the far more famous (and pricey) Chelsea Hotel. Dorm beds are $20 per person; private rooms start at $65. The Gershwin's reputation and popularity make reservations a must, and it's becoming a popular hangout for young travelers who are staying elsewhere in the city.

Just a few steps away from the Gershwin is the gamier but cheap *Madison Hotel* (☎ (212) 532-7373), 21 E 27th St – a good alternative for those without reservations. Very spare rooms with private bath cost $60/80.

The *Senton Hotel* (☎ (212) 684-5800), 39-41 W 27th St, has a garish neon sign and looks a bit dicey from the outside, but rooms have televisions, are reasonably clean and cost $40 with shared bath and $60 private.

Middle The *Chelsea Hotel* (☎ (212) 243-3700), 222 W 23rd St, once a low-cost hangout, is now cashing in on its fame as a literary landmark. The rooms are uneven in quality and the front desk clerk will snicker if you ask for Sid Vicious's room (since remodeled and renumbered). Actor Ethan Hawke – now a published author – is the Chelsea's most famous recent resident. There are some shared-bath rooms for $70 a night, but they're nearly always booked. Rooms with private bath have climbed in price in recent years and now start at $125.

The *Gramercy Park Hotel* (☎ (212) 475-4320), at the corner of E 21st St and Lexington Ave, advertises itself as a 1st-class place, and though the location overlooking Gramercy Park is perfect, it's a bit dowdy and the service tends to be slow and inattentive. The place does have a wonderfully dark lobby bar that's worth checking out if you're merely passing by. Singles start at $135 a night.

Top End The *Inn at Irving Place* (☎ (212) 533-4600), 56 Irving Place at E 17th St, is a charming and expensive 12-room town house that has a reputation for romance. Rates begin at $275 and go as high as $325 depending on the season.

Midtown
Budget The no-frills *Herald Square Hotel* (☎ (212) 279-4017), 19 W 31st St, has held its rates for about five years to $45 for a small room with a shared bath, $55 for private bath. Doubles begin at $75.

Hotel 31 (☎ (212) 685-3060), 120 E 31st St, is the sister establishment of the East Village's Hotel 17, with similar rates: $65 for shared bath and $100 for private bath.

Furnishings are a bit frayed at the 400-room *Pickwick Arms Hotel* (☎ (212) 355-0300), 250 E 51st St, but the place is popular with European travelers. Rates start at $65, and there's a decent restaurant on the premises serving a $5.95 buffet lunch.

There are a few good mid-range places not far from Herald Square. The *Wolcott Hotel* (☎ (212) 268-2900), 4 W 31st St, is a 280-room Beaux Arts hotel designed by John Duncan, the architect of Grant's Tomb. Rates are $70/75.

A welcome new addition to the choices in Midtown is the *Murray Hill Inn* (☎ (212) 545-0879), 143 E 30th St (between Lexington and Third Aves), a converted brownstone with 50 small rooms, each with TV. Cost is $45 with shared bath, $65 private bath.

The *Vanderbilt YMCA* (☎ (212) 756-9600), 224 E 47th St (between Second and Third Aves), is a very popular place just two blocks from the UN. Its facilities include a great gym, swimming pool and (slightly overpriced) cafeteria. Due to its location, cleanliness and low cost – $53 single, $66 double – book early if you want to stay here.

The *Hotel Metro* (☎ (212) 947-2500), 45 E 35th St off Madison Ave, combines '30s Art Deco (its lobby walls feature movie posters from Hollywood's golden era) with the comfort of a gentlemen's club. It has an attractive lounge and library area. Upstairs you'll find rather plain rooms, but the price ($125 to $175) and location (near the

The Gershwin is a popular spot for young travelers.

Morgan Library and the Empire State Building) make this 160-room hotel a worthy choice.

Just south of Columbus Circle is the *Westpark Hotel* (☎ (212) 246-6440), 308 W 58th St, with easy access to Central Park. It's tough booking a room there in the summer because of its word-of-mouth popularity with European travelers. Singles/doubles start at $75/88, with two-room suites available for as low as $140.

The *Mayfair* (☎ (212) 586-0300), 242 W 49th St (between Broadway and Eighth Ave), is another reasonable small hotel very near most attractions. This smoke-free, 78-room facility offers singles from $80 to $120 and doubles from $90 to $140 depending on the season.

The *Hotel Iroquois* (☎ (212) 840-3080), 49 W 44th St, is a poorer version of the more famous Algonquin, which stands nearby, and charges $90 and up depending on the season.

Middle The area of Park Ave south of Grand Central Terminal is an unremarkable but busy stretch between Midtown and the Flatiron district that has a number of reasonably priced and unfancy hotels. *Howard Johnson on Park Ave* (☎ (212) 532-4860), 429 Park Ave South, is a comfortable place with singles/doubles starting at $105/115.

The *Madison Towers* (☎ (212) 685-3700), 22 E 38th St just off Madison Ave, is very popular with Latin American tourists, who hang out in its wonderfully tacky Whaler Bar. Rates start at $120.

The *Ameritania Hotel* (☎ (212) 247-5000), 1701 Broadway, next door to the Ed

Sullivan Theater where the *Late Show with David Letterman* is televised, is popular with European bus tours. It's decorated like a futuristic disco, and the desk clerks usually knock off 10% from the $112/130 room rate if they are told you heard about the hotel in a guidebook.

The *Warwick* (☎ (212) 247-2700), 65 W 54th St, is a newly renovated hotel with a nice lounge overlooking Sixth Ave. Rooms start at $130 a night.

The *Woodward Hotel* (☎ (212) 247-2000), 210 W 55th St, is a quiet and efficient Best Western property, located near Carnegie Hall. It has singles/doubles from $115/135, and there's access to a good local gym.

The *Hotel Wellington* (☎ (212) 247-3900), at the corner of Seventh Ave and 55th St, just two blocks south of Carnegie Hall, has 700 unremarkable but reasonably priced rooms at $125/135. Just around the corner from the main branch of the New York Public Library is the *Quality Hotel* (☎ (212) 447-1500), 3 E 40th St, a 186-room business hotel that cuts deeply into its $152/167 regular rates on weekends, when occupancy drops.

Like all the hotels on Central Park South, the *St Mortiz* (☎ (212) 755-5800), 50 Central Park South, has a great location, but it's well past its prime and the staff seems woefully overworked. That's probably why you can get room deals for as little as $125 overlooking the park.

The *Salisbury Hotel* (☎ (212) 246-1300), 123 W 57th St, is virtually across the street from icons of both high and low culture: Carnegie Hall and Planet Hollywood. Rooms are $169, with suites available for $200.

The *Fitzpatrick Manhattan* (☎ (212) 355-0100), 687 Lexington Ave (between 56th and 57th Sts), is a 92-room hotel popular with Irish visitors. While it's located near Bloomingdale's and other Midtown attractions, the hotel's bar is pretty lousy and (shockingly)

serves bad Guinness. Rates have climbed recently – rooms run from $150 to $300.

Top End Most of the expensive Midtown hotels have rates starting at $200 that fluctuate greatly according to demand.

The legendary *Waldorf Astoria* (☎ (212) 355-3000), 301 Park Ave, is the place where members of the British Royal Family turn up for fundraising dinners; singles/doubles start at $225/250, though weekend specials bring the price down to about $180. The lobby is quietly elegant but surprisingly not as grand as you would expect; the restaurants and bars within are

KIM GRANT

The view up Lexington Ave from
the Gramercy Park Hotel

suitably expensive but not remarkable enough to justify the prices.

Morgan's (☎ (212) 686-0300), 237 Madison Ave, is a sleek and unmarked hotel still popular with the European *glitterati*. Rates are $200 and up for singles and $220 to $285 for doubles, with suites beginning at $395.

Publishing executives still love to lunch at the *Royalton* (☎ (212) 869-4400), 44 W 44th St, keeping the hotel's restaurant an A-list must, but the hotel itself is easy to book into. Rooms are $250 for singles and $275 and up for doubles.

Across the street, the *Algonquin* (☎ (212) 840-6800), 59 W 44th St, still attracts people thanks to its reputation as the spot for the Algonquin Round Table of '30s New York writers, but the $200-plus rooms are often small and cramped. The old furniture was replaced during a 1991 renovation.

The *Plaza* (☎ (212) 759-3000), 768 Fifth Ave, has recently been bought by a hotel group that will presumably rein in the garish decorative excesses of the previous owner, New York developer Donald Trump. But even at $250 a night and above, you're not likely to get anything better than a postage-stamp-sized view of Central Park unless you positively insist on one before checking in. The ground floor is always busy with nonresidents meeting for expensive drinks in the Oak Room or tea in the garden court. For about the same amount of money, you're better off across the street at the elegant *Sherry Netherland* (☎ (212) 355-2800), 781 Fifth Ave.

The *Peninsula* (☎ (212) 247-2200), 700 Fifth Ave at 55th St, once known as the Gotham Hotel, is one of the oldest surviving grand hotels in Midtown, dating back to 1904. It is totally renovated and has a world-famous spa and athletic club that sprawls over three floors. Rates are $300 and up for doubles only.

Across the street, the *St Regis* (☎ (212) 753-4500), Fifth Ave and 55th St, is well known for its 1st-class service and King Cole bar, which features a mural by Maxfield Parrish that was moved from the old

Knickerbocker Hotel in Times Square. Its double rooms cost $425.

Rates at the elegant limestone *Four Seasons* (☎ (800) 332-3442), 57 E 57th St, begin at $420/470 and continue up to $800 for a suite.

Times Square

Budget If you need a Midtown space on short notice, try the *Hotel Carter* (☎ (212) 944-6000), 250 W 43rd St, a 1000-room hotel with rates as low as $50 a night. Conditions in this huge hotel are anything but 1st class. The renovated and clean *Portland Square Hotel* (☎ (212) 382-0600), 132 W 47th St, is just steps away from the middle of Times Square and has $45 rooms with shared bath; private-bath rooms start at $70.

The *Broadway Bed and Breakfast* (☎ (212) 997-9200), 264 W 46th St, just across the street from Restaurant Row, is a former run-down Times Square-area hotel that has been turned into a reasonably priced and well-located small inn with 42 neat rooms. Singles/doubles are $78/85 and come with continental breakfast. The *Milford Plaza* (☎ (212) 869-3600), 270 W 45th St, is a Ramada-owned 1300-room standard hotel that is a favorite for out-of-town bus tours and airline crews. Rooms are $75/100, with special three-day weekend deals.

Middle *Days Inn Midtown* (☎ (800) 572-6232), at the corner of Eighth Ave and 48th St, and *Quality Hotel and Suites Midtown* (☎ (212) 768-3700), 157 W 47th St, are bland chain hotels with rates from $99 to $120.

The *Hotel Edison* (☎ (212) 840-5000), 228 W 47th St, was once a high-class spot for Broadway stars that caters to tourists now, though its colorful coffee shop is still a hangout for theater people. Rates are $95/105.

The *Paramount* (☎ (212) 764-5500), 235 W 46th St, was a hip place in the early '90s, but it's no longer difficult to get into the Whiskey Bar on the street level. Singles start at $125. ·

Top End Top-end hotels around Times Square charge upwards from $160 a night but don't really offer much distinction; they are charging for their location. All are rather loudly lit, and the lobbies are set back from the street to discourage outsiders. They include the *Marriott Marquis* (☎ (212) 398-1900), 1535 Broadway; the *Novotel* (☎ (212) 315-0100), 226 W 52nd St; and the *Double Tree Suites* (☎ (212) 719-1600), 47th St and Seventh Ave.

Upper West Side

The *Broadway American Hotel* (☎ (212) 362-1100), 2178 Broadway, attracts visitors with its $45 rooms with shared bath, but it's best to pay $89 for a private bath or go elsewhere because it's a renovated welfare hotel that still has more than 100 long-term residents.

The *Excelsior* (☎ (212) 362-9200), 45 W 81st St, is an old 169-room hotel that overlooks the Museum of Natural History. Rates run from $89 for a single, and two-room suites begin at $129. The *Mayflower* (☎ (212) 265-0060), 15 Central Park West at W 61st St, though a bit stodgy, has over 500 rooms and often offers special deals for three-day weekends.

The 96-room *Newtown* (☎ (212) 678-6500), 2528 Broadway, is a smaller-sized alternative to the big West Side hotels. Rates are $65/75.

The *Hotel Olcott* (☎ (212) 877-4200), 27 W 72nd St, is an old residence hotel well known as a bargain spot on the Upper West Side. The hotel is just steps away from the Dakota building and the 72nd St entrance to Central Park, and you'll have to book early to get its singles that start at $85.

Upper East Side

The 12-room *Gracie Inn* (☎ (212) 628-1700), 502 E 81st St, is an undiscovered country-style inn near the East River run by Sandra Arcara, with singles/doubles starting at $79/139. You get a good breakfast with the room.

The *Franklin* (☎ (212) 369-1000), 164 E 87th St, is a standard place with 53 rooms running from $115 to $125.

Relatively cheap for an elegant East Side hotel is the *Hotel Wales* (☎ (212) 876-6000), 1295 Madison Ave at E 92nd St, a century-old hotel building that was recently restored to its former glory. Its 100 rooms start at $160 a night and include a continental breakfast.

Some of New York's most elegant and expensive hotels are located on the Upper East Side. For around $275 or more a night you can enjoy the quiet elegance of the *Pierre* (☎ (212) 838-8000), at 61st St and Fifth Ave. Steps away from Madison Ave is the intimate and quiet 61-room *Lowell* (☎ (212) 838-1400), 28 E 63rd St, the of-the-moment place to stay for West Coast celebrities like Quentin Tarantino. Rates start at $350.

Also worth checking out – provided money is no object – are the *Plaza-Athenee* (☎ (212) 734-9100), 37 E 64th St, the *Hotel Westbury* (☎ (212) 535-2000), at Madison Ave and E 69th St, and the *Carlyle* (☎ (212) 744-1600), at Madison Ave and E 76th St. All three are elegant, located in the middle of the high-end shopping district, and cost $300 and more per room per night.

Places to Eat

If you decided to eat in a different restaurant every night in New York City, 46 years would pass before you ran out of options. Only Paris offers a greater selection of elegant culinary experiences; but at the opposite end, absolutely no other city can beat New York's selection of reasonably priced restaurants. Of course, mixed among these 17,000 restaurants are more than a few mediocre places, usually serving fast food versions of Chinese food or other ethnic dishes. The average cost of a 'sit-down' meal with drink, tax and tip is $30. Those looking to spend a bit more can get squeezed if attention isn't paid to how the meal is adding up: dinner at an unremarkable restaurant can add up to $100 for two.

Don't be shy about asking about cost: most waiters, whatever the price level of a restaurant, neglect to tell you the cost of off-menu 'specials' or recommended wines. And if you're looking for a night of drinking, do it at a bar, not a restaurant; proprietors like to gouge on alcohol prices, especially for specialty drinks such as margaritas.

The single best source for restaurant information is the *Zagat Survey*, available at bookstores all over the city, though its critical assessments tend to be overly enthusiastic about the city's more famous restaurants. Restaurant reviews also appear weekly in *Time Out* and *New York* magazines and in the Friday *New York Times*.

RESTAURANTS
Lower Manhattan

Pearl Palace (☎ (212) 482-0771), 60 Pearl St, is a no-frills Indian restaurant open seven days a week, 24 hours a day, that fuels brokers and support staff from nearby Wall St firms. They offer a bargain all-you-can-eat buffet lunch ($6.99) Monday to Friday from 11 am to 2:30 pm that includes a salad bar. *Zigolini's* (☎ (212) 425-7171), 66 Pearl St, specializes in filling focaccia sandwiches, all for under $7.50. Some of the specials are named after customers who suggested them.

The newer *Beckett's Bar & Grill* (☎ (212) 269-1001), 78 Pearl St, is a standard-issue Irish bar serving pints and pub food to local workers during its busy lunch hour.

There are dozens of places to eat at South Street Seaport, few of them better than an average McDonald's. The *North Star Pub* (☎ (212) 509-6757), 93 South St, is a passable imitation of a British pub with traditional fare, like bangers and mash for $9.95. It's packed with office workers on weekdays.

New York's Vendor Cuisine

Even the healthiest eater may be tempted to try some fast food from one of the thousands of streetside stands located in Midtown, which now serve much more than the traditional New York hot dog with onions ($1.50). It's possible to find vendors offering up fruit, healthy soups, Middle Eastern fare such as *falafels* (crushed and spiced chickpeas fried and served in toasted pita), chicken or breaded eggplant sandwiches, take-away Thai dishes and Italian sandwiches on focaccia bread. You'll find the vendors on side streets just off the main avenues in Midtown, and a filling meal and a soda will generally cost you between $3 and $8 provided you don't buy lunch near a museum or a tourist site such as the Statue of Liberty, where prices tend to run a dollar or three higher. Avoid the 'hot' pretzels though – they are almost invariably rock hard. ∎

Slightly more expensive, but worth the detour, is the *Bridge Cafe* (☎ (212) 227-3344), 279 Water St, underneath the Brooklyn Bridge. It has an extensive wine list and entrees in the $15 range.

Chinatown

Chinese Food Everyone in New York has their favorite restaurant in Chinatown. Former mayor Ed Koch is a proud patron of *Peking Duck House* (☎ (212) 227-1810), 22 Mott St. It was over the signature specialty that Koch helped then-Paris mayor Jacques Chirac lay plans to rid the French capital of dog droppings. (The meal was more successful than Chirac's subsequent program.) *Hay Wun Loy* (☎ (212) 285-8686), 28-30 Pell St, specializes in fresh fish right out of the tank and dim sum. *Hong Ying Rice Shop* (☎ (212) 349-6126), 11 Mott St, is a prototypical basement-level Chinatown eatery, serving dishes such as shrimp with black bean sauce for $8.95. Vegans should check out the *House of Vegetarian* (☎ (212) 226-6572), 68 Mott St. The barbecue 'pork' and 'duck' dishes for $6.95 taste so much like the real thing, you'll wonder if the entire menu is a put-on.

Joe's Shanghai (☎ (212) 233-8894), 9 Pell St, is a popular outpost of a famed restaurant in the borough of Queens, but stick to the delicious appetizers – such as the steamed dumplings – and avoid the mediocre main menu items.

Just a bit farther afield, on East Broadway running directly east from Chatham Square to the Manhattan Bridge, are a number of restaurants and food stands that cater mostly to locals, since visitors tend to flock to Mott St. You'll find moderately priced Hong Kong-style food at the *Nice Restaurant* (☎ (212) 406-9779), 35 E Broadway. Its 2nd-floor banquet room is a popular spot for Chinese wedding receptions.

Vietnamese & Thai Food In recent years a number of Vietnamese restaurants have found a home in Chinatown. *Nha Trang*

(☎ (212) 233-5948), 80 Baxter St, is often packed at lunch with jurors and lawyers from the nearby city courthouses, who eat at crowded tables with other strangers. A filling meal can be had for well under $10 if you stick with dishes like the $3.50 barbecued beef on rice vermicelli and the $2.75 shrimp spring rolls. The super-rich but delicious Vietnamese-style coffee with condensed milk is $1.50. A virtually identical menu is available next door at *New Pasteur* (☎ (212) 608-3656), 85 Baxter St.

Slightly more expensive – about $1 more per meal – but less greasy is *Nha Hang* (☎ (212) 233-8988), 73 Mulberry St.

The *Thailand Restaurant* (☎ (212) 349-3132), 106 Bayard St, serves up the most authentic Thai dishes outside of Bangkok. Particularly good is the $7.95 spicy vegetarian soup – it's the closest thing to a cure for the common cold.

Italian Food Chinatown also has some low-priced Italian restaurants, including *Giambone* (☎ (212) 285-1277), 42 Mulberry St. A southern Italian restaurant, Giambone was patronized by Mafia chieftain John Gotti nearly every afternoon

Dining in New York: An Insider's Guide

Having a meal in New York can be a daunting experience even for locals, in large part because the dining experience requires more than a mere knowledge of how large a tip to leave. Some of the following phenomena shouldn't occur at expensive, 1st-class places, and won't happen at all if you're dining in a busy take away without a wait staff. But here's a quick look at some of the more annoying things you'll encounter in some of the city's bistros and middle-range restaurants – and yes, your author *has* waited on tables for a living . . . .

The Hovering Busboy Bus persons often approach a diner not just once, or twice, but up to three times within a few minutes to take your plate away, as if their very jobs depended on clearing the table a nanosecond after your final bite. This habit worsens when the restaurant is not particularly busy.

Wine List Understudies You don't have to be a wine expert or snob to object to restaurants that offer (often high priced) wine lists that don't specify years or waiters who actually bring to the table a cheaper and more recent vintage than the one advertised. And even though the average cost of a glass of wine now starts at $8 and is climbing higher, many restaurants have started substituting low-quality Chilean wines that are available by the *bottle* in wine stores for prices far cheaper than the restaurant charges for a mere glass.

'Water-Induced Deafness' New York is famous for its clean, fresh tap water, and many people prefer it to overpriced bottled water, which, after all, became a tradition in European cities with dodgy public water supplies. Yet many waiters instantly forget a request for plain tap water and have to be asked repeatedly for same. Some locals will tell you

during his corruption trials, which took place at a nearby courthouse in Foley Square.

Little Italy

A good rule of thumb while looking for a restaurant in Little Italy is to avoid any place where the manager hangs out in the street trying to drum up business. During summer months, the two blocks of Mulberry St north of Canal St are closed to traffic to allow the small restaurants more space for outdoor seating. Most of the places with al fresco dining offer entrees for $15 and under, and if you stick with pasta, you can't go far wrong.

Benito 1 (☎ (212) 226-9171), 174 Mulberry St, is one of the better known choices here. By far the best spot to sit down for a while is *Cafe Roma* (☎ (212) 226-8413), 385 Broome St, where you can have cannoli and espresso in a quiet setting after a Chinatown or SoHo meal.

Many of the storied old eateries in this neighborhood, such as *Puglia* (☎ (212) 226-8912), 189 Hester St, with its raucous singing and huge crowds, and *Vincent's* (☎ (212) 226-8133), 199 Mott St, remain profitable on the assurance that their tourist-based clientele won't be making return visits anytime soon.

SoHo

Once the center of nouveau dining, many of the restaurants in SoHo are growing tired or are plagued by erratic food quality and inattentive service. Many restaurants don't accept reservations; and when you're told the wait is '20 minutes,' rest assured that's SoHo-speak for an hour.

Budget *Lupe's East LA Kitchen* (☎ (212) 966-1326), 110 Sixth Ave, is a reasonable Mexican restaurant that is popular among locals for lunch. It offers good burritos and enchiladas in the $6.50 range.

that this goes back to the early '90s, when several summer droughts prompted a rule that patrons were to get water only on request. But with the reservoirs full these days, this 'water-induced deafness' probably has more to do with the fact that a glass of H_2O is free and thus doesn't figure in a tip. (Hint: If you have to ask for water more than twice, you're getting bad service.) This is a condition most often found in waiters who are also aspiring actors.

Pepper Worship Though not exclusively a New York phenomenon, you'll notice that waiters deliver entrees armed with a pepper mill without regard to whether you've ordered a tuna fish salad or even *steak au poivre*! It seems some secret culinary society declared this a required action in all US restaurants sometime in the later '80s. But shouldn't the meal arrive at the table with the proper amount of pepper already on it?

Coat Checks There's nothing wrong with leaving your winter coat in a separate room staffed by someone to look after it, but beware of restaurants that simply hang coats on a rod in the hallway – they're looking to make money without providing any security. And if the coat check has a sign saying the restaurant is 'not responsible for personal property' literally hanging over your hat and coat, it means that in the event that your brand new leather coat is stolen, you'll get an apology but not much else.

The Final Insult When taking cash payment for a meal, many waiters will ask 'Do you want change from that?' to save themselves the trouble of an additional trip back to the table, even if you're paying a $21 tab with two $20 bills. Nobody seems to think such a question is presumptuous. And if a woman offers to pay with her credit card, don't be surprised if the waiter (or even waitress) processes the bill and thoughtlessly hands the completed slip to the *man* at the table. ■

Vegetarian For vegetarians, SoHo offers three notable restaurants: *Souen* (☎ (212) 807-7421), 219 Sixth Ave, has a wide selection of macrobiotic menu items, as well as less stringent vegetarian dishes. *Helianthus Vegetarian* (☎ (212) 598-0287), 48 MacDougal St, features Chinese and Japanese food and offers a lunch deal that includes a dumpling and rice with dishes like lemon mock chicken and sautéed udon for around $5.50. *Spring Street Natural* (☎ (212) 966-0290), 62 Spring St, is a louder and busier restaurant with a large menu that in addition to vegetarian selections includes healthy fish and chicken dishes for $15 and under.

Middle *Lucky Strike* (☎ (212) 941-0479), 59 Grand St, features French bistro fare, and the menu, painted on mirrors above the table, has remained unchanged for several years. It gets very crowded late on Friday and Saturday when a DJ plays the front room. *Fanelli's Cafe* (☎ (212) 226-9412), 94 Prince St, is one of the grittier places in the neighborhood. It's a dark, smoky bar with pressed tin ceiling and burgers for a reasonable $10.

Le Jardin Bistro (☎ (212) 343-9599), 25 Cleveland Place (one block east of Lafayette St, near Kenmare St; subway: Spring St), is a newcomer with French fare for $15. It has a very popular back garden, but unfortunately the management doesn't respect reservations and keeps customers waiting an unconscionably long time, and it also promotes illegal smoking in the dining room.

Top End *Cascabel* (☎ (212) 431-7300), 218 Lafayette St, offers a dramatic eating experience with its blood-red decor and adventurous menu. Everything is delicious – but costly (around $50 per person).

The *Kitchen Club* (☎ (212) 274-0025),

30 Prince St, is an intimate space where owner-chef Marja Samson works in full view of diners. She's a bit eccentric – if you spot a worm in your salad, she will respond with a lecture on the wonders of organic foods. The mushroom dumplings, Japanese box dinners and pumpkin ice cream are sublime.

Raoul's (☎ (212) 966-3518), 180 Prince St, has the attitude and pulse of a classic late-night bistro. The menu, written in chalk on a blackboard, is exclusively in French accompanied by Parisian-level prices – $40 or more per person with wine. Smokers are relegated to the isolated back garden room, which is entered by passing through the busy kitchen. Across the street is *Quilty* (☎ (212) 254-1260), 177 Prince St, an austere white space named after Humbert Humbert's adversary in Vladimir Nabokov's novel *Lolita*. The walls are decorated with butterflies under glass, an allusion to Nabokov's passionate nonliterary pursuit. A solid selection of fish and game items are on the menu for about $20.

Tribeca

In recent years Tribeca has overtaken SoHo as the trendiest dining spot in the city, but there is still a healthy selection of moderately priced restaurants.

Middle *Odeon* (☎ (212) 233-0507), 145 West Broadway, is an amazing phenomenon: a once-trendy '80s restaurant that has not only survived but thrived in this decade. It serves bistro fare such as lamb sandwiches and steak frites for under $18 until 2 am every day.

The former chef from Odeon has made a big debut on his own with *The Independent* (☎ (212) 219-2010), 179 West Broadway. There's an inexpensive lunch menu ($12 and under) and a wide array of bistro choices at night for about $5 more.

Riverrun (☎ (212) 966-3894), 176 Franklin St (subway: Franklin St), was one of the first restaurants in the area and features $2.95 pints during happy hour and a juke box that still costs just 10¢ per play. Unfortunately, this place's pub grub has become grossly bad in recent years and should be avoided. A far better alternative is the nearby *Walker's* (☎ (212) 941-0142), 16 N Moore St, a dark watering hole with three dining rooms and a very reasonable Sunday brunch. It serves straightforward fare – sliced turkey sandwiches and hamburgers for $6.95. Jazz combos play Sunday nights with no cover charge.

The *Liquor Store Bar* (no phone), 235 West Broadway, is a popular nighttime hangout in a small Federal-style building that its owners proudly claim has been in continuous commercial use since 1804. The bar is rather unimaginatively named after a previous business at the same site; locals, inspired by the furry animals often seen scampering down the street, call it the Rat Bar.

Bubby's (☎ (212) 219-0666), 120 Hudson St, is always packed on weekends for its breakfast fare, with locals hoping to spot actor Harvey Keitel, who lives around the corner. You may have to wait an hour for a table for brunch.

Top End Reservations are required weeks (and for Saturday months) in advance at *Chanterelle* (☎ (212) 966-6960), 2 Harrison St, which offers a fixed-price dinner menu for around $80 per person. Its changing menu often features a heavenly seafood sausage, and the combined experience of service and cuisine in the spare dining room is world class.

Montrachet (☎ (212) 219-2777), 239 West Broadway, doesn't offer much in the way of decor and is super expensive at night (Salmon entrees for $27). But the restaurant is worth remembering for the $20 lunch specials.

Greenwich Village

Picking a restaurant around Bleecker St between Broadway and Seventh Ave is difficult – there are many choices, and more than a few are mediocre. Tread warily and consider these selections, or head to the cheaper choices on Second and Third Aves in the East Village. Most of the following are within walking distance of the W 4th St subway station.

Budget Passersby can watch the homemade noodles being prepared at *Sammy's Noodles* (☎ (212) 924-6688), 453-461 Sixth Ave, which sprawls over several storefronts. Filling (and unhealthy) lunch specials start at $4.50, and none of the noodle dishes are more expensive than $6.95.

Despite its trendiness and late-night scene, *Bar Six* (☎ (212) 645-2439), 502 Sixth Ave, is actually a reasonable place to stop for lunch. Grilled chicken or rockfish sandwiches cost just $6.95 and include soup or salad.

Picasso Cafe (☎ (212) 929-6232), 359 Bleecker St, is another good budget choice, serving light crusted pizza and sandwiches for under $10 in a fine garden space right in the heart of the West Village.

The landmark *White Horse Tavern* (☎ (212) 989-3956), 567 Hudson St, has a popular outdoor dining area where decent pub grub is served. This is the place where poet Dylan Thomas is often said to have drunk himself to death in 1953. (He did

---

This Year's Model

Nobu (☎ (212) 219-0500), 105 Hudson St, the oh-so-trendy sushi restaurant, has taken chichi dining in Manhattan to a new level of insanity. In order to make a mere reservation, you must provide them with a credit card – they threaten to charge $25 per person if anyone neglects to show up. Its tasting menu, prepared by hot chef Nobuyuki Matsuhisa, begins at $60 a person, and while some say it's worth the price, the inattentive service makes the whole evening feel like a complete rip-off – you're better off going to the far cheaper sushi restaurants on E 9th St off Third Ave. For now Nobu is coasting on star power, but what will they do when Meryl Streep stops eating there? ∎

---

spend his last night on the town there, but died a few days later in a hospital.)

Middle *Dix et Sept* (☎ (212) 645-8023) is a mid-priced French bistro located, naturally enough, on the corner of Seventh Ave and 10th St. It proclaims itself to be 'Paris without the attitude,' but the restaurant's obnoxious bartenders didn't get the message, so give the bar a miss and head to the tables for solid fare.

Grange Hall (☎ (212) 924-5246), 50 Commerce St, just off Barrow St a block from Sixth Ave, is a converted neighborhood tavern with a beautiful wooden bar that serves organic foods. It's very popular and the wait can be as long as an hour without a reservation, but the prices are reasonable – the $7.95 smoked trout salad appetizer is a meal in itself. *Caffe Lure* (☎ (212) 473-2642), 169 Sullivan St, is a cramped and popular French bistro with a wood-burning oven. The individual pizzas, all under $11, are delicious, but avoid the place on hot summer nights – the oven turns the restaurant into a sauna. Nearby is *Tomoe Sushi* (☎ (212) 777-9346), 172 Thompson St, a wildly popular place that always seems to have a line. Its

---

The Pizza War

An odd little pizza war is taking place in New York among several unrelated pizzerias named Ray's. While all claim to be the 'original Ray's,' that distinction is generally thought to belong to the one located at Sixth Ave and 11th St. Oddly enough, though, no one quite seems sure what it was about this Ray's that prompted the good word of mouth. One decent Ray's claimant is located near the Puck Building on Prince St, but you're better off passing it by and patronizing *Lombardi's* (☎ (212) 941-7994), 32 Spring St, indisputably the oldest pizza restaurant in New York. Established in 1905, this brick-oven pizzeria serves only pizza pies and huge calzones, delicious half-moon dough shells stuffed with ricotta cheese and herbs. The fresh mushroom pie is served with three different types of the fungus. ■

---

sushi – reputed to be the best in the city – is $15 to $25.

A more undiscovered gem is *Piadina* (☎ (212) 460-8017), 57 W 10th St, where friendly waiters serve the namesake appetizer, an Italian version of quesadillas – melted cheese and other delicious additives between thin baked slices of bread.

Let's Do Brunch

Though it's said that New York is the city that never sleeps, it's not quite true. You'll notice that absolutely *nothing* happens before noon on Sundays. Then, at about 12:30 pm, everyone seems to have the same idea – buy the Sunday *Times* and head off to have brunch with friends. Almost every decent brunch spot south of 14th St seems to have long lines and crowded dining rooms. Most don't take reservations for brunch business, so be prepared to wait in line – or get to the restaurant at noon. ■

El Faro (☎ (212) 929-8210), 823 Greenwich St, is a classic old Spanish restaurant that's quiet during the week and impossibly crowded on Friday and Saturday nights. The decor hasn't changed in 20 years, nor have the waiters. Main dishes like the spicy shrimp diablo may seem pricey at $16, but they're enough to feed two people.

In the heart of the meat-packing district sits *Florent* (☎ (212) 989-5799), 69 Gansevoort St (off Washington St), a French-run bistro offering hanger steak, hamburgers and breakfast selections. On the weekend closest to July 14th, the restaurant takes over Gansevoort St for an open-air Bastille Day celebration featuring everything from drag queens to Frank Sinatra imitators. It's also a great place to pick up reduced admission flyers for downtown nightclubs.

Cornelia St, a small block between Bleecker and W 4th St, has four middle-range restaurants of note. *Cornelia St Cafe* (☎ (212) 989-4319), at No 29, is the oldest of the lot and a perfect space for brunch. Right next door is *Pó* (☎ (212) 645-2189), at No 31, a tiny spot with a Northern Italian flavor. *Home* (☎ (212) 243-9579), at No 20, has fresh grilled fish specials for around $12, and is quite famous for its tremendously rich chocolate pudding. *Le Gigot* (☎ (212) 627-3737), at No 18, is a cozy and popular newcomer with standard and hearty bistro fare.

Italian There are many middle-range Italian restaurants in Greenwich Village. Among the best is *Trattoria Spaghetto* (☎ (212) 255-6752), 232 Bleecker St at the corner of Carmine St, a converted old coffee shop with traditional red-checked vinyl tablecloths. Almost all the pasta dishes are $10.

Slightly more expensive, and certainly more colorful, is *Rocco* (☎ (212) 677-0590), 181 Thompson St just north of Houston St, where the friendly and attentive wait staff will be happy to provide your favorite dish even if it's not on the menu. This gathering place for local Village eccentrics has been around for 60 years.

Marinella (☎ (212) 807-7472), 49

Carmine St, not only has a multi-paged menu, but displays extensive daily specials on a blackboard that is wheeled from table to table. The northern Italian chicken, fish and veal entrees cost about $14.

East Village

In terms of price, pure choice and reliability, this area is the best in the city for travelers on a budget. It offers just about everything but fancy French dining.

Budget *Benny's Burritos* (☎ (212) 254-2054), 93 Ave A, decorated in '60s kitsch (lava lamps, pink walls and Formica tables), is a local pioneer in low-fat Cal-Mex food. The super-filling burritos and enchiladas are $7 and under, and include plenty of options for vegetarians. But watch out for the lethal margaritas. A larger and more crowded Benny's is located in the West Village at 113 Greenwich St (☎ (212) 727-0584).

Bereket (☎ (212) 475-7700), 187 E Houston St on the corner of Orchard (subway: Second Ave), is a 24-hour kebab eatery with a good selection of vegetarian dishes. It's a favorite with club hoppers heading to and from the newest no-name club on nearby Ludlow St.

Hotel Galvez (☎ (212) 358-9683), 103 Ave B, features healthy takes on Tex-Mex food and country folk music performers in the adjacent lounge. (Ave B is rapidly becoming the spot to visit as a cluster of clubs, restaurants and bars open up above Houston St north to E 10th St.)

The East Village has many delis and diners that serve filling meals at low prices. The late French-Italian actor Yves Montand's favorite hang-out in New York was the *Second Ave Deli* (☎ (212) 677-0606), 156 Second Ave, a quintessential Jewish deli offering great fare (the matzo ball soup comes with sprigs of fresh dill). This restaurant offers much better bargains than the more touristy alternatives in Midtown: the Carnegie Deli and Stage Deli.

There's also Katz's Deli (☎ (212) 254-2246), on the corner of Ludlow and Houston Sts, a Lower East Side institution since 1888. Entering Katz's, you receive a

---

Little Delhi

Sixth St between Second and First Aves has been dubbed 'Little Delhi' thanks to the 20 restaurants that have popped up on the block since the late 1970s. (Don't bother asking the proprietors if all the restaurants share the same kitchen – it's a tired joke they've heard a million times before.) The name of the street is a bit of a misnomer, since most of the immigrants who have opened shop there are from Bangladesh.

At one time, they were all crowded on weekend nights, but as Indian cuisine has become more common elsewhere in town (and the Indian population has shifted to the Jackson Heights section of Queens) these eateries have hit slower times. Of late there has been a mad war for lunch business, with many of the restaurants offering four- and five-course meals for as little as $4.95, including soft drink and coffee. In general, the restaurants offering live Indian music and/or a wine list wind up being more expensive than their alcohol-free counterparts. Arrive at the dry places with your own store-bought beer – there's an Indian market on the corner of First Ave and 6th St with a very good selection. ■

---

ticket upon entry and have it marked up with each purchase you order. If you're undecided about whether to order the corned beef or pastrami, the countermen will cut off a slice for you to taste. The food is still tasty, and Katz's was the setting for Meg Ryan's infamous orgasm scene in *When Harry Met Sally*.

Middle *Time Cafe* (☎ (212) 533-7000), 380 Lafayette St, is a pleasant surprise: a trendy nightspot, popular with models, that actually serves very good organic food, although the service can sometimes be inattentive. There's a good selection of pizzas at $10.95 and other entrees top out at about $18.00. *Fez*, the lounge immediately behind the restaurant, serves lighter Moroccan fare. *Roettele AG* (☎ (212) 674-4140), 126 E 7th St, is a Swiss restaurant incongruously located on a block in the East Village that retains much of its Polish character. Strapping waitresses serve healthy portions of *Sauerbraten* and *veau emincee* (sliced veal with mushrooms) for around $16 an entree.

John's of 12th St (☎ (212) 475-9531), 302 E 12th St, has been in business for more than 80 years. This warm wood-paneled restaurant with candlelight dining offers traditional Italian food and service. If you stick with the pasta selections, your meal will stay under $10, but the specials can go up as high as $18.

With its pressed-tin ceilings and faded paintings, *Lanza's* (☎ (212) 674-7014), 168 First Ave (near E 10th St), is a throwback to an earlier time in the East Village. Its five-course Italian dinner (for just $11.95) includes a selection of delicious desserts. If you're not hungry but want a strong espresso and an Italian pastry, try the nearby *DeRobertis* pasticceria (☎ (212) 674-7137), 176 First Ave, which has been in business since 1904.

Lucky Cheng's (☎ (212) 473-0516), 24 First Ave, is a Thai restaurant featuring drag queen 'waitresses' that has been over-taken by curious out-of-towners. Reservations are often not respected – you can encounter an hour-long wait – and the food is as temperamental as the he/she server. If you're looking for a high-concept food experience in the East Village, call *Princess Pamela's Southern Touch Restaurant* (☎ (212) 477-4460), 78 E 1st St, where you'll be treated to soul food, live entertainment most weekends, and often the Princess herself, who will be happy to sit down and share her opinions of the famous and the infamous who have eaten there – mention Idi Amin and you'll make an evening of it.

Japanese In recent years E 9th St has become something of a Little Tokyo with excellent sushi restaurants lining the street. *Hasaki* (☎ (212) 472-3327), 210 E 9th St, has the best reputation. Try there first, but if

Florent, in the heart of the meat-packing district

you find you have a long wait ahead of you, then go next door to *Sharaku* (☎ (212) 598-0403), 8 Stuyvesant St, where there are plenty of tables and a large menu featuring many Japanese specialties aside from the sushi.

Chelsea

It could be argued that Chelsea has the best and most varied dining experiences in the city. But for some of its more popular (and expensive) restaurants, you'll need to make weekend reservations weeks in advance.

Budget One of New York's oddest hybrid cuisines is the cheap and filling fare developed by Chinese immigrants who once lived in Cuba and moved to the US following the revolution in the late 1950s. The best of the Cuban-Chinese restaurants in Chelsea is *Sam Chinita* (☎ (212) 741-0240), on Eighth Ave and 17th St, with its diner atmosphere and items such as plantains and *ropa vieja*, well-cooked beef in a spicy sauce.

The 24-hour *Empire Diner* (☎ (212) 243-2736), 210 Tenth Ave, attracts many Chelsea club hoppers at night.

KIM GRANT

Village cafe scene

Middle *America* (☎ (212) 505-2110), 9 E 18th St, is a huge, noisy place with a multi-page menu that's worth checking out for the elevated bar in the back, which is covered by a skylight. Have a drink there and then head for the as-yet-undiscovered *Cafe Bondi* (☎ (212) 691-8136), 7 W 20th St, an isolated spot with a back garden that specializes in Sicilian cooking.

Alva (☎ (212) 228-4399), 36 E 22nd St, is a dark and sleek American bistro that has a light bulb motif in honor of the inventor Thomas Alva Edison. There is a reasonable wine list and fresh fish entrees for around $18.

Top End Two of the best places in Chelsea, or indeed the entire city, are the *Union Square Cafe* (☎ (212) 243-4020), 21 E 16th St, and the *Gramercy Tavern* (☎ (212) 477-0077), 42 E 20th St. These sister restaurants are renowned for providing five-star dining at three-star prices; as a consequence it's necessary to book weeks beforehand to eat on a weekend night. Gramercy Tavern – which has a much more erratic level of service and quality – serves a $57 fixed-price menu nightly.

Just as expensive are the Latin American *Patria* (☎ (212) 777-6211), 250 Park Ave South, and *Mesa Grill* (☎ (212) 807-7400), 102 Fifth Ave, with hot Southwestern fare.

Midtown
Budget *Madras Mahal* (☎ (212) 684-4010), 104 Lexington Ave, is but one of 10 Indian restaurants between 27th and 29th Sts, but this vegetarian spot is the only one in the city that conforms to kosher rules of preparation. There's a lunch buffet available for $6.95.

Just off the northeast corner of W 55th St and Eighth Ave is the *Soup Kitchen International* stand (☎ (212) 757-7730), whose gruff owner, Al Yeganeh, was parodied in an episode of the hit TV series *Seinfeld* as the 'Soup Nazi.' This colorful character requires that you announce your selection within seven seconds (the better to move the line of patrons along), but his hot and cold soup selections are absolutely delicious and come in three sizes ($6/8/10), and come accompanied by a fresh piece of bread, salad and fruit. Be aware that the queue can last up to 40 minutes at lunchtime no matter what the weather, and the proprietor tends to close his shop up for weeks at a time to take unannounced vacations.

La Fondue (☎ (212) 581-0820), 43 W 55th St, offers very reasonable lunches in a narrow dining space off Sixth Ave. Fondue for one costs $7.95, and daily lunch specials are available for $8.95 including a main course, salad and a glass of wine. Across the street, the slightly more expensive *La Bonne Soupe* (☎ (212) 586-7650), 48 W 55th St, has similar lunch specials with a French flavor. There are more than two dozen delis, pubs and moderately priced restaurants on 55th and 56th Sts between Sixth and Fifth Aves serving Midtown office workers. It's also worth checking out the *JP French Bakery* (☎ (212) 765-7575), 54 W 55th St, which offers coffee, Gallic pastries and sandwiches on fresh baguettes for $7 and under.

Middle The east side of Midtown is pretty desolate for decent fare, except along Second and First Aves in the 40s and 50s. *Billy's* (☎ (212) 753-1870), 948 First Ave at 52nd St, offers a glimpse of old New York dining. It is over 120 years old, with checkered tablecloths and wooden floors. But its common entrees are a bit pricey, in the $15 to $20 range. Less historic, and less expensive, is the *Mayfair* (☎ (212) 421-6216), 964 First Ave, which has a similar menu.

Sarge's (☎ (212) 679-0442), 548 Third Ave at 36th St, is a classic late-night deli that offers very filling lunch fare for under $8, including soup and beverage.

Le Quercy (☎ (212) 265-8141), 52 W 55th St, is an unpretentious, but authentic French bistro where you can get a good glass of steely Sancerre. A three-course lunch costs $19, with several options per course, including broiled monk fish and chicken grandmere.

Island Burgers and Shakes (☎ (212) 307-7934), 766 Ninth Ave, specializes in *churascos*, a juicy breast of chicken sandwich that comes in more than 50 different varieties for under $8.

Two popular delis are the *Carnegie Deli* (☎ (212) 757-2245), 854 Seventh Ave at W 54th St, and *Stage Deli* (☎ (212) 245-7850), 834 Seventh Ave at W 53rd St. The Carnegie is a tourist trap with an undistinguished menu featuring huge sandwiches for about $12, and the Stage is a pale imitation of the Carnegie.

Top End There are plenty of restaurants in Midtown that rely on expense-account executives, but few have the quality to match their prices. One that certainly does is *Aquavit* (☎ (212) 307-7311), 13 W 54th St. The main dining room is in a stunning six-story glass-enclosed atrium complete with a silent waterfall. The $55 fixed-price menu may seem steep, but it's worth every penny considering that the entrees, like venison with berry sauce, are sublime.

Le Bernadin (☎ (212) 489-1515), 155 W 51st St, is renowned for its ultra-fresh fish offerings. The food lives up to its reputation, but the setting, in a bland Midtown office block, doesn't quite justify the $48 lunch menu tab.

Vong (☎ (212) 486-9592), 200 E 54th St and Second Ave, offers pricey Asian fare to office workers in an elegant setting. It's best to go there for the lunch specials, all running around $20.

Times Square

The side streets off Times Square are filled with hamburger joints and a variety of middle-range ethnic restaurants of varying quality. You'll do okay if you stick to unambitious food choices or patronize the following selections.

It may not look like much from the outside, but *King Crab* (☎ (212) 765-4393), 871 Eighth Ave, specializes in delicious and cheap seafood dinner specials for under $12; it's a good option before the theater. *Mee Noodle Shop* (☎ 765-2929), 795 Ninth Ave, is part of the city's best chain of cheap Chinese restaurants, serving a hearty bowl of broth, noodles and meat for just $4.95. Mee offers the same menu at two other locations: 922 Second Ave at 49th St and 219 First Ave at 13th St.

Restaurant Row Restaurant Row is officially the block of W 46th St between Eighth and Ninth Aves, but locals use the name to refer to almost all the restaurants west of Times Square.

Some mediocre places – usually those serving glorified pub grub – survive thanks to their proximity to the theater district, but there are a few gems here, too. *Joe Allen* (☎ (212) 581-6464), at No 326, serves entree salads, sandwiches and soup in a brick-walled room lined with the posters of famous Broadway flops. It's impossible to get into the place before the theater without a reservation, but it clears out completely for walk-ins by the 8 pm curtain time. *Orso* (☎ (212) 489-7212), right next door at No 322, is also run by Joe Allen and serves more expensive Tuscan food at about $17 to $20 per entree. It's popular with theater people and has a daily late-night seating at 10:30 pm for those coming out of performances. *Barbetta* (☎ (212) 246-9171), at No 321, is in an old townhouse that may have once been a brothel. You can get a $25 fixed-price menu in its quiet garden. *Hourglass Tavern* (☎ (212) 265-2060), at No 373, is a tiny place with reasonably priced stews and fish dishes that is (inaccurately) described as an expensive restaurant in the John Grisham novel *The Firm*.

Just around the corner is *Zen Palate* (☎ (212) 582-1669), 663 Ninth Ave, which serves an exclusively vegetarian menu.

Hell's Kitchen The formerly dangerous blocks along and around Ninth Ave are being rapidly gentrified. There are dozens of new, moderately priced places to patronize offering all kinds of ethnic cuisines.

Mike's (☎ 246-4115), 650 Tenth Ave, is a Cajun-influenced cheap bistro with ever-changing decorative themes that have turned the place into a pinball machine and a Christmas shrine to Madonna (the singer, not the Virgin Mother).

Puttanesca (☎ (212) 581-4177), 859 Ninth Ave at 56th St, is typical of the Italian restaurants in this neighborhood. The pasta dishes are all around $10 and can be followed by some rather delicious desserts. Dinner for two with drinks will run $45 or less. But perhaps the best new addition is *Bricco* (☎ (212) 245-7160), 304 West 56th off Eighth Ave. This two-story place is quite reasonable – the dishes tend to be $15 and under, with wine $22 a bottle – and the quality of service and fare high, so there's great value for money.

The area of Ninth Ave from 38th to 40th Sts may be unique in the city, as it offers at least 12 different cuisines within three blocks, a reflection of the many recent immigrants who, working as cab drivers or pushcart vendors, frequent the area after their shifts. Along the avenue or just off it, you can find Italian, Indian, Chinese, West African, Haitian, Filipino, Pakistani, Mexican, Cuban and Cajun eateries! Among the mainstays are the *Cupcake Cafe* (☎ (212) 465-1530), 522 Ninth Ave at 39th St, which makes specialty wedding cakes and serves an array of fancy pastries, and *Guido's* (☎ (212) 564-8074), a pasta restaurant located across the street in the Supreme Macaroni Company building at 511 Ninth Ave. A block farther south is *Manganaro's* (☎ (212) 563-5331), 488 Ninth Ave, a wood-floored Italian grocery that serves cheap pasta dishes and heroes for under $5.

Upper West Side

Budget The Upper West Side has dozens of cheap Chinese restaurants, pubs and fast food joints. The most reliable Chinese selection is *Empire Szechuan* with seven city locations, including 251 W 72nd St (☎ (212) 496-8460) and 193 Columbus Ave above 68th St (☎ (212) 496-8778). These bustling places serve generally healthy fare and offer lunch specials for around $7.

Tibet Shambala (☎ (212) 721-1270), 488 Amsterdam Ave, has a menu split evenly between meat and vegetarian dishes for $8.95 and under (salad and rice included).

Cafe Lalo (☎ (212) 496-6031), 201 W 83rd St, has a 14-page menu of slightly expensive pastries, but you can spend an entire rainy afternoon here reading the dozens of newspapers and magazines on offer.

Top End The neighborhood's moderate restaurants tend to have mediocre food and inattentive service. If you're in that price range, head a little farther south on Ninth Ave to 40th St and pick a place with an interesting window-displayed menu. But if you're looking to splurge, try either of the neighborhood's well-known and expensive restaurants: *Cafe Luxembourg* (☎ (212) 873-7411), 200 W 70th St, is impossible to get into without a reservation before performances at Lincoln Center, when it offers a $19.95 special dinner.

The romantic *Cafe des Artistes* (☎ (212) 877-3500), 1 W 67th St, has seen countless marriage proposals over the years. The restaurant features a famous mural of naked nymphs prancing through Central Park, which almost obscures the generally high quality of the entrees in the $20 range. Men must wear jackets after 6 pm.

Tavern on the Green (☎ (212) 873-3200), at W 67th St and Central Park West, is the most profitable restaurant in the US, pulling in an astounding $32 million annually from visitors who want to admire its flood-lit topiary statues in the back garden. The restaurant has improved food quality from atrocious to not bad, but the wait staff is alternately patronizing or inattentive. If you must visit, absolutely insist on sitting outside or by a window and expect to pay about $50 a person, even for brunch.

Harlem

Harlem is justifiably famous for its soul food, but there's also a growing West African influence in the neighborhood. Vegetarians or those seeking low-fat choices will have a hard time. Most of the following restaurants are within walking distance of the 125th St subway stations. Most places serve big portions at incredibly cheap prices.

Soul Food By far the most famous restaurant in Harlem is *Sylvia's* (☎ (212) 996-0660), 328 Lenox Ave, which has a gospel brunch on Sunday afternoon

KIM GRANT

Tavern on the Green, the USA's
most profitable restaurant

(reservations required). *Copeland's* (☎ (212) 234-2357), 547 W 145th St (off Broadway; subway: 1/9 to 145th St), is famous for its $12.95 midweek nighttime buffet; eating à la carte (entrees run as high as $17) means a higher tab. *Copeland's Country Kitchen* is a sister restaurant at 203-205 W 125th St, just steps away from the Apollo Theater.

You can get the real deal at much better value at *Singleton's Barbecue* (☎ (212) 694-9442), 525 Lenox Ave, where the $5.50 lunch specials offer pig's feet, smothered chicken livers and other delicacies with a choice of two vegetables. *M & G Soul Food Diner* (☎ (212) 864-7326), 383 W 125th St, is open 24 hours a day, seven days a week. Its grumpy waitresses serve up breakfasts ($4.50) from midnight until 1 pm and huge portions round the clock. *Louise Family Restaurant* (☎ (212) 864-8400), 217 Lenox Ave, is another good choice for breakfast.

Caribbean & West African Food *Pan Pan* (☎ (212) 926-4900), 500 Lenox Ave, offers spicy Jamaican meat patties for $1.25 and coffee-and-roll breakfasts for $1. Members of the Senegalese staff at *Darou Minam* (☎ (212) 864-9024), 1943 Powell Blvd, don't speak English very well, but the delicious West African dishes they serve up transcend all language barriers. Their specialty is *Mafe* – lamb prepared in a peanut sauce – for just $5. *Keur Samba* (☎ (212) 864-6161), 120-126 W 116th St just off Lenox Ave, is considered the best French African restaurant in the neighborhood for its spicy fish stews that start at $7.

Italiaii Several landmark remnants of Italian East Harlem remain in business, though the Italian residents moved out decades ago and return here only to eat. Check out *Morrone's Bakery* (☎ (212) 722-2972), 324 E 116th St, for great peasant bread. *Rao's Restaurant* (☎ (212) 722-6709), 455 E 114th St, is an expensive restaurant with just 12 tables that's famous for claiming to be booked months in advance (the rules are bent if you're Woody Allen or a local politician). If you want to

go, show up early in the evening well dressed and polite. If you're in jeans, check out *Patsy's Pizzeria* (☎ (212) 534-9783) at 2287 First Ave (open Monday through Saturday from 10 am to 10 pm, Sunday noon to 10 pm).

Upper East Side

Visitors should be aware that the East Side, particularly in the Midtown area of the 50s and 60s, has an overabundance of lousy restaurants that survive on the patronage of Midtown hotel visitors. Here are a few rules of thumb for moderate to high-priced restaurants in the area, which apply to all the East Side up to Spanish Harlem. The cuisine choices are predominately Chinese, Italian or French. In *general*, the Chinese restaurants offer lousy, '60s-era Chinese fare (that is, Americanized food like Egg Foo Young) in black lacquer settings that appeal to well-heeled old patrons. The Italian restaurants offer regional dishes and tend to be moderate, though willing to charge far too much for pasta entrees ($12 to $20). (For an exception see Hosteria Fiorella below.) The French restaurants up here are generally of decent quality, but are almost uniformly expensive, just like their Parisian counterparts.

Budget *Favia Lite* (☎ (212) 223-9115), 1140 Second Ave, is a healthy Italian restaurant near the 59th St Bridge that serves surprisingly tasty pasta entrees, listing calories and fat content for every menu item. The large grilled chicken pizza costs $15; skimmed milk or soy mozzarella is available at no extra charge.

There are dozens of moderately priced restaurants on Second and Third Aves between 60th and 86th Sts that offer lunch specials for under $10. *Cafe Greco* (☎ (212) 737-4300), 1390 Second Ave (between 71st and 72nd Sts), is a typical example of the norm, serving continental dishes and a good weekend brunch.

Middle Many small, wood-paneled restaurants with a French flavor line Madison Ave north of 60th St and several nearby

Theme Restaurants

There has been an explosion of tourist-trap restaurants in the Midtown area around 57th St, transforming what was once one of the most exclusive shopping districts on earth. Some high-end shops such as Burberry's and Chanel are still located there, but the area has become home to a growing number of logo-peddling theme palaces. Some are simply ludicrous (the unsuccessful Fashion Cafe, a restaurant supposedly created by supermodels who are famous for not eating) or just plain fake (Hansen's 'olde style' Brewery).

The formula behind these places follows a plan mapped out by Robert Earl, the British businessman behind the Hard Rock Cafe and Planet Hollywood. These glittery palaces have celebrity 'owners,' usually movie or sports stars with a minor financial interest, who show up with their friends at the opening. Schwarzenegger, Stallone and Willis only show up for restricted-list parties for their latest films, but videos of the visitations are played forever, as the gullible line up for hours in the vain hope of seeing Sly chow down on a chili burger.

Needless to say, you have a better chance of seeing a celebrity walk by you on the street as you wait to get into the restaurant (and wait you will – the theme joints keep you waiting for 20 minutes even if they're empty).

Moreover, it's impossible to judge the service and simple fare on offer at the restaurants, since their heavy volume increases the chance that you'll come across a badly cooked meal or a waiter with an attitude. Expect, at any rate, to be steered, if not pressured, into buying merchandise: these places see a profit margin of 15% on the food, but realize a 50% gain on the T-shirts.

Hard Rock Cafe The granddaddy of all theme restaurants (☎ (212) 459-9320), 221 W 57th St, has been in New York since 1983 and offers glimpses of rock memorabilia of dubious provenance. Just how many times did Elvis really strum that guitar, anyway?

It's open Sunday to Thursday from 11:30 am to midnight and Friday and Saturday from 11 am to 2 am.

Planet Hollywood This place (☎ (212) 333-7827), 140 W 57th St, displays film artifacts and costumes in a noisy, flashing-light atmosphere that resembles a futuristic disco. No

side streets. Two fine places to find a bit of Paris (including a well-dressed clientele and slightly pricey entrees ranging from $17 to $24) are *La Goulue* (☎ (212) 988-8169), 746 Madison Ave near 64th St, and *Madame Romaine de Lyon* (☎ (212) 759-5200), 132 E 61St off Park Ave. It's possible to have a moderately priced and pleasant meal at either by sticking to the appetizer side of the menu or having lighter fare such as omelets.

The ambiance is French, the menu is French and the prices are high at *Quatorze Bis* (☎ (212) 535-1414), 323 E 79th St, but it would help if the waiter knew how to pronounce *Coq au Vin*. A true Parisian bistro experience can be had at *Trois Jean* (☎ (212) 988-4858), 154 E 79th St. You'll be surrounded by native French speakers as you sample wonderful wine by the glass ($8) and try poached salmon on the $14.95 daily lunch menu. There's also an expensive and over-the-top truffle menu for those with a bit of extra pocket change.

The ambiance and food is *tres* French at *Voulez-Vous* (☎ (212) 249-1776), 1462 First Ave at 76th St, but the wait staff is friendly and helpful, with prices running to about $30 per person with wine.

Hosteria Fiorella (☎ (212) 838-7570), 1081 Third Ave at 64th St, is a cut above the expensive but unremarkable Italian fare you find in this neighborhood. It's not cheap ($15 an entree and up), but it specializes in well-prepared seafood reservations are taken, and you stand in line outside for about 45 minutes just to get to another line inside. There are enough movie items visible through the window and on display in the gift shop next door to justify giving the restaurant a miss. It's open 11 am to 1 am every day.

Motown Cafe Named for the Detroit record label, the Motown Cafe (☎ (212) 489-0097), 104 W 57th St, opened in 1995. The background music, as expected, is quite good (often accompanied by a karaoke-style show where dancers lip-synch to big Motown hits) and the food, displayed on a menu that resembles an old LP cover, is more than passable. The food is reasonably priced and has a Southern influence (collard greens, ribs and sweet-potato fries). It's open daily from 11:30 am to 2:30 am.

Harley-Davidson Cafe This shrine to the motorcycle company (☎ (212) 245-6000), 1370 Sixth Ave, features gas tanks signed by celebrities and pictures of anyone who owned, rode on or even stood near a Harley-Davidson. It serves trashy fare such as a Reese's Chocolate Peanut-Butter Pie and is so commercial the menu's available for sale at $10. Open daily from 11 am to 2 am.

Jekyll & Hyde Club This place (☎ (212) 541-9505), 1409 Sixth Ave, is refreshingly free of celebrity connections and features waiters dressed as vampires and ghouls, along with a flashy show where a Frankenstein's monster comes to life. Complain about the long wait to get in and your waiter will point to a skull and say, 'That guy was dying to get in.' If that's your idea of a funny line, this place is for you.

It's open Monday, Tuesday and Thursday from 11:30 am to 2 am, Wednesday and Sunday from 11 am to 2 am and Friday and Saturday from 11 am to 3 am.

Official All Star Cafe In Times Square, the Official All Star Cafe (☎ (212) 840-8326), 1540 Broadway at 45th St, is an enormous restaurant-cum-sports stadium with sports memorabilia such as Andre Agassi's ponytail, a backboard smashed by Shaquille O'Neal and Monica Seles' tennis racquets. It has 60 TV monitors, serves more than 50 types of hamburgers and features the Charlie Sheen Room, filled with the actor's baseball collection. It's open daily from 11 am to 2 am. ■

dishes and offers an antipasto bar filled with homemade choices that vegetarians or those who aren't greatly hungry will love ($15.95 for six choices). Everything's good here, though you'll want to avoid the overpriced thin-crust pizzas ($12). A sister restaurant called *Trattoria Dell'Arte* (☎ (212)-245-9800), 900 Seventh Ave, is just across the street from Carnegie Hall. But pick the East Side location to avoid the crowds of fur-clad concertgoers who pack Trattoria nearly every night.

Top End *Arcadia* (☎ (212) 223-2900), 21 E 62nd St, is one of the best dining experiences in the city – well worth every penny you spend (which can run to $80

per person). The food has a French American taste to it, you can't go wrong with anything on the menu, and the service is attentive but not intrusive. It's an intimate space, adorned by a mural of the four seasons by Paul Davis, and it can be a little crowded if you're seated in the middle; when making reservations ask for a side banquet.

Aureole (☎ (212) 319-1660), located in a lovely townhouse at 34 E 61st St, may be the most refined restaurant in the city. Certainly you'll want to wear a suit to dinner if you're a man – and a fancy new one at that. The menu is delicately prepared American cuisine, and it can be enjoyed for a $32 fixed-price lunch.

Bronx

Arthur Ave-Belmont Some of the restaurants in this eight-block neighborhood have been in business since just after WWI, including *Mario's* (☎ (718) 584-1188), 2342 Arthur Ave, and *Ann & Tony's* (☎ (718) 933-1469), 2407 Arthur Ave, a family-style Neapolitan restaurant with pasta specials for $12 and under. There are often lines outside of the more famous *Dominick's* (☎ (718) 733-2807), 2335 Arthur Ave, a cash-only place where the crusty waiters serve large portions at long tables for around $12 a dish. (There are no menu prices, the waiters present you with a final figure at the end of the meal.)

City Island Locals hang out at the *Rhodes Restaurant* (☎ (718) 885-1538), 288 City Island Ave, open every night until 2 am and serving standard pub specials and burgers for around $8. A lighter choice for breakfast is the City Island Diner (☎ (718) 885-0362), 304 City Island Ave.

At *Anna's Harbor Restaurant* (☎ (718) 885-1373), 565 City Island Ave, and the neighboring *Sea Shore Restaurant*, both on the western side of the island, transient boaters can 'dock and dine' at dedicated slips.

Brooklyn

Brooklyn Heights-Cobble Hill Brooklyn Heights has two excellent bring-your-own-bottle restaurants: *Acadia Parish* (☎ (718) 624-5154), 148 Atlantic Ave near Clinton St, serves filling Cajun fare. Nearby is *La Bouillabaisse* (☎ (718) 522-8275), 145 Atlantic Ave, where the signature dish and other French fare often attract lines out the door. For those who don't want to bother with shopping around for something to drink with a meal, there's the newest outpost of the *Park Slope Brewing Co* (☎ (718) 522-4801), 62 Henry St, which serves a dozen local microbrews and sandwiches for $7 and under.

You can enjoy a $3 pint during happy hour from 4 to 7 pm at *Pete's Waterfront Ale House* (☎ (718) 522-3794), 136 Atlantic Ave, which proclaims itself the 'home of warm beer, lousy food and an ugly owner.'

Absolutely the most authentic restaurant for recent émigrés from Yemen is the *Yemen Cafe* (☎ (718) 834-9533), 176 Atlantic Ave, with filling lamb and chicken curry dishes for $10 and under. This place, filled with local Yemenis drinking green tea and shooting the breeze, is a must for anyone spending some time in Brooklyn Heights

At Fulton Landing stands the famous *River Cafe* (☎ (718) 522-5200), 1 Water St, a romantic restaurant with delicately prepared American cuisine and a $65 fixed-price dinner menu – you'll need to make early reservations for a window seat. Just as good, but much cheaper, is *Patsy's* (☎ (718) 858-4300), 19 Old Fulton St, a shrine to Frank Sinatra disguised as

DAVID ELLIS

Brooklyn Heights watering hole

a pizzeria that serves delicious big pies for $13.

A performance at BAM can be followed by a meal at the cafeteria-style *Junior's* (☎ (718) 852-5257), at the corner of Flatbush and DeKalb Aves, the place to get New York's best cheesecake, or at *Gage and Tollner* (☎ (718) 875-5181), 372 Fulton St, one of New York's oldest restaurants (established 1879), which reopened in March of 1996 after an extensive renovation.

Along Court St, there's *Cousin's Cafe* (☎ (718) 596-3514), at No 160, a bar serving unadorned sandwiches for lunch that features jazz combos on weekend nights. You can also get a good-value meal at the no-frills *Sam's Restaurant* (☎ (718) 596-3458), No 238, where the menu advises that 'if your wife can't cook, don't divorce her – eat at Sam's.' The *Court Bakery* (☎ (718) 875-4820), No 298, is famous for filling pastries, including the cream-filled lobster tail.

The *Cafe on Clinton* (☎ (718) 625-5908), 268 Clinton St, is worth checking out for its great neighborhood bar and daily dinner specials, which are $10 before 6:30 pm.

The best balance of price and quality can be found at the *Red Rose Cafe* (☎ (718) 625-0963, 315 Smith St (subway: Carroll St); it serves pasta and seafood platters for $10 and under. An astoundingly good bargain in a friendly neighborhood.

Park Slope Vegetarians are served by *Healthy Henrietta's* (☎ (718) 622-2924), 787 Union St, with specialties such as scrambled tofu and vegetable burritos for under $8. The *Lemongrass Grill* (☎ (718) 399-7100), 61A Seventh Ave, has spicy and generous Thai dishes, including a wide selection of meatless choices, for $12 and under. The *Park Slope Brewing Co* (☎ (718) 788-1756), 356 Sixth Ave at 5th St, serves hearty pub grub and local brews.

Eastern Parkway The streets near the Brooklyn Museum of Art have a number of West Indian restaurants, including the *Wizard* (☎ (718) 399-9141), 806 Washington Ave, which serves pumpkin soup and $2 meat patties. *Tom's Restaurant* (☎ (718) 636-9738), 782 Washington Ave, is a legendary, 60-year-old place that is a must for its egg cream sodas and hearty breakfasts, all under $5. Gus, the friendly owner, seems to know everyone and serves favored customers a free toasted corn muffin smothered in honey.

Coney Island Two blocks away from the boardwalk is *Totonno's* (☎ (718) 372-8606), 1524 Neptune Ave, one of the city's best brick-oven pizza restaurants. Totonno's is open only Thursday to Sunday from noon to whenever he runs out of fresh mozzarella cheese. *Gargiulos* (☎ (718) 266-4891), 2911 W 15th St, is a noisy family-style place once famous for its huge Styrofoam Octopus, reputedly stolen from the New York Aquarium. The octopus is gone, but you can get filling southern Italian dishes for about $15.

Brighton Beach Some of Brighton Beach's restaurants cater to a certain sector of the Soviet émigré population, such as *Cafe Pearl* (☎ (718) 891-4544), 303 Brighton Beach Ave, which serves Georgian specialties for about $12, or the *Winter Garden* (☎ (718) 934-6666), on the Boardwalk, which attracts Muscovites. The bakeries on Brighton Beach Ave sell fantastic dark Moscow bread for $1.50 a loaf. You can enjoy a sticky sweet cheery drink while watching videos of Russian variety programs at *Caffe Cappuccino* (☎ (718) 646-6207), 290 Brighton Beach Ave.

At night, several raucous nightclubrestaurants offer set menus and elaborate floor shows. Two of the most famous are the *National* (☎ (718) 646-1225), 273 Brighton Beach Ave, which charges $55 per person on Friday, Saturday and Sunday nights for its eye-popping, completely over-the-top variety show and dinner, well oiled by carafes of vodka, and *Primorski* (☎ (718) 891-3111), 282 Brighton Beach Ave, with a cheaper set menu ($20 on weekdays, $25 on weekends) – but if you lose track of the vodka consumption the bill is sure to be much larger.

Williamsburg Williamsburg is home to the renowned *Peter Luger's Steak House* (☎ (718) 387-7400), 178 Broadway (subway: Marcy Ave), an old warehouse of a restaurant that has the reputation of serving New York's best beef. This out-of-the-way place takes cash only and dinner with drinks costs about $45 per person.

In Williamsburg (subway: Bedford Ave) you can visit *Plan-eat Thailand* (☎ (718) 599-5758), 184 Bedford Ave, and enjoy Southeast Asian dishes for $8 to $10 while listening to live jazz and checking out the work of local artists on the walls. (This place was called Planet Thailand until bozo lawyers from Planet Hollywood threatened to sue them.) At *Oznot's Dish* (☎ (718) 599-6596), 79 Berry St, the Mediterranean-flavored menu offers dishes for under $10. *Bean* (☎ (718) 387-8222), 167 Bedford Ave, is a bustling and inexpensive vegetarian restaurant.

Queens

Many of Queens' international dining options are covered in the Ethnic Neighborhood Tour sidebar in Things to See & Do.

Astoria You can have a cheap dinner at the 24-hour *Uncle George's* (☎ (718) 626-0593), 33-19 Broadway, which serves daily specials of barbecued pork and potatoes for $8 and red snapper for $12 a plate. The taste of the restaurant's *tzatziki*, the Greek dip made of yogurt, garlic and cucumber, will last in your mouth for hours. Vegetarians fare well at the slightly more upscale *Akroyiali Taverna* (☎ (718) 932-7772), 33-04 Broadway, which has large salads with fresh feta cheese and *spanakopita* (spinach pie) for $7. Just down the street is the smoky and sleek patisserie *Omonia* (☎ (718) 274-6650), 32-20 Broadway, where it's possible to linger over an espresso, close your eyes and hear nothing but Greek spoken around you. A similar experience can be found at the *Galaxy Cafe* (☎ (718) 545-3951), 34-02 Broadway, and

the *Kolonaki Cafe* (☎ (718) 932-8222), 33-02 Broadway, which is named after Kolonaki Square in Athens, the meeting place for Greece's idle rich.

Flushing It's hard to offer a comprehensive list of the best of Flushing's many restaurants. Here it's best to adventure on your own, taking a look at the menus posted in the windows. *Joe's Shanghai* (☎ (718) 539-3838), 136-21 37th Ave, is known throughout the city for its steaming bowls of handmade dumplings and noodle dishes. *Sam Won Garden* (☎ (718) 321-0101), 136-17 38th Ave, across from the municipal parking lot, is open 24 hours and offers a menu of sushi and Korean barbecue. Two people can feast there for about $30. Whole fish meals are the specialty at *Golden Pond* (☎ (718) 886-1628), 37-17A Prince St, west of the subway station. A dim sum feast can be found at *KB Garden* (☎ (718) 961-9088), 136-28 39th Ave.

Staten Island

There are a cluster of cheap restaurants near the ferry terminal. The *Sidestreet Saloon* (☎ (718) 448-6868), 11 Schuyler St, just a few minutes' walk from the ferry, is a popular lunch spot for workers from the borough courthouse across the street. The *Cargo Cafe* (☎ (718) 876-0539), at the corner of Slossen Terrace and Bay St three blocks east of the ferry terminal, has lunch specials like fish and chips for $4.25.

La Caleta (☎ (718) 447-0397), 75 Bay St, has Spanish seafood specials and chicken dishes for $8 and under. Nearby, the *Clipper* (☎ (718) 273-5100), 38 Bay St, is a diner open daily from 6 am to midnight (open Friday and Saturday until 3 am), with most dishes under $10. *Gilly's Luncheonette* (☎ (718) 448-0579), 9 Hyatt St immediately behind Staten Island Borough Hall, has sandwiches for $4 and under.

RH Tug's (☎ (718) 447-6369), 1115 Richmond Terrace, is a nice spot for waterfront al fresco lunching just three minutes west of the Snug Harbor Cultural Center. Sandwiches run about $8.

DINERS

New York City has literally hundreds of diners, the kind with fast service at a table and countertop, cheap prices and a wide array of gut-busting choices. (So isn't it ironic – and a bit dumb – that there are actually faux New York diners like Brooklyn Diner, across the street from the Hard Rock cafe, right in Manhattan?)

One staple on all diner menus is the cheap 'breakfast special' – usually eggs, bacon, toast and coffee for under $4, served until 11 am or sometimes 24 hours a day. You might consider abandoning the overpriced fare at your hotel to have breakfast at the nearest diner. The following is a geographically diverse selection of true diners.

Greenwich Village The closet-sized *Bagel* (☎ (212) 255-0106), 170 W 4th St, is a cramped but charming Village institution. Nearby is *Joe Jr's* (☎ (212) 924-5220), at the corner of Sixth Ave and W 12th St, a place to watch the passing street parade from a booth and keep an eye out for the celebrity clientele, which includes actor Matthew Broderick.

East Village The 24-hour *Veselka* (☎ (212) 228-9682), 144 Second Ave, is a Polish diner with a great local following. It's decorated with murals by local artists and has great soups; the grill chefs treat making pancakes as a performance art. Among the many other Eastern European diners in this neighborhood is the great *Odessa* (☎ (212) 473-8916), 119 Ave A, a favorite hangout for young clubgoers and elderly émigrés looking for seriously filling fare.

Midtown The *Star Diner* (☎ (212) 245-3030), 839 Seventh Ave, is one of the best authentic eateries in Midtown, where there are more than a few overpriced cafes catering to the tourist trade. It's nothing fancy, just good, solid food at decent prices.

Cab drivers hang out before and after their shifts at the *Munson Diner* (☎ (212) 246-0964), 600 W 49th St at Eleventh Ave, where the burgers are greasy, the waitresses call you 'Hon' and the door to the women's bathroom is locked, in order to keep the street ladies from conducting their business on the premises.

If you're stuck waiting for a bus out of Port Authority, have a meal at the *Westway Diner* (☎ (212) 582-7661), 614 Ninth Ave at 44th St, a great 24-hour place with a good selection of dinner entrees.

Broadway types, including top producers and playwright August Wilson, hang out in the *Edison Diner* (☎ (212) 840-5000), 228 W 47th St, located in the lobby of the Edison Hotel. It's well known for its hearty chicken soup.

Upper West Side There are a great many cheap coffee shops on Broadway above 86th St, but most of those that once stood closer to Columbus Circle have disappeared due to development. There's also *EJ's Luncheonette* (☎ (212) 873-3444), 447 Amsterdam Ave above 81st St, a contrived new version of the traditional lunch counter, where the prices and quality live up to the promise. It's incredibly crowded for weekend brunch.

Upper East Side The *Lexington Candy Shop* (☎ (212) 288-0057), 1226 Lexington Ave at 83rd St, evokes the 1930s with its old-fashioned telephone booths and soda fountain. One of the cheaper options in this tony neighborhood full of pricey bistros is the *Skyline Diner* (☎ (212) 861-2540) at Lexington Ave and E 75th St, which is open 24 hours.

CAFES

There's nothing better than passing a rainy day within the confines of a warm cafe, preferably with a good book. And in an era of overcrowded Starbucks shops and Starbucks wannabes that serve really bad coffee, it's hard to find the perfect spot. The following places are some of my downtown favorites, with reasonably priced cafe drinks and light fare:

SoHo Word of mouth among French expatriates has given *Le Gamin* (☎ (212) 254-4678), 50 MacDougal St, a distinctly Gallic

KIM GRANT

Sidewalk catering – for the eat-and-run crowd

flavor, and if you want to fall in love with someone from Paris, head here. You'll also love the selection of magazines – if you can get a table. There's another branch at Ninth Ave and 21st St (☎ (212) 243-8864).

If you're shut out, buy a paper yourself and walk a block to the quieter *Once Upon a Tart* (☎ (212) 387-8869), 135 Sullivan St, where the tarts (naturally) and scones are superb.

Greenwich Village There are some two dozen cafes in Greenwich Village. One of the best is *Bleecker Street Pastry* (☎ (212) 242-4959), 245 Bleecker St, where you can linger over a cappuccino and sweet cake-like Italian croissant for $4, while watching locals peruse their morning papers. *Jon Vie* (☎ (212) 242-4440), 492 Sixth Ave, is a traditional French bakery where you can get a caloric pastry and coffee for $1.95 before 11 am.

French Roast (☎ (212) 533-2233), 78 W 11th St, is a 24-hour cafe serving light sandwiches and desserts at reasonable prices. It's a good place to peruse the New York newspapers. The dark and historic *Caffe Reggio* (☎ (212) 475-9557), 119 MacDougal St, is often crowded on weekends, but worth checking out during quiet weekday afternoons.

The Adore (☎ (212) 243-8742), 17 E 13th St off Fifth Ave, is a wonderful cafe with a sun-swept 2nd-floor dining area with stone walls and a wood floor that looks like a French country home. You can eavesdrop on the academics and shrinks who live and work in this area while enjoying the chocolate-filled croissants and coffee for under $5. (It's closed Sunday.)

See the Greenwich Village Walking Tour in Things to See & Do for more cafes in this part of town.

East Village Two Irish bars welcome coffee drinkers during the slower daylight hours: *The Scratcher*, 209 E Fifth St (subway: Astor Place), is popular with native-born Irish expats. This true Dublin-style pub is a quiet place to read the newspaper over coffee during the day, but it's crowded and raucous at night. It serves brunch Thursday to Sunday. There's also *Swift*, 34 E 4th St just off the Bowery, another wildly popular Irish bar with live bands and the best pint of Guinness in New York City.

FOOD STORES

New York City's food stores are uniformly small and over priced, but you can cobble together a decent and healthy lunch from one of the fruit stands set up on major avenues all over the city, especially on Sixth Ave near the office buildings in Midtown and on Third Ave above 59th St near the large apartment blocks. There are numerous fruit stands on the Upper West Side along Broadway, where you can stock up on provisions for a Central Park picnic. (Remember that grapes and the like should be washed, since they've been exposed to air pollution all day.)

Gourmet Garage has two locations – in SoHo (☎ (212) 941-5850), 453 Broome St, and on the Upper East Side (☎ (212) 535-5889), 301 E 64th St just east of Second Ave – which offer a very good selection of (expensive) fruit, breads and cheeses. The store also sells healthy portions of rice and beans for $4 and elaborate sandwiches like tandoori chicken for around $5. *Zabar's* (☎ (212) 787-2000), on the corner of Broadway and W 80th St, is perhaps the city's most popular food emporium, with very good prices on items such as smoked salmon. A few blocks south, *Fairway Market* (☎ (212) 595-1888), 2127 Broadway at W 74th St, tends to have low prices on cheese and prepared salads. On the East Side, try the *Vinegar Factory* (☎ (212) 987-0885), 431 E 91st St, for a similar range of gourmet food choices.

If you're buying a week's worth of provisions, check out the *Fruit & Vegetable Stand* on the southeast corner of Broadway and Houston Sts, just next to the subway entrance. It offers bulk prices on bags of merchandise (eight lemons for $1; five oranges for $1.50) and is open Monday to Saturday from 8 am to about 6 pm.

Picnickers and apartment dwellers should check out the huge new *Chelsea Market*, in an old cookie factory on Ninth Ave between 15th and 16th Sts. Breads, soups, bagels, cheese, wine and kitchen supplies are on offer here in the biggest food complex in all of downtown. The building itself offers an interesting mix of industrial architecture (using bits of the factory) and commissioned industrial-style art within its block-long space.

Entertainment

No single source could possibly list everything that happens in New York City, but *Time Out* tries hard and is the single best guide to nightlife. High culture events get big play in the Sunday and Friday *New York Times* and the *New Yorker*; dance clubs and smaller music venues take out numerous ads in the *Village Voice*. The free sheet *New York Press* also has roundups of cultural events.

NYC On Stage (☎ (212) 768-1818) is an information line listing music and dance events that is available 24 hours.

The Broadway Show Line (☎ (212) 563-BWAY/2929) provides descriptions of plays and musicals both on and off the Great White Way; you can use it to obtain information on ticket prices and make credit card purchases.

Ticket Services

Ticketmaster (☎ (212) 307-7171 for concerts, (212) 307-4100 for the performing arts) has a lock on sales for most major concerts and sporting events, despite the rock group Pearl Jam's valiant attempt to file an antitrust complaint against the company's handling fees, which can add up $7 to the ticket price.

You can order by phone or visit Ticketmaster outlets at Bloomingdale's, the HMV and Tower record stores and the Sony Building at 550 Madison Ave.

Unfortunately, some box offices – like the one at Radio City Music Hall – have been adding 'venue service charges' to ticket prices bought on-scene, narrowing the gap between box-office prices and fees charged by Ticketmaster.

Theater

While Times Square is ostensibly the center of New York's legitimate theater, the productions around Times Square are increasingly dominated by the holy trinity of overblown spectaculars: Andrew Lloyd Webber, Cameron MacIntosh and the Disney Company.

Though long-running productions like *Cats, Miss Saigon* and *Beauty and the Beast* attract large audiences, old theaters better suited to drama (the *Biltmore, Brooks Atkinson* and *Barrymore)* sit empty for lack of serious content. The high costs and critical frustrations of Broadway led even Broadway giant Neil Simon – who has a theater named for himself on 52nd St – to debut his *London Suite* in a Union Square theater in 1994.

All this movement has blurred the distinction of what is and what isn't a 'Broadway' show. But in general, Broadway productions are those that take place in the large theaters around Times Square – either plays featuring big stars or musical spectaculars – which attract more than nine million patrons each year. Of late, Broadway has featured a number of edgier, dance-oriented productions, including *Rent, Bring in Da Noise, Bring in Da Funk* and the revival of *Chicago*, but the longest-running shows tend to be mainstream in appeal.

'Off Broadway' usually refers to dramas that are performed in smaller (200 seats or fewer) spaces elsewhere in town, a big business in itself that now boasts annual attendance of 3.5 million people a year. Prominent spots for Off Broadway performances include: *PS 122* (☎ (212) 477-5288), 150 First Ave (near E 9th St; subway: Astor Place), located in a converted public school; the *Circle in the Square Theater* (☎ (212) 307-2705), 1633 Broadway at 50th St; the *Samuel Beckett Theater*, 410 W 42nd St (near Ninth Ave); and the *Performing Garage* (☎ (212) 966-3651), 33 Wooster St (subway: Spring St).

'Off-Off Broadway' events are readings, experimental performances and improvisations held in spaces with less than 100 seats with an as-yet unmeasured annual patronage.

Discount Theater Tickets

The TKTS booth in the middle of Times Square (☎ (212) 768-1818) sells same-day tickets to Broadway and Off Broadway musicals and drama. Tickets sell at either half price or 75% off regular box office rates as determined by the producers, plus a $2.50 service charge per ticket. The booth accepts cash or traveler's checks only.

The booth has an electric marquee listing the available shows. On Wednesday and Saturday matinee tickets go on sale at 10 am, and on Sunday the windows open at noon for afternoon performances.

Evening tickets go on sale every day at 3 pm, and a line begins to form up to an hour before the booth opens. (A good tip: Wait until 7 pm to buy your tickets, when the best available house seats go on sale for many productions. Lines tend to be shorter on Wednesday evenings because many visitors have already taken in an afternoon performance.)

While waiting in line you'll be accosted by hawkers offering handbill discounts for theatrical events at much smaller venues elsewhere in town, in the event that the big show you're hoping to see is sold out that day. (It's impossible to get tickets to the most popular shows on Saturday.) There is a smaller, less crowded TKTS outlet at 2 World Trade Center that maintains the same hours.

In 1996, the TKTS booth also began selling tickets to recitals, dance group appearances and performances of the New York Philharmonic. So even if you're not interested in brassy Broadway shows, it's still worth checking out. ∎

Cinemas

New Yorkers take film very seriously, so going to the cinema can be a trying experience in the evening and on weekends. Though prices are now $8.50, most first-run films sell out early on Friday and Saturday nights. You're likely to have to stand in one line to buy a ticket and another to get into the theater. What's worse, movie chains publish semifictitious start times in order to leave about 20 minutes to sell you popcorn and soda. You can at least avoid one queue by calling ☎ (212) 777-FILM/3456 and prepaying for the movie of your choice for an additional $1 charge per ticket; you get the ticket by swiping your credit card through a machine upon arrival.

Despite the attendant hassles, New York offers the cinéaste plenty of choices, and you can still duck into a movie house on a rainy or hot afternoon (though movie-mad New Yorkers under the age of 65 can't get admission discounts).

The *Sony Theaters Lincoln Square*, at Broadway and 68th St, includes a collection of 12 large-screen theaters and a 3D Imax theater. Sony (☎ (212) 336-5000) and Cineplex Odeon (☎ (212) 505-2463) have multiplexes throughout Manhattan. The *Angelika Film Center* (☎ (212) 995-2000), at the corner of Mercer and Houston Sts (subway: Broadway-Lafayette St), and the *Lincoln Plaza Cinemas* (☎ (212) 757-2280), opposite Lincoln Center at Broadway and 63rd St, specialize in foreign films and are always crowded on weekends.

Independent films and career retrospectives are held at the three-screen *Film Forum* (☎ (212) 727-8110), 209 W Houston St (subway: Houston St), and Lincoln Center's *Walter Reade Theater* (☎ (212) 875-5600), which has very comfortable, screening-room quality seats.

Far-out fringe works and films that have yet to get US distribution can be seen at *Anthology Film Archives* (☎ (212) 505-5181), 32 Second Ave (subway: Second Ave).

Classical Music & Opera

The New York Philharmonic (☎ (212) 721-6500) plays at Lincoln Center's *Avery Fisher Hall*, at W 64th St and Broadway, and has been getting rave reviews under the direction of German-born conductor Kurt Masur, though the aging and conservative Philharmonic audience still resists programs that deviate from the standard repertory. The audience is also pretty rude: nanoseconds after the final note, patrons go running up the aisles in order to beat the traffic home. Tickets range from $15 to $60.

Visiting philharmonics and the New York Pops orchestra perform at *Carnegie Hall* (☎ (212) 247-7800), W 57th St and Seventh Ave. A schedule of monthly events is available in the lobby next to the box office, and you can usually get tickets as low as $12 for nonsubscription events. The American Symphony Orchestra, the Chamber Music Society of Lincoln Center and the Little Orchestra Society hold their seasons at *Alice Tully Hall* (☎ (212) 721-6500) at Lincoln Center.

More intimate venues for classical music include the *Merkin Concert Hall* (☎ (212) 362-8719), 129 W 67th St, *Symphony Space* (☎ (212) 864-5400), 2536 Broadway at 95th St, and *Town Hall* (☎ (212) 840-2824), 123 W 43rd St.

The *Metropolitan Opera* (☎ (212) 362-6000) holds its season from September to April in its namesake Lincoln Center theater. It's nearly impossible to get into the first few performances of operas that feature such big stars as Jessye Norman and Plácido Domingo, but once the B team takes over, tickets become available. Aficionados have been complaining for years about a general drop in the vocal quality on stage, but the sets for classics like *Aida* are uniformly spectacular. Center orchestra tickets start at $115, but you can get a seat in the upper balcony for $16. Standing room is also available on a limited basis.

The more daring and lower-cost New York City Opera (☎ (212) 870-5630) takes the stage at the *New York State Theater*, next door to the Met, for a split season that runs for a few weeks in early autumn and picks up again in the late spring.

Dance & Ballet

New York is home to more than half a dozen world-famous dance companies. The New York City Ballet, established by Lincoln Kirstein and George Balanchine in 1948, performs at Philip Johnson's New York State Theater in Lincoln Center (☎ (212) 870-5570) during the winter. During the spring, the American Ballet Theater (☎ (212) 477-3030) takes over at the Metropolitan Opera House for a short season.

City Center (☎ (212) 581-1212), a Moorish palace on W 55th St between Sixth and Seventh Aves, is home to the Alvin Ailey American Dance Theater every December and hosts engagements by the National Ballet of Spain and other foreign companies. The most offbeat dance venue is the *Joyce Theater* (☎ (212) 242-0800), a renovated cinema in Chelsea at 175 Eighth Ave and W 19th St. The season includes visits by such bold physical groups as the Erick Hawkins and Merce Cunningham dance companies.

Live Music

When major singers and 'super groups' that regularly fill arenas play a smaller venue in New York, their record company usually buys up all the tickets and hands them out as freebies, so don't feel disappointed if you missed Bruce Springsteen's surprise club appearance. It's easier to get tickets to see lesser lights. Major concerts are announced months in advance and are usually held at Madison Square Garden (☎ (212) 456-6000), Radio City Music Hall (☎ (212) 247-4777) or the Beacon Theater (☎ (212) 496-7070), 2124 Broadway (subway: 72nd St), a converted movie palace on the West Side.

The Concert Hotline (☎ (212) 249-8870) tells you who's playing in the clubs, but the narrator's rapid-fire delivery may be difficult to follow if English is not your native language.

Jazz The basement-level *Village Vanguard* (☎ (212) 255-4037), 178 Seventh Ave (subway: Christopher St), may be the world's most famous jazz club; it has hosted literally every major star of the past 50 years. The cover charge runs $15 to $20

DAVID ELLIS

Lenox Lounge in Harlem – remnant of swingin' times

with a two-drink minimum. Legendary trumpeter Doc Cheatham, now in his 90s, plays the Sunday jazz brunch at *Sweet Basil* (☎ (212) 242-1785), 88 Seventh Ave South, which hosts week-long visits by other big stars. *Smalls* (☎ (212) 929-7565), 183 W 10th St, is a unique place without a liquor license that hosts an incredible $10, 10-hour jazz marathon every night from 10 pm to 8 am that attracts top talent coming off gigs in other mainstream joints. Another intimate space is *Zinno* (☎ (212) 924-5182), 126 W 13th St. *Detour* (☎ (212) 533-6212), 349 E 13th St at First Ave, is a fine spot with daily jazz and no cover charge.

By far the most expensive club is the *Blue Note* (☎ (212) 475-8592), 131 W 3rd St, featuring big stars playing short sets with music charges up to $60. You can hear acid jazz and other fringe music at the *Knit-ting Factory* (☎ (212) 219-3055), 74 Leonard St in Tribeca. The wildly popular Mingus Big Band plays every Thursday at *Fez* (☎ (212) 533-2680), 380 Lafayette St (subway: Bleecker St), which hosts experimental music every other night of the week. *Iridium* (☎ (212) 956-4676), 44 W 63rd St, is trying to make a name for itself by breaking new jazz acts. See also the Harlem jazz clubs below.

Harlem Jazz Clubs Harlem's Cotton Club era is long gone, but there are still several places to hear jazz, both modern and traditional. Because of declining patronage, most have performances on weekend nights; call ahead to check times and possible cover charges. The old *Lenox Lounge* (☎ (212) 722-9566), at Lenox Ave and 125th St, is worth visiting anytime for its remarkable Art Deco interior. *Showman's*

Cafe (☎ (212) 864-8941), 2321 Frederick Douglass Blvd, features jazz combos and R&B vocalists. The same mix of styles, along with a late-night menu, can be found at *Wells Restaurant* (☎ (212) 234-0700), 2247 Powell Blvd. *Lickety Split* (☎ (212) 283-9093), 2361 Powell Blvd, specializes in Caribbean bands. A new version of the *Cotton Club* (☎ (212) 663-7980), 666 W 125th St (subway: 1/9 to 125th St) is located on the west side of Harlem. Check it out: even the house band is magnificent.

Tipping in Clubs

Nightclubs in New York are notorious for trying to obscure the fact that you are only obligated to tip on waiter service. At the end of a set, you're likely to be handed a credit card slip or bill that includes the music charge for each person in the total. This is standard procedure at expensive places like the Blue Note jazz club. Tip generously if you wish, but deduct the music charge before calculating it. ■

Rock Well-known intimate concert spaces include the *Bottom Line* (☎ (212) 228-6300), 15 W 4th St in the Village. The prototypical punk club *CBGB* (☎ (212) 982-4052), 315 Bowery, incubator of such famous acts as the Talking Heads and the Ramones, is still going strong after two decades. It's one of the few places in New York that looks, feels and smells *exactly* like you imagined it would.

Big names turn up at the small *Mercury Lounge* (☎ (212) 260-4700), 217 E Houston St, and at *Tramps* (☎ (212) 727-7788) in Chelsea at 51 W 21st St, a 1000-seat club that's over 20 years old.

Irving Plaza (☎ (212) 777-6800), 17 Irving Place (subway: Union Square), is an increasingly popular venue for well-known foreign acts (Tricky, Everything But the Girl). Its presence in a formerly sleepy neighborhood has inspired the opening of many new bars on 15th St that attract an NYU undergraduate crowd, few of whom seem to be over 21 years of age.

New clubs turn up in the Lower East Side all the time – check out the flyers in the neighborhood's bars and restaurants.

Blues, Folk & World Music The *55 Bar* (☎ (212) 929-9883), 55 Christopher St, is an authentic smoky joint that never charges a cover. Visiting blues masters play at *Chicago Blues* (☎ (212) 924-9755), at 14th St and Eighth Ave, and the uptown *Manny's Car Wash* (☎ (212) 369-2583), 1558 Third Ave (subway: 86th St).

International artists are brought to New York by the World Music Institute (☎ (212) 545-7536) for concerts at the *Washington Square Church*, 135 W 4th St, and other venues throughout the city. The Deadhead tradition lives on at *Wetlands* (☎ (212) 966-4225), 161 Hudson St (subway: 1/9 to Canal St). College radio favorites play *Far Side* (☎ (212) 673-9143), 269 E Houston St (subway: Second Ave) on the Lower East Side. The *Back Fence* (☎ (212) 475-9221), 155 Bleecker St, which never charges a cover, is the best folk venue among many in the center of Greenwich Village. The *Fast Folk Cafe* (☎ (212) 274-1636), 41 N Moore

Nights Out in Brooklyn

In addition to the many events at the Brooklyn Academy of Music, *Arts at St Ann's Church* (☎ (718) 858-2424), at the corner of Montague and Clinton Sts in Brooklyn Heights, is a year-round series of concerts with tickets running about $20. Recent performers include country singer Kathy Mattea and boogie-woogie maestro Dr John. *Bargemusic* (☎ (718) 624-4061) is the name for the chamber music program held at Fulton Landing under the Brooklyn Bridge that has two performances each week during the summer. Concerts and performances by small dance companies are held at the *Brooklyn Center for the Performing Arts* at Brooklyn College (☎ (718) 951-4500), Campus Rd and Hillel Place (subway: Flatbush Ave-Brooklyn College). ■

St (subway: Franklin St), is a new all-acoustic venue sponsored by *Fast Folk Magazine*.

SOB's (☎ (212) 243-4940), 204 Varick St (subway: Houston St), specializes in Afro-Cuban sounds and is the home of salsa master Tito Puente. Uptown, the place to go is the *Latin Quarter* (☎ (212) 864-7600), at Broadway and W 95th St.

Bars

A proper listing of New York City's better drinking places would take up most of an entire book.

There are plenty of boring bars that are located all over the city, most of which have Irish names, such as the horrendous Blarney Stone chain. You'll be able to size

these places up immediately after you walk in – they're usually undistinguished places with lumpy red-naugahyde furniture and steam tables of bad food, and they're usually patronized by a small crowd of chain-smoking alcoholics. (A few places that fit the above description but have some charm are listed below.) Midtown pick-up bars almost always have silly names (ie, Mumbles or Chuckles).

Most bars are open until 2 am, though some keep the beer flowing until 4 am on Friday and Saturday.

What follows is a highly selective list of places to find great beer and a good time.

Lower Manhattan *The Greatest Bar on Earth* (☎ (212) 524-7011), at Windows on

No Smoking – And They Mean It!

In 1994, New York passed a stringent anti-smoking law that restricted cigarette use in restaurants with 35 seats or more to bar areas in separate rooms equipped with an air-filter system. Despite dire predictions from some proprietors that the antismoking laws would lead to a wave of bankruptcies, the law went into effect at a time when the economy was on an upswing and business began booming at restaurants all over town.

One unfortunate side effect of the law is that smokers have been driven almost exclusively to bars and lounges in the city, where you can smoke without restriction. (And cigarette companies have taken to handing out free samples at these spots to boost their business.) On weekend evenings in some bars, the second-hand smoke is so strong that it stings your eyes and makes your clothes reek like an ashtray, even if you've just stayed for a single beer. In response to this, there has been an increase in 'no smoking' bars like the one at Time Cafe in the East Village, and even some famous clubs like the Bottom Line have banned smoking outright. If things go on like this, the image of the 'smoky nightclub' will be a thing of the past. ■

the World on the 107th floor of One World Trade Center, has an exceedingly silly name, but you can't beat the view and the beer is moderately priced ($5) for the setting.

Bridge Cafe, 279 Water St (subway: City Hall), an 1847 tavern near the South Street Seaport, was declared by the *New York Times* to be the oldest tavern in the city. The food is surprisingly good, but a bit expensive.

SoHo & Tribeca *Ñ*, 33 Crosby St (subway: Grand St), is a dark and easy-to-miss tapas bar with a friendly staff. But don't go there hungry or you'll wind up spending more than you wanted to. The *Ear Inn*, 326 Spring St (subway: Spring St), is located in the old James Brown House (not the Godfather of Soul). This old place near the Hudson River attracts sanitation workers and office dwellers with its great shepherd's pie and inexpensive lunch choices. *Cafe Noir*, 32 Grand St (subway: Grand St), is a good place to munch on North African appetizers while watching the passing SoHo parade from the open-air bar railing.

Gay Entertainment

Nightlife Gay clubs and bars catering to every taste are listed in the free sheets *HX/Homo Xtra* and *Next*, which are given away free at most restaurants and bars. Other gay-oriented publications include the literary magazine *Christopher Street* and *Metrosource*, a lifestyle magazine given away free in bars. There is also the lesbian oriented *HX For Her* free sheet now widely available.

On the whole, gay drinking places tend to cater only to men, but the more popular gay dance clubs welcome women, even though they are largely cruise joints and usually have a unisex bathroom; obviously straight men entering lesbian bars and clubs are likely to encounter open hostility. Popular clubs in the Chelsea area include *Champs* (☎ (212) 633-1717), 17 W 19th St, a gathering place for the clean-cut crowd, and *Splash* (☎ (212) 691-0073), 50 W 17th St, where well-toned boys put on a water show. There's an array of cruise joints here as well: *Rome* (☎ (212) 242-6969), 290 Eighth Ave, *Barracuda* (☎ (212) 645-8613), 275 W 22nd St, and *King* (☎ (212) 366-5464), 579 Sixth Ave, which has a male-only 3rd-floor grope room.

A wildly popular new club is *g* (☎ (212) 929-1085), 223 W 19th St, a sleek, modern lounge that welcomes a fair number of straights during the week. On weekends it's totally packed with an exclusively gay crowd.

For dancing, it's best to go to a gay night at a mainstream club (many of the following are listed under Dance Clubs). *Twilo* (☎ (212) 268-1600), 530 W 27th St, is a popular place with a $20 cover. The club is also the site of a popular new Sunday afternoon tea dance. *Limelight* is gay on Wednesday and Friday, and *Webster Hall* becomes Lavender Lounge on Wednesday. *Tunnel's* clientele gets gayer as the night grows longer – some gays set their alarms for dawn on Sunday and party at Tunnel well into Sunday afternoon.

The rough trade has traditionally met in forbidding bars along the West Side piers in Chelsea, but hangouts not already decimated by the AIDS pandemic are now closing because of increased property values. The *Spike* (☎ (212) 243-9688), 120 Eleventh Ave, and the *Eagle's Nest* (☎ (212) 691-8451), 142 Eleventh Ave, still survive, but the *Lure* (☎ (212) 741-3919), 409 W 13th St, is currently the most popular leather bar. None of these places welcome the curious.

The Christopher St area in Greenwich Village (subway: 1/9 to Christopher St) is the site of many popular restaurants and bars, including the *Monster* (☎ (212) 924-3558), 80 Grove St, and *Uncle Charlie's* (☎ (212) 255-8787), 56 Greenwich Ave, crowded places with large after-work clienteles. The *Stonewall Inn* (☎ (212) 463-0950), 53 Christopher St, though not the bar of the famous rebellion, stands near the same site. Bars catering to

Greenwich Village *Chumley's*, 86 Barrow St (subway: Christopher St), is a hard-to-find but famous speakeasy serving decent (cash only) pub grub. It was among the first places in the city to serve American microbrews exclusively. The *Corner Bistro*, 331 W 4th St (subway: Christopher St), is a famous West Village bar with carved wooden tables where you can eat charred hamburgers until 2 am.

East Village *The Scratcher*, 209 E Fifth St (subway: Astor Place), is popular with Irish people. It's a true Dublin-style pub, a quiet place to read the newspaper during the day over coffee, but crowded and raucous at night. *Swift*, 34 E 4th St just off the Bowery, is another wildly popular Irish bar with live bands and the best pint of Guinness in New York City. *KGB*, 85 E 4th St, is a 2nd-floor living room site for literary meetings.

McSorley's Old Ale House, 15 E 7th St, is the well-known subject of Joseph Mitchell's *New Yorker* stories. A cramped and stodgy old bar, it refused to admit women until the 1970s; these days it often has a long line of tourists and NYU

---

older gays include *Julius* (☎ (212) 929-9672), 159 W 10th St, and *Marie's Crisis* (☎ (212) 243-9323), 59 Grove St, which features show tunes.

Henrietta Hudson (☎ (212) 924-3347), 438 Hudson St, is open until 4 am every night, and *Crazy Nanny's* (☎ (212) 366-6312), 21 Seventh Ave South, calls itself a 'place for gay women – biological or otherwise.' *The Clit Club* (☎ (212) 529-3300) meets Friday at The Bar Room, 432 W 14th St, and has been the leading lesbian hot spot for years. *Rubyfruit* (☎ (212) 929-3343), 531 Hudson St, is a favorite with older women.

Uptown, the scene is much more discreet. There are several gay businessmen's places on the East Side, including the *Townhouse* (☎ (212) 754-4649), 206 E 58th St, which is basically a place to meet young hustlers. *M* (☎ (212) 935-2150), 256 E 49th St, is a Midtown spot with drink specials for the working crowd. Professionals also patronize the *Tool Box* (☎ (212) 427-3106), 1748 Second Ave at E 91st St. On the West Side, *The Works* (☎ (212) 799-7365), 428 Columbus Ave, is a popular cruising spot known for its Sunday beer blasts.

Restaurants Virtually all of the restaurants in Greenwich Village and Chelsea are gay-friendly – see Places to Eat. There are three popular restaurants on Eighth Ave within a few blocks of each other south of 23rd St that are better known for their scenes than the food: *The Viceroy* (☎ (212) 633-8484), *Candy Bar* (☎ (212) 229-9702) and *Food Bar* (☎ (212) 243-2020). *Eighteen and Eighth* (☎ (212) 242-5000), named after its location, has cheap lunches for under $8 and flirtatious male waiters.

You can pick up reduced-admission club flyers at the gay-friendly restaurants *Florent* (see Greenwich Village in Places to Eat) and *Manatus* (☎ (212) 989-7042), 340 Bleecker St, an all-night place.

Nearby on Bedford St are three restaurants with recognizably gay clienteles: *Mary's* (☎ (212) 741-3387), at No 42, an old Italian restaurant; *Universal Grill* (☎ (212) 989-5621), at No 44, and *Seventh Ave South* (☎ (212) 647-7636), at No 46. Each is packed on weekends for dinner and brunch.

Aggie's (☎ (212) 673-8994), 146 W Houston St, is a coffee shop popular with lesbians – single females tend to receive better service than anyone else.

Gyms These remain popular meet-and-greet places. The Chelsea Gym (☎ (212) 255-1150), 267 W 17th St, and the David Barton Gym (☎ (212) 727-0004), 552 Sixth Ave, are among the many places that offer day workouts for about $15. ■

■■■■■■■■■■■■■■■■■■■■■■■■■

Five Eclectic Clubs

The following clubs defy categorization simply because they offer different events nearly every night of the week. Here's a quick look and a (sometimes partial) listing of what goes on behind the door.

Arlene Grocery is run by the former owner of the now-closed Sine, a legendary cafe that was the nexus for the Irish immigrant crowd. This old bodega hosts a different kind of act nearly every night (from folk rock to poetry readings), either free or for a small cover charge. 95 Stanton St (subway: Second Ave), ☎ (212) 473-9831

Fez, directly under the Time Cafe restaurant, hosts the wildly popular Mingus Big Band every Thursday. On other nights you can catch drag queen shows, readings of novels in progress and lounge music concerts. 380 Lafayette St (subway: Bleecker St), ☎ (212) 533-2680

The Knitting Factory is home to 'fringe' performances during the JVC Jazz fest each June, and it's a nice spot to hang out even when there's no performance. 74 Leonard St in Tribeca (subway: Franklin St), ☎ (212) 219-3055

Luna Lounge, near Arlene Grocery, is on a street that's become one of the livelier weekend hangouts in the city. Basically a bar for downtowners, this spot becomes a super-hot comedy club at 7 pm on Monday nights, when top young comedians try out their newest material for free. 171 Ludlow St (subway: Second Ave), ☎ (212) 260-2323

The Nuyorican Poets Cafe is a pioneering East Village performance space located between Aves B and C and featuring one-act plays, readings of works in progress and, yes, even poetry. 236 E 3rd St (subway: Second Ave), ☎ (212) 465-3167 ■

■■■■■■■■■■■■■■■■■■■■■■■■■

undergraduates waiting to get in. Don't bother waiting unless you simply must get a whiff of 100 year's worth of stale beer that the sawdust on the floor hasn't absorbed (you're best off dropping by in the afternoon).

You can get a nice slice of East Village life by having a late-night drink in *7B*, a horseshoe-shaped bar at the southeast end of Tompkins Square Park. During the day, it's a quiet place for old men to hang out; at night it's nothing less than a grunge pickup joint fueled by malt liquor beer specials. It has been featured in a number of films, including *The Verdict* and *Crocodile Dundee*.

Midtown   *Landmark Tavern*, 626 Eleventh Ave (subway: Times Square), is more a restaurant than a bar. It serves the best fish and chips in the city and a decent brunch. The 1868 structure housed the tavern owner's family (see the 2nd-floor living room) and is located on the far West Side near the Intrepid Air and Space Museum. *McHale's Bar and Cafe*, 730 Eighth Ave, is an old guy's bar and cafe in the theater district with character and a great neon sign. *Rudy's* (☎ (212) 974-9169), 627 Ninth Ave, practically glories in its reputation as a spot for booze hounds. This joint not far from the Port Authority Bus Terminal serves $1.50 drafts and $5 pitchers of American beer. *Full Moon Bar* (☎ (212) 974-0973), W 46th St and Eighth Ave, is a similar no-frills saloon with $1 hamburgers, 50¢ hot dogs and cold Bud for $2.

Slightly more upscale is the *Film Center Cafe* (☎ (212) 262-2525), 635 Ninth Ave, which has a happy hour of $2 pints from 4 to 6 pm on weekdays.

Upper West Side   *Dublin House*, 225 W 79th St (subway: 79th St), shouldn't be remarkable, but it is, thanks to the odd combination of old men and Columbia University undergrads who patronize the place. *Night Cafe* (☎ (212) 864-8889), 938 Amsterdam Ave, attracts the Columbia graduate-student crowd.

Brooklyn Beer Drinking

For an absolutely fascinating look at the Brooklyn beer drinking culture, visit *Farrell's Bar & Grill* (☎ (718) 788-8779), 215 Prospect Park West (subway: 15th St-Prospect Park). The drinking begins before noon in this male-dominated local joint, and only Budweiser is on offer in either 75¢ glasses or 32-oz Styrofoam cups (you can also quaff shots of whiskey). The 60-year-old Farrell's once banned chairs – the theory being that if you couldn't stand up, you could no longer be served. There are a few seats now, but most patrons still do their drinking leaning against the bar.

Also keep your eye open for ads for city beer fests – one big festival takes place in the shadow of the Brooklyn Bridge in the early summer months, and there's another held indoors in Manhattan in the autumn (usually at the Irving Plaza club). The $20 admission gets you free samples and entertainment from a bevy of bar bands. ■

Upper East Side *Kinsale Tavern*, 1672 Third Ave (subway: 96th St), is a gathering place with over 20 beers on tap that attracts European rugby and soccer fanatics with early-morning live satellite broadcasts of matches during the winter months. (Many bars on Second and Third Aves offer the same television transmissions.) In a city packed with Irish pubs, *The British Open*, 320 E 59th St (subway: 59th St-Lexington Ave), in the shadow of the Queensboro Bridge, draws fans of golf and the Royal Family. Unfortunately, they have taken to charging an outrageous $7 for a pint of British draught beer. You'll have cheaper (and weaker) beer at the nearby *Subway Inn*, 143 E 60th St, just above the 59th St-Lexington Ave subway station, an old bar that looks like it hasn't changed in 40 years, right down to the barmen's white shirts and thin black ties.

Lounges

Throughout the 1990s there has been a big growth in lounges catering to both gay and mixed crowds. Lounges are exclusively defined by their crowds – those downtown offering cigars and bourbon attract office workers; Chelsea lounges are almost exclusively gay.

Patrons tend to be a bit better dressed in these places, with the significant exception of hole-in-the-wall joints in the East Village and the Lower East Side. Some of the lounges feature live music – places that charge admission to hear performers are listed in the Live Music section. Most bars are open until 2 am, some till 4 am on Friday and Saturday.

Greenwich Village *Hudson Bar and Books*, 636 Hudson St, is a narrow faux library that has free jazz on weekend evenings. This place has two club-like uptown cousins: *Beekman Bar and Books*, 889 First Ave near the United Nations, and *Lexington Bar and Books*, 1020 Lexington Ave. The latter enforces a pretentious jackets-only policy. *Bar d'O*, 29 Bedford St (subway: W 4th St), is a sleek lounge with drag acts several nights a week and a lesbian night on Tuesday, when it's not unusual to see girls start fighting at the bar. It attracts a chic crowd of gays and straights who arrive at about 11 pm to begin their night of revels. The bar is just about empty in the early evening.

East Village The *10th St Lounge*, 212 E 10th St (subway: Union Square), is a sleek, publicity-shunning place that was once very in with East Villagers. Wear black – and hide this tourist guide – in order to fit in at this pleasantly austere place to have a drink. *147 Ludlow St* (subway: Delancey St) is a place so cool it doesn't have a name. A DJ plays nightly till 4 am. You'll find a bunch of new places on Ludlow and Stanton Sts in the Lower East Side – check out the neighborhood on a weekend night.

Chelsea Try the martinis at *Opera* (☎ (212) 229-1618), 539 W 21st St between Tenth and Eleventh Aves, or drop by the *Third Floor Cafe*, 315 Fifth Ave (subway: 34th St-Sixth Ave), a sleek new coffee and wine bar in the Flatiron district that's open to 2 am Friday and Saturday.

Midtown At the Rainbow Room's *Promenade Lounge*, on the 65th floor of the GE Building, 30 Rockefeller Plaza, you must wear a jacket and decent clothing, but for the price of admission to visit the top of the Empire State Building, you get a stunning view that *includes* that landmark and a drink to go along with it.

The *Top of the Tower*, 3 Mitchell Place, (subway: 50th St-Lexington) is a lounge on the 26th floor of the Beekman Tower Hotel that offers a clear view of the east side, including the Chrysler Building and the fabulous '30s-era Pepsi ad across the East River. *44*, 44 W 44th St (subway: 42nd St), is in the lobby of the Royalton Hotel. It has an appropriately snooty atmosphere, but the tiny circular bar located immediately to the right after the entrance is a great hideaway spot for a martini.

Upper East Side *Bemelmans' Bar*, 35 E 76th St (subway: 77th St), is an elegant space in the Carlyle Hotel where you'll feel uncomfortable without a jacket (there's a cover charge for evening performances). Ludwig Bemelmans, the author-illustrator of the Eloise stories, lived in the hotel and painted the murals on the walls here. The lounge at *The Mark Hotel*, 22 E 77th St, is a quiet, green velvet space that epitomizes Upper East Side elegance.

Dance Clubs

If a club is around long enough to be listed here, it's almost by definition no longer hot. The monthly magazine *Paper* is the best source for clubs. You should also keep an eye out for club and band flyers on walls and billboards while walking through the East Village – it is often the only way to find out about some clubs that for legal reasons do not have phones or advertise. Most of the following are located below 14th St and attract a mixed gay and straight crowd.

It generally costs about $20 to get into the clubs from Thursday to Saturday. Don't even think about going to any of these places before 11 pm, even on a weeknight; things don't truly pick up until 1 am

KIM GRANT

or later. Some of the phone numbers listed are pretty useless since the clubs don't generally pick up.

Cab drivers are a good source for the locations of cutting-edge clubs. Those working the nightshift know exactly where to pick up fares in the wee hours of the morning, and they can at least tell you the locations of undiscovered night spots. Just make sure the driver knows you're asking about dance clubs, not bordellos.

Buddha Bar is an unremarkable space popular for its live music salsa nights and Juicy, the Sunday night lesbian lounge. 150 Varick St (subway: Houston St), ☎ (212) 255-4433

Don Hill's is a transvestite favorite for its $10 Olivia Newton-John nights. 511 Greenwich St at Spring St (subway: Spring St), ☎ (212) 334-1390

Limelight is, like other Limelights, a deconsecrated church; it's been in trouble with city authorities since a patron OD'd on the premises. It's currently closed due to federal drug investigations but may reopen by the time you read this. 660 Sixth Ave (subway: 23rd St), ☎ (212) 807-7850

Nell's is the original European velvet lounge; it attracts a rougher crowd now and there's a metal detector at the door. 246 W 14th St (subway: 14th St-Eighth Ave), ☎ (212) 675-1567

Palladium, in a former Academy of Music concert hall, was a big '80s disco before becoming almost exclusively dedicated to live hip hop and house music. It's now in danger of being torn down for an NYU dorm. 126 E 14th St (subway: Union Square), ☎ (212) 473-7171

Roxy is an old favorite featuring roller skating that refuses to die. 515 W 18th St at Tenth Ave (subway: 14th St-Eighth Ave), ☎ (212) 645-5156

Save the Robots is a hard core, very late-night place that's now featuring Japanese pop. 25 Ave B (subway: Second Ave), ☎ (212) 995-0968

System offers mostly house music in the old Cat Club performance space. 76 E 13th St (subway: Union Square), ☎ (212) 388-1060

Tatou is a bordello-like lounge that's dissed by New Yorkers because of its reputation as a watering hole for Europe's idle rich. 151 E 50th St (subway: 50th St-Lexington), ☎ (212) 753-1144

Tunnel is a massive three-floor club featuring Junior Vasquez, the city's most popular DJ, on Saturday night. 220 Twelfth Ave at 27th St (subway: 23rd St-Eighth Ave), ☎ (212) 695-7292

Webster Hall is a huge, five-level club with midget go-go dancers; it's also famous for its Lavender Lounge gay nights and Psychedelic Thursdays. 125 E 11th St (subway: Union Square), ☎ (212) 353-1600

Comedy Clubs

It's generally acknowledged that stand-up comedy has been in a pathetic state for several years with unfunny, amateurish comics playing to half-empty houses all over town. If you're looking for mainstream laughs, stick with the top-level comedians who play *Caroline's* (☎ (212) 757-4100), 1626 Broadway in Times Square. (The club has also opened the Comedy Nation bar and lounge right next door.) There's also *Chicago City Limits* (☎ (212) 888-5233), 1105 First Ave, and *Catch a Rising Star* (☎ (212) 244-3005), the legendary launching ground for many comedy stars of the 1970s. It has moved to nicer quarters at 253 W 28th St and offers decent pub fare and musical performers on some nights.

Those looking for more cutting edge comedy should head to the Lower East Side and try the weekly shows at *Surf Reality* (☎ (212) 673-4182), 172 Allen St (between Stanton and Rivington Sts), and the *Luna Lounge* (☎ (212) 260-2323), 171 Ludlow St (subway: Second Ave). There's usually no cover at these 'alternative' spaces.

SPECTATOR SPORTS

Baseball

Baseball's recent labor woes led to a serious decline in the sport's attendance nationwide, and you can usually get same-day tickets to any New York Mets (☎ (718) 507-8499) or New York Yankees (☎ (718) 293-6000) game, unless the teams are in a late-season pennant race. The 162-game season lasts from early April to early October, and when one team is on the road, the other is at home. The Mets play in wind-swept Shea Stadium in Flushing Meadows, Queens (subway: Willets Point-Shea Stadium); it's a 35-minute journey from Midtown. The Yanks play at their legendary namesake park in the South Bronx (subway: 161st St-Yankee Stadium), just 15 minutes from Midtown. Most games begin at 7:30 pm and tickets range from $6.50 to $20. In 1997, the two rival teams began playing a limited number of regular season interleague games for the first time. (For more on the stadiums and their surrounding neighborhoods, see the Queens and Bronx sections.)

Basketball & Hockey

The NBA New York Knicks (☎ (212) 465-6741) and the NHL New York Rangers (☎ (212) 465-6741) play at 19,000-seat Madison Square Garden, Seventh Ave and W 33rd St. Both teams sell huge amounts of season tickets, and so visitors must book generally bad seats through Ticketmaster or deal with the many scalpers who hover around the area. They try to get a premium on seats that already cost up to $75. When dealing with scalpers, the best strategy is to wait until after the 7:30 pm game time, when prices should drop.

Tennis

The US Open, the year's final Grand Slam event, takes place during the two weeks leading up to Labor Day at the National Tennis Center (☎ (718) 760-6200), in Flushing Meadows-Corona Park in Queens (subway: Shea Stadium-Willets Point). Corporations buy up boxes for the Open, and the approach to the newly built USTA main court is a gauntlet of scalpers offering tickets at outrageous prices. It's possible to get tickets at the box office for early-round matches.

The USTA rents out courts at the tennis center to amateurs year round with the off-peak price starting at $25 an hour. With the exception of Open weeks, you play on the same courts used by the pros for practice.

Horse Racing

When Off Track Betting (OTB) offices were established in the 1970s, turnstile figures at New York-area racetracks plummeted. Now the Sport of Kings is the Sport of Cigar-Smoking Retirees. The winter racing season takes place at Aqueduct Racetrack (☎ (718) 641-4700) in Brooklyn (subway: Aqueduct) Wednesday to Monday from November to May.

It's more pleasant to visit Belmont Park

(☎ (718) 641-4700), just beyond the Queens border in Nassau County, during the summer months from Tuesday to Sunday. The main event of the Belmont season is the Belmont Stakes, held in early June, the third leg of thoroughbred racing's Triple Crown. A special Long Island Rail Road train leaves Penn Station for Belmont several times each racing day and costs $7 roundtrip (☎ (718) 217-5477).

Shopping

WHAT TO BUY
Books

There are Barnes & Noble 'superstores' opening all over town. Among the many locations are: Union Square (☎ (212) 253-0810), Astor Place (☎ (212) 420-1322), 675 Sixth Ave at W 22nd St (☎ (212) 727-1227), and 2289 Broadway at W 82nd St (☎ (212) 362-8835). Each features over 200,000 titles, a music

KIM GRANT

Shopper's dream

department, comfortable seating and a cafe where patrons can read magazines for free. The stores are open daily from 9 am to 10 pm.

The Gotham Book Mart (☎ (212) 719-4448), 41 W 47th St, is one of the city's premier stand-alone shops; its trademark shingle declares that 'wise men fish here.' Coliseum Books (☎ (212) 757-8381), 1771 Broadway, has a huge selection of paperback fiction and out-of-print titles. Shakespeare and Co is a general-interest shop with three locations: downtown at 716 Broadway (☎ (212) 529-1330), in the financial district at 1 Whitehall St (☎ (212) 742-7025) and on the Upper East Side at 939 Lexington Ave (☎ (212) 570-0201).

Three Lives (☎ (212) 741-2069), a Greenwich Village institution at 154 W 10th St, stocks a good number of biographies. Books and Co (☎ (212) 737-1450), 939 Madison Ave, is a distinguished store that has attracted dozens of major authors for readings; photos of their appearances line the walls. It's open Monday to Saturday from 10 am to 7 pm and Sunday noon to 6 pm.

St Marks Book Shop (☎ (212) 260-7853), 31 Third Ave, specializes in political literature, poetry and academic journals.

The handsome Rizzoli store sells art books and general interest titles at two locations: 31 W 57th St (☎ (212) 759-2424) and 454 West Broadway (☎ (212) 674-1616).

Used The Strand (☎ (212) 473-1452), 828 Broadway, boasts of having eight miles of used books and review copies. Just around the corner a block east is the fine, small *Alabaster Bookshop* (☎ (212) 982-3550) 122 Fourth Ave.

Easy Streets

Shoppers in New York may notice that some streets have come to be dominated by retail stores selling only one particular type of merchandise. The reasons for this phenomenon are varied – in some cases, zoning laws have clustered the shops in one spot, or cheap rents have attracted the merchants. Sometimes a certain neighborhood simply gets a 'reputation,' prompting like-minded retailers to locate there. Whatever the reason, here are the places to head if you're interested in the following types of things to buy:

Caps, T-Shirts, Sunglasses & Gloves – These are sold by street vendors all over the city, but a number of them gather along Broadway between Houston and Canal Sts on weekends. What they sell depends on the season, but the price for just about everything is $5.

Jewelry – Groups of cooperative stalls sell jewelry on W 47th St between Sixth and Fifth Ave. Since the stores are dominated by Orthodox Jews, the street is shuttered early on Friday and largely closed on weekends. The vendors here are very skilled in looking pained while offering you the 'best deal' possible – while still making a healthy profit. A similar row of Chinese-owned jewelry shops are clustered near Bowery and Canal Sts (open weekends).

Funky Clothing & Bric-a-Brac – This sort of thing can be had in the many East Village shops, with the center of this growing district being E 9th St between Ave A and First Ave. A number of young clothing designers are trying to make a name for themselves in eponymous shops in this neighborhood, and it's of particular interest for fashion-conscious women.

Hardware, Electronics – Stores can be found along the length of Canal St that are great for light electronics, like extension cords and plugs. Avoid purchasing anything that requires a warranty here (like cameras and stereo equipment), since the shopkeepers do not have good reputations, and *never* buy a phone or video camera from a roving street vendor – it's a scam.

Musical Instruments – Several legendary music shops are clustered on W 48th St between Sixth and Seventh Aves, including Manny's and Sam Ash, which sell just about anything you can play, new and used (shops are closed on Sunday). Guitar lovers will also want to head downtown to Matt Umanov, 273 Bleecker St (subway: W 4th St).

Shoes – Doc Martens fans and the rest of the construction-boot crowd head to W 8th St between Sixth Ave and Broadway, where some 30 shoe stores offer reasonable prices on workhorse shoes and sneakers.

For other examples of the easy street phenomenon, check out the sections on cameras and kitchenware in this chapter and the sidebar on Little Delhi in Places to Eat. ■

The Argosy (☎ (212) 753-4455), 116 E 59th St, features estate sales and rare prints (it's closed Sunday). The dusty and colorful Chelsea Books and Records (☎ (212) 465-4340) can be found at 111 W 17th St. The East Village Books & Records Shop (☎ (212) 477-8647), 101 St Mark's Place, has a good selection of used titles and 50% of profits go to local community groups.

Travel Travel titles and maps can be found at the Traveller's Bookstore (☎ (212) 664-0995) in the Time Warner building, 22 W 52nd St. The Complete Traveller (☎ (212) 685-9007), 199 Madison Ave (corner of W 35th St), also offers an interesting selection of first editions and old Baedecker guides.

Civilized Traveler has two locations, on the Upper West Side at 2003 Broadway

KIM GRANT

way (☎ (212) 875-0306) and at 2 World Financial Center, 25 Liberty St (☎ (212) 786-3301).

Gay Every decent bookstore now includes a gay and lesbian department. A Different Light Bookstore (☎ (212) 989-4850), 151 W 19th St, has 15,000 titles on gay themes. It's open from 10 am to midnight and features a small cafe, several author readings a week and a free Sunday night movie series.

Gay Pleasures Books (☎ (212) 255-5756), 546-548 Hudson St, features gay titles and stock magazines and all the entertainment weeklies.

Specialty Titles Applause Theater Books (☎ (212) 496-7511), 211 W 71st St, carries screenplays and film essays. The Drama Book Shop (☎ (212) 944-0595), in Times Square at 723 Seventh Ave, has the city's largest selection of plays.

Books of Wonder (☎ (212) 989-3270), 16 W 18th St, carries children's titles and young adult fiction and is open Monday to Saturday from 10 am to 7 pm and Sunday 11 am to 6 pm.

East-West Books (☎ (212) 243-5994), 78 Fifth Ave, has a large stock of titles on Buddhism and Asian philosophies.

Whodunit lovers are served by the Mysterious Bookshop (☎ (212) 765-0900), 129 W 56th St, and Murder Ink (☎ (212) 362-8905), 2486 Broadway.

Those interested in architecture should check out Urban Center Books (☎ (212) 935-3592), in the historic Villard Houses at 458 Madison Ave.

Cameras

New York's camera prices are hard to beat, but some of the camera stores in Midtown have reputations for bait-and-switch tactics, so if you go in to buy a Canon lens and the salesperson begins offering a cheaper no-name alternative that's supposedly 'better,' beware. You should also know that it's nearly impossible to get them to knock down published prices as all the camera stores know exactly what their rivals are charging. And because the industry is dominated by shops owned and operated by Orthodox Jews, they usually close in observation of the Sabbath early Friday and all day Saturday and are shuttered during all major Jewish holidays.

You won't meet with a sleazy salesperson at the following places: B&H Photo-Video (☎ (800) 947-9979), 119 W 17th St, is New York's most popular camera store but suffers from zoo-like crowding, gruff help and a pay-first, pick-up-second bureaucracy. The trick is to go in knowing what you want – salespeople don't have the time for a lot of demonstration. It's open Monday and Tuesday 9 am to 6 pm, Wednesday and Thursday 9 am to 7:15 pm, Friday from 9 am to 1 pm and Sunday 10 am to 4:45 pm. Lens and Repro (☎ (212) 675-1900), 33 W 17th St, is a quieter place with a staff eager to explain things to the non-expert. Adorama (☎ (212) 627-8487), on the 2nd floor at 42 W 18th St, rents out photo and video equipment on a daily, weekly and monthly basis. 17th St Photo (☎ (212) 366-9870), 34 W 17th St (2nd floor), also has a patient staff. Olden (☎ (212) 725-1234), 1265 Broadway in Herald Square, is open seven days for camera appraisals and sales. If you're purchasing Leica products and other super high-end stuff, stick to B&H and

Ken Hansen Photo (☎ (212) 317-0923), 509 Madison Ave at E 53rd St, 18th floor, which specializes in Leicas and other top-end equipment. It's open Monday to Friday from 8:30 am to 5 pm.

Computers

Like camera equipment, New York offers great deals on computers. In addition to generally good prices, out-of-staters can beat the taxes by shipping their purchases home, and folks from abroad beat higher domestic prices and value-added taxes.

But shopping for computers in New York is not for the faint of heart. To get the best deals, check out the ads in the Tuesday science section in the *New York Times* and head to the store with a very firm idea of the equipment you want and the price you're willing to pay for it. Like camera equipment, it's crucial not to let a salesperson try to talk you into accepting a cheaper 'substitute' computer, unless you're very familiar with the recommendation.

There are quite a few computer stores in New York, and it's smarter to stick with well-known outlets like those listed here. Do try to avoid the disreputable stores along lower Fifth Ave, and under no circumstances buy equipment that does not come with an adequate warranty from a reputable manufacturer.

J&R Computer World (☎ (212) 238-9100), 15 Park Row (subway: City Hall), has a good reputation for selection and price, but the level of service depends on the salesperson you encounter. Try to avoid shopping there on busy weekends. ICS (☎ (212) 924-5579), 1123 Broadway, has some of the best deals on MacIntosh products and laptops. It's open Monday to Friday from 9 am to 6 pm and Saturday from noon to 4 pm. Comp USA (☎ (212) 764-6224), 420 Fifth Ave, has a good range of printers and aisles of computer software. The Staples (☎ (212) 944-6744) at 1075 Sixth Ave is one of several branches selling computer peripherals, fax machines, printers and office supplies at decent prices.

Antiques

The Annex Flea Market (☎ (212) 243-5343) takes place every Saturday and Sunday from 10 am to 5 pm on Sixth Ave and W 26th St. See the Chelsea section in Things to See & Do. The Chelsea Antiques Building (☎ (212) 929-0909), 110 W 25th St, has indoor stalls of first-edition books, furniture and other items.

There are several antique furniture stores on E 59th St between Second and Third Aves. More stores can be found in the area of Broadway just below Union Square and along E 12th St. Vendors that sell lighting, rare books, prints and other items of interest can be found at the Metropolitan Art Auction (☎ (212) 463-0200), 110 W 19th St.

Top-level auctions are held at Christie's (☎ (212) 546-1000), 502 Park Ave, which held a popular and bizarre sale in 1995 of items from Frank Sinatra's attic, and Sotheby's (☎ (212) 606-7000), 1334 York Ave. Friday's *New York Times* contains announcements of exhibitions.

Leatherwear

Low-cost knockoffs of Coach bags and leather backpacks are available in numerous stores along Broadway just above Houston St, on Bleecker St and on W 4th St immediately off Sixth Ave. Shoe stores selling Doc Martens, hiking boots and other sturdy walkers can be found on W 8th St between Fifth and Sixth Aves – check ads in the *Village Voice* for specials.

Higher priced shoe stores can be found in SoHo among the clothing boutiques.

Jewelry

High-end jewelry shoppers should visit Cartier, Harry Winston and Tiffany and Co, all on Fifth Ave between 52nd and 57th Sts. If you're looking for diamonds and pearls at lower prices, you should visit the Diamond District (see the Easy Streets sidebar).

KIM GRANT

Orchard St, Lower East Side

Cheap Clothing

Dozens of shops sell off-brand clothing at wholesale prices in the Garment District, centered on W 37th St between Eighth and Ninth Aves. For casual wear, many people head to nearby Urban Outfitters (☎ (212) 475-0009), 628 Broadway. If you're looking for more than just jeans, head to the famous Canal Jean Company (☎ (212) 226-1130), 504 Broadway (just up from Canal St). It offers backpacks, army jackets, parkas and a variety of used clothing, including suit jackets and overcoats directly out of the Salvation Army bin for as little as $5. For bargains on Levis, go to Dave's Army and Navy (☎ (212) 989-6444), 779 Sixth Ave. It's packed on Saturday afternoons with foreign visitors stocking up on $25 pairs of Levis.

Music

Tower Records (☎ (212) 505-1500), with its main branch at 692 Broadway, has the best selection of music, but you pay generally higher prices (about $15) there than at HMV, which has a downtown store in Herald Square (☎ (212) 620-0900) and uptown branches on Lexington Ave and E 86th St (☎ (212) 348-0800) and 72nd St and Broadway (☎ (212) 721-5900). Both chains are being given a run for their money by the massive new Virgin Megastore (☎ (212) 332-0400), at W 45th St and Broadway in Times Square.

Shops specializing in CDs for under $10 along with bootlegs and imported music are found on Bleecker St in the West Village. Triton, at No 247, and Route 66 Records (☎ (212) 627-7212), across the street at No 258, are among the best in the city. Uptown, NYCD (☎ (212) 724-4466), 426 Amsterdam Ave, runs a permanent special where if you buy four CDs, you get the fifth one free. Other Music (☎ (212) 477-8150), 15 E 4th St, brazenly opened right across the street from a major Tower Records outlet, but thrives thanks to its selection of offbeat CDs.

Traditionalists should head to Carmine St in Greenwich Village, where stores still sell old lps. Footlight Records (☎ (212) 533-1572), 113 E 12th St, has a magnificent collection of out-of-print albums, Sinatra bootlegs and foreign movie soundtracks on CD.

Kitchenware

It might seem odd to come to New York and buy cookware and kitchen products, but you can really beat department and catalogue prices on items like espresso machines, Kitchenaids, Cuisinarts, chef's knives, pepper mills and even pizza peels (the wooden paddle that places them inside the oven) by shopping the restaurant supply stores on Bowery just below Houston St. The downside is that some of these places sell glassware by the box and are closed Saturday. Two places that sell retail and are open all week are Bari (☎ (212) 925-3845), 240 Bowery, and Chef's Restaurant Supply (☎ (212) 254-6644), 294 Bowery. Some New Yorkers recommend Bridge Kitchenware (☎ (212) 688-4220), 214 E 52nd St, but the place is presided over by a grouchy old man, whom some regard as 'colorful,' and the prices and selections aren't worth it.

WHERE TO SHOP

If you can't get it in New York, it's not available. But it helps to know the places where you can get the best or the cheapest.

Bloomingdale's This New York institution (☎ (212) 705-2000), at E 59th St and Lexington Ave, may think of itself as a New York version of Harrods, but this incredibly cramped, crowded and badly designed department store matches it in attitude and almost nothing else. It does not duplicate the famous London emporium's architectural splendor, magnificent food hall or grand selection of merchandise.

Still, 50,000 people visit daily, and you might as well check it out, too, if they're advertising a clothing sale and to see the designer shops. It's also entertaining in a weird way to walk through the bizarre 1st-floor perfume section, where dozens of clerks try to spray you with the latest scent while repeating the sales pitch in an automaton-like fashion. They are said to spray 500 ounces of fragrance into the air each day.

Bloomingdale's is open Monday to

KIM GRANT

Bloomies

Friday from 10 am to 8:30 pm, Saturday from 10 am to 7 pm, and Sunday from 11 am to 7 pm.

Century 21 Located across the street from the World Trade Center, Century 21 (☎ (212) 227-9092), 25 Church St (subway: Cortlandt St), has big bargains on designer clothing, perfume, sportswear and kitchen products. It's one of the few discount places where the selection of men's wear is as extensive as the women's department. You never know exactly what's on offer, but you will be guaranteed to find marked down Armani shirts and Betsey Johnson dresses on the racks.

Shopping at the store – which doesn't advertise, opens early and is closed on Sunday – is a ritual for downtown office workers and people waiting out their two weeks of jury duty at the nearby courthouses.

It's open Monday to Wednesday from 7:45 am to 7 pm, Thursday from 7:45 am to 8:30 pm, Friday from 7:45 am to 8 pm and Saturday from 10 am to 7 pm.

FAO Schwarz It may not be the only toy store in the city, but you wouldn't know it from the weekend crowds at FAO Schwarz (☎ (212) 644-9400), 767 Fifth Ave. It *is* the most expensive and elaborate one, and there's usually a 25-minute wait to get in during the holiday season. The Barbie salon at the back of the store (entrance on Madison Ave) is wildly popular – you never realized how much stuff that doll had in her closet. It's open Monday to Saturday from 10 am to 6 pm (Thursday to 8 pm) and Sunday 11 am to 6 pm.

The Enchanted Forest (☎ (212) 925-6677), 85 Mercer St, is a smaller and delightful store catering to kids in SoHo. It specializes in teddy bears and hand puppets from $25 and under.

Kiehl's This quirky pharmacy (☎ (212) 475-3400), 109 Third Ave, has a patient staff that has been selling organic skin-care products since 1851. This precursor to the Body Shop has a very loyal clientele, and celebrities such as Richard Gere can be spotted in the place buying products and admiring the late owner's eccentric collection of antique Harley-Davidson motorcycles.

Macy's This popular department store (☎ (212) 695-4400) has for years claimed to be the world's largest (Moscow's Gum department store and several others probably have a more legitimate right to that title). Still, most New Yorkers have an affectionate regard for Macy's, one of the city's last surviving general-interest retailers, in large part because of its sponsorship of a fireworks festival on the 4th of July and the annual Thanksgiving Day Parade. Though Macy's has experienced financial problems in recent years, the store's stock hasn't diminished, and it continues to hold its famous Wednesday 'One Day Sales.'

Paragon Athletic Goods This sporting goods store (☎ (212) 255-8036), 867 Broadway (subway: Union Square), not only has the best selection of sports merchandise, but it regularly beats prices found at chain stores such as the Sports Authority. Particularly notable for its end-of-season sales on tennis racquets and running shoes, Paragon also has the best selection of in-line skates in the city and a helpful staff that will literally spend an hour helping you choose the best kind.

Warner Bros Studio Store This store (☎ (212) 754-0300), at the corner of 57th St and Fifth Ave, is like a theme restaurant that dispenses with food and simply sells corporate identity. Whether or not you care for items like a Sylvester stapler or a Bugs Bunny coffee mug depends on your regard for the old Looney Toon cartoon characters. You can also buy authenticated animation cels for upwards of $2500. Plenty of people love this store and have made it one of the most profitable retail outlets in New York City.

It's open Monday to Saturday from 10

am to 7 pm and Sunday from noon to 6 pm. In 1996, the Walt Disney company opened a similar theme store (☎ (212) 702-0702) just two blocks south at 711 Fifth Ave.

Fifth Ave

The Midtown portion of Fifth Ave is not as exclusive as it once was, as the arrival of the Warner Bros store indicates, but four landmark stores remain:

Bergdorf Goodman – Sells jewelry and the *couture* collections from a variety of companies including Armani, Calvin Klein and Christian Dior. A newer men's store across the street offers Charvet and Turnbull & Asser clothing. No 754, ☎ (212) 753-7300

Henri Bendel – Sells a curious and expensive mix of accessories and clothing, mainly for women. No 712, ☎ (212) 247-1100

Saks Fifth Ave – Known for its January sale, it has a vast ground floor selling space and a helpful staff. No 611, ☎ (212) 753-4000

Tiffany's – Not as snooty as you might expect, and if you look hard enough, you can take home a reasonably priced small item and get the impressive Tiffany's box. No 727, ☎ (212) 755-8000

Madison Ave

The funkiest boutiques may be in SoHo, but more formal shopping can be found on Madison Ave above E 42nd St. On the Upper East Side, Madison Ave is as close as New York comes to a *Place Vendôme* Parisian experience, as designers try to outdo each other in their showplace stores, most clustered above E 60th St. There are fewer crowds on Sunday, but you won't be able to drop in on any of the avenue's first-rate art galleries, which are closed that day. Here's a list of stores you'll find between E 42nd St and E 77th St.

Bang & Olufson – The most expensive and best-designed electronic equipment in the world. 952 Madison Ave, ☎ (212) 879-6161

Barney's – The flagship of the hip and haughty clothing chain store that's famous for treating potential customers as too fat, too poor, and, in the men's department, too straight. No 660, ☎ (212) 826-8900

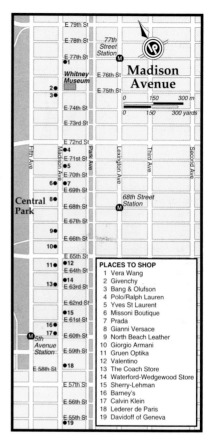

PLACES TO SHOP
1 Vera Wang
2 Givenchy
3 Bang & Olufson
4 Polo/Ralph Lauren
5 Yves St Laurent
6 Missoni Boutique
7 Prada
8 Gianni Versace
9 North Beach Leather
10 Giorgio Armani
11 Gruen Optika
12 Valentino
13 The Coach Store
14 Waterford-Wedgewood Store
15 Sherry-Lehman
16 Barney's
17 Calvin Klein
18 Lederer de Paris
19 Davidoff of Geneva

Brooks Brothers – A legendary store selling conservative clothing and formal wear for men; includes a smaller women's department. No 346, ☎ (212) 682-8800

Calvin Klein – The media savvy designer opened this flagship store in early 1995. No 654, ☎ (212) 292-9000

The Coach Store – The place for expensive leather bags, wallets and belts that never go on sale. No 710, ☎ (212) 319-1772

Davidoff of Geneva – Everything for the smoker except Cuban cigars. No 535, ☎ (212) 751-9060

DAVID ELLIS

Antique dealer, Houston St

Gianni Versace – The other high priest of Italian style has two shops for fashion-obsessed rockers on Madison Ave, one for men, one for women. No 816, ☎ (212) 744-5572

Giorgio Armani – Refusing to be outdone by anyone, Armani opened up his own massive flagship store in 1996. E 65th St and Madison Ave, ☎ (212) 988-9191

Givenchy – The place for traditional French suits and accessories. No 954, ☎ (212) 772-1040

Gruen Optika – The best store in the city for one-of-a-kind eyewear. No 740, ☎ (212) 988-5832

Lederer de Paris – Leather goods and diaries from France. No 613, ☎ (212) 355-5515

Missoni Boutique – The popular Italian designer's expensive knitwear is sold here. No 836, ☎ (212) 517-9339

North Beach Leather – California-style leather outfits featuring bright colors. No 772, ☎ (212) 772-0707

Polo/Ralph Lauren – An old mansion makes an appropriate setting for Lauren's clothing aimed at aristocratic wannabes. Madison Ave and E 72nd St, ☎ (212) 606-2100

Prada – The Milan company's expensive and trendy offerings (shoes are $300 and up) are available here. Madison Ave and E 70th St, ☎ (212) 327-0488

Sherry-Lehman – A world-class wine and spirit store that also has reasonable prices (it's closed on Sunday). No 679, ☎ (212) 838-7500

Valentino – One of the world's best-known *couture* desingers. No 823, ☎ (212) 744-0200

Vera Wang – Bridal wear for New York's High Society. 991 Madison Ave, ☎ (212) 628-3400

The Waterford-Wedgwood Store – One of Madison Ave's premier shops for fine China and blown glass. No 713, ☎ (212) 759-0500

Worth and Worth – The place for men's hats, custom-made umbrellas and scarves. No 331, ☎ (212) 867-6058

Yves St Laurent – Selections from the legendary (and out-of-fashion) master of French *couture* are sold here. No 855, ☎ (212) 472-5299

Flea Markets

You can rummage through old movie posters, bicycles, antique cameras, silver and just about everything else in empty parking lots on Sixth Ave above W 24th St, Saturday and Sunday.

Junk Stores

That's what New Yorkers call the Woolworth knock-off outlets that sell 99¢ household items (light bulbs, soap, batteries, utensils) and/or minor items of clothing (socks, hats, gloves). The major drags for these stores are along W 14th St between Seventh Ave and Union Square, and E 86th St between First and Lexington Aves.

Excursions

Long Island

Long Island (population 2,609,212) is a study in geographic and economic contrasts. It begins with crowded and urban Brooklyn (Kings County) and Queens (Queens County) on the western shore, and it then gives way to blander suburban housing and strip malls in neighboring Nassau County. The terrain becomes flatter and less crowded in rural Suffolk County, which comprises the eastern end of the island. Suffolk County itself contains two peninsulas – commonly called the North and South 'forks' – divided by Peconic Bay.

The island was first a series of whaling and fishing ports, as well as the exclusive outpost for New York's ultra-rich, who built estates along the secluded coves on the north shore of Nassau County (called the 'Gold Coast'). In the years following WWII, Nassau became increasingly more populated, as thousands of middle-class families moved to the suburbs. Levittown, the prototypical planned community, attracted 55,000 people in the booming 1950s.

In Suffolk County, economic development patterns were geographically reversed. The North Fork is home to salaried workers and owners of small farms, while the South Fork is dominated by several villages (Hampton Bays, Southampton, Bridgehampton, East Hampton and Amagansett), known collectively as the Hamptons, where actors, writers and entertainment executives gather to schmooze away the summer season on private estates and in expensive restaurants.

For most visitors, a trip to Long Island means a trip to the beach, whether the destination is crowded Jones Beach or Fire Island in Nassau, or quiet Shelter Island, Greenport or the more showy Hamptons enclaves. All are within easy reach via public transportation, which is the best option for summer weekends, when traffic jams are particularly hellish. However, if you're interested in exploring Long Island's historic mansions, or sampling wine in the vineyards of the North Fork, it's best to have a car.

Getting There & Away

Car The Long Island Expressway (LIE; I-495) cuts through the center of the island and ends by joining two smaller roads. The older Rt 25 (also known as the Jericho Turnpike) runs roughly parallel to I-495, then continues to the end of the North Fork at Orient Point. Rt 27 (also known as the Sunrise Hwy) runs along the bottom of Long Island, becomes the Montauk Hwy and ends up at the end of the South Fork at Montauk Point.

Bus The Hampton Jitney (☎ (800) 936-0440, (516) 283-4600) leaves several times daily for Long Island's South Fork from three locations on the East Side of Manhattan, including E 41st St between Lexington and Third Aves. Sunrise Coach Lines (☎ (800) 527-7709) services the North Fork from its stop at E 44th St and Third Ave. Both average a one-way fare of $15, and drivers usually know ways of circumventing summer weekend traffic, making these buses a good alternative to driving a car.

A number of private bus companies serve points within Long Island – call ☎ (516) 766-6722 for information on transportation in Nassau County; for Suffolk County, call ☎ (516) 360-5700.

Train The Long Island Rail Road (LIRR; ☎ (516) 822-5477, (718) 217-5477) carries 250,000 passengers daily to 134 stations throughout Long Island from New York

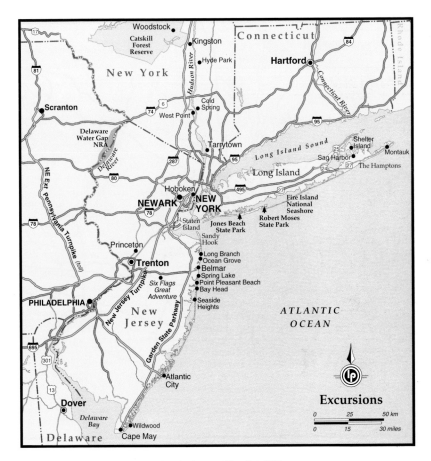

Excursions

City's Penn Station. Trips to the farthest points on the railroad – Greenport in the North Fork and Montauk in the South Fork – cost $15.25/7.50 adult/child one way, with off-peak rates of $10.25.

In the summer, the LIRR offers roundtrip deals to the south shore beaches, but be aware that the lines at the station ticket office are very long on Friday nights and Saturday mornings. You can always buy tickets well in advance (so drop by in the late morning to pick up tickets for an intended Friday evening departure).

Tourist Offices

The Long Island Convention and Visitors Bureau (☎ (800) 441-4601) publishes an annual free travel guide. You can obtain maps, restaurant listings and lodging guides from the local chambers of commerce by calling:

Southampton	☎ (516) 283-0402
East Hampton	☎ (516) 324-0362
Shelter Island	☎ (516) 749-0399
Montauk	☎ (516) 668-2428
Greenport-Southold	☎ (516) 477-1383

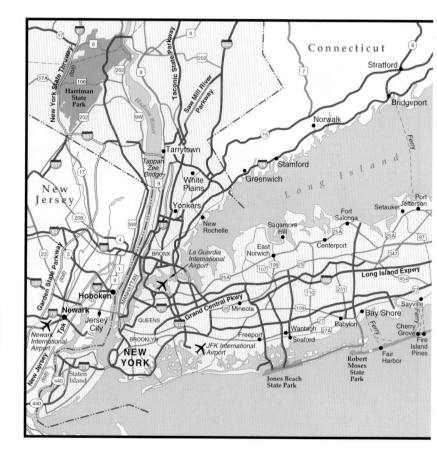

Activities

It's possible to **bike** along Rt 25 on the North Fork, and along the side roads in the Hamptons, especially along the seven-mile Rt 114 (the Sag Harbor Turnpike) from East Hampton to Sag Harbor. Shelter Island is also a perfect spot for biking and **hiking** the Mashomack Nature Preserve. You can embark on long, uninterrupted **walks** along the beautiful shoreline from East Hampton to Montauk. **Surfers** head to the Georgica Jetties, Montauk and Shinnecock Inlet. Directions and information on conditions can be obtained in season by

calling ☎ (516) 283-SURF/7873. Two-hour **kayak** explorations of Peconic Bay are offered by Shelter Island Kayak Tours (☎ (516) 749-1990) for $45 per person.

OYSTER BAY & CENTERPORT

The quiet village of Oyster Bay is a refuge for the rich just one hour away from New York City – the hills overlooking the water are dotted with million-dollar residences placed a tasteful distance from one another. In 1885, Theodore Roosevelt built a 23-room mansion on **Sagamore Hill** (☎ (516) 922-4447), which eventually

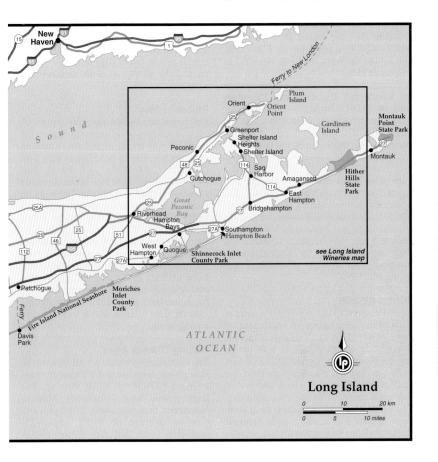

Long Island

served as the summer White House during his tenure in office from 1901-09. It was in this dark Victorian mansion that Roosevelt brokered an end to the Russo-Japanese War, for which he won the Nobel Peace Prize.

Roosevelt was in many ways the first president of the modern era – he used a telephone to remain in contact with Washington, which is still on view in his study. Though TR was also the first chief executive to concern himself with conservation, animal rights activists will no doubt turn pale at the many mounted heads, antlers and leopard skins on display, along with the inkwell made from a rhinoceros foot.

Roosevelt died at Sagamore Hill in 1919 and is buried in a cemetery a mile away. A red-brick Georgian house on the grounds houses his gold Nobel medal. Later occupied by Theodore Roosevelt Jr, it is now a museum charting the 26th president's political career.

Sagamore Hill is open daily from April to October and Wednesday to Sunday during the winter from 9 am to 5 pm. Tours of the Roosevelt home leave on the hour; admission is $2, seniors and children under

16 get in free. To get there, take the 41N exit from the Long Island Expressway and travel on Rt 106, turn right on E Main St, and follow the signs on Cove Neck Rd to Sagamore Hill.

Continuing east on Rt 25A brings you to the **Vanderbilt Mansion and Planetarium** (☎ (516) 854-5555) in Centerport. Also known as Eagle's Nest, this was the estate of Willie Vanderbilt, one of the last major heirs to the Staten Island family railroad fortune. Willie spent most of his life – and money – collecting sea creatures and curiosities from the South Pacific and Egypt, many of which are on display. The mansion is now owned by Nassau County, which holds community events on the 43-acre site. It's open Tuesday to Sunday from noon to 5 pm. Admission to the mansion is $8/6, with a $4 charge for children; a combination ticket for the planetarium and mansion is $11.

JONES BEACH

Jones Beach (☎ (516) 785-1600) is without a doubt the *least* exclusive beach area on Long Island. Tens of thousands of people converge on its six-mile stretch of ocean, and there's parking for nearly 25,000 cars in its lots. Though it's always mobbed, the sand at Jones Beach is clean, and it's an enjoyable respite from the sweltering city. The LIRR offers $15 roundtrip fares from Penn Station in the city to the Freeport station on Long Island; the trip takes under 40 minutes and includes a shuttle bus to Jones Beach.

ROBERT MOSES STATE PARK & FIRE ISLAND

Robert Moses State Park, at the westernmost end of the Fire Island National Seashore (☎ (516) 289-4810), is the only spot on the island accessible by car. The park is similar in scale (and level of crowding) to neighboring Jones Beach. You can get there by taking Exit 53 off the LIE and traveling south across the Moses Causeway. The rest of Fire Island is a summer-only cluster of villages accessible only by ferry from three points on mainland Long

Island. Fire Island is probably the country's leading gay resort area, centered around Cherry Grove. Fire Island's main drag is the car-free village of Ocean Beach, packed on weekends with strollers and shoppers.

Places to Stay

Fire Island accommodations are expensive, but you really wouldn't want to stay on the mainland and travel in and out. Camping spots include *Heckscher Park* in East Islip (☎ (516) 581-4433) and *Watch Hill* (☎ (516) 597-6455) on Fire Island. *Houser's Hotel* (☎ (516) 583-7799), at Bay Walk on Ocean Beach, has 12 rooms with rates from $135 to $200 a night. The *Ocean Beach Hotel* (☎ (516) 583-9292) is a 21-unit facility open from May to September charging $65 to $185 per room. The year-round *Four Seasons B&B* (☎ (516) 583-8295), 468 Dehnoff Walk in Ocean Beach, requires a two-day stay during the summer and $300 for a weekend stay ($250 during the off season). This price includes breakfast and afternoon tea.

Getting There & Away

The three ferry terminals are all close to the Bay Shore, Sayville and Patchogue (pronounced PATCH-og) LIRR stations. The ferry season runs from early May to November; trips take about 20 minutes and cost an average of $10/5 adults/kids roundtrip, with discount season passes available. Three ferry companies connect Fire Island and the mainland:

Fire Island Ferries (☎ (516) 665-3600) sail from Bay Shore to Saltaire, Fair Harbor and Ocean Beach.

Sayville Ferry Service (☎ (516) 589-8980) runs from Sayville to Cherry Grove and Fire Island Pines.

Davis Park Ferry Company (☎ (516) 475-1665) travels from Patchogue to Davis Park and Watch Hill.

THE HAMPTONS

Prominent artists, musicians and writers have long been attracted to the beautiful beaches and rustic Cape Cod-style homes in the Hamptons, but the easy-money '80s brought an influx of showier summertime visitors who made their fortunes in the fashion industry and on Wall St. In recent years, the Hamptons have become truly 'hot,' as West Coast entertainment moguls purchased large homes here, following in the footsteps of Steven Spielberg. Year-round residents seem annoyed and amused by the show in equal measure. Many of the attractions, restaurants and hotels in the Hamptons close the last week in October and remain shut until late April. B&B prices drop – and traffic jams along the Montauk Hwy disappear – about two weeks after Labor Day.

Southampton

Southampton village doesn't have half the flash of its neighbors to the east, but it's a pleasant place to spend an afternoon in search of history and art. You can get maps and brochures for the town at the chamber of commerce office at 76 Main St, located among a group of high-priced craft shops and decent restaurants. Just a few steps away from the tourist office is the **Halsey Homestead**, a saltbox house built in 1648, just eight years after the first European settlers arrived in the area. It's open to the public from June to September, Tuesday to Saturday from 11 am to 4:30 pm and Sunday from 2 to 4:30 pm.

The **Parrish Art Museum** (☎ (516) 283-2111), 25 Jobs Lane, is just a short walk away from Main St. It has been open to the public since 1898, and its gallery features the work of major artists. The museum is open Tuesday to Saturday from 11 am to 5 pm and Sunday from 1 to 5 pm. In the winter the museum is closed on Tuesday and Wednesday. Suggested admission is $3.

Sag Harbor

Sag Harbor, seven miles north of Bridge-hampton, is an old whaling town on Peconic Bay that's far less beach-oriented than the other Hampton towns. Its **Whaling Museum** (☎ (516) 725-0770) is just west of the shops on Main St. It's open from May to October, Monday to Saturday from

10 am to 5 pm and Sunday from 1 to 5 pm; admission is $3/1.

Sag Harbor's *American Hotel* (☎ (516) 725-3535), on Main St, has only eight rooms starting at $150 a night, but the ground-floor restaurant and bar is a hangout for weekending worthies.

East Hampton & Amagansett

The heart of trendy Long Island is East Hampton, where you can shop at the Coach leather store, catch readings and art exhibitions at the **Guild Hall** (☎ (516) 324-0806) and dine at the *Maidstone Arms* (☎ (516) 324-5006), 207 Main St, the most elegant and expensive restaurant in town. Driving or biking down Main Beach along Ocean Ave will afford glimpses of the larger saltbox estates with water views. You can see some other grand (private) houses by turning right at **Lilly Pond Lane** and peeking through the breaks in the high shrubbery. Amagansett is basically an extension of East Hampton distinguished by the huge flagpole in the center of the Montauk Hwy. The *Stephen Talkhouse* (☎ (516) 267-3117), 161 Main St, is a 20-year-old concert venue (Elvis Costello and others have appeared here) that has an active bar scene on nonperformance nights.

Montauk

Montauk is a long, flat 13-mile drive away from Amagansett along Rt 27. If you're a biker looking for a challenge, peel off to the right and take the **Old Montauk Hwy**, an undulating road overlooking the ocean that passes by several resorts, including the 175-room *Gurney's Inn* (☎ (516) 668-3203), a spa with rates starting at $260.

Montauk itself is more honky-tonk than the rest of the Hamptons, with more reasonable restaurants and a rougher bar scene. The LIRR train terminus is a long 10-minute walk to the center of town. **Montauk Downs** (☎ (516) 668-3781) has a fine public golf course that charges $20 per person for a round; there are long waits for tee times in the summer. If you drive out to Montauk Point State Park, stop at the scenic overlook and avoid the parking lot at the very end, which charges for a view that's not really worth the money, unless you intend to visit the unimpressive **Montauk Lighthouse Museum** for an additional fee of $2/1.

Places to Stay

There's camping at *Hither Hills State Park* (☎ (516) 668-2461).

In the Hamptons, there's virtually no price difference between places calling themselves B&Bs and smaller inns – most have rates well over $130 in high season. The recently renovated *Mill House Inn* (☎ (516) 324-9766), 33 N Main St, East Hampton, run by Dan and Katherine Hartnett, has eight themed rooms starting at $100 a night off season and $185 in summer.

The Fariel family has run the *Sea Breeze Inn* (☎ (516) 267-3159) in Amagansett since 1957. It's located just a block away from the LIRR train station, and its 12 rooms are all clean (some with shared bath). Rates are $60 to $140, with weekly discounts available. Owner Rob Fariel hangs out with guests in the 1st-floor bar and can proffer flawless advice on where to eat and what to see in the area.

The motels in more isolated Montauk run a bit cheaper during the summer – about $125 a night – but many are booked solid on a monthly basis by groups of students employed at the resorts and restaurants.

Places to Eat

There are a few cheap seafood stands on Rt 27 near Napeague Beach (between Amagansett and Montauk) that serve fish sandwiches, fresh steamers and fried clams for $10 and under during the summer months. The most popular are the *Lobster Roll* (☎ (516) 267-3740), with its distinctive 'Lunch' sign, and *Cyril's*, a restaurant presided over by an ex-Marine with a handlebar mustache, which serves an excellent sesame shrimp meal. In Montauk, the *Shagwong Restaurant* (☎ (516) 668-3050) on Main St serves good tavern-style meals year round. The more expensive Hamptons options include the *Laundry* (☎ (516) 324-

3199), 31 Race Lane one block from the East Hampton train.

SHELTER ISLAND

Smack in between the north and south forks is Shelter Island, a pretty community with a third of its land mass dedicated to the **Mashomack Nature Preserve**. There's an attractive town center in Shelter Island Heights, a cluster of Victorian buildings on the north side of the island. The North Ferry Company (☎ (516) 749-0139) runs boats to Shelter Island every 15 minutes from the North Fork terminal (near the LIRR station in Greenport) from 6 am to 11:45 pm; a car and driver costs $6.50, additional passengers $1. The trip takes seven minutes. South Ferry Inc (☎ (516) 749-1200) goes to Sag Harbor from 6 am to 1:45 am; a car and driver is $7, passengers $1.

Bike Rental

At Piccozzi's Bike Shop (☎ (516) 749-0045), on Bridge St (a five-minute walk from the ferry – call ahead in the summer to reserve), bikes can be rented for $18 a day, and they are sturdy enough for a strenuous trek across Shelter Island or back to Greenport for a 20-mile exploration of the North Fork and Orient Point.

Places to Stay & Eat

Local B&Bs include the *Azalea House* (☎ (516) 749-4252), 1 Thomas Ave, which has five rooms with rates from $50 to $125. *Shelter Island B&B* (☎ (516) 749-0842), 7 St Mary's Rd, has four rooms (two with a private entrance) for $60 on weekends. You can get very good off-season rates at the *Ram's Head Inn* (☎ (516) 749-0811) on Ram Island Dr on Shelter Island. It charges $70 for a private bath in midweek off peak; during the summer rates jump to $125 or more a room.

The dining choices on Shelter Island are very seasonal. The *Dory* (☎ (516) 749-8871), near the Shelter Island Heights Bridge, is a smoky bar that serves simple fare on a waterfront patio. *Shelter Island Pizza* (☎ (516) 749-0400), on Rt 114, is just about the only place open every day year round.

NORTH FORK

Greenport is the main town in the North Fork, where you can catch a ferry to/from Shelter Island. The people in Greenport live there year round, and many are farmers or employees of the local Grumman aerospace company, one of the region's biggest employers, though layoffs have rocked the town recently. Efforts to offset the slumping farming and manufacturing economy in the North Fork led to the establishment of several vineyards during the '80s. Now, Greenport is the perfect base to begin an exploration of the area's wineries.

Wineries

Today there are 16 vineyards in eastern Long Island, all but three of them located in the North Fork near Rt 25. Just look for the distinctive green 'wine trail' road signs that crop up just past Riverhead; nine of the vineyards are clustered within two miles of the town of Cutchogue (pronounced KUTCH-og). You can get more information on touring the wine trail by contacting the

Long Island Wine Council at ☎ (516) 475-5492. Be aware that the vineyards get very crowded during summer weekends, and most vineyards are open weekends only during the winter. In season, try to visit during the week – and have a hearty breakfast before quaffing a lot of wine, since you'll have to drive or bike from one place to another. The largest facility is **Pindar Vineyards** (☎ (516) 734-6200) in Peconic, which offers frequent tours of the 250 acres of vines daily from 11 am to 6 pm. They also have evening wine festivals several times a year where light food is served for a small charge. Also offering daily tastings are **Peconic Bay Vineyards** (☎ (516) 734-7361), which has an array of tasty dry Chardonnays and dessert wines, and **Bedell Cellars** (☎ (516) 734-7537), a leader in the quest for a decent Long Island red.

Orient

Just east of Greenport is the tiny hamlet of Orient, about three miles in from Orient Point ferry terminal; follow the signs for the 'Orient

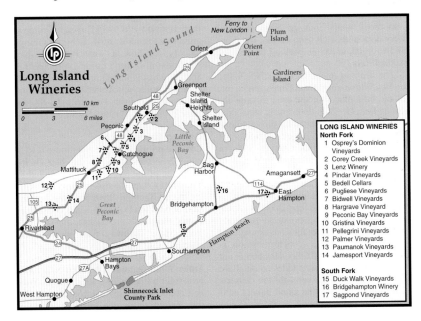

Long Island Wineries

LONG ISLAND WINERIES

North Fork
1 Osprey's Dominion Vineyards
2 Corey Creek Vineyards
3 Lenz Winery
4 Pindar Vineyards
5 Bedell Cellars
6 Pugliese Vineyards
7 Bidwell Vineyards
8 Hargrave Vineyard
9 Peconic Bay Vineyards
10 Gristina Vineyards
11 Pellegrini Vineyards
12 Palmer Vineyards
13 Paumanok Vineyards
14 Jamesport Vineyards

South Fork
15 Duck Walk Vineyards
16 Bridgehampton Winery
17 Sagpond Vineyards

Business District' at the Civil War monument at the side of Rt 25. There's not much of a business district in this tiny 17th-century hamlet, just an old wooden post office and a general store. But Orient is a remarkably well-preserved collection of white clapboard houses and former inns. It's everything a colonial town is supposed to be – quiet, manageable and very pretty. Farther out of town, you can bike past the Oyster Ponds just east of Main St and also check out the beach at Orient Beach State Park.

The Cross Sound Ferry Company (☎ (516) 323-2525) takes passengers and autos from the tip of the North Fork to New London, Connecticut; reservations are recommended. Autos cost $28, passengers $13 one way. The company also offers an auto-free hydrofoil shuttle from the terminal to the Foxwoods Casino and Resort in Connecticut.

Places to Stay & Eat

The best place to stay in Greenport is the *White Lions Inn* (☎ (516) 477-8819), 433 Main St. This large old home has five rooms (two with shared baths) and is just a four-block walk from the Shelter Island ferry dock and LIRR train station. Rates are $65 to $110, with free parking at the back of the house.

The *Seafood Barge* (☎ (516) 765-3010), on Rt 25 three miles from Greenport, is one of the best places in the area to taste the sweet Peconic Bay scallops, a local specialty that was devastated by brown tide in 1994. The restaurant, which overlooks the Port of Egypt Marina, charges $18 for dinner entrees and offers a selection of lunch specials for $8.95.

In Greenport, restaurants are clustered around the marina. *Claudio's* (☎ (516) 477-0715), across from the ferry dock, is a landmark that gets quite noisy at the long wooden bar, but the food is considered mediocre by locals. A better option is *Aldo's* (☎ (516) 477-1699), 103-105 Front St, which is also pricey ($19 entrees like lamb loin), but it serves sublime desserts and biscotti made in the small bakery next to the restaurant.

The Hudson Valley

There are many charming spots just north of New York City in this region, which refers to the villages and towns that dot the Hudson River south of Albany. Autumn is a particularly beautiful time here, and many city dwellers rent cars to see the changing colors.

Remember that even though the towns are easily reached by the Metro North commuter line out of Grand Central Station, there is little reliable public transportation between localities or to sites set back from the river. You'll need to have a car for the fullest exploration of the area.

Just over New York's eastern border are Connecticut's Litchfield Hills, and farther north are Massachusetts' Berkshire Hills. These are very popular tourist destinations, especially in the summer, when outdoor activities and festivals abound. The area is dotted with inns and B&Bs, and all of it is detailed in Lonely Planet's *New England*.

The regional Hudson Valley Tourist Board (☎ (800) 232-4782) issues a guide to attractions and annual events. Orange County, location of West Point Military Academy, also has a guide (☎ (800) 762-8687). Most tourist brochures can be obtained at the New York State Information Center at Harriman, Exit 16 off I-87 (the New York State Thruway).

Getting There & Away

Car The principal scenic river route is Rt 9, which hugs the east side of the river. On the west side of the river the road is called Rt 9W. Most towns are also reached by taking the faster Taconic State Parkway, which runs north from Ossining and is considered one of the state's prettiest roads. The New York State Thruway runs west of the Hudson.

Train While Amtrak (☎ (800) 872-7245) passenger trains run the length of the river and connect with several communities on the eastern shore, the best bet is Metro

North (☎ (212) 532-4900, (800) 638-7646) commuter trains from Grand Central Station (take the 'Hudson Line').

Metro North runs special summer and autumn tourist packages on weekends that include train fare and transportation to and from specific sites such as Hyde Park and the Vanderbilt Mansion. (The fare is $17.75 for adults, $14.50 for seniors and $4 for children.) There's even a train that drops you off on the Appalachian Trail on Saturday morning and picks you up again in the early evening. Call for details.

River Cruises New York Waterway (☎ (800) 533-3779) boats offer several tour packages of the Hudson Valley that depart from Manhattan's Pier 78 at 10:45 am. One seven-hour trip visits several Tarrytown historic homes for $35/$17.50 for adults/children. A cruise to the 40-room Rockefeller estate Kykuit is $25, all inclusive. Cruises are offered daily except Tuesday from May to November.

Bike The country roads east of the Hudson River are perfect for biking. For further information, find *Mountain Biking Destinations in the NY Metropolitan Area* by Joel Sendek (Urban Country Publications) or *25 Bicycle Tours in the Hudson Valley* by Peter Kick (Back Country Books).

TARRYTOWN

This town is forever associated with author Washington Irving, whose *Legend of Sleepy Hollow* was set here in his home town. In fact, the village of North Tarrytown changed its name to Sleepy Hollow in late 1996 in order to attract more tourists. Information on the area can be obtained by the Sleepy Hollow Chamber of Commerce (☎ (914) 631-1705), 54 Main St, Sleepy Hollow (open Monday to Friday, 9 am to 5 pm), and the Historic Hudson Valley organization (☎ (914) 631-8200, (800) 448-4007), which is the non-profit caretaker for five historic sites in the Lower Hudson Valley: Sunnyside, Philipsburg Manor, Kykuit, Van Cortlandt Manor and the Union Church of Pocantico Hills. There are many historic homes near Tarry-

town, the most fabulous of which is the **Kykuit**, the riverside Rockefeller family estate (☎ (914) 631-8200). Tickets are $18 for adults, $16 for seniors and students, and they can be ordered by phone ahead of time. It's open April to November. Reservations are essential.

Places to Stay & Eat The cheapest and prettiest spot in town is on the hilltop grounds of *Marymount College* (☎ (914) 332-8209, 631-3200), 100 Marymount Ave. In the summer, dormitory rooms are available for $25 a night per person. The *Tarrytown Hilton Inn* (☎ (914) 631-5700), 455 S Broadway (Hwy 9), is one of the more attractive Hiltons to be found and seems to have acknowledged its historic locale; even the bar has a homey-antique touch. Rooms are pricier here, in the $115 to $175 range, and large suites are in the $200 to $400 range.

One of best diners in the valley is *Bella's Restaurant & Donut Shop* (☎ (914) 332-0444), 5 S Broadway near the corner of Main St. The doughnuts will tempt those who swore off doughnuts years ago. The diner also offers goulash, pot roast, hearty soups and sandwiches. The *Main Street Cafe* (☎ (914) 332-9834), 24 Main St, is a moderately upscale American bistro with interesting sandwiches.

COLD SPRING

Cold Spring is typical of the depressed Hudson Valley towns that are slowly waking up as urban dwellers discover their simple charms. There are antique shops, inns and restaurants along its hilly Main St and a waterfront walk that's literally in the shadow of a mountain on the west side of the river. Cold Spring and nearby Beacon are the areas featured (in a fictional disguise) in the Richard Russo novel *Nobody's Fool* and the Paul Newman movie of the same name.

A walking tour (☎ (914) 265-2756) leaves from 63 Chestnut St, from mid-May to mid-November, every Sunday at 2 pm. To join, call ☎ (914) 265-2756, or inquire at any of the antique shops on Main St.

Metro North trains run from Grand Central Station to Cold Spring about every 90 minutes or so; the trip takes just over an hour. The village can be reached with a car by taking the scenic Rt 9D (if you're coming from west of the river, turn left after crossing the Bear Mountain Bridge). Rt 9D runs directly along the east side of the Hudson and parallels the larger Rt 9, which runs a few miles inland farther east. From Rt 9 (north or south), take Rt 301 directly into the center of town.

Places to Stay & Eat There are several very nice, if pricey, B&Bs here, including the *Pig Hill B&B* (☎ (914) 265-9247), 73 Main St, a pink-brick Victorian in the middle of the village. Summer rates vary for rooms with private bath and fireplace ($150/125 on weekends/weekdays) to rooms with a shared bath ($130/100). Non-summer rates start at $80.

The Depot (☎ (914) 265-5000), at 1 Depot Rd, is located in the old railway station right by the Metro North tracks, so you can't miss it. The pub grub is good and runs in the $10 to $18 range, but avoid the pricier bland dinner entrees. For a full-scale dinner try *Riverview* (☎ (914) 265-4778), which overlooks the Hudson at 45 Fair St and serves $10 pasta and seafood dishes, or *76 Main St* (☎ (914) 265-7676). Vegetarians should check out the *Foundry Cafe* (☎ (914) 265-4504), 55 Main St, which also features microbrews.

WEST POINT

Generations of American soldiers have been groomed at the United States Military Academy since its establishment in 1802, including US Grant, Douglas MacArthur and Dwight Eisenhower. Today the cadet corps are made of men and women who live on its impressive campus of red-brick and graystone Gothic and Federal-style buildings, churches and temples. The West Point Visitors Center (☎ (914) 938-2638) is actually in Highland Falls, about 100 yards south of the military academy's Thayer Gate. It's open daily from 9 am to 4:45 pm for maps and tour information.

HYDE PARK

The peaceful hillsides of Hyde Park overlook the eastern edge of the Hudson and are home to three significant attractions: the Franklin D Roosevelt Home and Library, the Eleanor Roosevelt National Historic Site and the Vanderbilt Mansion National Historic Site.

The **Franklin D Roosevelt Home and Library** (☎ (914) 229-8114, (800) 337-8474), 511 Albany Post Rd, is the first US presidential library. FDR (1882-1945) made Hyde Park his summer White House during his four terms. The museum features old photos, FDR's voice on tape (from the fireside chats and several speeches), a special wing in memory of Eleanor Roosevelt and FDR's famous 1936 Ford Phaeton car, with its special hand controls that enabled the wheelchair-bound president to drive. President and Mrs Roosevelt (1884-1962) are interred in the Rose Garden on the grounds.

The museum is open daily: November through April from 9 am to 5 pm, and May through October from 9 am to 6 pm. Admission is $5 for adults, $4 for seniors and free for kids under 16.

Because FDR's mother lived at Hyde Park until her death in 1941, Eleanor Roosevelt, who did not get along with her mother-in-law, stayed at her own home called Val-Kill, which is Dutch for 'valley stream.' It's now known as the **Eleanor Roosevelt National Historic Site** (☎ (914) 229-9115), located two miles east of Hyde Park. After the president's death, Eleanor made this her permanent home. The peaceful grounds are dotted with sugar maple and pine trees, and a dirt

road leads to the cottage from the entrance off Rt 9G. It's open daily from May through October and weekends only in April, November and December; free.

The **Vanderbilt Mansion National Historic Site** (☎ (914) 229-9115) is two miles north of Hyde Park on Rt 9. The spectacular 54-room Beaux Arts home, with many original furnishings still intact, was a mere weekend and summer cottage for members of the railroad dynasty. It's open year round, daily from 9 am to 5 pm from April until November; and closed Tuesday and Wednesday during the winter; admission is $2 for adults, free for seniors and children under 16.

New Jersey

HOBOKEN

This town of 33,000, situated directly across the Hudson River from Manhattan, is a gentrified community of well-preserved brownstones popular with young professionals. It is known locally for its raucous bar and club scene and is also the birthplace of Frank Sinatra. The classic film *On the Waterfront* was shot here in 1954.

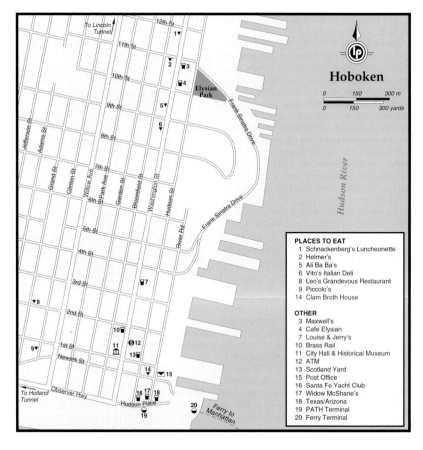

PLACES TO EAT
1 Schnackenberg's Luncheonette
2 Helmer's
5 Ali Ba Ba's
6 Vito's Italian Deli
8 Leo's Grandevous Restaurant
9 Piccolo's
14 Clam Broth House

OTHER
3 Maxwell's
4 Cafe Elysian
7 Louise & Jerry's
10 Brass Rail
11 City Hall & Historical Museum
12 ATM
13 Scotland Yard
15 Post Office
16 Santa Fe Yacht Club
17 Widow McShane's
18 Texas/Arizona
19 PATH Terminal
20 Ferry Terminal

Hoboken is easily explored on foot, and a grid system makes getting around quite simple. Most of Hoboken's shops and restaurants are located within a few blocks of the ornate old Erie Lackawanna Train Terminal, where the PATH trains stop, or along Washington St. The town's history is outlined at the **Hoboken City Hall & Historical Museum** (☎ (201) 420-2026), 1st and Washington Sts, open Monday to Friday from 9 am to 4 pm.

Places to Eat

Schnackenberg's Luncheonette (☎ (201) 659-9834), 1110 Washington St between 11th and 12th Sts, is a wonderful place dating from the 1940s with prices from the 1970s: most items are $5.

Vito's Italian Deli (☎ (201) 792-4944), 806 Washington St between 8th and 9th Sts, makes great mozzarella sandwiches and other large heros. *City Hall Bake Shop* (☎ (201) 659-3671), on Washington St between Newark and 1st Sts, serves baked goods and coffee. *Piccolo's* (☎ (201) 653-0564), 92 Clinton St between Newark and 1st Sts, has been serving delicious cheesesteak sandwiches at the same location since 1955. *Ali Ba Ba's* (☎ (201) 653-5319), 912 Washington St between 9th and 10th Sts, serves Middle Eastern food for $12 to $20.

More expensive options include the *Clam Broth House* (☎ (201) 659-6767), 38 Newark St, and *Helmer's* (☎ (201) 963-3333), 1036 Washington St at the corner of 11th St, a traditional German bar-restaurant established in 1936 that has an impressively large beer selection.

West of Washington St, 2nd St has become a living example of gentrified Hoboken, as former gin mills have been reopened or renovated as restaurants and food-serving taverns. One enduring symbol of the old neighborhood is *Leo's Grandevous* restaurant and tavern (☎ (201) 659-9467), which has occupied 200 Grand St since 1939. It's near the spot where Frank Sinatra grew up, and its bar area features a large number of autographed portraits of 'The Voice.' The menu is quite reasonable,

with delicious hot Italian heroes under $5 and pasta specials from $8.

Entertainment

An old Hoboken bar from the turn of the century, *Maxwell's* (☎ (201) 798-4064), 1039 Washington St at 11th St, is, for many people, the best reason to visit Hoboken. Maxwell's has a small back room that has been featuring the best up-and-coming rock acts since 1978 from Thursday to Saturday nights. Notable bands who played here prior to making it big include REM, Sonic Youth and Nirvana. Bruce Springsteen filmed his 'Glory Days' video (directed by Hoboken resident John Sayles) at Maxwell's.

Built in 1896, the *Cafe Elysian* (☎ (201) 659-9110), 1001 Washington St at 10th St, has a beautiful old bar that became a beauty parlor and an ice cream parlor to survive the Prohibition years. Some of the regulars – many of whom park their motorcycles out front – look like extras in the movie *On the Waterfront*, which was partly filmed at this place. *Louise & Jerry's* (☎ (201) 656-9698), 329 Washington St between 3rd and 4th Sts, is a classic basement-level hangout with a coin-operated pool table and happy hour specials. The *Brass Rail* (☎ (201) 659-7074), 135 Washington St at 2nd St, features a 2nd-floor restaurant serving decent French food, with live jazz Thursday to Saturday nights.

The bars across from the PATH station attract large crowds of young professional patrons. *Texas/Arizona* (☎ (201) 420-0304), on River Rd on the corner of Hudson Place, and *Santa Fe Yacht Club* (☎ (201) 420-8317), 44 Hudson Place, both serve Mexican specials and a broad range of beers. Between them, the raucous *Widow McShane's* (☎ (201) 659-9690) offers a more traditional Irish pub setting, as does *Scotland Yard* (☎ (201) 222-9273), 72 Hudson St, which has British beer on tap.

Getting There & Away

PATH trains stop at the Erie Lackawanna Train Terminal in Hoboken, as do ferries operated by New York Waterway ferries (☎ (800) 533-3779), which travel between Hoboken and the World Financial Center in Lower Manhattan. Ferries leave every 20 minutes at peak times. The trip takes eight minutes and costs $2 each way.

NEWARK

With its rapidly growing international airport and a location across the Hudson River from New York City, Newark (population 314,000) is known by many tourists as the start or finish point to a visit to the region. Long beset by municipal corruption and a variety of urban ills, Newark is not a popular spot for tourists, though officials hope to attract more people once the huge New Jersey Performing Arts Center opens in late 1997.

You should visit Newark via Amtrak, PATH train or New Jersey Transit, since most of the city's attractions are centered around or within walking distance of the Newark Penn Station (not to be confused with New York's Penn Station). The cheapest choice – the $1 PATH train – is also the most convenient. The area east of the train station is called the **Ironbound district**, a vibrant, multiethnic community that was once surrounded by the major railroad lines. It has long been a home for European immigrants, and since the 1960s it has been home to a large block of new arrivals from Portugal, who have established their own restaurants, shops and fresh food markets on and around Ferry St.

There is no conventional tourist office in Newark, but a map and a guide to the city can be obtained by contacting the City Hall Public Information Office (☎ (201) 733-8165), 920 Broad St, Room 214, Newark, NJ 07102. The office is open weekdays from 9 am to 5 pm and welcomes drop-ins looking for the same packet of information.

Newark Museum

Founded in 1909, the Newark Museum (☎ (201) 596-6550), 49 Washington St, features permanent galleries with frequently changing exhibits. In 1989 the museum opened 60,000 sq feet of new exhibition space designed by the architect Michael Graves. The museum has a world-renowned Tibetan Collection featuring a Buddhist altar, consecrated in 1990 by the Dalai Lama. There are also significant objects from Japan, Korea, China, India and other Himalayan areas. It is, all told, the largest and most comprehensive selection of Tibetan art in the US. Other galleries include American Painting & Sculpture from the 18th to 20th centuries, and the Decorative Arts collection features glass, ceramics and textiles from the Renaissance to the present. There are also well-known pieces of American silver, furniture and pottery, along with important objects from the Victorian era. In the museum's garden is a 1794 schoolhouse, the Newark Fire Museum and a collection of contemporary sculpture.

It's open Wednesday to Sunday from noon to 5 pm; admission is free. The museum is on Washington St at Central Ave in the University Heights section of downtown Newark. You can walk to the museum or take bus Nos 44 or 72 from Penn Station. Parking is available; be sure to have your parking ticket stamped at the museum's information desk.

Places to Eat

The best places to dine are the Portuguese and Spanish eateries in the Ironbound district near Penn Station. With the good value, authentic decor and swift, efficient service, you really feel like you have been transported to Lisbon. Lunchtime is the real bargain, when you can enjoy excellent specials for $5 to $10. The oldest restaurant here, *Iberia Tavern & Restaurant* (☎ (201) 344-7603), 82-84 Ferry St, is spotlessly clean with seats at the bar and tables. Across the street, their newer branch, *Iberian Peninsula Restaurant* (☎ (201) 344-5611), 67-69 Ferry St, features the same menu plus barbecued dishes.

You can enjoy a hearty *riodizio de*

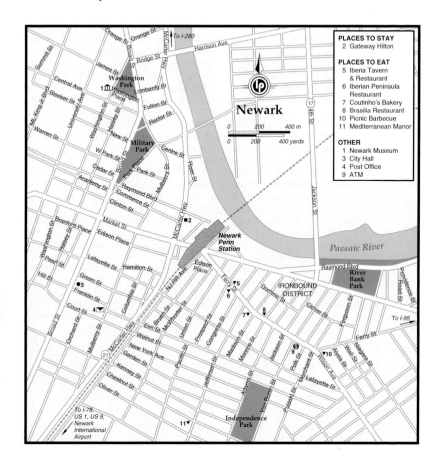

PLACES TO STAY
2 Gateway Hilton

PLACES TO EAT
5 Iberia Tavern
  & Restaurant
6 Iberian Peninsula
  Restaurant
7 Coutinho's Bakery
8 Brasilia Restaurant
10 Picnic Barbecue
11 Mediterranean Manor

OTHER
1 Newark Museum
3 City Hall
4 Post Office
9 ATM

churrasco, or all-you-can-eat Brazilian barbecue, for just $15 at *Brasilia Restaurant* (☎ (201) 465-1227), 132 Ferry St, between Madison and Monroe Sts. *Mediterranean Manor* (☎ (201) 465-1966), 255 Jefferson St, features live Portuguese *fado* music.

If you just want a quick bite to eat or prefer to spend less, try *Picnic Barbecue* (☎ (201) 589-4630), 232 Ferry St, between Wilson Ave and Alyea St. There are a couple of Portuguese bakeries serving up snacks like *bolo de arroz* (sweet rice pudding cakes), including *Coutinho's Bakery* (☎ (201) 344-7384), 121 Ferry St.

PRINCETON

This attractive town is known throughout the world for its Ivy League university, which educates 6000 students each year on its wall-enclosed campus. Worth visiting for a day or as a stop on the way to and from Philadelphia, Princeton has some lovely architecture, interesting historic sites and a nice array of shops and restaurants along Nassau St.

The Princeton Convention and Visitors Bureau (☎ (609) 683-1760), 20 Nassau St, offers maps and brochures for those planning a visit.

Princeton University

Free tours of the campus are offered by Orange Key Tours (☎ (609) 258-3603). Their office is in MacLean House, which is not well sign-posted – it's the light-mustard-colored building adjacent to the gate across from Palmer Square. The office is open Monday to Saturday from 9 am to 5 pm and on Sunday from 1 to 5 pm; tours operate Monday to Saturday at 10 and 11 am, 1:30 and 3:30 pm, Sunday at 1:30 and 3:30 pm. This is a volunteer organization staffed by students, and the tours include a history of the university along with some

information for any prospective students about academic and social life on the campus. Reservations are not necessary but notification is appreciated.

A collection of 20th-century sculpture that includes works by Henry Moore and Pablo Picasso is scattered throughout the campus. The university is also the site of an **art museum** in McCormick Hall (☎ (609) 452-3787). Exhibits include paintings and sculpture from ancient times through to contemporary periods. There is a free guided tour Saturday at 2 pm. It's open Tuesday to Saturday from

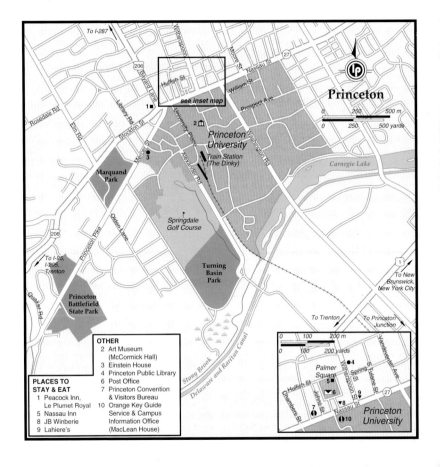

OTHER
2 Art Museum
   (McCormick Hall)
3 Einstein House
4 Princeton Public Library
6 Post Office
7 Princeton Convention
   & Visitors Bureau
10 Orange Key Guide
   Service & Campus
   Information Office
   (MacLean House)

PLACES TO
STAY & EAT
1 Peacock Inn,
   Le Plumet Royal
5 Nassau Inn
8 JB Winberie
9 Lahiere's

10 am to 5 pm, Sunday from 1 to 5 pm. Admission is free.

Historic Homes

There are several historic homes in Princeton, including **Drumthwacket** (☎ (609) 683-0057), on Rt 206, the home of New Jersey's governor. Built in 1835 by Charles Olden, a Civil War-era governor, it was refurbished by the New Jersey Historical Society. Free tours are offered of the 1st-floor public rooms on Wednesday from noon to 2 pm. Be sure to call ahead as these tours are not always operating. Admission is free, but donations are welcomed. **Albert Einstein's home** was the house on 112 Mercer St, but it is not open to the public. It is currently owned by a member of the Institute for Advanced Studies where Einstein studied. Einstein used a 2nd-floor room at the back of the house for a study.

Princeton Battlefield State Park

This park commemorates the historic battle of Princeton, fought on January 3, 1777, a decisive victory for George Washington and a major turning point in the American Revolution. This is one of the few battlefields of the Revolution to remain virtually unchanged. An illustrated plan stands next to the flagpole, and graves of soldiers killed during the battle are to the north of the memorial columns. It's interesting to note that because Princeton was a Loyalist town, it was looted after the battle by the victorious rebel troops. The park is open daily from dawn to dusk and admission is free. Be sure to get a copy of the free leaflet describing the battle from Bainbridge House.

Places to Stay & Eat

It's expensive to stay in Princeton. The 18th-century *Peacock Inn* (☎ (609) 924-1707), 20 Bayard Lane, has 17 comfortable rooms; rates are $90 with shared bath, $105 to $125 with private bath, including continental breakfast. *Nassau Inn* (☎ (609) 921-7500), Palmer Square, is a 1756 home with extensions. Weekday rates start at $155; slightly lower on weekends.

The *Whole Earth Center* (☎ (609) 924-7429), east of campus at 360 Nassau St, is a deli offering vegetarian and natural food choices. *JB Winberie* (☎ (609) 921-0700), One Palmer Square, is a restaurant and bar with entrees under $12, a daily happy hour and an all-you-can-eat Sunday brunch buffet for $11.95. *Lahiere's* (☎ (609) 921-2798), 11 Witherspoon St, is probably the best place in town, serving French-continental cuisine for lunch and dinner. It's closed Sunday. Lunch is from $25 to $40 per person; fixed-price dinner $38. *Le Plumet Royal* (☎ (609) 924-1707), at the Peacock Inn, 20 Bayard Lane, has a special $25 menu, with à la carte selections running from $40 to $60. It's open daily for lunch and dinner with Sunday brunch.

Getting There & Away

Suburban Transit buses (☎ (609) 249-1100) leave from New York City's Port Authority to Palmer Square, Princeton. New Jersey Transit and Amtrak offer several daily trains to Princeton. Passengers must transfer at Princeton Junction to a smaller shuttle train (known to locals as 'the dinky') to make the five-minute trip to Princeton itself. That train stops right next to the University campus. By car, Princeton is reached by taking the NJ Turnpike to Exit 9; follow Rt 1 south to Princeton and take the 'Washington Rd' exit (Rt 571) to Nassau St.

THE JERSEY SHORE

The New Jersey coast stretches 127 miles from Sandy Hook in the north to Cape May in the south. It's the most visited area of the state, and thanks to its beaches and the casinos of Atlantic City, it accounts for most of the 178 million total trips taken by tourists. Along the way are towns that run from beautiful to seedy – from quiet and Victorian Spring Lake to loud and youth-oriented Belmar. This is a summer-only destination: every oceanfront town in New Jersey shuts down for the season about two weeks after Labor Day and remains dead until the following May.

Given its proximity to New York City

(90 minutes or less) the Jersey Shore is a perfect place for a quick trip away from the urban bustle. Each town offers different kinds of on-the-water activities, so match your interests to the following list, and select your destination accordingly:

Fishing
    Belmar, Point Pleasant
Surfing
    Manasquan, Long Branch
Swimming
    Bay Head, Belmar
Quiet Weekending
    Spring Lake, Bay Head, Ocean Grove

Getting There & Away New Jersey beaches from Long Branch to Bay Head are served by New Jersey Transit North Jersey Coast train service. From May to Labor Day, New Jersey Transit has frequent train service from New York City (Penn Station), Hoboken and Newark to shore points at Long Branch, Ocean Grove, Belmar, Manasquan, Point Pleasant and Bay Head A combination roundtrip train ticket and one-day beach pass to these points costs $12 from Hoboken or Newark or $15 from New York with shuttle buses running from some stations to the beach, which is usually about a half mile away.

To get to the shore by car, take the Lincoln Tunnel or George Washington Bridge out of New York City to the NJ Turnpike. At Woodbridge, exit to the Garden State parkway, which runs to all Jersey Shore points as well as Atlantic City and Cape May at the south of the state.

Ocean Grove

This one-sq-mile town began as a Methodist tent-revival community in the 1890s. For years, no cars (with the exception of the newspaper delivery truck) were allowed on Sunday, and crusty 'peace officers' strictly enforced the ban on Sabbath swimming. All that ended in 1979 when the Supreme Court ruled that the town charter was unconstitutional. Its wooden 6500-seat Great Auditorium (tickets: ☎ (908) 988-0645) stands at the center of town at the western end of Ocean Pathway. It was built to house sermons by visiting ministers and still hosts music concerts by touring troupes, such as the Preservation Hall Jazz Band. The auditorium, built in 1894 in just 92 days, also played a role as the Hotel Stardust in the 1980 Woody Allen film *Stardust Memories*.

The tourist office (☎ (908) 774-4736) is at 64 Main Ave in the offices of the *Times*, the local weekly newspaper. It's only open during the summer Monday to Friday from 10 am to 4 pm. Off season, contact the chamber of commerce (☎ (800) 388-4768). During the summer season a tourist information booth is set up near the Great Auditorium.

To get to Ocean Grove by train, take New Jersey Transit to the depressed shore town of Asbury Park – the station is about three blocks from the border of Ocean Grove.

Fighting Mother Nature

Throughout the last decade, New Jersey's oceanfront communities have worked hard to prevent erosion of the shoreline by monitoring tides, planting sand grass and rebuilding sea walls during the off season. Many environmentalists think these efforts are too costly and ultimately fruitless, but given the importance of the beachfronts to the local economy, the efforts will continue. Federally backed replenishments *are* successful in the short term, but the winter of 1996 and its two major blizzards brought unexpected devastation to the area. Atlantic City lost more than three feet of beach despite the presence of dozens of 'geotubes' – 12-foot-tall artificial sand dunes made of plastic. The geotubes may not have kept the sand from shifting, but they did keep the roiling waters from damaging beachfront casinos. Still, the cost of replenishing the damaged beach in Atlantic City alone ran more than $7 million. ■

DAVID ELLIS

Beach umbrellas dot the eroding Jersey Shore

Places to Stay & Eat There are many places to stay in Ocean Grove, and most offer reductions for long stays. The following places are open only in season, unless otherwise noted.

The *Pine Tree Inn* (☎ (908) 775-3264), 10 Main Ave half a block from the beach, is the quintessential Victorian B&B. All of the furniture is tasteful and antique. All rooms have sinks, some have private baths and porches, it's very clean, and bicycles are available for guests. The single/double rates are $45/95, with reductions off season. The *Sandpiper* (☎ (908) 774-6261), 19 Ocean Pathway, is one of the nicest and most reasonable places to stay in Ocean Grove. Singles/doubles are $25/50. *House by the Sea* (☎ (908) 775-2847), 14 Ocean Ave, is the nicest of the hotels facing the shore. Single and double rates are the same:

$42 to $58 from Sunday to Thursday and $52 to $68 on Friday and Saturday.

The *Raspberry Cafe* (☎ (908) 988-0833), 60 Main Ave, is the place with the best breakfast food in town for under $10. *Main Avenue Deli* (☎ (908) 502-0400), 54 Main Ave, sells pizza. *Freedman's Bakery* (☎ (908) 774-8235), 55 Main Ave, specializes in morning baked goods and coffee.

Belmar

Belmar is a popular gathering place for people in their 20s, but following a riot after an MTV-sponsored beach party a few years ago, the town has tried to curtail its Fort Lauderdale image. A new law closes down all bars at midnight, and the police are pretty aggressive about cracking down on loud parties and drinking in public. Belmar is popular with the local gay population, which gathers on the northern end of the beach at 2nd Ave near the border with Avon. But as yet, there are no discernible gay gathering places in town. The local chamber of commerce (☎ (908) 681-1176) has information on events and activities.

Activities Besides the beach ($4 daily; $40 for the season, $10 for seniors), there's a small amusement area with a rooftop miniature golf course on Ocean Ave between 14th and 15th Aves. It's open until about 11 pm and costs $5 per person. The Skate Rental (☎ (908) 681-7767) store in the Mayfair Hotel rents in-line skates and bicycles for $20 a day. They also rent boogie boards for $12 a day. Iron City Gym (☎ (908) 681-8098), on Ocean Ave between 8th and 9th Aves, has day passes for $8 per day; open year round. Charter Boats leave the busy Belmar Marina (☎ (908) 681-2266) seven days a week, year round, from 7 am to 7:30 pm. The cost is generally from $21 to $33 to join a regularly scheduled departure. Captain Paul Hepler (☎ 908) 928-4519) runs charters from the marina, and the Fisherman's Den tackle shop (☎ (908) 681-6677) rents small motor boats for $25 a day from 6 am.

Places to Stay & Eat Most of the places in town have the crowded and casual look and feel of rooming houses. *Carol's Guest House* (☎ (908) 681-4422), 201 11th Ave, is cheapest at $25 per person, per night, including continental breakfast, with lower weekly rates. The year-round *Mayfair Hotel* (☎ (908) 681-2620), 1000 Ocean Ave on the corner of 10th Ave, has a big lobby, a kitchen and a pool. Rooms with private/ shared bath are $85/75 Friday and Saturday; $45 other days. If you want to stay across from the marina, the *Belmar Motor Lodge* (☎ (908) 681-6600, fax 681-6604) is at Rt 35 and 10th Ave. A standard modern motel, its rooms have TV, phone and air-con. Rates range from $53 to $88. *Havens & Hampton* (☎ (908) 681-1231), 5th and Main Sts, features dining in a room overlooking the Shark River inlet. Fresh seafood dishes start at $12, and lobster specials depend on the

catch. *Ollie Klein's* (☎ (908) 681-1177), 708 River Rd, has a similar menu on the south side of the Main St bridge.

The *Circus Drive-In* (☎ (908) 449-2650), near Belmar on Rt 35, is an old-fashioned '50s-style drive-in where the waiter serves food to patrons still sitting in their cars (open only during the summer season).

Entertainment *Bar Anticipation* (☎ (908) 681-7422), 703 16th Ave, is a massive, mostly outdoor bar complex. 'Bar A' is Belmar's pick-up place, with 10 bars, live music and swimsuit competitions. The bouncers are burly and surly. *D'Jais* (☎ (908) 681-5855) is a large dance club at the corner of Ocean and 18th Aves. It's open seven days a week from May to September. *Reggie's*, on Ocean Ave between 11th and 12th Aves, attracts a slightly older singles crowd; open from May to October with live music on weekends.

Spring Lake
Known locally as the 'Irish Riviera,' Spring Lake has a bevy of expensive, elegant, quiet and charming Victorian inns, B&Bs and hotels. Maps and information are available from the chamber of commerce (☎ (908) 449-0577), PO Box 694, Spring Lake, NJ 07762. Beach passes (☎ (908) 449-8005) cost $3.50 daily and $43 for the season; children 11 and under go free.

Places to Stay & Eat Spring Lake's hotels and B&Bs tend to be among the most expensive on the Jersey Shore, with daily rates over $100.

High-Tech Boardwalk
After storms destroyed Spring Lake's two-mile boardwalk, town officials decided to replace it with a gray material that looks like wood plank but is actually a composite of recycled plastic bags and wood-pallet chips. This springy surface lasts longer and, better yet, doesn't give you splinters. ■

Victoria House (☎ (908) 974-1882), 214 Monmouth Ave, has 10 well-appointed rooms, most at $120 a night with a two-night minimum in summer. The *Johnson House* (☎ (609) 449-1860), 25 Tuttle Ave, has singles/doubles from $90/110, with shared bath from $65, along with free parking. A Victorian-era house, the *Spring Lake Inn* (☎ (609) 449-2010), 104 Salem Ave, features an 80-foot wraparound porch. It's your best bet if you're on a budget and want to stay in Spring Lake. It's only open from July 4 to Labor Day, but is large, airy and clean. Doubles with bath and air-con are $65 to $95; some rooms have shared bath from $35 to $65. *La Maison* (☎ (908) 449-0969), at 404 Jersey Ave on a residential block, is an opulent, eight-room B&B. Rates are $95 to $159; an efficiency cottage is available for weekly stays. The *Hewitt Wellington Hotel* (☎ (908) 974-1212, fax 974-2338) is at 200 Monmouth Ave overlooking the lake. It's a large, white, wood structure with a wraparound porch, small pool and restaurant. Off-peak/peak season doubles start at $70/110. Open April to October.

The *Beach House* (☎ (908) 449-9646), facing the sea at 901 Ocean Ave, is a good place to quaff specialty drinks on the porch. It's open May to October. *Whispers* (☎ (908) 449-3330), in the Hewitt Wellington Hotel, serves pasta, chicken, veal and seafood dishes for $17 to $22. The restaurant in the *Sandpiper Hotel* (☎ (908) 449-6060), 7 Atlantic Ave, serves a large Sunday seafood brunch buffet for $14.

Point Pleasant Beach

Point Pleasant Beach has a nice boardwalk, active nightlife and two privately owned beaches. **Risden's Beach** (☎ (908) 892-8410) goes from the southern end of the boardwalk to a point just north of Trenton Ave. Its weekday/weekend cost is $3.50/4.50; children four to seven are 50¢; and the seasonal pass is $50. Risden's also provides two large bath houses (☎ (908) 892-9743, 892-9580) along their section of the beach. **Jenkinson's Beach** (☎ (908) 892-3274) runs from Trenton Ave north to

the Manasquan River inlet and includes an amusement park and a small aquarium. The beach fees are $4/5 weekday/weekend; children five to 11 are $1. Charter fishing boats run out of Ken's Landing (☎ (908) 892-9787, 899-5491), 30 Broadway, and departure times and cost are posted there. A half-day trip usually runs between $18 and $25. Some boats also run 90-minute night cruises along the shore for $8/5 for adults/children. Clark's Landing (☎ (908) 223-6546) also has charter boats. Scuba divers should check out the Inlet Dive Center (☎ (908) 899-4545), 318 Broadway. Underwater Discovery (☎ (908) 295-5800), 201 Broadway, offers rentals and lessons.

The chamber of commerce (☎ (908) 899-2424), 517-A Arnold Ave, has general information.

Places to Stay & Eat *Atlantic Motel* (☎ (908) 899-7711, fax 899-4342), 215 Broadway, costs $65/99 weekdays/weekends, and its rooms face away from the road, so they're less noisy. *Mariner's Cove* (☎ (908) 899-0060), 50 Broadway, costs $89/109 weekdays/weekends; $10 for each additional person in the room. *Surfside Motel* (☎ (908) 899-1109), 101 Broadway, is $88 during the week and higher on weekends.

The nicest place to eat is *Jack Baker's* (☎ (908) 892-9100), 101 Channel Dr Point. Its booths overlook the brook heading to and from the sea on the Manasquan Inlet, and you can eat reasonably priced seafood for $15 and under, with numerous lunch specials (book ahead on summer weekends).

Bay Head

The quietest town on the Jersey Shore is Bay Head, the terminus of the North Jersey Coast train line. It is a quiet community with Cape Cod-style homes along the beach. Although there is public access to the ocean, there's no boardwalk, and it's very peaceful even in high season. Beach passes are available from the Bay Head Improvement Association (☎ (908) 892-4179) on the western end of Mount St, though the address is 532 Lake Ave. The cost is $4.25 per day or $50/35 for full and half season, but you have to buy season tickets in pairs; children under 11 are free.

Places to Stay & Eat *Bentley Inn* (☎ (908) 892-9589), 694 Main Ave, has seasonal rates of $49 to $89. *Conover's Bay Head Inn* (☎ (908) 892-4664), 646 Main Ave, has rates that include breakfast: $70 to $115 on weekdays, $105 to $165 on weekends.

The *Greenville Hotel & Restaurant* (☎ (908) 892-3100) is a year-round Victorian hotel at 345 Main Ave. In-season rates are from $77 to $102 during the week and from $132 to $202 weekends. *Bluff's Hotel & Restaurant* (☎ (908) 892-1114) is right on the beach at 575 East Ave; rooms are $145 to $200.

GREAT ADVENTURE THEME PARK

This massive Six Flags Great Adventure theme park (☎ (908) 928-1821) is in Jackson Township west of the Jersey Shore towns, and it features a 350-acre drive-through safari with 1500 animals from seven continents, along with a theme park with over 100 rides, shows and attractions. In the early 1980s, the park had a reputation for attracting out-of-control teenagers, but then it was bought by Time Warner, which invested $100 million and touted its image as 'bigger than Disney World and a whole lot closer.'

The company recently sold Great Adventure to private investors, but you'll still get the sense that it's one big advertisement for the Warner Bros studio, with the Lethal Weapon water ride and Looney Tunes characters such as Bugs Bunny roaming the grounds. There's a popular log flume and several harrowing roller coasters.

On summer weekends, Great Adventure has very long lines at its most popular rides, so it's important to go early or on a weekday. Throughout the season concerts by rock, country and jazz artists are included in the admission price.

The amusement area is open from April to October from 10 am to midnight, with the Wild Safari Park open from 9 am to 4 pm. Admission is $28 for both the rides and safari park; children under 54 inches tall pay $19. Adult season tickets are $59.95, and $199 for a family of four. Six Flags is located off Exit 7A on the NJ Turnpike or Exit 98 to I-195 on the Garden State Parkway.

ATLANTIC CITY

Since casino gambling came to Atlantic City (population 38,000) in 1977, the town has become the most popular tourist destination in the USA, with 37 million annual visitors spending some $4 billion at its 12 casinos and restaurants. Proximity accounts for much of that popularity, since nearly one-third of the population of the US lives within 300 miles of Atlantic City. While the casino industry has created 45,000 jobs and has enjoyed record profits since 1993, little of this money has benefited the town, despite the many promises of prosperity made 20 years ago. Unemployment still stands at 15%, homelessness is still a big problem and the four-block stretch of town from the end of the Atlantic City Expressway to the beachfront casinos is still a depressing collection of empty lots, rough-looking

---

Monopoly

Many people know that Monopoly, arguably the world's most popular board game, uses the names of Atlantic City properties. The one area listed on the board not found in Atlantic City – Marvin Gardens – is in nearby Margate. But Monopoly's creator, Charles Darrow, misspelled the spot, which is actually Marven Gardens. Darrow (who reputedly 'borrowed' ideas freely from two other board games called 'Finance' and 'The Landlord's Game') sold the right to Monopoly to Parker Bros in 1935. Since then, the company has sold more than 160 million copies in 25 languages, often tailoring the board to reflect famous sites in local markets. ■

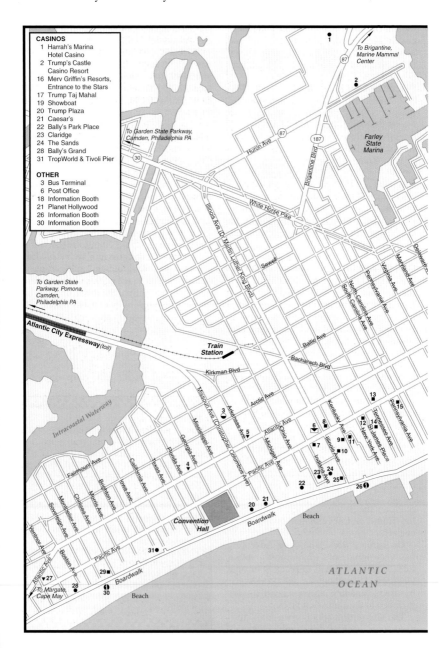

CASINOS
1 Harrah's Marina
  Hotel Casino
2 Trump's Castle
  Casino Resort
16 Merv Griffin's Resorts,
  Entrance to the Stars
17 Trump Taj Mahal
19 Showboat
20 Trump Plaza
21 Caesar's
22 Bally's Park Place
23 Claridge
24 The Sands
28 Bally's Grand
31 TropWorld & Tivoli Pier

OTHER
3 Bus Terminal
6 Post Office
18 Information Booth
21 Planet Hollywood
26 Information Booth
30 Information Booth

To Brigantine,
Marine Mammal
Center

Farley
State
Marina

To Garden State Parkway,
Camden, Philadelphia PA

Huron Ave

White Horse Pike

Brigantine Blvd

Sewell

Delaware

Maryland Ave

Virginia Ave

Pennsylvania Ave

North Carolina Ave

South Carolina Ave

To Garden State
Parkway, Pomona,
Camden,
Philadelphia PA

Atlantic City Expressway (toll)

Intracoastal Waterway

Train
Station

Kirkman Blvd

Baltic Ave

Bacharach Blvd

Arctic Ave

Missouri Ave (Christopher Columbus Ave)

Illinois Ave (Dr Martin Luther King Blvd)

Arkansas Ave

Atlantic Ave

Ohio Ave

Michigan Ave

Pacific Ave

Georgia Ave

Florida Ave

California Ave

Iowa Ave

Texas Ave

Indiana Ave

Kentucky Ave

Tennessee Ave

St James Place

New York Ave

Pennsylvania Ave

Fairmount Ave

Montpelier Ave

Morris Ave

Chelsea Ave

Brighton Ave

Sovereign Ave

Ventnor Ave

Atlantic Ave

Boston Ave

Pacific Ave

Convention
Hall

Boardwalk

Beach

To Margate,
Cape May

ATLANTIC
OCEAN

Beach

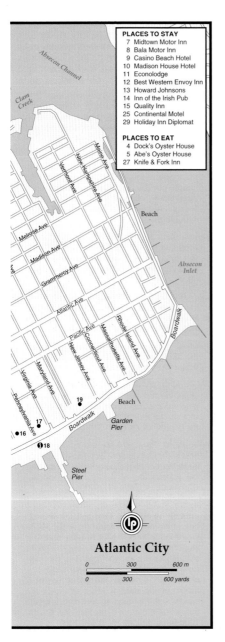

PLACES TO STAY
7 Midtown Motor Inn
8 Bala Motor Inn
9 Casino Beach Hotel
10 Madison House Hotel
11 Econolodge
12 Best Western Envoy Inn
13 Howard Johnsons
14 Inn of the Irish Pub
15 Quality Inn
25 Continental Motel
29 Holiday Inn Diplomat

PLACES TO EAT
4 Dock's Oyster House
5 Abe's Oyster House
27 Knife & Fork Inn

Atlantic City

bars and abandoned warehouses. The bottom line is that for nongamblers there is no reason to visit Atlantic City unless you're on your way to Cape May or Philadelphia. For one thing, casino security people do not look kindly upon those simply wandering through the gaming areas without any intention of playing – which is probably just as well, since watching other people spend their money playing noisy 25¢ slot machines gets old very quickly. (You must be 21 or over to gamble.)

The Visitors Information Center (☎ (609) 344-8338) is at 1716 Pacific Ave (between Indiana Ave and MLK Blvd). Five information booths stand along the Boardwalk between the Taj Mahal to the north and the Grand Casino to the south. There is also a desk inside Convention Hall providing many brochures for local hotels; it's open daily from 10 am to 7 pm.

Places to Stay

Atlantic City's room rates vary depending on the season. In the winter, it's possible to stay in a top hotel such as Merv Griffin's Resorts for as little as $70 a night. The trick is to walk up to the reception desk and act uncertain if you plan to stay the night. You will most likely be offered a room at a deep discount, provided you look well-dressed enough to spend money in the casino. The AmeriRoom Reservations hotline (☎ (800) 888-5825) specializes in packages that usually include meals, show tickets and complimentary chips. The city offers its own reservations service at ☎ (800) 447-6667, with rooms at all price levels and package deals. If you want a nondescript room for less than $50, try one of the city's many motels.

Middle The following motels charge the following rates for singles/doubles: winter midweek from $25 to $30, winter weekends from $50 to $80; summer midweek from $35 to $45, summer weekends from $60 to $100. Holiday weekends range from $60 to $200.

Bala Motor Inn
MLK Blvd and Pacific Ave
☎ (609) 348-3031

Best Western Envoy Inn
Pacific and New York Aves
☎ (609) 344-7117

Casino Beach Hotel
154 Kentucky Ave between the
Boardwalk and Pacific Ave
☎ (609) 348-4000

Continental Motel
the Boardwalk at MLK Blvd
☎ (609) 345-5141

Days Inn
the Boardwalk and Morris Ave
☎ (609) 344-6101

Econo Lodge
117 S Kentucky Ave between the
Boardwalk and Pacific Ave
☎ (609) 344-9093, (800) 323-6410

Economy Motel
Pacific and Hartford Aves
☎ (609) 348-9111

Holiday Inn-Diplomat
the Boardwalk and Chelsea Ave
☎ (609) 348-2200

Howard Johnson Inn
Tennessee and Pacific Aves
☎ (609) 344-4193

Madison House Hotel
123 Illinois (MLK Blvd) near the
Sands Casino
☎ (609) 345-1400

Miami Hotel
Kentucky Ave between Boardwalk
and Pacific Ave
☎ (609) 344-2077

Midtown Motor Inn
Indiana and Pacific Aves
☎ (609) 348-3031

Quality Inn
S Carolina and Pacific Aves
☎ (609) 345-7070

Top End Atlantic City's casino hotels dominate the expensive choices. Rates run from $90 to $370 depending on the season and day of the week, usually with meals, shows, free use of health spa and casino chips.

Bally's Grand – the southernmost casino, formerly known as the Golden Nugget, has just over 500 rooms. Boston Ave between the Boardwalk and Pacific Ave (☎ (609) 347-7111)

Bally's Park Place Casino Hotel & Tower – this 1200-room casino occupies the site of the 1860 Dennis Hotel, which is incorporated into the newer facility; it's the site of many heavyweight boxing matches. Park Place and the Boardwalk (☎ (609) 340-2000)

Caesar's Atlantic City Hotel Casino – this 1000-room hotel is also the site of Atlantic City's Planet Hollywood-theme restaurant, which is just off the gaming area. Arkansas Ave and the Boardwalk (☎ (609) 348-4411)

Claridge Casino Hotel – one block west of the Boardwalk, accessible by a moving walkway that operates in one direction only: into the casino, not out. There are 500 rooms and a three-floor, claustrophobic casino area. Indiana Ave and the Boardwalk (☎ (609) 340-3400)

Merv Griffin's Resorts – a 670-room Victorian hotel that served as a hospital during WWII and the center of 'Camp Boardwalk.' N Carolina Ave and the Boardwalk (☎ (609) 340-6000)

Sands Hotel, Casino & Country Club – a black glass box that was originally named the Brighton Hotel when it opened. Brighton Park and Indiana Ave (☎ (609) 441-4000)

Showboat – a riverboat-theme interior dominates the 700 rooms. Delaware Ave and the Boardwalk (☎ (609) 343-4000)

TropWorld Casino & Entertainment Resort – one of the biggest places in town, with its own indoor theme park (Tivoli Pier), a 90,000-sq-foot casino and 1020 rooms. Iowa Ave and the Boardwalk (☎ (609) 340-4000)

Trump Plaza Casino Hotel – this modern tower next to the Convention Center has 560 rooms and a Warner Bros Studio Store overlooking the Boardwalk. Mississippi Ave and the Boardwalk (☎ (609) 441-6700)

Trump Taj Mahal – by far the most extravagant property in Atlantic City, and the second-largest casino in the world (after the MGM Grand in Las Vegas). Nine two-ton limestone elephants welcome visitors, and 70 bright minarets crown the rooftops. The German-crystal chandeliers in the casino and lobby alone cost $14 million, and despite the garish nature of the interior, the room rates are similar to those found in more modest facilities; it's also the site of the Hard Rock Cafe. 1000 Boardwalk (☎ (609) 449-1000)

The Boardwalk

Atlantic City's famous Boardwalk was the first in the world, built in 1870 by local business owners who wanted to cut down on the sand being tracked into hotel lobbies by guests returning from the beach. A man named Alexander Boardman came up with the idea, and the planks became known as Boardman's Walk – later shortened to 'Boardwalk.' ∎

Places to Eat

Some of the best bargains can be found at the various buffet restaurants offered by the casinos to keep patrons inside. They all range under $20 – just check the many advertisements on the boardwalk.

Atlantic City's two top seafood restaurants are *Docks Oyster House* (☎ (609) 345-0092), 2405 Atlantic Ave, and *Abe's Oyster House* (☎ (609) 344-7701), at Atlantic and Arkansas Aves, with entrees from $30. The *Knife & Fork Inn* (☎ (609) 344-1133), at the junction of Atlantic and Pacific Aves near Albany Ave, serves seafood and steaks for $45 and up; closed Sunday.

Getting There & Away

New Jersey Transit also runs buses from New York City to the depot on Arctic Ave between Columbus and Arkansas Aves. The one-way/roundtrip fare is $21.45/23. For a better deal, check out the casino buses from New York, which run about $22 roundtrip but include food vouchers and $10 worth of quarters for the slots. From New York's Port Authority, contact Academy (☎ (212) 971-9054) or Greyhound (☎ (800) 231-2222). By car, take the Garden State Parkway to Exit 38, which is the Atlantic City Expressway.

Architectural Glossary

Brownstone – A townhouse, built of reddish-brown sandstone.

DAVID ELLIS
Classic Brownstones, Park Slope, Brooklyn

Classical – Architectural styles derived from the Greeks and Romans.

Corinthian – The most ornate style of Greek architecture characterized by a capital adorned with carved acanthus leaves, and a slender column incised with flutes – semicylindiral grooves that run the length of the shaft.

Doric – The oldest order of classic Greek architecture, marked by austere, fluted columns.

Federal – Post-Revolutionary American architecture, distinguished by refined and elegant variations on the Georgian style, with elliptical fanlights and rectangular sidelights around the door.

Georgian – Colonial-era style marked by classical, Renaissance and Baroque inspired details, and stately equilibrium.

Gothic – The Gothic revival, or neo-Gothic movement, took root in the mid-19th century. Builders yearned for the romance of the Middle Ages, and structures were easily identified by their earthen colors, steep, pitched roofs, gables and pointed arches.

Greek-Revival – Based on Classic architectural forms, with its prime examples looking like transplanted Aegean temples. It was used in everything from New York's Federal Hall to urban row houses.

Ionic – Classic Greek architectural order used on the Acropolis, with columns topped by scrolled, ram-horn shaped capitals.

Renaissance – From the mid-19th through the early 20th century, Renaissance Revival and Beaux Arts architecture paid glorious homage to the grand 15th to 16th century homes, churches and palaces of Europe.

skyscraper – Quite simply, a very tall building – though the term was coined when buildings rarely were more than 10 stories high.

KIM GRANT

Index

MAPS

TEXT

SIDEBARS

New York City Map Section

KIM GRANT

Stained glass mural of Empire State Building,
located in the buildings lobby

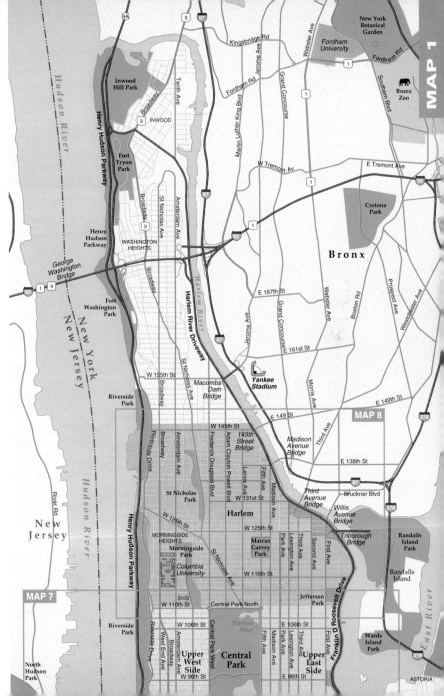

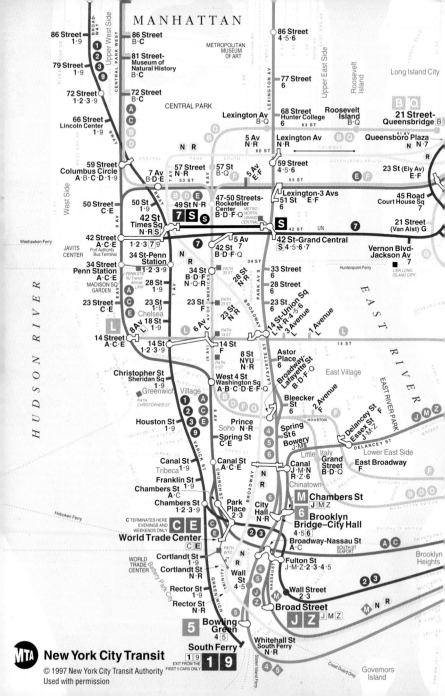

MANHATTAN

86 Street 1·9
86 Street B·C
81 Street–Museum of Natural History B·C
79 Street 1·9
72 Street 1·2·3·9
72 Street B·C
66 Street Lincoln Center 1·9
59 Street Columbus Circle A·B·C·D·1·9
50 Street C·E
50 St 1·9
49 St N·R
42 St Times Sq N·R·S
42 Street A·C·E
34 Street Penn Station A·C·E
34 St-Penn Station 1·2·3·9
28 Street C·E
28 St 1·9
23 Street C·E
23 St 1·9
18 St 1·9
14 Street A·C·E
14 St 1·2·3·9

Upper West Side
CENTRAL PARK WEST
BROADWAY
7 AV
8 AV
CENTRAL PARK SOUTH
West Side
57 Street N·R·Q·W
7 Av B·D·E
57 St B·Q·F
42 St-Times Sq
1·2·3·7·9
Port Authority Bus Terminal
34 St N·Q·R·W
28 St N·R
23 St N·R
34 St B·D·F·M·N·Q·R
23 St F·M
23 St N·R

JAVITS CENTER
PENN STA NJ Transit Amtrak LIRR
MADISON SQ GARDEN

7 AV
6 AV (AV OF THE AMERICAS)

METROPOLITAN MUSEUM OF ART

86 Street 4·5·6
77 Street 6
68 Street Hunter College 6
Lexington Av N·R
5 Av N·R
59 Street 4·5·6
Lexington-3 Avs 51 St 6
47-50 Streets-Rockefeller Center B·D·F·Q
5 Av E·F
42 St-Grand Central S·4·5·6·7
5 Av 7
42 St B·D·F·Q·7
33 Street 6
28 Street 6
23 Street 6
14 St-Union Sq L·N·R·4·5·6
3 Avenue L
1 Avenue L
Astor Place 6
Bleecker St 6
Spring St 6
Canal St J·M·N·R·Z·6
14 ST

Lexington Av
Hunter College

Roosevelt Island

Long Island City

Queensboro Plaza N·W·7
21 Street-Queensbridge B
23 St (Ely Av) E·F
45 Road Court House Sq 7
21 Street (Van Alst) G
Vernon Blvd-Jackson Av 7

EAST RIVER

Christopher St Sheridan Sq 1·9
Houston St 1·9
Canal St 1·9
Franklin St A·C
Chambers St 1·9
Chambers St 1·2·3·9

Greenwich Village
Tribeca

West 4 St Washington Sq A·B·C·D·E·F·Q
Prince St N·R
Spring St C·E
Canal St A·C·E
Park Place 2·3
City Hall N·R
Chambers St J·M·Z
Brooklyn Bridge-City Hall 4·5·6

Soho
Little Italy
Chinatown

Grand Street B·D·Q
East Broadway F
Delancey St F
Essex St J·M·Z

Lower East Side
East Village
East River Park

World Trade Center
C TERMINATES HERE EVENINGS AND WEEKENDS ONLY
Cortlandt St 1·9
Cortlandt St N·R
Rector St 1·9
Rector St N·R
Wall St 4·5
Broadway-Nassau St A·C
Fulton St J·M·Z·2·3·4·5
Wall Street 2·3
Broad Street J·Z
Whitehall St South Ferry N·R

Bowling Green 4·5
South Ferry 1·9

Brooklyn Heights

New York City Transit
© 1997 New York City Transit Authority
Used with permission
EXIT FROM THE FIRST 5 CARS ONLY

Governors Island

HUDSON RIVER

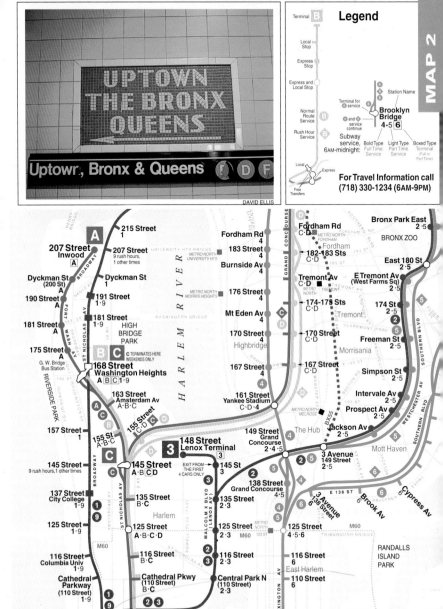

DAVID ELLIS

Legend

Terminal **B**

Local Stop

Express Stop

Express and Local Stop

Station Name

Terminal for service

Brooklyn Bridge
4·5 **6**

and service continue

Normal Route Service

Rush Hour Service

Subway service, 6AM–midnight:
Bold Type Full Time Service · Light Type Part Time Service · Boxed Type Terminal (Full or Part Time)

Local · Express

Free Transfers

For Travel Information call
(718) 330-1234 (6AM–9PM)

MAP 2

A 207 Street Inwood Ⓐ

A 215 Street 1

207 Street 9 rush hours, 1 other times Ⓐ

Dyckman St (200 St) Ⓐ

Dyckman St 1

190 Street Ⓐ

191 Street 1·9

181 Street Ⓐ

181 Street 1·9

HIGH BRIDGE PARK

UNIVERSITY HTS BRIDGE

METRO NORTH UNIVERSITY HTS

WASHINGTON BRIDGE

175 Street Ⓐ
G. W. Bridge Bus Station

B **C** C TERMINATES HERE WEEKENDS ONLY

168 Street Washington Heights Ⓐ Ⓑ Ⓒ 1·9

157 Street 1

163 Street Amsterdam Av A·B·C

Ⓐ

155 Street C·D·D

Ⓑ Ⓒ

155 St A·B·C

C **D**

145 Street 9 rush hours, 1 other times

145 Street A·B·C·D

C

137 Street City College 1·9 Ⓐ Ⓐ

135 Street B·C

125 Street 1·9 Ⓐ Ⓐ

125 Street A·B·C·D

Harlem

116 Street Columbia Univ 1·9 Ⓐ Ⓐ

116 Street B·C

Cathedral Parkway (110 Street) 1·9 Ⓐ Ⓐ

Cathedral Pkwy (110 Street) B·C

103 Street 1·9

103 Street B·C

96 Street 1·2·3·9

96 Street B·C

148 Street Lenox Terminal ③

3

145 St EXIT FROM THE FIRST 4 CARS ONLY ③

135 Street 2·3

125 Street 2·3 METRO NORTH 125 ST M60

116 Street 2·3

Central Park N (110 Street) 2·3

MALCOLM X BLVD (LENOX AV)

Ⓐ ②

③

②

Upper West Side

MANHATTAN

BROADWAY

ST NICHOLAS AV

RIVERSIDE PARK

CENTRAL PARK WEST

HARLEM RIVER

Fordham Rd 4

183 Street 4

Burnside Av 4

176 Street 4

Mt Eden Av 4

170 Street 4

167 Street 4

Ⓐ

161 Street Yankee Stadium C·D·4

149 Street Grand Concourse 2·4·5

138 Street Grand Concourse 4·5

125 Street 4·5·6 METRO NORTH

116 Street 6 East Harlem

110 Street 6

103 Street 6

96 Street 6

LEXINGTON AV

GRAND CONCOURSE

Fordham Rd C·D

METRO NORTH FORDHAM

Fordham

182–183 Sts C·D

Tremont Av C·D

METRO NORTH TREMONT

174–175 Sts C·D

170 Street C·D

Highbridge

167 Street C·D

149 Street 2·5

The Hub

3 Avenue 149 Street 2·5

Mott Haven

BYS5

3 Avenue 138 Street ②

E 138 ST

Brook Av

3 Avenue 138 Street ⑥

Cypress Av

125 Street 4·5·6 M60

RANDALLS ISLAND PARK

East Harlem

WARDS ISLAND PARK

M60

TRIBOROUGH BRIDGE

Bronx Park East 2·5

BRONX ZOO

East 180 St 2·5

E Tremont Av (West Farms Sq) 2·5

174 St 2·5

Tremont ②

Freeman St 2·5

Morrisania

Simpson St 2·5

Intervale Av 2·5

Prospect Av 2·5

Jackson Av 2·5

⑤

⑥

SOUTHERN BLVD

WESTCHESTER AV

SOUTHERN BLVD

PLACES TO STAY
7 Best Western Seaport Inn
9 Millennium Hotel

PLACES TO EAT
6 Bridge Cafe
12 North Star Pub
17 Fraunces Tavern
18 Zigolini's
19 Pearl Palace

OTHER
1 Federal Courthouse
2 Public Toilet
3 Police Headquarters
4 Brooklyn Bridge
   Pedestrian Entrance
5 Post Office
8 New York Waterways Ferry
10 Century 21
11 Federal Reserve Bank
13 Pier 17
14 India House
15 National Museum of
   the American Indian,
   US Customs House
16 Beckett's Bar & Grill
20 Shrine of St Elizabeth Ann
   Seton, New York Unearthed
21 Statue of Liberty
   Ferry Ticket Booth
22 Staten Island Ferry Terminal

Tribeca

to MAP 4

Harrison St
Jay St
Hudson St
West Broadway
West Broadway

Hudson River Esplanade

Greenwich St

Chambers St

Hudson River Park

Warren St

Park Place

Park Place

Battery Park City Waterfront Promenade

Murray St

Murray St

West Broadway

North End Ave

Vesey St

5

Ferry to Hoboken, NJ

World Financial Center

North Tower **World Trade Center**

Marriott World Trade Center

South Tower

8

North Cove

Liberty St

Cedar St

Washington St

Greenwich St

Albany St

Albany St

Carlisle St

Battery Park City Waterfront Promenade

Rector St

South End Ave

Battery Place

W Thames St

Hudson River

Second Place

West St

Castle Clinton

21

Ferry to Ellis Island

Ferry to Statue of Liberty

0   150   300 m
0   150   300 yards

MAP 3

Lower
East
Side

Lower
Manhattan

Thomas St

Broadway

Duane St

Reade St

Chambers St

Worth St   Chatham Square

Park Row

Thomas Paine Park

Foley Square

African Burial Ground

Sun Building

CIVIC CENTER

Surrogate's Court

Warren St

Murray St

Tweed Courthouse

City Hall

NYC Info Booth

NYC Info Booth

Municipal Building

Ave of the Finest

Frankfort St

City Hall Park

Woolworth Building

Barclay St

St Paul's Chapel

Fulton St

Dey St

Cortlandt St   Maiden Lane

Thames St

Trinity Church

Bank of New York

Broadway

New St

Morris St

Bowling Green

Battery Park

Park Row

Beekman St

Nassau St

William St

Ann St

Gold St

Cliff St

Ped Mall

Beekman St

Water St

Front St

Fulton St

South St

Peck Slip

Dover St

Spruce St

Robert F Wagner Place

Brooklyn Bridge

Franklin D Roosevelt Drive

John St

Platt St

Liberty St

Cedar St

Pine St

Maiden Lane

Nassau St

Federal Hall

Wall St

Morgan Guaranty Building

New York Stock Exchange

Exchange Place

Standard Oil Building

Beaver St

Whitehall St

Stone St

Bridge St

Pearl St

Water St

Broad St

William St

Gouverneur Lane

Old Slip St

Coenties Slip

Vietnam Veterans Plaza

Schermerhorn Row

Burling Slip

Fletcher St

Maiden Lane

Front St

South St

Wall St

South St

Fulton Fish Market

South Street Seaport

East River

to MAP 9
Brooklyn Heights

to MAP 4

Pearl St

Park Row

St James Place

Henry St

Oliver St

Madison St

Monroe St

Catherine St

Cherry St

Water St

South St

Market St

Peter Minuit Plaza

State St

Brooklyn Battery Tunnel

Ferry to Staten Island

1
2
3
4
5
6
7
8
9
10
11
12
13
14
15
16
17
18
19
20
22

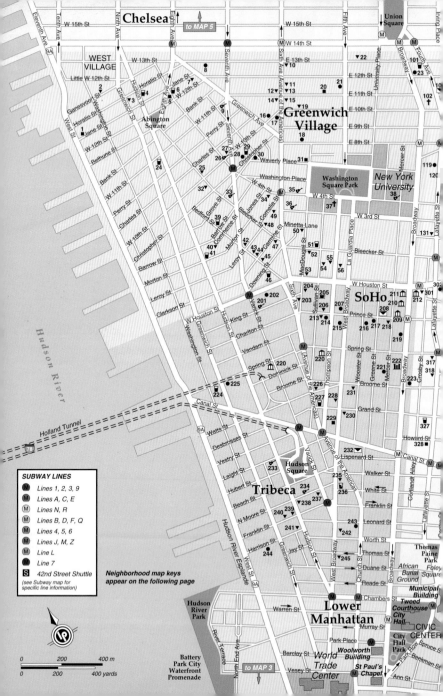

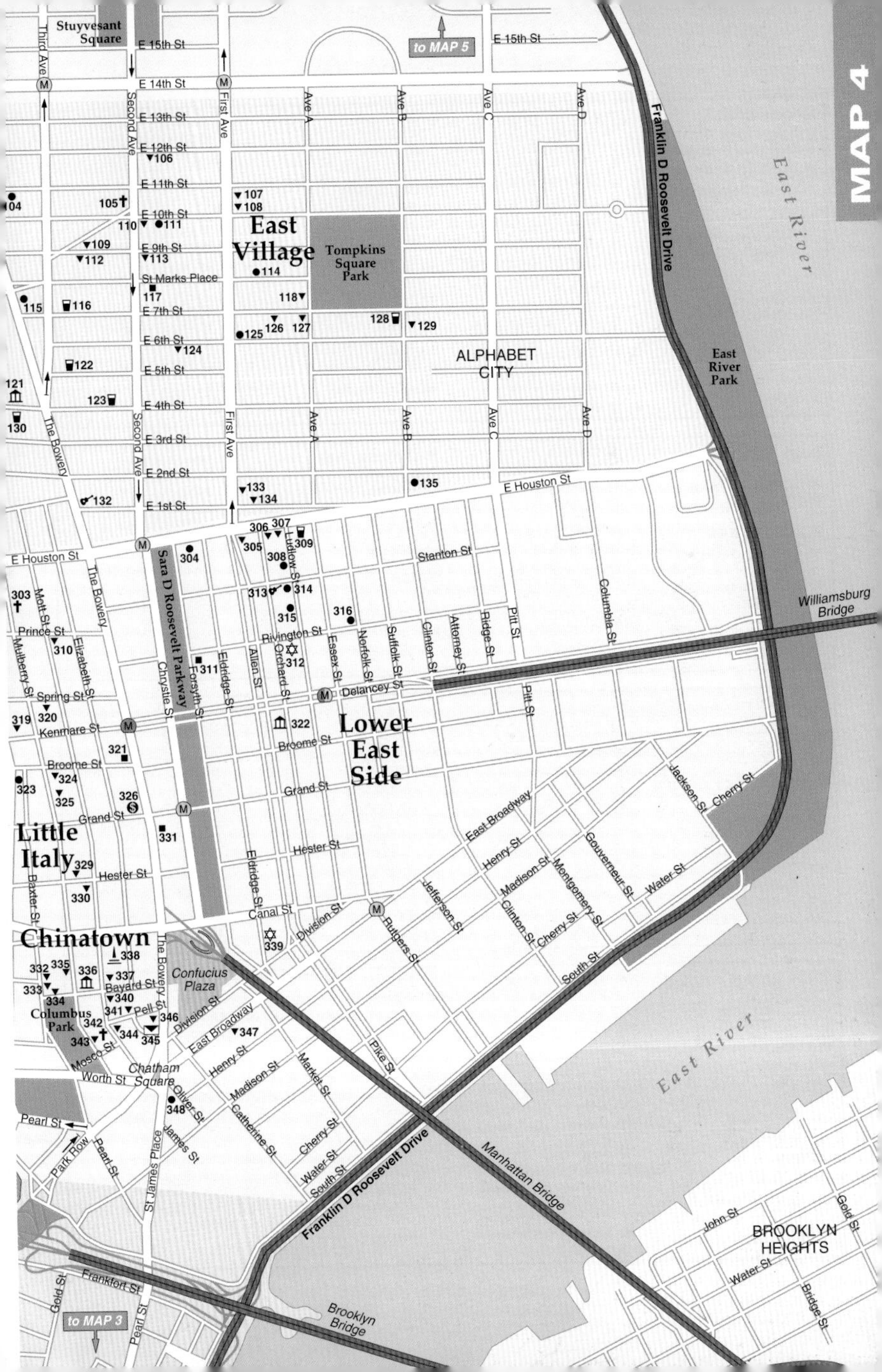

MAP 4

Stuyvesant Square

to MAP 5

E 15th St
E 15th St

E 14th St

E 13th St
Second Ave
First Ave
Ave A
Ave B
Ave C
Ave D

E 12th St
▼106

E 11th St
▼107
▼108

E 10th St
▼109
●111
110

E 9th St
▼112
▼113

East Village

Tompkins Square Park

●114

St Marks Place
117

118▼

E 7th St
▼115
♥116
▼124
126 127
●125

128♥
▼129

E 6th St

E 5th St
♥122

E 4th St
123♥

121
♨
130

The Bowery
Second Ave
First Ave

E 3rd St

E 2nd St

E 1st St
▼133
▼134

●135

E Houston St

ALPHABET CITY

East River Park

East River

Franklin D Roosevelt Drive

♥132

E Houston St

The Bowery
Mott St
Mulberry St
Elizabeth St

Sara D Roosevelt Parkway

Chrystie St
Forsyth St
Eldridge St
Allen St
Orchard St
Ludlow St
Essex St
Norfolk St
Suffolk St
Clinton St
Attorney St
Ridge St
Pitt St

Stanton St

Columbia St

Williamsburg Bridge

306 307
305
304
308
309
313
315
314
316
311
✡312

Rivington St

Delancey St

303
†

Prince St

310

Spring St
319 320
Kenmare St

Broome St
▼324
323
325

326
Ⓢ
331

321

Grand St

Broome St

Grand St

Lower East Side

♨322

Hester St

East Broadway
Henry St
Madison St
Gouverneur St
Water St

Jefferson St
Clinton St
Montgomery St

Jackson St
Cherry St

South St

Little Italy
329
330

Hester St

Baxter St

Canal St

Eldridge St

Division St

Ⓜ

Rutgers St

✡339

Canal St

Chinatown
332 335
333
334
Columbus Park
336
♨
337
Bayard St
340
341▼
342
343
344 345
346

↓338

Confucius Plaza

The Bowery

Mott St
Elizabeth St
Mulberry St

Pell St

Doyers St

East Broadway
▼347

Henry St
Madison St
Market St
Catherine St

Pike St

Chatham Square
348

Mosco St
Worth St

Pearl St

Park Row
James St

St James Place

Oliver St

Cherry St
Water St
South St

East River

Manhattan Bridge

Franklin D Roosevelt Drive

Pearl St

Frankfort St

John St
Water St
Gold St

BROOKLYN HEIGHTS

Bridge St

Gold St

to MAP 3

Brooklyn Bridge

Map 4 Neighborhood Keys

Greenwich Village Key

PLACES TO STAY
1 Riverview Hotel
5 Incentra Village
20 Larchmont Hotel
31 Washington Square Hotel

PLACES TO EAT
2 Florent
3 El Faro
7 Benny's Burritos
10 Joe Jr's Restaurant
11 Bar Six
12 'Original' Ray's Pizza
13 Jon Vie
14 Sammy's Noodles
15 French Roast
19 Piadina
22 The Adore
25 Picasso Cafe
27 Dix et Sept
32 Manatus
34 Bagel Diner
40 Grange Hall
42 Seventh Avenue South Restaurant
43 Mary's
44 Marinella
45 Universal Grill
47 Trattoria Spaghetto
48 Bleecker Street Pastry
49 Le Gigot
50 Minetta Tavern
52 Le Figaro
53 Aggies
54 Cafe Lure
55 Rocco
56 Tomoe Sushi

BARS/CLUBS
4 Hudson Bar & Books
6 Corner Bistro
9 Village Vanguard
24 White Horse Tavern
26 Small's
29 Stonewall Inn
33 Sweet Basil
35 Washington Square Church
36 Blue Note
38 Bottom Line
39 Chumley's
41 Henrietta Hudson's
46 Bar d'O
51 Back Fence

OTHER
8 Gay & Lesbian Community Service Center
16 Patchin Place
17 Jefferson Market Library
18 Shoe and Leather Shops
21 Forbes Galleries
23 Strand Bookstore
28 Stonewall Place
30 Northern Dispensary
37 Judson Memorial Church

East Village

PLACES TO STAY
117 St Marks Hotel

PLACES TO EAT
106 John's of East 12th Street
107 DeRobertis
108 Lanza's
109 Sharaku
110 Second Ave Deli
112 Hasaki
113 Veselka
118 Odessa Diner
124 Little Delhi
126 Roetelle AG
127 Benny's Burritos
129 Hotel Galvez
131 Time Cafe
133 Lucky Cheng's
134 Princess Pamela's Southern Touch

BARS/CLUBS
101 System
104 Webster Hall
116 McSorley's
122 Scratcher
123 KGB
128 7B Bar
130 Swift Bar
132 CBGB

OTHER
102 Grace Church
103 Post Office
105 St Marks in-the-Bowery
111 10th St Baths
114 East Village Books & Records
115 Cooper Union
119 Colonnade Row
120 Joseph Papp Public Theater
121 Old Merchant's House Museum
125 East Village Launderette
135 Save the Robots

SoHo • Tribeca

PLACES TO STAY
229 Soho Grand Hotel

PLACES TO EAT & DRINK
201 SOB's
203 Souen Restaurant
204 Helianthus Vegetarian Restaurant
205 Once Upon a Tart
206 Quilty
213 Raoul's
218 Fanelli Cafe
224 Ear Inn
226 Lupe's East LA Kitchen
227 Cafe Noir
228 Félix
230 Lucky Strike
231 Gourmet Garage
233 Wetlands
234 Fast Folk Cafe
235 Montrachet
236 Liquor Store Bar
237 Walkers
238 Bubby's
239 Nobu
240 Riverrun Cafe
241 Chanterelle
242 The Independent
245 Odeon

OTHER
202 Film Forum
207 Rizzoli Bookstore
208 Post Office
209 Guggenheim/SoHo
210 New Museum of Contemporary Art
211 African Museum
212 Alternative Museum
214 Ward-Nasse Gallery
215 Leo Castelli Gallery
216 Howard Greenberg Gallery
217 Haas's Mural
219 Singer Building
220 Fire Museum
221 Enchanted Forest
222 St Nicholas Hotel
223 Haughwout Building
225 Don Hill's
232 Post Office
243 Clocktower Gallery
244 Harrison Street Houses

Little Italy • Chinatown • Lower East Side

PLACES TO STAY
311 Off SoHo Suites Hotel
321 Pioneer Hotel
328 Holiday Inn Downtown
331 World Hotel

PLACES TO EAT & DRINK
301 Fruit & Veggie Stand
305 Yonah Shimmel Bakery
306 Bereket
307 Katz's Deli
309 Mercury Lounge
310 Kitchen Club
317 Spring Street Natural
318 Cascabel Restaurant
319 Le Jardin Bistro
320 Lombardi's Pizza
324 Cafe Roma
325 Benito I Restaurant
327 Ñ Bar
329 Puglia
330 Vincent's
332 Nha Hang
333 New Pasteur
334 Thailand Restaurant
335 Nha Hang
337 House of Vegetarian
340 Peking Duck House
341 Hay Wun Loy
343 Giambone
344 Hong Ying Rice Shop
346 Joe's Shanghai
347 Nice Restaurant

OTHER
302 Puck Building
303 Old St Patrick's
304 Russ & Daughters
308 Luna Lounge
312 First Roumanian-American Congregation
313 Arlene Grocery
314 Amy Downs
315 147 Ludlow Street
316 Schapiro's Wines
322 Lower East Side Tenement Museum
323 Old Police Headquarters
326 Bowery Savings Bank
336 Chinatown History Museum
338 Eastern States Buddhist Temple
339 Eldridge St Synagogue
342 Church of the Transfiguration
345 Post Office
348 First Shearith Cemetery

DAVID ELLIS

Washington Square Park

KIM GRANT

Sidewalk antique sale, Greenwich Village

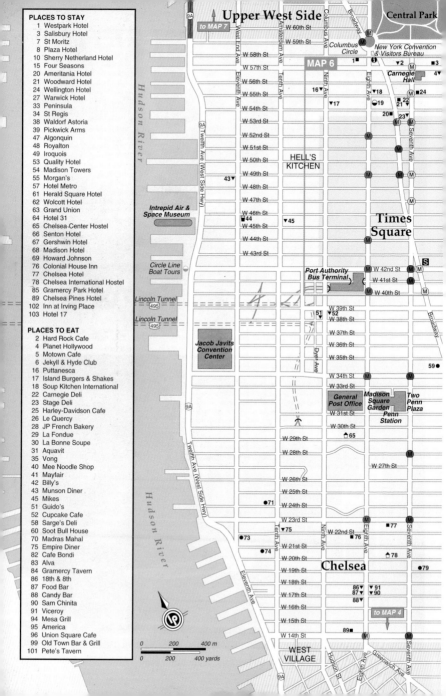

MAP 6

Upper West Side — **Central Park** — **Times Square** — **Hell's Kitchen** — **Chelsea** — **West Village**

PLACES TO STAY
1 Westpark Hotel
3 Salisbury Hotel
7 St Moritz
8 Plaza Hotel
10 Sherry Netherland Hotel
15 Four Seasons
20 Ameritania Hotel
21 Woodward Hotel
24 Wellington Hotel
27 Warwick Hotel
33 Peninsula
34 St Regis
38 Waldorf Astoria
39 Pickwick Arms
47 Algonquin
48 Royalton
49 Iroquois
53 Quality Hotel
54 Madison Towers
55 Morgan's
57 Hotel Metro
61 Herald Square Hotel
62 Wolcott Hotel
63 Grand Union
64 Hotel 31
65 Chelsea-Center Hostel
66 Senton Hotel
67 Gershwin Hotel
68 Madison Hotel
76 Howard Johnson
76 Colonial House Inn
77 Chelsea Hotel
78 Chelsea International Hostel
85 Gramercy Park Hotel
89 Chelsea Pines Hotel
102 Inn at Irving Place
103 Hotel 17

PLACES TO EAT
2 Hard Rock Cafe
4 Planet Hollywood
5 Motown Cafe
6 Jekyll & Hyde Club
16 Puttanesca
17 Island Burgers & Shakes
18 Soup Kitchen International
22 Carnegie Deli
23 Stage Deli
25 Harley-Davidson Cafe
26 Le Quercy
28 JP French Bakery
29 La Fondue
30 La Bonne Soupe
31 Aquavit
35 Vong
40 Mee Noodle Shop
41 Mayfair
42 Billy's
43 Munson Diner
45 Mikes
51 Guido's
52 Cupcake Cafe
59 Sarge's Deli
60 Soot Bull House
70 Madras Mahal
75 Empire Diner
82 Cafe Bondi
83 Alva
84 Gramercy Tavern
86 18th & 8th
87 Food Bar
88 Candy Bar
90 Sam Chinita
91 Viceroy
94 Mesa Grill
95 America
96 Union Square Cafe
99 Old Town Bar & Grill
101 Pete's Tavern

Intrepid Air & Space Museum
Circle Line Boat Tours
Lincoln Tunnel 495
Jacob Javits Convention Center
Port Authority Bus Terminal
General Post Office
Madison Square Garden
Two Penn Plaza
Penn Station
New York Convention & Visitors Bureau
Carnegie Hall
Columbus Circle

Hudson River

0 200 400 m
0 200 400 yards

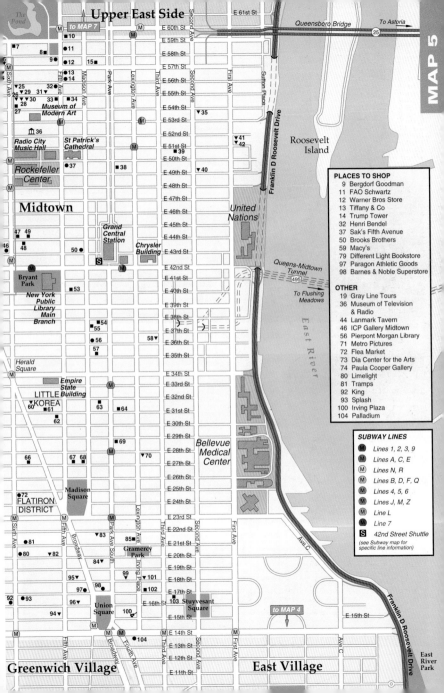

Hustle and bustle in Times Square

The Yellow River, Manhattan-style

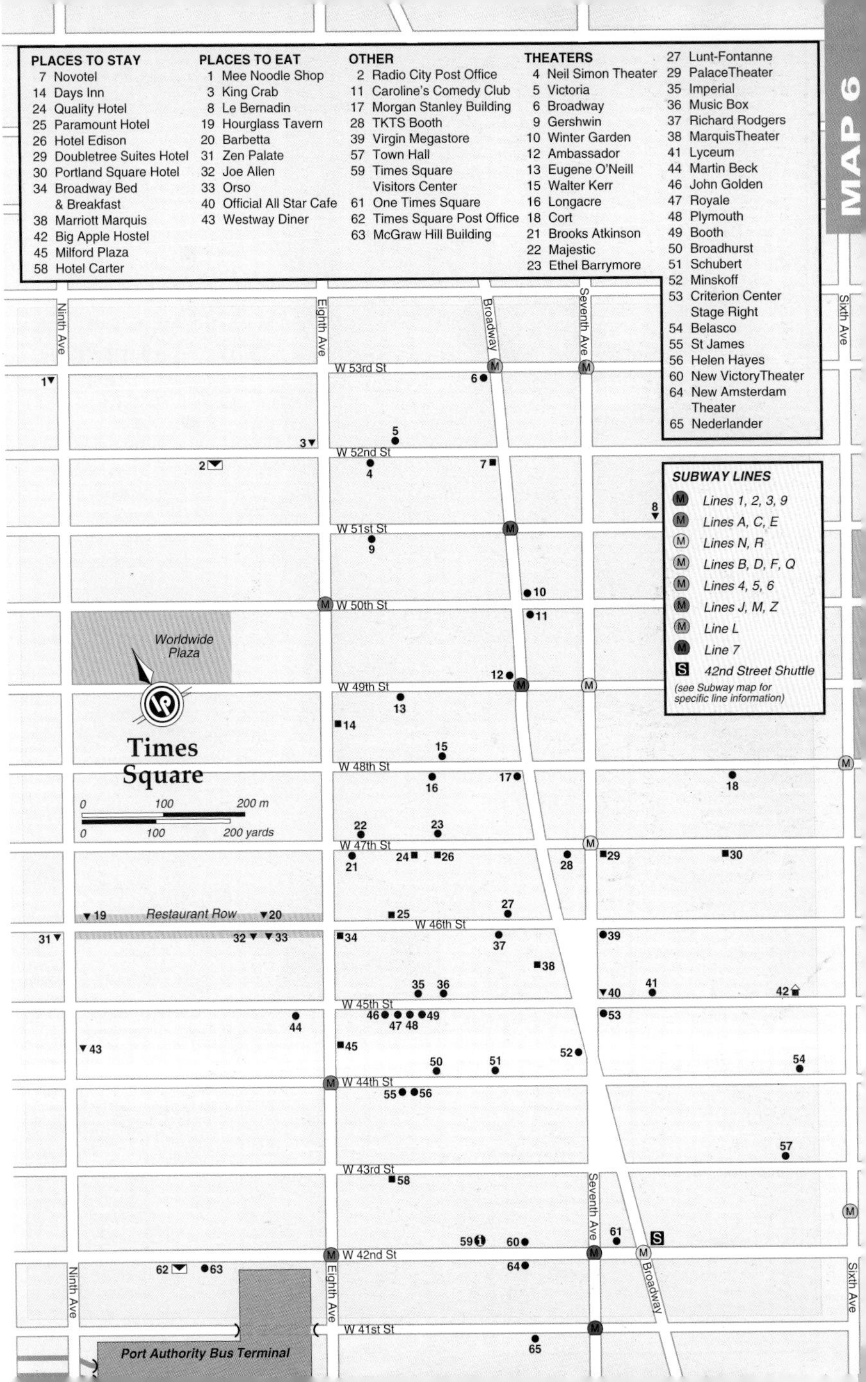

MAP 6

PLACES TO STAY
7 Novotel
14 Days Inn
24 Quality Hotel
25 Paramount Hotel
26 Hotel Edison
29 Doubletree Suites Hotel
30 Portland Square Hotel
34 Broadway Bed
   & Breakfast
38 Marriott Marquis
42 Big Apple Hostel
45 Milford Plaza
58 Hotel Carter

PLACES TO EAT
1 Mee Noodle Shop
3 King Crab
8 Le Bernadin
19 Hourglass Tavern
20 Barbetta
31 Zen Palate
32 Joe Allen
33 Orso
40 Official All Star Cafe
43 Westway Diner

OTHER
2 Radio City Post Office
11 Caroline's Comedy Club
17 Morgan Stanley Building
28 TKTS Booth
39 Virgin Megastore
57 Town Hall
59 Times Square
   Visitors Center
61 One Times Square
62 Times Square Post Office
63 McGraw Hill Building

THEATERS
4 Neil Simon Theater
5 Victoria
6 Broadway
9 Gershwin
10 Winter Garden
12 Ambassador
13 Eugene O'Neill
15 Walter Kerr
16 Longacre
18 Cort
21 Brooks Atkinson
22 Majestic
23 Ethel Barrymore
27 Lunt-Fontanne
29 PalaceTheater
35 Imperial
36 Music Box
37 Richard Rodgers
38 MarquisTheater
41 Lyceum
44 Martin Beck
46 John Golden
47 Royale
48 Plymouth
49 Booth
50 Broadhurst
51 Schubert
52 Minskoff
53 Criterion Center
   Stage Right
54 Belasco
55 St James
56 Helen Hayes
60 New VictoryTheater
64 New Amsterdam
   Theater
65 Nederlander

SUBWAY LINES
Ⓜ Lines 1, 2, 3, 9
Ⓜ Lines A, C, E
Ⓜ Lines N, R
Ⓜ Lines B, D, F, Q
Ⓜ Lines 4, 5, 6
Ⓜ Lines J, M, Z
Ⓜ Line L
Ⓜ Line 7
Ⓢ 42nd Street Shuttle
(see Subway map for
specific line information)

Ninth Ave
Eighth Ave
Broadway
Seventh Ave
Sixth Ave

W 53rd St
W 52nd St
W 51st St
W 50th St
W 49th St
W 48th St
W 47th St
W 46th St
W 45th St
W 44th St
W 43rd St
W 42nd St
W 41st St

Worldwide
Plaza

Times
Square

0   100   200 m
0   100   200 yards

Restaurant Row

Port Authority Bus Terminal

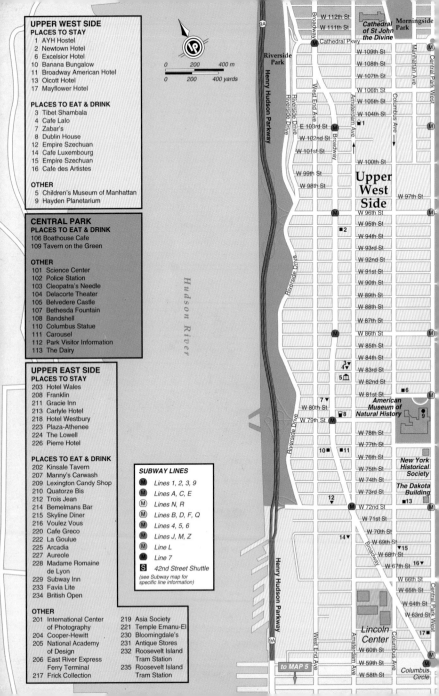

UPPER WEST SIDE
PLACES TO STAY
1 AYH Hostel
2 Newtown Hotel
6 Excelsior Hotel
10 Banana Bungalow
11 Broadway American Hotel
13 Olcott Hotel
17 Mayflower Hotel

PLACES TO EAT & DRINK
3 Tibet Shambala
4 Cafe Lalo
7 Zabar's
8 Dublin House
12 Empire Szechuan
14 Cafe Luxembourg
15 Empire Szechuan
16 Cafe des Artistes

OTHER
5 Children's Museum of Manhattan
9 Hayden Planetarium

CENTRAL PARK
PLACES TO EAT & DRINK
106 Boathouse Cafe
109 Tavern on the Green

OTHER
101 Science Center
102 Police Station
103 Cleopatra's Needle
104 Delacorte Theater
105 Belvedere Castle
107 Bethesda Fountain
108 Bandshell
110 Columbus Statue
111 Carousel
112 Park Visitor Information
113 The Dairy

UPPER EAST SIDE
PLACES TO STAY
203 Hotel Wales
208 Franklin
211 Gracie Inn
213 Carlyle Hotel
218 Hotel Westbury
223 Plaza-Athenee
224 The Lowell
226 Pierre Hotel

PLACES TO EAT & DRINK
202 Kinsale Tavern
207 Manny's Carwash
209 Lexington Candy Shop
210 Quatorze Bis
212 Trois Jean
214 Bemelmans Bar
215 Skyline Diner
216 Voulez Vous
220 Cafe Greco
222 La Goulue
225 Arcadia
227 Aureole
228 Madame Romaine
    de Lyon
229 Subway Inn
233 Favia Lite
234 British Open

OTHER
201 International Center
    of Photography
204 Cooper-Hewitt
205 National Academy
    of Design
206 East River Express
    Ferry Terminal
217 Frick Collection
219 Asia Society
221 Temple Emanu-El
230 Bloomingdale's
231 Antique Stores
232 Roosevelt Island
    Tram Station
235 Roosevelt Island
    Tram Station

SUBWAY LINES
Ⓜ Lines 1, 2, 3, 9
Ⓜ Lines A, C, E
Ⓜ Lines N, R
Ⓜ Lines B, D, F, Q
Ⓜ Lines 4, 5, 6
Ⓜ Lines J, M, Z
Ⓜ Line L
Ⓜ Line 7
Ⓢ 42nd Street Shuttle
(see Subway map for
specific line information)

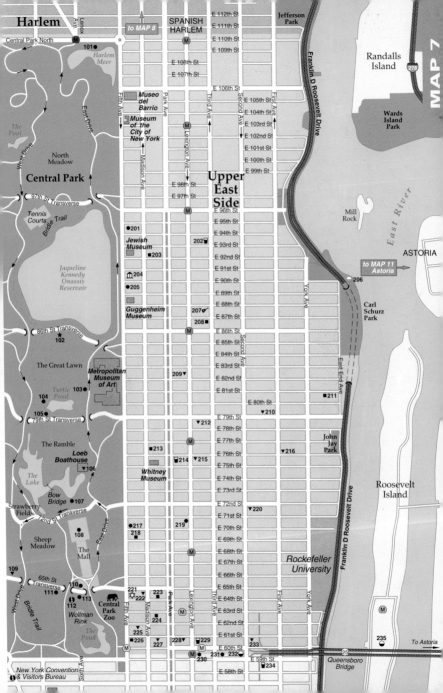

Riverside Park

Henry Hudson Parkway

W 148th St
W 147th St
W 146th St

W 147th St
W 146th St

W 145th St
2

M W 145th St ▼1
Broadway
Amsterdam Ave
Convent Ave
St Nicholas Ave
Edgecombe Ave
8 Ave/Fredrick Douglass Blvd
Clayton Powell Blvd
Lenox Ave
M

W 144th St
W 143rd St
W 142nd St

W 145th St
W 144th St
W 143rd St
W 142nd St
W 141st St

St Nicholas Park

W 141st St
W 140th St
W 139th St
W 138th St
W 137th St
W 136th St
W 135th St

W 140th St
W 139th St
W 138th St
W 137th St
W 136th St
W 135th St

†3
▼4
5▼
6●
▼7

Hamilton Place

Riverside Drive

W 134th St
W 133rd St
W 132nd St
W 131st St
W 130th St

W 134th St
W 133rd St
W 132nd St
W 131st St
W 130th St

Convent Ave

▼8

Harlem

Hudson River

9▼

Convent Ave

W 129th St
W 128th St
W 127th St
W 126th St

W 130th St
W 129th St
W 128th St
W 127th St
W 126th St

16▼

M

Tiemann Place

W 125th St

St Nicholas Ave

▼11
13●   14
W 125th St
M

LaSalle St

12▼   W 124th St

15
▼17
M

10
W 123rd St
W 123rd St

Grant's Tomb

MORNINGSIDE HEIGHTS

W 122nd St

Riverside Church

W 121st St
W 121st St

Morningside Park

W 120th St

Riverside Park

Morningside Drive
Morningside Ave
Manhattan Ave

W 119th St
W 118th St
W 117th St

18

Columbia University

Claremont Ave

▼19

●23

M W 116th St
W 116th St
W 115th St
W 114th St

†20 ▼21   22
M

Frederick Douglass Blvd
Adam Clayton Powell Blvd
St Nicholas Ave
Lenox Ave

W 115th St
W 114th St
W 113th St
W 112th St
W 111th St

Broadway
Amsterdam Ave

W 113th St
W 112th St
W 111th St

Riverside Park

Henry Hudson Parkway

Cathedral of St John the Divine

Cathedral Parkway

Central Park North

M

Central Park

Harlem

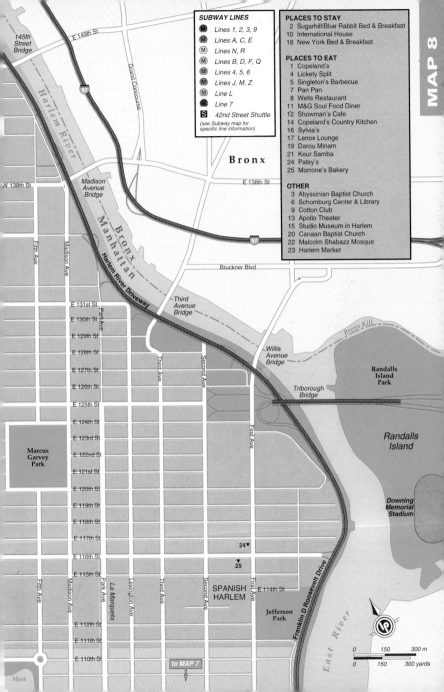

MAP 8

SUBWAY LINES

M Lines 1, 2, 3, 9
M Lines A, C, E
M Lines N, R
M Lines B, D, F, Q
M Lines 4, 5, 6
M Lines J, M, Z
M Line L
M Line 7
S 42nd Street Shuttle
(see Subway map for specific line information)

PLACES TO STAY
2 Sugarhill/Blue Rabbit Bed & Breakfast
10 International House
18 New York Bed & Breakfast

PLACES TO EAT
1 Copeland's
4 Lickety Split
5 Singleton's Barbecue
7 Pan Pan
8 Wells Restaurant
11 M&G Soul Food Diner
12 Showman's Cafe
14 Copeland's Country Kitchen
16 Sylvia's
17 Lenox Lounge
19 Darou Minam
21 Keur Samba
24 Patsy's
25 Morrone's Bakery

OTHER
3 Abyssinian Baptist Church
6 Schomburg Center & Library
9 Cotton Club
13 Apollo Theater
15 Studio Museum in Harlem
20 Canaan Baptist Church
22 Malcolm Shabazz Mosque
23 Harlem Market

145th Street Bridge

E 149th St

Harlem River

Grand Concourse

Bronx

Madison Avenue Bridge

W 138th St

E 138th St

Bronx Manhattan

Harlem River Driveway

Bruckner Blvd

Third Avenue Bridge

E 131st St
E 130th St
E 129th St
E 128th St
E 127th St
E 126th St
E 125th St
E 124th St
E 123rd St
E 122nd St
E 121st St
E 120th St
E 119th St
E 118th St
E 117th St
E 116th St
E 115th St

Willis Avenue Bridge

Bronx Kill

Randalls Island Park

Triborough Bridge

Randalls Island

Downing Memorial Stadium

Fifth Ave
Madison Ave
Park Ave
Third Ave
Second Ave
First Ave

Marcus Garvey Park

24▼
▼25

SPANISH HARLEM

E 114th St

Fifth Ave
Madison Ave
Park Ave
La Marqueta
Lexington Ave
Third Ave
Second Ave
First Ave

Franklin D Roosevelt Drive

Jefferson Park

East River

E 112th St
E 111th St
E 110th St

Meer

to MAP 7

0   150   300 m
0   150   300 yards

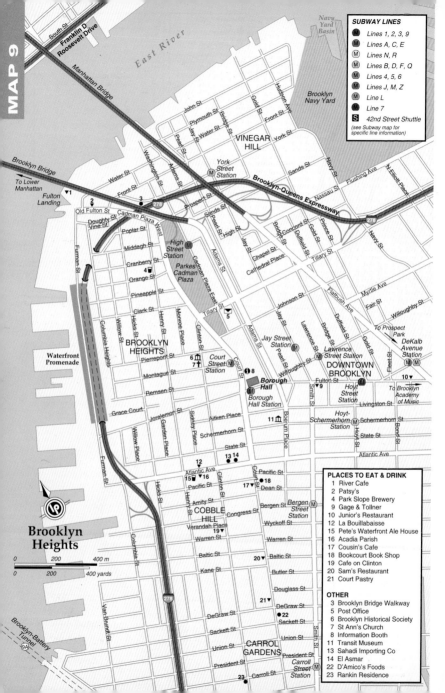

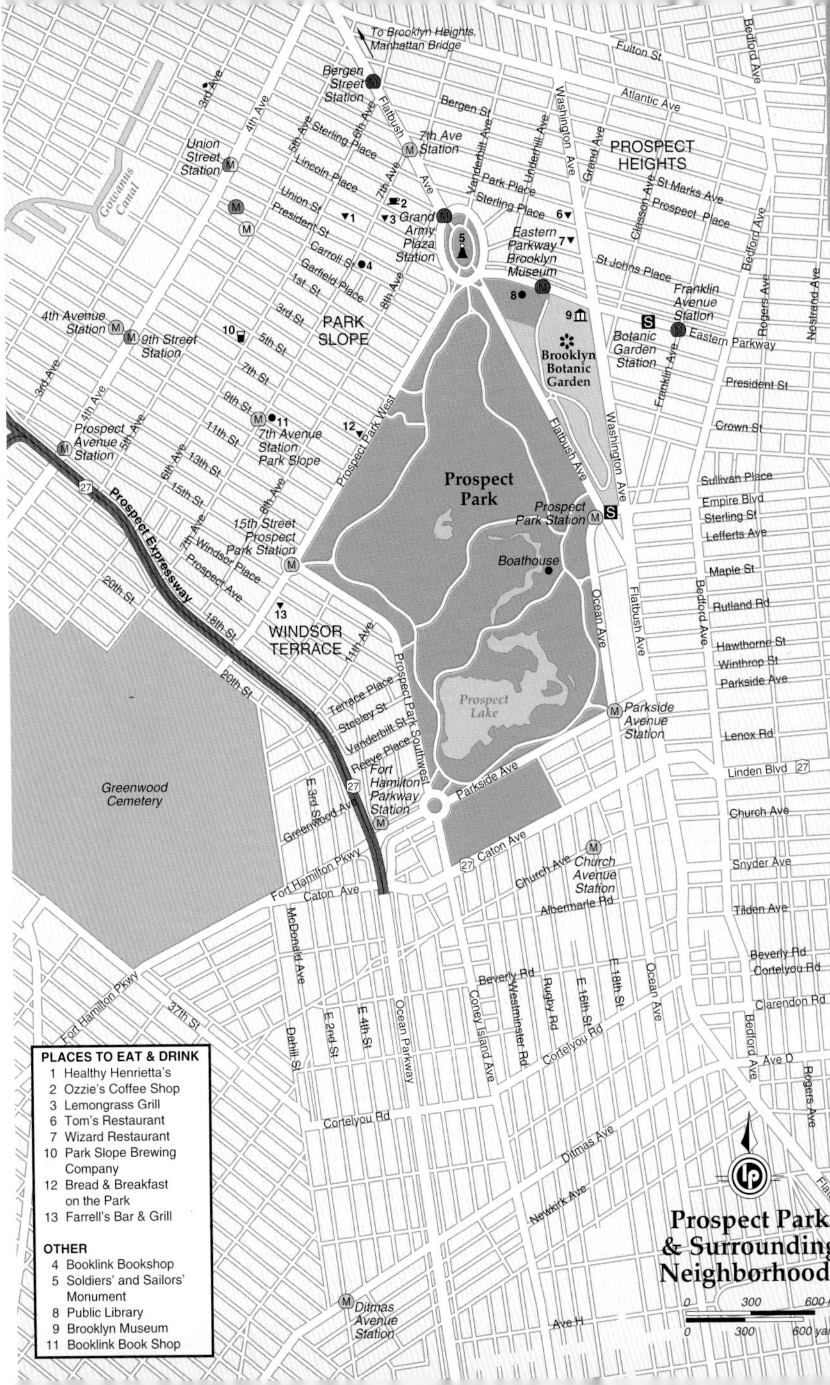

MAP 10

To Brooklyn Heights,
Manhattan Bridge

Fulton St

Bergen Street
Station

Bedford Ave

Atlantic Ave

Bergen St

PROSPECT
HEIGHTS

Sterling Place

7th Ave
Station

Lincoln Place

Park Place

St Marks Ave

Prospect Place

Union St

Sterling Place

▼1

President St

▼3 Grand
Army
Plaza
Station

▼2

6▼

Eastern
Parkway Brooklyn
Museum

7▼

St Johns Place

Franklin
Avenue
Station

Carroll St

5

Garfield Place

Garfield Place

Clinton Ave

4th Avenue
Station

9th Street
Station

10

5th St

PARK
SLOPE

8●

Eastern Parkway

9 🏛

Botanic
Garden
Station

Botanic
Garden

President St

Brooklyn Botanic
Garden

Crown St

7th St

9th St

Prospect
Avenue
Station

●11

7th Avenue
Station
Park Slope

12▼

Prospect Park West

Sullivan Place

Empire Blvd

Prospect Park

Sterling St

Lefferts Ave

15th Street
Prospect
Park Station

Maple St

Windsor Place

Prospect
Park Station

Rutland Rd

Boathouse

Hawthorne St

Prospect Expressway

WINDSOR
TERRACE

▼13

Winthrop St

Parkside Ave

Ocean Ave

Bedford Ave

Prospect
Lake

Parkside
Avenue
Station

Lenox Rd

Greenwood
Cemetery

Terrace Place

Linden Blvd

Vanderbilt Place

Church Ave

Reeve Place

Fort
Hamilton
Parkway
Station

Parkside Ave

Fort Hamilton Pkwy

Caton Ave

Snyder Ave

Church
Avenue
Station

Albermarle Rd

McDonald Ave

Caton Ave

Tilden Ave

Beverly Rd

Cortelyou Rd

Beverly Rd

Clarendon Rd

Cortelyou Rd

Ocean Parkway

Ditmas Ave

Ave D

Cortelyou Rd

Newkirk Ave

Rogers Ave

Ditmas
Avenue
Station

Ave H

PLACES TO EAT & DRINK
1 Healthy Henrietta's
2 Ozzie's Coffee Shop
3 Lemongrass Grill
6 Tom's Restaurant
7 Wizard Restaurant
10 Park Slope Brewing
   Company
12 Bread & Breakfast
   on the Park
13 Farrell's Bar & Grill

OTHER
4 Booklink Bookshop
5 Soldiers' and Sailors'
   Monument
8 Public Library
9 Brooklyn Museum
11 Booklink Book Shop

**Prospect Park
& Surrounding
Neighborhoods**

0   300   600 m
0   300   600 yards

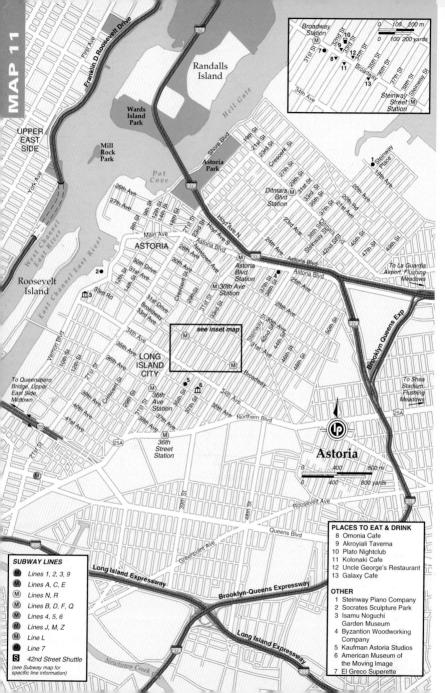

MAP 11

Randalls Island

UPPER EAST SIDE

Wards Island Park

Mill Rock Park

Pot Cove

Astoria Park

Franklin D Roosevelt Drive

First Ave

York Ave

West Channel East River

East Channel East River

Roosevelt Island

2

3

ASTORIA

Main Ave

Ditmars Blvd Station

Astoria Blvd Station

30th Ave Station

1 Steinway Place

To La Guardia Airport, Flushing Meadows

see inset map

LONG ISLAND CITY

36th Ave Station

36th Street Station

To Queensboro Bridge, Upper East Side, Midtown

To Shea Stadium, Flushing Meadows

5

6

Northern Blvd

Astoria

Roosevelt Ave

Queens Blvd

Brooklyn-Queens Expressway

Long Island Expressway

Long Island Expressway

Greenpoint Ave

Newtown Creek

Inset map:

Broadway Station

10
7 9 3
8 12
11
Broadway
13

Steinway Street Station

31st St, 32nd St, 33rd St, 34th Ave, 35th St, 36th St, 37th St, 38th St

PLACES TO EAT & DRINK

8 Omonia Cafe
9 Akroyiali Taverna
10 Plato Nightclub
11 Kolonaki Cafe
12 Uncle George's Restaurant
13 Galaxy Cafe

OTHER

1 Steinway Piano Company
2 Socrates Sculpture Park
3 Isamu Noguchi Garden Museum
4 Byzantion Woodworking Company
5 Kaufman Astoria Studios
6 American Museum of the Moving Image
7 El Greco Superette

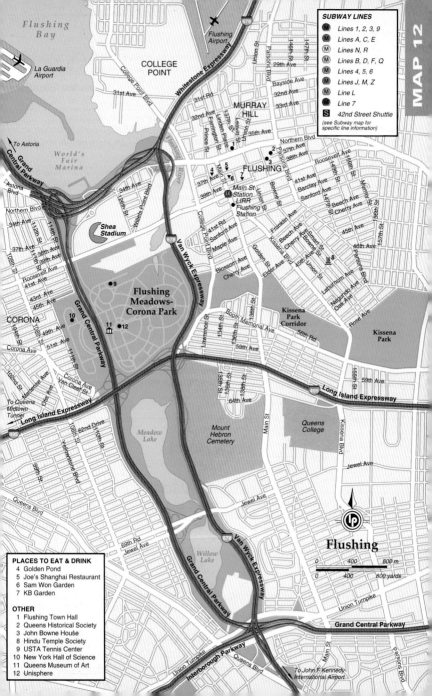

MAP 12

SUBWAY LINES

- Ⓜ Lines 1, 2, 3, 9
- Ⓜ Lines A, C, E
- Ⓜ Lines N, R
- Ⓜ Lines B, D, F, Q
- Ⓜ Lines 4, 5, 6
- Ⓜ Lines J, M, Z
- Ⓜ Line L
- Ⓜ Line 7
- Ⓢ 42nd Street Shuttle

(see Subway map for specific line information)

Flushing Bay

La Guardia Airport

To Astoria

World's Fair Marina

COLLEGE POINT

Flushing Airport

MURRAY HILL

FLUSHING

Main St Station LIRR / Flushing Station

Shea Stadium

CORONA

Flushing Meadows-Corona Park

Kissena Park Corridor

Kissena Park

Meadow Lake

Mount Hebron Cemetery

Queens College

Willow Lake

Flushing

To Queens Midtown Tunnel

To John F Kennedy International Airport

| 0 | 400 | 800 m |
| 0 | 400 | 800 yards |

PLACES TO EAT & DRINK
4 Golden Pond
5 Joe's Shanghai Restaurant
6 Sam Won Garden
7 KB Garden

OTHER
1 Flushing Town Hall
2 Queens Historical Society
3 John Bowne House
8 Hindu Temple Society
9 USTA Tennis Center
10 New York Hall of Science
11 Queens Museum of Art
12 Unisphere

THE LONELY PLANET STORY

Lonely Planet published its first book in 1973 in response to the numerous 'How did you do it?' questions Maureen and Tony Wheeler were asked after driving, busing, hitching, sailing and railing their way from England to Australia.

Written at a kitchen table and hand collated, trimmed and stapled, *Across Asia on the Cheap* became an instant local bestseller, inspiring thoughts of another book.

Eighteen months in South-East Asia resulted in their second guide, *South-East Asia on a shoestring*, which they put together in a backstreet Chinese hotel in Singapore in 1975. The 'yellow bible', as it quickly became known to backpackers around the world, soon became *the* guide to the region. It has sold well over half a million copies and is now in its 9th edition, still retaining its familiar yellow cover.

Today there are over 350 titles, including travel guides, walking guides, language kits & phrasebooks, travel atlases and travel literature. The company is the largest independent travel publisher in the world. Although Lonely Planet initially specialised in guides to Asia, today there are few corners of the globe that have not been covered.

The emphasis continues to be on travel for independent travellers. Tony and Maureen still travel for several months of each year and play an active part in the writing, updating and quality control of Lonely Planet's guides.

They have been joined by over 80 authors and 200 staff at our offices in Melbourne (Australia), Oakland (USA), London (UK) and Paris (France). Travellers themselves also make a valuable contribution to the guides through the feedback we receive in thousands of letters each year and on our web site.

The people at Lonely Planet strongly believe that travellers can make a positive contribution to the countries they visit, both through their appreciation of the countries' culture, wildlife and natural features, and through the money they spend. In addition, the company makes a direct contribution to the countries and regions it covers. Since 1986 a percentage of the income from each book has been donated to ventures such as famine relief in Africa; aid projects in India; agricultural projects in Central America; Greenpeace's efforts to halt French nuclear testing in the Pacific; and Amnesty International.

'I hope we send people out with the right attitude about travel. You realise when you travel that there are so many different perspectives about the world, so we hope these books will make people more interested in what they see. Guidebooks can't really guide people. All you can do is point them in the right direction.'

– Tony Wheeler

LONELY PLANET PUBLICATIONS

Australia
PO Box 617, Hawthorn 3122, Victoria
tel: (03) 9819 1877 fax: (03) 9819 6459
e-mail: talk2us@lonelyplanet.com.au

USA
150 Linden St
Oakland, CA 94607
tel: (510) 893 8555 TOLL FREE: 800 275-8555
fax: (510) 893 8572
e-mail: info@lonelyplanet.com

UK
10a Spring Place,
London NW5 3BH
tel: (0171) 428 4800 fax: (0171) 428 4828
e-mail: go@lonelyplanet.co.uk

France:
1 rue du Dahomey, 75011 Paris
tel: 01 55 25 33 00 fax: 01 55 25 33 01
e-mail: bip@lonelyplanet.fr

World Wide Web: http://www.lonelyplanet.com
or *AOL keyword: lp*